(ex·ploring)

1. Investigating in a systematic way: examining. 2. Searching
into or ranging over for the purpose of discovery.

# Microsoft® SharePoint®
# for Office 2016

## BRIEF

Daniela Marghitu

Barbara Stover

Series Created by Dr. Robert T. Grauer

 **Pearson**

330 Hudson Street, NY, NY 10013

**Vice President of IT & Career Skills:** Andrew Gilfillan

**Senior Portfolio Manager:** Samantha Lewis

**Team Lead, Project Management:** Laura Burgess

**Project Manager:** Barbara Stover

**Development Editor:** Barbara Stover

**Editorial Assistant:** Madeline Houpt

**Director of Product Marketing:** Brad Parkins

**Director of Field Marketing:** Leigh Ann Sims

**Field Marketing Managers:** Molly Schmidt

**Senior Operations Specialist:** Diane Peirano

**Interior and Cover Design:** Cenveo

**Senior Product Model Manager:** Eric Hakanson

**Production and Digital Studio Lead:** Heather Darby

**Course Producer, MyITLab:** Amanda Losonsky

**Digital Project Manager, MyITLab:** Becca Lowe

**Media Project Manager, Production:** Tanika Henderson

**Full-Service Project Management:** iEnergizer/Aptara®, Ltd.

**Composition:** iEnergizer/Aptara®, Ltd.

**Cover Image Credits:** cunico/Fotolia (*compass rose*); mawrhis/Fotolia (*checker pattern*); wavebreakmedia/Shutterstock (*students*); Sergey Nivens/Fotolia (*world*); dotshock/Shutterstock (*business people*)

Credits and acknowledgments borrowed from other sources and reproduced, with permission, in this textbook appear on the appropriate page within text.

Microsoft and/or its respective suppliers make no representations about the suitability of the information contained in the documents and related graphics published as part of the services for any purpose. All such documents and related graphics are provided "as is" without warranty of any kind. Microsoft and/or its respective suppliers hereby disclaim all warranties and conditions with regard to this information, including all warranties and conditions of merchantability, whether express, implied or statutory, fitness for a particular purpose, title and non-infringement. In no event shall Microsoft and/or its respective suppliers be liable for any special, indirect or consequential damages or any damages whatsoever resulting from loss of use, data or profits, whether in an action of contract, negligence or other tortious action, arising out of or in connection with the use or performance of information available from the services.

The documents and related graphics contained herein could include technical inaccuracies or typographical errors. Changes are periodically added to the information herein. Microsoft and/or its respective suppliers may make improvements and/or changes in the product(s) and/or the program(s) described herein at any time. Partial screen shots may be viewed in full within the software version specified.

Microsoft® and Windows® are registered trademarks of the Microsoft Corporation in the U.S.A. and other countries. This book is not sponsored or endorsed by or affiliated with the Microsoft Corporation.

**Library of Congress Cataloging-in-Publication Data**

Names: Marghitu, Daniela, author. | Stover, Barbara, author.
Title: Microsoft SharePoint for Office 2016 brief / Daniela Marghitu, Barbara
  Stover.
Description: Boston : Pearson, [2017] | Series: Exploring series | Includes
  index.
Identifiers: LCCN 2017006830| ISBN 9780134497624 (pbk.) | ISBN 0134497627
  (pbk.)
Subjects: LCSH: Intranets (Computer networks) | Computer file sharing. |
  Microsoft Office. | Computer file sharing. | Web services.
Classification: LCC TK5105.875.I6 M375 2017 | DDC 004.6/82—dc23 LC
  record available at https://lccn.loc.gov/2017006830

4    18

ISBN 10:    0-13-449762-7
ISBN 13: 978-0-13-449762-4

# About the Authors

## Daniela Marghitu

Dr. Daniela Marghitu is a faculty member in the Computer Science and Software Engineering Department at Auburn University, where she has worked since 1996. She has published six Information Technology textbooks, over 100 peer reviewed journal articles and conference papers, and she has given numerous presentations at national and international professional events in the USA, England, France, Spain, Portugal, Germany, and Romania. She is the founder-director of the Auburn University Educational and Assistive Technology Laboratory (LEAT), an institutional partner of AccessComputing (http://www.washington.edu/accesscomputing/), AccessCS10k and AccessEngineering NSF funded Alliances. She is the CO-PI of NSF INCLUDES: South East Alliance for Persons with Disabilities in STEM (https://cws.auburn.edu/apspi/pm/includes), CO-PI and Technology Coordinator of the NSF Alabama Alliance for Students with Disabilities in STEM (https://cws.auburn.edu/apspi/pm/stem), the PI of NSF Auburn University Computer Science for All (http://cs4all.eng.auburn.edu), Computer Science for All Girls (http://cs4allg.eng.auburn.edu), Computer Science for All Bulldogs (http://csallb.eng.auburn.edu), and Computer Science for All Romanians (http://cs4allro.eng.auburn.edu) research and inclusive K12 outreach projects. She is the recipient of the 2011 AccessComputing Capacity Building Award, the 2012 Auburn University Access award, the 2012 SDPS Outstanding Achievement Award, the 2013 Microsoft Fuse Research award, and the 2015 DO-IT Trailblazer award. Official site: http://eng.auburn.edu/~daniela

## Barbara Stover

Barbara's professional life is focused on education. As a professor at Marion Technical College in Marion, Ohio, she taught Microsoft Office applications and Web technologies. She serves as an adjunct faculty member at George Washington University in Washington D.C., in the Educational Technology Leadership Masters degree program. She has authored several textbooks and edited many others.

# Dedications

To my family–Stefania, Dan, Elena, and Dumitru.

**Daniela Marghitu**

To you, the student, embarking on the adventure of a lifetime—your career. Wishing you success!

**Barbara Stover**

# Contents

# Acknowledgments

The Exploring team acknowledges and thanks all the reviewers who helped us throughout the years by providing us with their invaluable comments, suggestions, and constructive criticism.

Adriana Lumpkin
Midland College

Alan S. Abrahams
Virginia Tech

Alexandre C. Probst
Colorado Christian University

Ali Berrached
University of Houston–Downtown

Allen Alexander
Delaware Technical & Community College

Andrea Marchese
Maritime College, State University of New York

Andrew Blitz
Broward College; Edison State College

Angel Norman
University of Tennessee, Knoxville

Angela Clark
University of South Alabama

Ann Rovetto
Horry-Georgetown Technical College

Astrid Todd
Guilford Technical Community College

Audrey Gillant
Maritime College, State University of New York

Barbara Stover
Marion Technical College

Barbara Tollinger
Sinclair Community College

Ben Brahim Taha
Auburn University

Beverly Amer
Northern Arizona University

Beverly Fite
Amarillo College

Biswadip Ghosh
Metropolitan State University of Denver

Bonita Volker
Tidewater Community College

Bonnie Homan
San Francisco State University

Brad West
Sinclair Community College

Brian Powell
West Virginia University

Carol Buser
Owens Community College

Carol Roberts
University of Maine

Carolyn Barren
Macomb Community College

Carolyn Borne
Louisiana State University

Cathy Poyner
Truman State University

Charles Hodgson
Delgado Community College

Chen Zhang
Bryant University

Cheri Higgins
Illinois State University

Cheryl Brown
Delgado Community College

Cheryl Hinds
Norfolk State University

Cheryl Sypniewski
Macomb Community College

Chris Robinson
Northwest State Community College

Cindy Herbert
Metropolitan Community College–Longview

Craig J. Peterson
American InterContinental University

Dana Hooper
University of Alabama

Dana Johnson
North Dakota State University

Daniela Marghitu
Auburn University

David Noel
University of Central Oklahoma

David Pulis
Maritime College, State University of New York

David Thornton
Jacksonville State University

Dawn Medlin
Appalachian State University

Debby Keen
University of Kentucky

Debra Chapman
University of South Alabama

Debra Hoffman
Southeast Missouri State University

Derrick Huang
Florida Atlantic University

Diana Baran
Henry Ford Community College

Diane Cassidy
The University of North Carolina at Charlotte

Diane L. Smith
Henry Ford Community College

Dick Hewer
Ferris State College

Don Danner
San Francisco State University

Don Hoggan
Solano College

Don Riggs
SUNY Schenectady County Community College

Doncho Petkov
Eastern Connecticut State University

Donna Ehrhart
State University of New York at Brockport

Elaine Crable
Xavier University

Elizabeth Duett
Delgado Community College

Erhan Uskup
Houston Community College–Northwest

Eric Martin
University of Tennessee

Erika Nadas
Wilbur Wright College

Floyd Winters
Manatee Community College

Frank Lucente
Westmoreland County Community
College

G. Jan Wilms
Union University

Gail Cope
Sinclair Community College

Gary DeLorenzo
California University of Pennsylvania

Gary Garrison
Belmont University

Gary McFall
Purdue University

George Cassidy
Sussex County Community College

Gerald Braun
Xavier University

Gerald Burgess
Western New Mexico University

Gladys Swindler
Fort Hays State University

Hector Frausto
California State University Los Angeles

Heith Hennel
Valencia Community College

Henry Rudzinski
Central Connecticut State University

Irene Joos
La Roche College

Iwona Rusin
Baker College; Davenport University

J. Roberto Guzman
San Diego Mesa College

Jacqueline D. Lawson
Henry Ford Community College

Jakie Brown Jr.
Stevenson University

James Brown
Central Washington University

James Powers
University of Southern Indiana

Jane Stam
Onondaga Community College

Janet Bringhurst
Utah State University

Jean Welsh
Lansing Community College

Jeanette Dix
Ivy Tech Community College

Jennifer Day
Sinclair Community College

Jill Canine
Ivy Tech Community College

Jill Young
Southeast Missouri State University

Jim Chaffee
The University of Iowa Tippie College
of Business

Joanne Lazirko
University of Wisconsin–Milwaukee

Jodi Milliner
Kansas State University

John Hollenbeck
Blue Ridge Community College

John Seydel
Arkansas State University

Judith A. Scheeren
Westmoreland County Community College

Judith Brown
The University of Memphis

Juliana Cypert
Tarrant County College

Kamaljeet Sanghera
George Mason University

Karen Priestly
Northern Virginia Community College

Karen Ravan
Spartanburg Community College

Karen Tracey
Central Connecticut State University

Kathleen Brenan
Ashland University

Ken Busbee
Houston Community College

Kent Foster
Winthrop University

Kevin Anderson
Solano Community College

Kim Wright
The University of Alabama

Kristen Hockman
University of Missouri–Columbia

Kristi Smith
Allegany College of Maryland

Laura Marcoulides
Fullerton College

Laura McManamon
University of Dayton

Laurence Boxer
Niagara University

Leanne Chun
Leeward Community College

Lee McClain
Western Washington University

Linda D. Collins
Mesa Community College

Linda Johnsonius
Murray State University

Linda Lau
Longwood University

Linda Theus
Jackson State Community College

Linda Williams
Marion Technical College

Lisa Miller
University of Central Oklahoma

Lister Horn
Pensacola Junior College

Lixin Tao
Pace University

Loraine Miller
Cayuga Community College

Lori Kielty
Central Florida Community College

Lorna Wells
Salt Lake Community College

Lorraine Sauchin
Duquesne University

Lucy Parakhovnik
California State University, Northridge

Lynn Keane
University of South Carolina

Lynn Mancini
Delaware Technical Community College

Mackinzee Escamilla
South Plains College

Marcia Welch
Highline Community College

Margaret McManus
Northwest Florida State College

Margaret Warrick
Allan Hancock College

Marilyn Hibbert
Salt Lake Community College

Mark Choman
Luzerne County Community College

Maryann Clark
University of New Hampshire

Mary Beth Tarver
Northwestern State University

Mary Duncan
University of Missouri–St. Louis

Melissa Nemeth
Indiana University-Purdue University
Indianapolis

Melody Alexander
Ball State University

Michael Douglas
University of Arkansas at Little Rock

Michael Dunklebarger
Alamance Community College

Michael G. Skaff
College of the Sequoias

Michele Budnovitch
Pennsylvania College of Technology

Mike Jochen
East Stroudsburg University

Mike Michaelson
Palomar College

Mike Scroggins
Missouri State University

Mimi Spain
Southern Maine Community College

Muhammed Badamas
Morgan State University

NaLisa Brown
University of the Ozarks

Nancy Grant
Community College of Allegheny
County–South Campus

Nanette Lareau
University of Arkansas Community
College–Morrilton

Nikia Robinson
Indian River State University

Pam Brune
Chattanooga State Community College

Pam Uhlenkamp
Iowa Central Community College

Patrick Smith
Marshall Community and Technical College

Paul Addison
Ivy Tech Community College

Paula Ruby
Arkansas State University

Peggy Burrus
Red Rocks Community College

Peter Ross
SUNY Albany

Philip H. Nielson
Salt Lake Community College

Philip Valvalides
Guilford Technical Community College

Ralph Hooper
University of Alabama

Ranette Halverson
Midwestern State University

Richard Blamer
John Carroll University

Richard Cacace
Pensacola Junior College

Richard Hewer
Ferris State University

Richard Sellers
Hill College

Rob Murray
Ivy Tech Community College

Robert Banta
Macomb Community College

Robert Dušek
Northern Virginia Community College

Robert G. Phipps Jr.
West Virginia University

Robert Sindt
Johnson County Community College

Robert Warren
Delgado Community College

Rocky Belcher
Sinclair Community College

Roger Pick
University of Missouri at Kansas City

Ronnie Creel
Troy University

Rosalie Westerberg
Clover Park Technical College

Ruth Neal
Navarro College

Sandra Thomas
Troy University

Sheila Gionfriddo
Luzerne County Community College

Sherrie Geitgey
Northwest State Community College

Sherry Lenhart
Terra Community College

Sophia Wilberscheid
Indian River State College

Sophie Lee
California State University, Long Beach

Stacy Johnson
Iowa Central Community College

Stephanie Kramer
Northwest State Community College

Stephen Z. Jourdan
Auburn University at Montgomery

Steven Schwarz
Raritan Valley Community College

Sue A. McCrory
Missouri State University

Sumathy Chandrashekar
Salisbury University

Susan Fuschetto
Cerritos College

Susan Medlin
UNC Charlotte

Susan N. Dozier
Tidewater Community College

Suzan Spitzberg
Oakton Community College

Suzanne M. Jeska
County College of Morris

Sven Aelterman
Troy University

Sy Hirsch
Sacred Heart University

Sylvia Brown
Midland College

Tanya Patrick
Clackamas Community College

Terri Holly
Indian River State College

Terry Ray Rigsby
Hill College

Thomas Rienzo
Western Michigan University

Tina Johnson
Midwestern State University

Tommy Lu
Delaware Technical Community College

Troy S. Cash
Northwest Arkansas Community College

Vicki Robertson
Southwest Tennessee Community

Vickie Pickett
Midland College

Weifeng Chen
California University of Pennsylvania

Wes Anthony
Houston Community College

William Ayen
University of Colorado at Colorado Springs

Wilma Andrews
Virginia Commonwealth University

Yvonne Galusha
University of Iowa

Special thanks to our content development and technical team:

Barbara Stover                    Janet Pickard

Elizabeth Lockley                 Steven Rubin

# Preface

## The Exploring Series and You

Exploring is Pearson's Office Application series that requires students like you to think "beyond the point and click." In this edition, we have worked to restructure the Exploring experience around the way you, today's modern student, actually use your resources.

The goal of Exploring is, as it has always been, to go farther than teaching just the steps to accomplish a task—the series provides the theoretical foundation for you to understand when and why to apply a skill. As a result, you achieve a deeper understanding of each application and can apply this critical thinking beyond Office and the classroom.

## The How & Why of This Revision

**Outcomes matter.** Whether it's getting a good grade in this course, learning how to use Microsoft Office and Windows 10 so students can be successful in other courses, or learning a specific skill that will make learners successful in a future job, everyone has an outcome in mind. And outcomes matter. That is why we revised our chapter opener to focus on the outcomes students will achieve by working through each Exploring chapter. These are coupled with objectives and skills, providing a map students can follow to get everything they need from each chapter.

**Critical Thinking and Collaboration are essential 21st-century skills.** Students want and need to be successful in their future careers—so we used motivating case studies to show relevance of these skills to future careers.

**Students today read, prepare, and study differently than students used to.** Students use textbooks like a tool—they want to easily identify what they need to know and learn it efficiently. We have added key features, such as Tasks Lists (in purple) and Step Icons, and tracked everything via page numbers that allow efficient navigation, creating a map students can easily follow.

**Students are exposed to technology.** The new edition of Exploring moves beyond the basics of the software at a faster pace, without sacrificing coverage of the fundamental skills that students need to know.

**Students are diverse.** Students can be any age, any gender, any race, with any level of ability or learning style. With this in mind, we broadened our definition of "student resources" to include MyITLab, the most powerful and most ADA-compliant online homework and assessment tool around with a direct 1:1 content match with the Exploring Series. Exploring will be accessible to all students, regardless of learning style.

## Providing You with a Map to Success to Move Beyond the Point and Click

All of these changes and additions will provide students an easy and efficient path to follow to be successful in this course, regardless of where they start at the beginning of this course. Our goal is to keep students engaged in both the hands-on and conceptual sides, helping achieve a higher level of understanding that will guarantee success in this course and in a future career.

In addition to the vision and experience of the series creator, Robert T. Grauer, we have assembled a tremendously talented team of Office Applications authors who have devoted themselves to teaching the ins and outs of Microsoft Word, Excel, Access, and PowerPoint. Led in this edition by series editor Mary Anne Poatsy, the whole team is dedicated to the Exploring mission of moving students **beyond the point and click**.

# Key Features

The **How/Why Approach** helps students move beyond the point and click to a true understanding of how to apply Microsoft Office skills.

- **White Pages/Yellow Pages** clearly distinguish the theory (white pages) from the skills covered in the Hands-On Exercises (yellow pages) so students always know what they are supposed to be doing and why.

- **Case Study** presents a scenario for the chapter, creating a story that ties the Hands-On Exercises together.

The **Outcomes focus** allows students and instructors to know the higher-level learning goals and how those are achieved through discreet objectives and skills.

- **Outcomes** presented at the beginning of each chapter identify the learning goals for students and instructors.

- **Enhanced Objective Mapping** enables students to follow a directed path through each chapter, from the objectives list at the chapter opener through the exercises at the end of the chapter.
  - **Objectives List:** This provides a simple list of key objectives covered in the chapter. This includes page numbers so students can skip between objectives where they feel they need the most help.
  - **Step Icons:** These icons appear in the white pages and reference the step numbers in the Hands-On Exercises, providing a correlation between the two so students can easily find conceptual help when they are working hands-on and need a refresher.
  - **Quick Concepts Check:** A series of questions that appear briefly at the end of each white page section. These questions cover the most essential concepts in the white pages required for students to be successful in working the Hands-On Exercises. Page numbers are included for easy reference to help students locate the answers.
  - **Chapter Objectives Review:** Appears toward the end of the chapter and reviews all important concepts throughout the chapter. Newly designed in an easy-to-read bulleted format.

**End-of-Chapter Exercises** offer instructors several options for assessment. Each chapter has approximately 11–12 exercises ranging from multiple choice questions to open-ended projects.

- **Multiple Choice, Key Terms Matching, Practice Exercises, Mid-Level Exercises, Beyond the Classroom Exercises, and Capstone Exercises** appear at the end of all chapters.

# Resources

## Instructor Resources

The Instructor's Resource Center, available at **www.pearsonhighered.com**, includes the following:

- **Instructor Manual** provides one-stop-shop for instructors, including an overview of all available resources, teaching tips, as well as student data and solution files for every exercise.

- **Solution Files with Scorecards** assist with grading the Hands-On Exercises and end-of-chapter exercises.

- **Prepared Exams** allow instructors to assess all skills covered in a chapter with a single project.

- **Rubrics** for Mid-Level Creative Cases and Beyond the Classroom Cases in Microsoft Word format enable instructors to customize the assignments for their classes.

- **PowerPoint Presentations** with notes for each chapter are included for out-of-class study or review.

- **Multiple Choice, Key Term Matching, and Quick Concepts Check Answer Keys**

- **Test Bank** provides objective-based questions for every chapter.

- **Scripted Lectures** offer an in-class lecture guide for instructors to mirror the Hands-On Exercises.

- **Syllabus Templates**
  - Outcomes, Objectives, and Skills List
  - Assignment Sheet
  - File Guide

## Student Resources

### Student Data Files

Access your student data files needed to complete the exercises in this textbook at **www.pearsonhighered.com/exploring.**

### Available in MyITLab

- **Multiple Choice quizzes** enable you to test concepts you have learned by answering auto-graded questions.

- **eText** available in some MyITLab courses and includes links to videos, student data files, and other learning aids.

- **Key Terms** quizzes enable you to test your understanding of key terms in each chapter.

(ex·ploring)

SERIES

1. Investigating in a systematic way: examining. 2. Searching
into or ranging over for the purpose of discovery.

# Microsoft® SharePoint®
# for Office 2016

BRIEF

## SharePoint

# Introduction to SharePoint 2016

**LEARNING OUTCOME**

- You will integrate Microsoft Office 365 and SharePoint Online.

**OBJECTIVES & SKILLS:** After you read this chapter, you will be able to:

# CASE STUDY | Daniela's Table Collaboration

Daniela's Table, a new Public Broadcasting Service (PBS) cooking show, is scheduled to air in the coming months. Daniela Lewis, a published cookbook author, is the on-air chef for the show. You have worked with Daniela as a media specialist for the past two years, mostly focusing on the layout of her cookbooks. Now your responsibilities have been expanded to support this new cooking show. You will lead a team that builds a website to provide viewers with recipes, video tips, and show schedules.

The team members for this project include an art designer, Laura McAfee, who lives and works in Quebec, Canada. Victor Merico is the copy editor, hired on an as-needed basis. Mary George is the recipe tester and photographer. Mary works from her professional home kitchen in Memphis, Tennessee. To bring this geographically diverse team together, you will use SharePoint Online and other tools included in Office 365. These applications enable you to collaborate regardless of your location using desktop or mobile computing technologies. You will begin this exciting phase of the project by exploring SharePoint Online and Office 365 tools.

# Using Office 365 and SharePoint Online

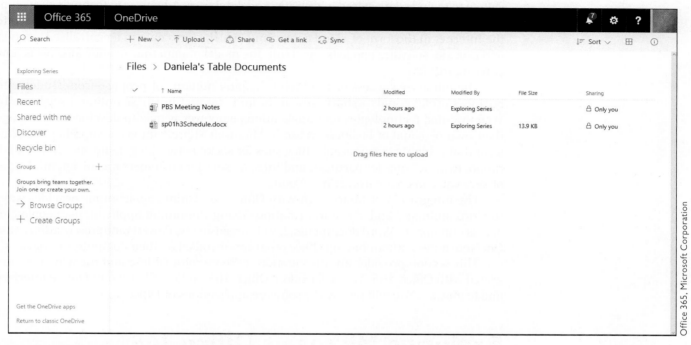

| | ↑ Name | Modified | Modified By | File Size | Sharing |
|---|---|---|---|---|---|
| | PBS Meeting Notes | 2 hours ago | Exploring Series | | 🔒 Only you |
| | sp01h3Schedule.docx | 2 hours ago | Exploring Series | 13.9 KB | 🔒 Only you |

Office 365, Microsoft Corporation

**FIGURE 1.1** Daniela's Table Collaboration Site

# CASE STUDY | Daniela's Table Collaboration

| Starting Files | Files to be Submitted |
|---|---|
| sp01h3Schedule | sp01h1Profile_LastFirst |
| sp01h3WKRE-TV_Logo | sp01h1Help_LastFirst |
| | sp01h2Documents_LastFirst |
| | sp01h2Notebook_LastFirst |
| | sp01h2Teamsite_LastFirst |
| | sp01h3Folder_LastFirst |
| | sp01h3Newsfeed_LastFirst |
| | sp01h3Task_LastFirst |
| | sp01h3People_LastFirst |
| | sp01h3Calendar_LastFirst |
| | sp01h3Schedule_LastFirst |
| | sp01h3Planning_LastFirst |
| | sp01h3Email_LastFirst (email message) |

# Introduction to SharePoint

Isaac Asimov's science-fiction writings from the 1940s through the 1980s describe a concept of data collection that encompasses all human knowledge and searchable by anyone. In many ways, this vision has come true with the advent of the Internet, computers, and mobile devices. Early models of computing called for people to be connected to a central computer, where data and software were made available to them through dumb terminals. In the 1980s, personal computers sidetracked this vision, and people purchased hardware and software for individual use. The data was stored locally and shared in a limited way. With the advent of the World Wide Web, the way data is stored shifted to include data stored in websites and databases. Advances in technology, including smartphones and other mobile devices, shifted an even greater amount of data to the Internet in the form of cloud computing, which stores data in a centralized location and provides software applications. Truly, the model of data that Asimov forecast is now entering fruition.

The immense success of the Web is helping millions of people—from students to business professionals—share, research, and conduct business online. User-friendly, Web-oriented technologies and applications empower people to develop and manage their own personal or business websites. Microsoft SharePoint is a comprehensive platform that is highly customizable. Blog sites for social networking, team sites for collaboration, extranet sites for partners, and Internet sites for customers are all potential types of sites you can create using SharePoint.

The integration of SharePoint with Office 365 Online applications provides ways to store, manage, and share information. Using the online applications, people can access and update Word documents, Excel spreadsheets, PowerPoint presentations, and OneNote notes without having Office programs installed on their computers or devices.

This section provides an introduction to SharePoint Online and the way it is integrated with Office 365. You will explore Office 365 and the SharePoint Online interface and team sites. You will review the software applications of Office 365.

## Exploring Microsoft Office 365

**STEP 1 ▸▸** **Microsoft Office** is a collection of server platforms, desktop applications, and online services that work together to improve productivity, make information sharing more effective, and facilitate the business decision-making process. Office 365 provides these services through **cloud computing**, where the applications are accessed through a Web browser and file storage is on servers you connect to through the Internet. This enables people to view, edit, and store documents using a variety of computing devices, such as PCs, laptops, tablets, or smartphones. All that is required to use the applications is an Internet connection and an Office 365 account. Office 365 enables organizations to create solutions to their business problems in an easily managed, cost-effective way.

**Microsoft Office 365** is a suite of apps that enables you to create documents and collaborate by sharing the documents with others. You select and purchase a subscription that contains the tools you need for the type of work you have. For instance, to complete the SharePoint exercises in this book, you need an Office 365 Business Essentials account or an Office 365 Educational account through your college or university. Subscriptions for Office 365 plans can be purchased on a monthly or an annual basis. To review the plans, visit www.office365.com.

Businesses and individuals find that using Office 365 has advantages. Software updates are applied without user or information technology (IT) staff intervention. Microsoft guarantees a 99.9% uptime, which means that you will be able to work whenever it is convenient for you. Email accounts are hosted by Microsoft, as are public websites and SharePoint intranet sites (depending on the type of account you purchase). You have access to Web conferencing and instant messaging (IM). Office Online enables you to edit and share documents using your Android phone or iPhone. **OneDrive for**

***Business*** enables you to create, sync, store, and share up to 1 TB of data in the cloud. As a business grows, additional users and more storage space can easily be added to the system.

The client system requirements for using Office 365 include using a current browser and a version of Microsoft Office. You can use the most recent version or the previous version of Microsoft Internet Explorer, Microsoft Edge, or Mozilla Firefox, or the latest version of Google Chrome or Apple Safari. Any Microsoft Office suite that is currently being supported will fit the client system requirements. For instance, Office 2010, Office 2013, and Office 2016 are currently supported suites.

**To log in to the services, after obtaining access to Office 365, complete the following steps:**

1. Open your Web browser and type login.microsoftonline.com in the address bar.
2. Type your account email address in the someone@example.com box. This email address is the one you created as you set up your Office 365 account, or it was assigned to you by the system administrator.
3. Type your password into the Password box and click Sign in. To protect the security of your account, do not click the check box to remain signed in.

The navigation bar across the top of the interface includes controls for Office 365, as shown in Figure 1.2. The left side of the navigation bar enables you to access the Office 365 apps. Click Office 365 on the left side of the navigation bar at any time to return to the Welcome screen. The right side of the navigation bar contains a notification area for your Office 365 account, a gear icon for managing your settings, and a question mark icon for getting help. At the far right on the top navigation bar is a photograph icon that provides access to your personal information settings and enables you to sign out of Office 365.

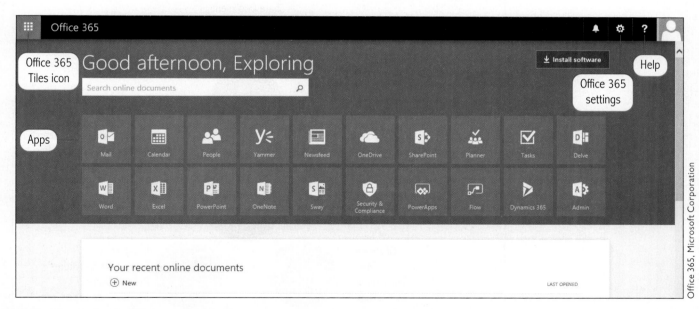

**FIGURE 1.2** Office 365 Welcome Screen

***SharePoint*** is the Microsoft central information sharing and business collaboration platform for organizations. SharePoint sites can be deployed both inside the organization (using intranets) and outside the organization's firewall (using extranets and the Internet) so employees, customers, and business partners can work together. Microsoft SharePoint 2016 includes SharePoint Online 2016 and SharePoint Server 2016. SharePoint Designer 2013 is a desktop application used to customize SharePoint websites. The OneDrive for Business sync app is an application that enables you to work on sites on your local computer. Each part of the platform has a specific purpose:

- SharePoint Online 2016 is a cloud-based service that enables people and organizations, such as businesses or governments, to collaborate, store, and manage documents within the organization and to provide a public website.

- SharePoint Server 2016 includes services that are managed on the organization's server. This product is an expensive and more complex product. It is recommended for large companies and Internet portals.

- SharePoint Designer 2013 is a free desktop application used to create sites for SharePoint Online and SharePoint Server. It enables you to add more features to websites and to customize the layouts of the sites to match your organization's branding. SharePoint Designer will not be updated for 2016 but can still be used with SharePoint Online sites.

- The OneDrive for Business sync app works with SharePoint Online to enable you to view and edit sites offline by putting a copy in a folder on your local computer.

Microsoft **SharePoint Online**, a component of Office 365, provides you with the commonly used features of SharePoint while relieving you of the burden of installing the software and maintaining servers. Using the Internet, you access the interface that enables you to build SharePoint sites. The sites reside on Microsoft servers in a secure environment.

The SharePoint capabilities—used to create solutions that bring together people, information, systems, and business processes—are summarized by Microsoft into categories, as shown in Figure 1.3, and include Share, Discover, Build, Organize, and Manage.

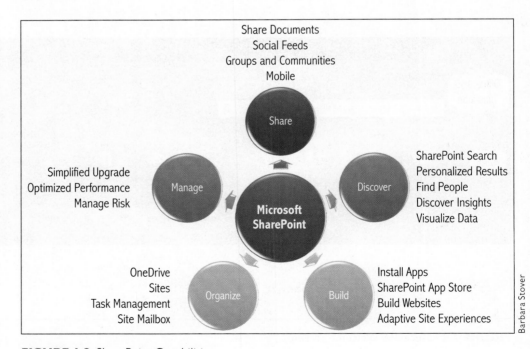

**FIGURE 1.3** SharePoint Capabilities

# Accessing and Exploring SharePoint Online

STEP 2 » Using a browser such as Microsoft Edge or Internet Explorer, you can access the SharePoint Online interface and begin building sites. A **SharePoint collection** is formed by a mandatory top-level site and one or more optional subsites. A **top-level site** is the topmost site (or parent site) in a site collection, as shown in Figure 1.4. A **subsite** (or child site) is a site that is created within a top-level site. A **SharePoint site** is a collection of related webpages, apps, and other components, such as lists and libraries, that enable you to organize and manage documents and information and to create workflows for the organization. **Team sites** facilitate collaboration among people in an organization by providing tools for information sharing and management.

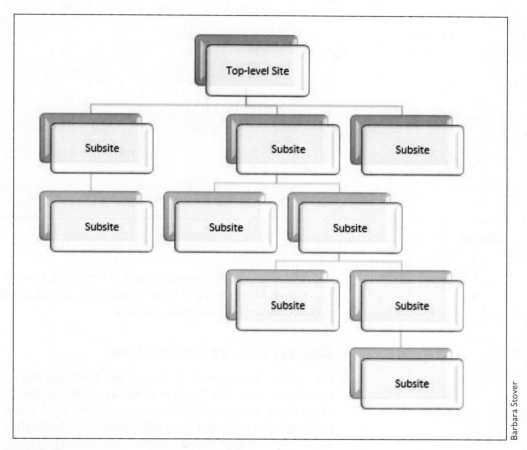

FIGURE 1.4 SharePoint Site Collection

SharePoint sites include a variety of components and services that can be used to solve business problems. It enables the user to create and customize a site. With little training or skills, a user can create sites, add apps and other components, and apply formatting to customize the site to meet the demands of organizations. SharePoint Online provides the tools you need for creating sites. Sign in to your Office 365 account and click the SharePoint tile displayed on the Welcome screen to access SharePoint Online. The Sites page displays the navigational structure and options you use to create new sites and edit existing sites, as shown in Figure 1.5. Think of the Sites page as your portal into all the sites you control or in which you participate. New sites you create will be shown on this page.

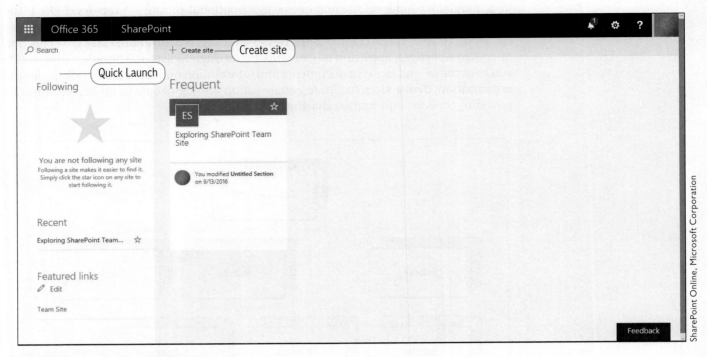

**FIGURE 1.5** SharePoint Online Window

Sites you are following are listed in the Quick Launch on the left side of the window. The **Quick Launch** is a common pane throughout all sites in SharePoint and provides easy access to elements within the site.

## Search SharePoint Online

One of the strongpoints of SharePoint Online is the ease with which you can search for information. The **Search field**, available at the top of the Quick Launch on the SharePoint page, enables you to search the sites you have permission to access. For instance, if you cannot remember which site holds the New Employee Welcome document, you can type the key words into the search field, and the search results list the sites or files where it can be found. Search filters focus searches on sites, people, and files, as shown in Figure 1.6.

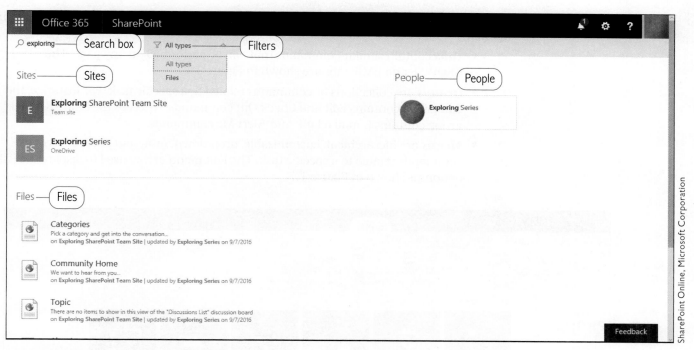

FIGURE 1.6 SharePoint Online Search

**To use the Search field, complete the following steps:**

1. Click in the Search box at the top of the Quick Launch.
2. Type the keyword(s) to use for the search, and then press Enter or click the arrow.

The outcome of the search is shown on a results page where the search filters are displayed across the top of the findings so that you can further refine the results. For instance, you may begin with a search, and then realize what you are looking for is a file. Click Files on the filter bar of the search results page, and a refined search results page displays.

> **TIP: SETTING UP A TRUSTED SITE**
> It is advisable to setup your SharePoint Online site as a Trusted Site in Internet Explorer. Click the Tools gear icon on the browser window, and then click Internet options. Click the Security tab, and then click Trusted sites. Click Sites, and then type the URL of your top-level site. Click Add. Click Close, and then click OK.

Beginner through professional developers can easily create, customize, and publish a professional-looking site using SharePoint Online. For instance, after leaving a meeting, you decide that you want to create a site so that your colleagues can review some new policy documents and comment on those documents. You simply create a new site, add the documents, and then share the site with your coworkers. You can select whether to share the site with everyone in the organization, or you can invite specific people by typing names or email addresses. SharePoint automatically adds tools and options to the site for customization.

## Use the SharePoint Online Ribbon

SharePoint Online features the Microsoft Office Fluent User Interface (UI), including the Ribbon. The Ribbon provides you with the user-friendly interface for accessing the SharePoint Online commands and tools. The **SharePoint Online Ribbon** is a fixed-position toolbar that appears across the top of each page and displays many of the most commonly used tools, controls, and commands. The Ribbon has three categories of components, as shown in Figure 1.7:

- *Tabs* contain similar commands that can be performed on any page. The BROWSE and PAGE tabs are shown in Figure 1.7.

- *Groups* are collections of commands related to a specific task. For instance, the Edit group contains Edit and Check Out commands, whereas the Share & Track group contains E-mail a Link and Alert Me commands.

- *Menus* are hierarchical, customizable, drop-down, or fly-out collections of commands related to a specific task. The Edit menu arrow used to display the Edit options is shown in Figure 1.7.

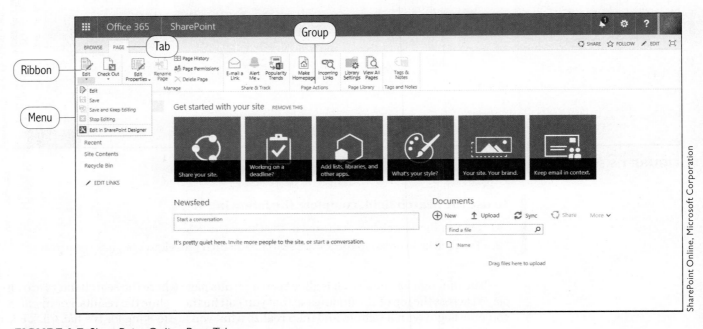

**FIGURE 1.7** SharePoint Online Page Tab

Commands are organized under the Ribbon tabs. By default, when viewing a site, the BROWSE tab will be the active tab. This tab does not display any Ribbon command options, as shown in Figure 1.8. The BROWSE tab displays the site page and navigation to additional pages in the site.

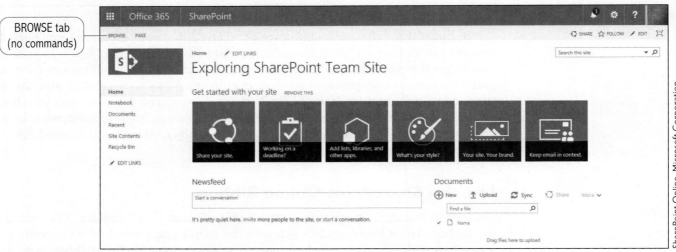

**FIGURE 1.8** SharePoint Online BROWSE Tab

SharePoint Online can be set to display in classic view or new view, which changes the options and their placement. To use a Ribbon, you often must switch to the classic SharePoint view. Click the link to Return to classic SharePoint at the bottom of the Quick Launch to display the view. To return to the new view (also known as the *new experience*), click Documents on the Quick Launch, click Library Settings in the Settings group on the Library tab and select Advanced settings. Scroll to the List experience section, select New experience, and then click OK. It can take some time for this setting to take effect.

The number and types of controls that appear on the Ribbon are context related and depend in part on the type of page you are viewing, the level of control the SharePoint Administrator has granted to you, and the configuration of your site. For example, the Documents page, shown in Figure 1.9 in classic view, includes the LIBRARY tab, meaning you have permission to add documents to the library. As you select Ribbon tabs, available commands are displayed. When you finish working with Ribbon commands, click the BROWSE tab to display the site page and navigation. To return to the top-level page for the site, click Home on the Quick Launch.

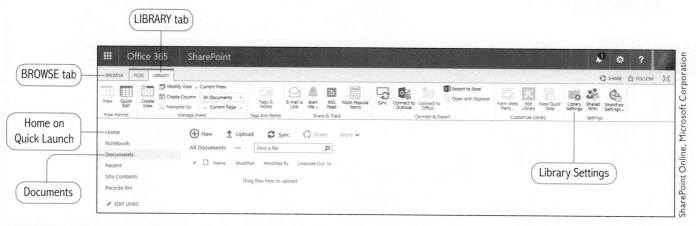

**FIGURE 1.9** SharePoint Online Documents Page Displayed in Classic View

The Settings menu contains options for managing the site based on the features available within the site and your permissions within the site. It also provides functions, such as create a new page or add an app, that may not be available on the Ribbon. You can access the Settings menu on every SharePoint page by clicking Settings (gear icon) on the top navigation bar and selecting Site settings, as shown in Figure 1.10.

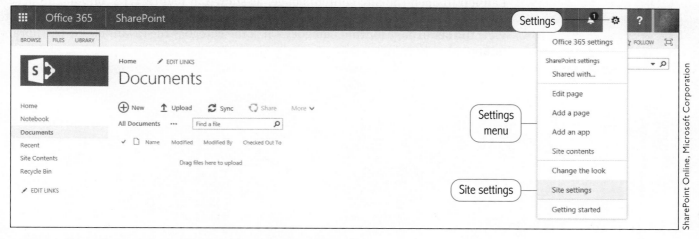

**FIGURE 1.10** SharePoint Online Settings in classic SharePoint view

# Viewing and Editing SharePoint Online Settings

The Site Settings page—displayed by clicking Site settings on the Settings menu—contains categories and options. Each category, shown in Figure 1.11, has links to several specific settings or subcategories. Many of the subcategories, such as Users and Permissions–People and groups, enable you to manage SharePoint lists. Other subcategories, such as Users and Permissions–Site collection administrators, provide dialog boxes with option settings.

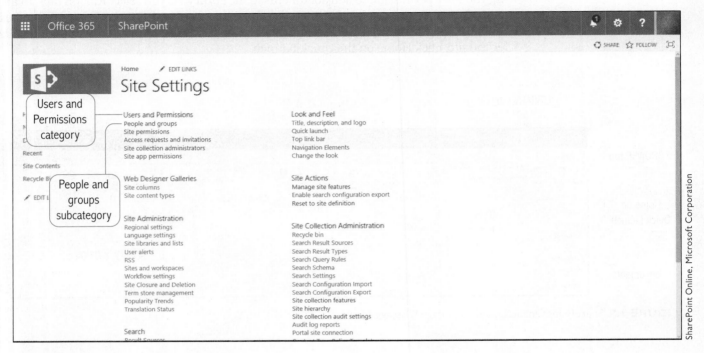

**FIGURE 1.11** SharePoint Online Site Settings

The Site contents page lists all the apps, documents, form templates, site assets, site pages, and style library items currently available to a user based on permission levels. The last date each item was modified is shown. Click Site contents in the Quick Launch to open the Site contents page, as shown in Figure 1.12, or you can access Site contents from the Settings menu. Click the category name of any listed item to view the detail page for that category. Click the category tile to launch the list, library, or app.

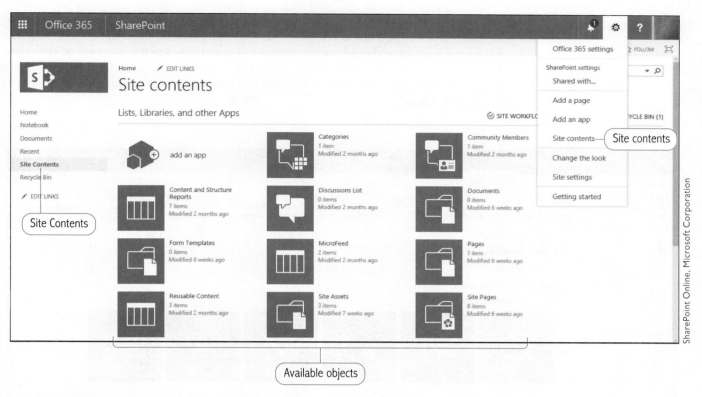

**FIGURE 1.12** SharePoint Online Site Contents Page Displayed in Classic View

Using SharePoint Online in a browser, click Edit on the PAGE tab on the Ribbon to edit pages. An alternative method for editing pages is to click Settings and select Edit page from the Settings menu. The Ribbon also contains an Edit button on the far-right side of the bar, which toggles into a Save icon when you open a page for editing. The FORMAT TEXT and INSERT tabs display on the Ribbon, as shown in Figure 1.13, with tools with which you may be familiar from working with other Office applications, ranging to some that are more specific to working with webpages.

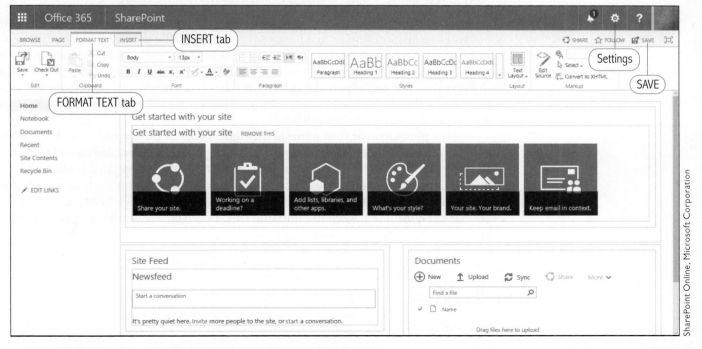

**FIGURE 1.13** SharePoint Online Editing Tabs Displayed in Classic View

The **status bar**, below the Ribbon, gives the user instant information in context, such as whether the page is checked out. The **notification area** appears on the right side of the Ribbon and displays messages that communicate the progress of the operation for a few seconds. For example, if you click the Check Out command in the Edit group, the status bar and notification area will look similar to the way they are displayed in Figure 1.14.

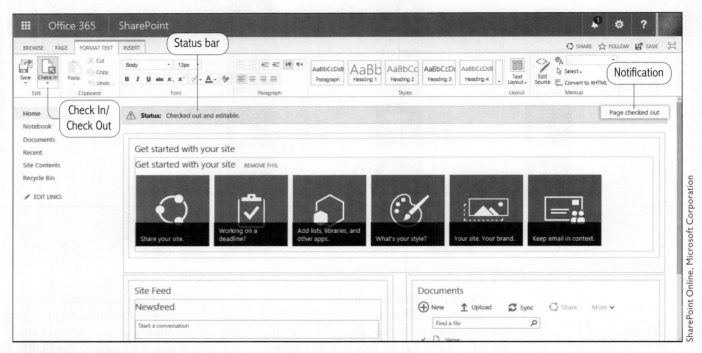

**FIGURE 1.14** SharePoint Online Status Bar and Notification Area Displayed in Classic View

## View and Edit Your SharePoint Online Profile

**STEP 3 ▶▶** Your online user profile presents your coworkers or team members with information about you in a fashion similar to a business card. This public profile includes basic information, contact information, and details. Some of the information is static and cannot be changed, such as the name used to set up your account. This basic information is shared with everyone. You can supply the details for other types of information and select who is able to view this information. User profiles are searched by SharePoint when users type names or keywords into the Search box.

Click the photo icon or your name at the right corner of the top navigation bar, select About me, and then click *Update profile* to open your profile in Delve. As you edit the information in your profile, remember that you are editing your Office 365 profile, and not just your SharePoint profile. The Delve page includes information such as your name, work phone number, a personal description, a picture, and topics where you are expert, as shown in Figure 1.15. Keep in mind that this should be a professional representation of you.

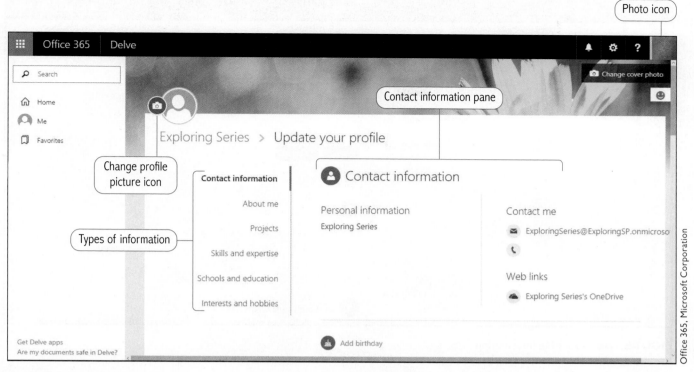

**FIGURE 1.15** Profile Information

Photographs in .bmp, .jpg, or .png format can be uploaded to your profile page. The optimal picture size is 96 × 96 pixels. Use a photograph that presents you as a business professional. When someone wants to review your profile, the user clicks your photograph.

**To upload a photograph, complete the following steps:**

1. Click the photo image in the right corner of the top navigation bar from any SharePoint or Office 365 page, and select About me.
2. Click the Change profile picture icon (refer to Figure 1.15).
3. Click Change your photo on the Edit Details page, which opens the Outlook My account page.
4. Click Upload photo.
5. Navigate to the location of the photograph on your local computer and select it.
6. Click Open. The photograph you selected will display in the Choose a picture window.
7. Click Upload.

Your personal description should focus on your career and offer details such as your title, current projects, and accomplishments within your field. To update this information, click in the About me box, as shown in Figure 1.16. When you have completed the editing of your personal description, click Save.

**FIGURE 1.16** About Me Information

**TIP: SAVING YOUR USER PROFILE**
As you save profile information, a dialog box may open informing you that changes to your profile may take some time. Click OK to continue with the updates.

Contact information is an important part of your profile and enables team members to get in touch with you in a variety of ways. Some information was added as your account was created and cannot be changed. You can add information, including your mobile phone number, fax number, home phone number, office location, and birthday, on this page. You also can select whether your fax number, home phone number, and office location are available to everyone or if it is private to you. Click the *Who can see this* arrow and select the option you want, as shown in Figure 1.17. You may have additional options based on how the administrator sets up your account. Click Save Home to add the information to your Contact me pane.

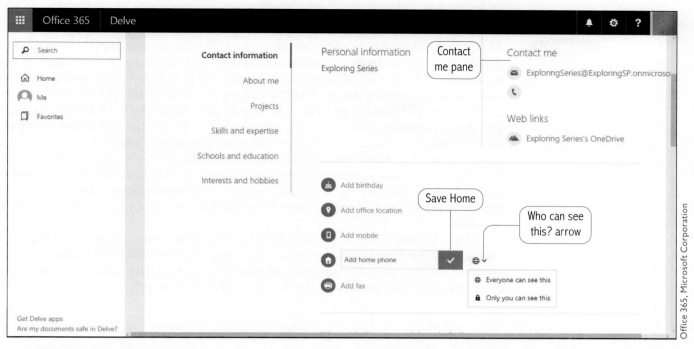

**FIGURE 1.17** Contact Information

Related to your personal description is the Skills and expertise section, as shown in Figure 1.8, which enables you to list your job responsibilities or areas of expertise. Type keywords in this box, to describe your skills, and click Add skill after each skill. These keywords can later be accessed by a user searching for a type of information on the SharePoint site. The Schools and education section enables you to list the schools you have attended, while the Interests and hobbies section can be used to list what you like to do in your spare time.

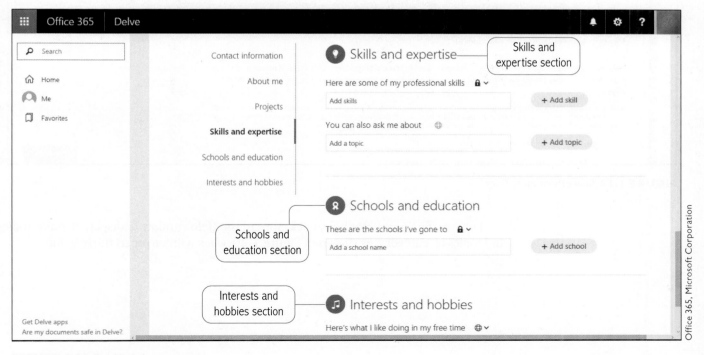

**FIGURE 1.18** Profile Information

# Getting Help

STEP 4 >> Although the SharePoint Online interface is user friendly, you may want additional information on a topic or setting. SharePoint Online, as with all Microsoft Office applications, includes an extensive set of help files that assist you in accomplishing anything from a simple task to a complex project. The help files are accessed through the Microsoft website.

To access the SharePoint Help pane, as shown in Figure 1.19, click Help (the question mark) on the right side of the top navigation bar. Within the SharePoint Help pane, click the Help link to open the Microsoft Office Support website which enables you to type topics to research in the Search Office help box. Help topics display for the keywords you type. You can browse community forum postings on the Microsoft Community page by clicking Community on the Help pane. You can type keywords into the search box, or browse by product or topic on the page. Depending on the keywords, you may see articles or videos.

At the bottom of the SharePoint Help pane there are links to Legal, and Privacy & cookies. The legal information includes the Acceptable Use Policy, the Customer Portal Terms of Use, a Privacy Notice, and Trademark information. The Privacy & Cookies page describes the privacy policies for the data throughout Office 365.

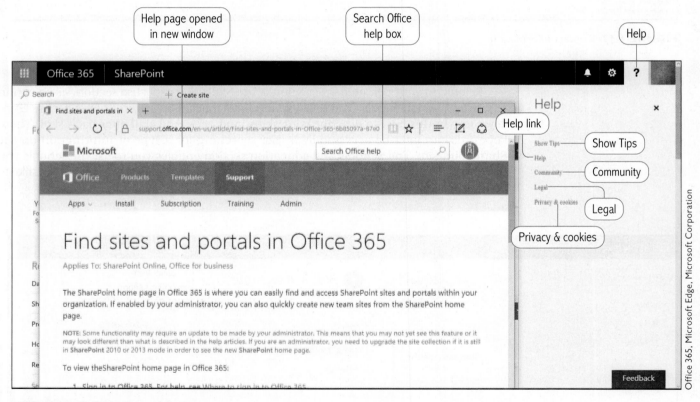

**FIGURE 1.19** SharePoint Help Pane

For specific SharePoint help, click Apps in the Help window to display popular topics and topics by category, as shown in Figure 1.20. Click a link to open the help file.

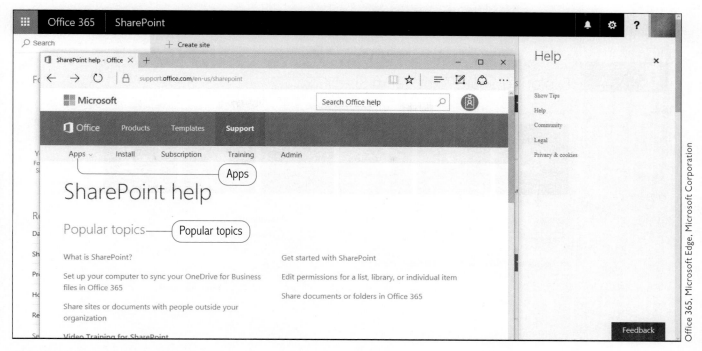

**FIGURE 1.20** SharePoint Help Search Results

***ScreenTips***, shown in Figure 1.21, display small boxes with descriptive and helpful text when you point to a command or control. Some controls roll up with additional information. For instance, Figure 1.22 shows a helpful hint for using the What's your style control on the Team Site page. When a Ribbon is available, Enhanced ScreenTips provide additional descriptive text, as shown in Figure 1.23.

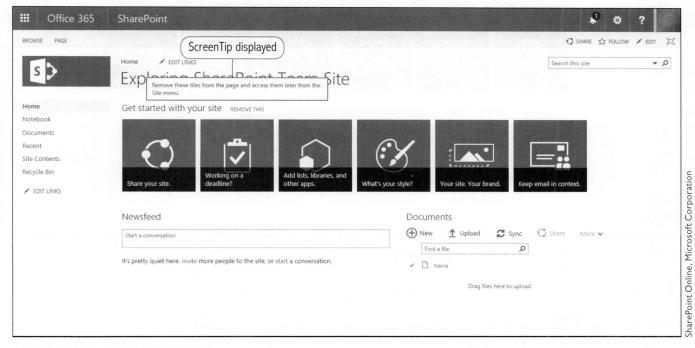

**FIGURE 1.21** SharePoint ScreenTip

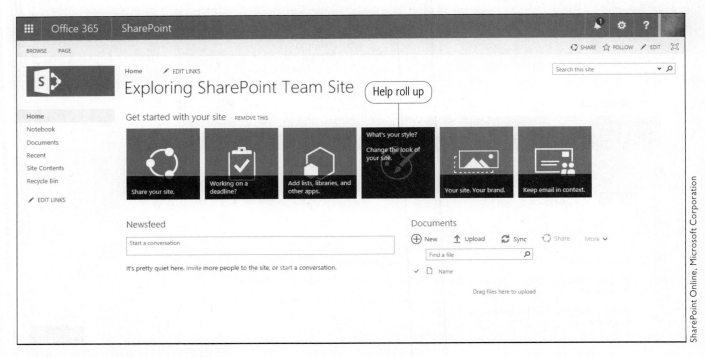

**FIGURE 1.22** SharePoint Help Roll Up

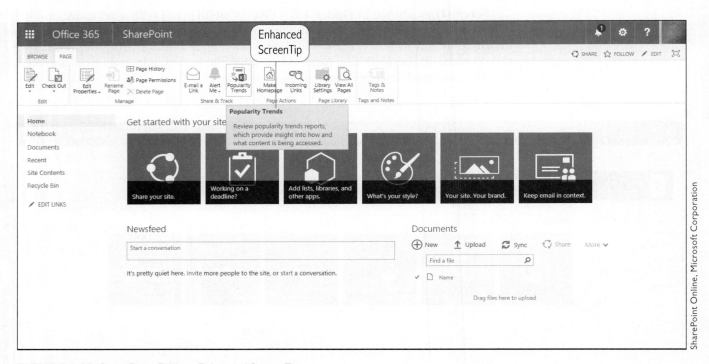

**FIGURE 1.23** SharePoint Ribbon Enhanced ScreenTip

**Quick Concept**

1. Describe two services that cloud computing provides. *p. 4*

2. What are some key advantages to using SharePoint Online team sites? *p. 7*

3. Explain the difference between the Search field and SharePoint Help. *p. 9, 18*

# Hands-On Exercises

**Skills covered:** Log onto Office 365 • Access SharePoint Online • Search SharePoint Online • Use the Ribbon • View Settings • Edit Settings • Use the SharePoint Help Window

## 1 Introduction to SharePoint

As you prepare to set up the new collaboration site for Daniela's Table, you review how to access your Office 365 account and your SharePoint Online workspace so that you can help members of your team get started.

---

### STEP 1 ›› EXPLORE MICROSOFT OFFICE 365

Before you can start exploring SharePoint Online, you must log in to your Office 365 account. Refer to Figure 1.24 as you complete Step 1.

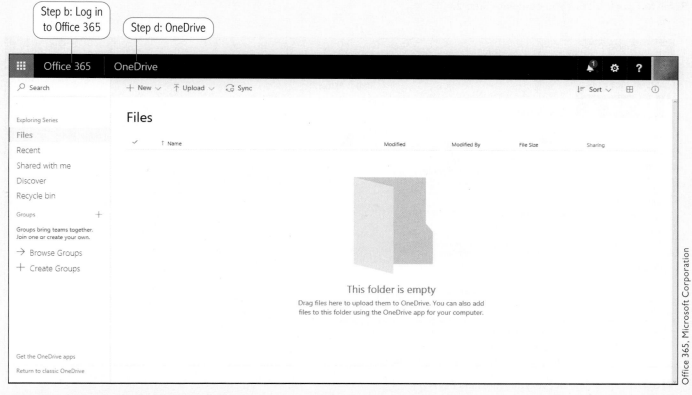

FIGURE 1.24 OneDrive Opened in Office 365

a. Open Microsoft Edge. Type **login.microsoftonline.com** in the address bar and press **Enter**.

b. Type your Office 365 **user name** and press **Enter**. Type your **password** and press **Enter**.

The Office 365 window displays with tips to help you get started on the Getting Started pane.

> **TROUBLESHOOTING:** Check with your instructor for your user name and password information.

**c.** Click the **Mail tile** on the Office 365 welcome screen.

Your mailbox may contain email messages or it may appear empty, depending on the setup of your account. Respond to any pop-up messages that you receive regarding security.

**d.** Click **Office 365** on the top navigation bar and click the **OneDrive tile**.

> **TROUBLESHOOTING:** If a Getting Started with OneDrive tab opens, click Next to continue with the exercise.

A new tab opens in the window. Documents or folders are shown in this window when you have added files and folders to OneDrive.

---

### STEP 2 ›› ACCESS AND EXPLORE SHAREPOINT ONLINE

To take full advantage of the SharePoint Online user interface, you will review the home page and search the site for information. Refer to Figure 1.25 as you complete Step 2.

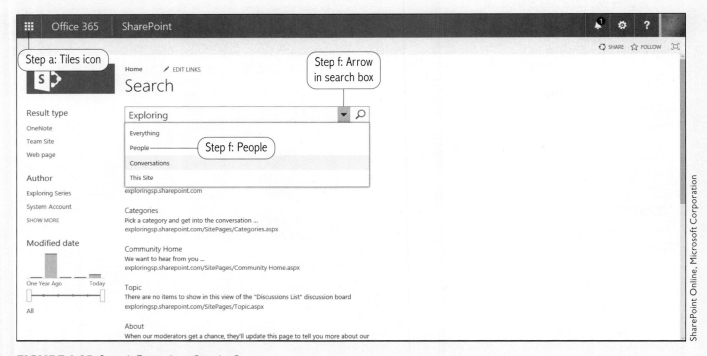

**FIGURE 1.25** Search Everything Results Page

**a.** Click the **Tiles icon** next to Office 365 on the top navigation bar, and select **SharePoint**.

Your SharePoint Online home page loads with links to a team site replacing the OneDrive tab.

> **TROUBLESHOOTING:** Click NOT NOW if an introductory page opens.

**b.** Click the **Team Site tile** in the right pane of the window or the **Team Site link** on the Quick Launch.

The team site loads with the Get started with your site, Newsfeed, and Documents areas.

**c.** Click the **PAGE tab** and review the options.

The PAGE tab displays editing and managing options for the page displayed in the window.

**d.** Click the **BROWSE tab** and observe the difference in the window.

**e.** Click in the **Search this site box**, type **your first name**, and click the **magnifying glass**.

**f.** Click the arrow in the search box, and click **People**.

Your profile information displays, possibly with just your first and last names. Additional profile information will be added in the next step.

### STEP 3 ›› VIEW AND EDIT YOUR PROFILE

So that your team can access information about you, you will update your SharePoint Online profile page to include areas of interest. Refer to Figure 1.26 as you complete Step 3.

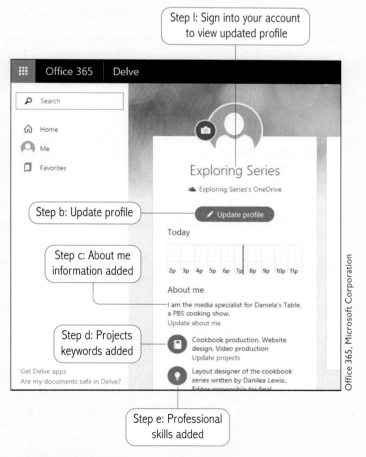

**FIGURE 1.26** Office 365 Profile

**a.** Click the photograph icon next to your name in the People search.

Your profile page opens in Delve, displaying the default information that was included when your account was created.

**b.** Click **Update profile** to open the Update your profile page and review the available information.

> **TROUBLESHOOTING:** Depending on the way your account is set up, you may see slightly different screens and click different buttons. To edit your profile, you can use Edit profile, rather than Update profile if that is the option on the page.

Access rights to viewing your basic information were set as your account was created for some items. For other items, you can determine whether other people can see the information.

**c.** Click in the **About me box** and type **I am the media specialist for Daniela's Table, a PBS cooking show.** (Be sure to include the period.)

**d.** Click in the **Projects** box and type **Cookbook production** and click **Add project**. Type **Website design** in the Projects box and click **Add project**. Type **Video production** in the Projects box and click **Add project**.

You have typed keywords that can be used to search for people with various skills.

**e.** Click in the **Here are some of my professional skills box** in the Skills and expertise section. Type **Layout designer of the cookbook series written by Daniela Lewis**, and click **Add skill**. Type **Editor responsible for final production standards.** in the Here are some of my professional skills box and click **Add skill**. (Include the periods.)

This information will be made available to everyone who views your profile.

**f.** Click in the **Schools and education box**, and type **your college or university name**.

Additional schools can be typed in this box, click Add school between each entry.

**g.** Click the **lock icon** next to the Schools box and select **Everyone can see this**. Click **Add school**.

> **TROUBLESHOOTING:** Click the lock icon above the box if you do not see the Everyone arrow, and change the setting to *Everyone can see this*.

You have set the privacy on the information to enable anyone to see this profile information.

**h.** Scroll up and click the **How can I change language and regional settings link,** and then click the **here link.** Click the **More options icon ( . . .)** and click **Language and Region**.

**i.** Click **Always use my personal settings** option in the Region section to select it.

> **TROUBLESHOOTING:** You may be blocked from changing to personalized settings by your administrator. If so, skip to step m.

**j.** Click the **Time Zone arrow** (above the Region section), and select the **Time Zone** of your location.

**k.** Click **Save all and close**. Click **OK** in response to the Profile Changes dialog box message.

**l.** Sign out of your Office 365 account and close the browser. Reopen the browser, sign into your account, and click the SharePoint tile. Type your name in the Search box, press **Enter**, and click your name in the People section of the results. Using the Snipping Tool, take a screen snip that shows your profile information. Save the file as **sp01h1Profile_LastFirst**. You will submit this file at the end of the Hands-On Exercises.

> **TROUBLESHOOTING:** Changes to your profile will not display until you sign out and close the browser, and then sign back into your account.

**m.** Close the Delve tab on the browser and return to a SharePoint tab.

**STEP 4 ›› GET HELP**

From beginner to advanced level, all SharePoint Online users will need to take advantage of the Help features at some time. You and your team members will need to know how to access the Help features. You will learn how to use SharePoint Help. Refer to Figure 1.27 as you complete Step 4.

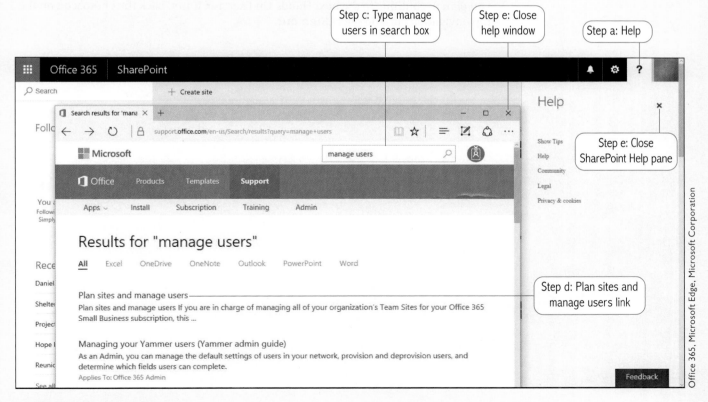

**FIGURE 1.27** SharePoint Help

**a.** Click **SharePoint** on the top navigation bar to return to the SharePoint home page. Click the **Help question mark** on the top navigation bar, click **Help** in the Help pane, and type **profile privacy** in the Search Office help box. Click the **magnifying glass icon**.

The SharePoint Help window contains a topic list of profile help information.

> **TROUBLESHOOTING:** If the SharePoint home page is not displayed, click the Tiles icon next to Office 365 on the top navigation bar and select the SharePoint tile.

**b.** Click the **Update your profile privacy settings link**. Review the information.

> **TROUBLESHOOTING:** If this topic is not available, select another topic to review.

**c.** Type **manage users** in the search box in the Microsoft support webpage box and press **Enter**.

Even though the help result topics are contextual, you can search for information that is not related to the page you are viewing.

**d.** Click the **Plan sites and manage users link** in the topics list. Read the article. Using the Snipping Tool, take a screen snip that shows the beginning of the article. Save the file as **sp01h1Help_LastFirst**. You will submit this file at the end of the Hands-On Exercises.

**e.** Close the browser window that contains the help file information.

**f.** Click **Close** in the top-right corner of the SharePoint Help pane.

**g.** Click **SharePoint** on the top navigation bar to return to the SharePoint home page if you plan to continue to the next Hands-On Exercise. If not, click the photo icon on the top navigation bar and select **Sign out**.

# Explore SharePoint Online Sites

Studies show that a successful twenty-first-century professional must learn to innovate. Developing creative adaptations using emerging technology and being able to collaborate effectively toward gaining competitive advantages have proved to be a successful approach toward building a rewarding professional career. SharePoint technologies have a tremendous impact on the Web developer community, and enable businesses of any size to develop innovative business applications. SharePoint sites are the foundation of all SharePoint installations and include a variety of components and services that can be used to solve business problems. SharePoint developers, from beginner to advanced, benefit from these features of SharePoint:

- Developers can easily create, customize, and publish a professional business site.
- The Office Ribbon user interface makes it easy to navigate and find the features.
- SharePoint Online enables users to access content, edit it, and quickly sync the edits to the server for distribution to team members or to a business or organization website.
- Windows mobile devices, such as Windows phones, enable users to access SharePoint Online, making content available to users while away from a desktop computer.
- Office Online apps can be used to access, edit, and save Microsoft Word, Excel, PowerPoint, and OneNote documents in a browser without loss of formatting.
- SharePoint sites are supported by current browsers, including mobile browsers, enabling users to work together regardless of the type of browser they have.
- SharePoint enables interoperability with non-Microsoft software applications within the SharePoint environment.
- SharePoint has accessible templates and tools that comply with the Web Content Accessibility Guidelines (WCAG 2.0) and the United Nations Convention on the Rights of Persons with Disabilities.

The United Nations Convention on the Rights of Persons with Disabilities recognized access to information and communications technologies—including the Web—as a basic human right. Accessible websites feature support for people with a range of disabilities including hearing, movement, sight, and cognitive ability. Refer to the appendices of this textbook to learn more about the Web design guidelines that are included in the World Wide Web Consortium's (W3C) Web Accessibility Initiative (WAI) and the U.S. federal law, subsection 1194.22 of Section 508, concerning Web-based intranet and Internet information and applications. You will also be introduced to some of the most popular assistive and adaptive technologies in the appendices.

This section introduces you to SharePoint Online tools for creating sites. You will learn about the categories of sites and explore a team site.

## Understanding Templates and the SharePoint Top-Level Team Site

SharePoint Online enables you to create sites that fit your needs. Users can create sites, add lists and libraries, and apply formatting to customize the site to meet the demands of the organization and the people who are collaborating.

Templates enable you to get a quick start on the development of a site. A **template** provides the SharePoint developer with a beginning set of tools and a layout for a site or workspace. The templates are grouped into three categories: Collaboration, Enterprise, and Duet Enterprise in SharePoint Online. SharePoint Server contains an additional category of templates called Publish. The SharePoint Online categories and template types are shown in Table 1.1.

**TABLE 1.1   Template Categories**

| Category | Template |
|---|---|
| Collaboration | **Team Site:** Facilitates team collaboration. This type of site provides tools for information sharing and management, as well as other team collaboration activities.<br>**Blog:** Used to post information for comment and discussion. Discussions on specific topics are captured and managed on blog sites.<br>**Project Site:** Focuses team collaboration on a specific project. All status, communication, and documents relevant to the project are stored in the project site.<br>**Community Site:** Enables community members to congregate and discuss common interests. Members can explore and filter discussions, and gain reputation points for contributions they make to the community site. |
| Enterprise | **Document Center:** Used to manage documents in a central location.<br>**Records Center:** Facilitates records management.<br>**Enterprise Search Center:** Enables an enterprise-wide search experience through general, people, conversation, and video searches.<br>**Basic Search Center:** Provides general search capabilities. |
| Duet Enterprise | **SAP Workflow Site:** Enables management of financial, asset, and cost accounting; production operations and materials; personnel; plants; and archived documents. |

By default, your Sites page contains a team site that you can customize to fit the needs of your organization. The highly customizable sites enable you to add components that help you manage information, facilitate collaboration, and enable workflow. These components include the following:

- **Lists** are collections of announcements, links, surveys, discussion boards, or tasks. Lists contain structured and tabular data. Built-in lists, such as Announcements, Calendar, and Links, appear by default when the site is created. You can customize these lists and also create new lists.

- **Libraries** are collections of documents, pictures, or forms that can be shared with others. Libraries contain unstructured data such as image, video, and audio files. By default, SharePoint sites contain a generic document library called *Documents*, which is an available link on the Quick Launch. Using SharePoint document libraries, you can filter and group documents as well as view metadata. You can create new custom libraries for a particular business category or subject.

- **Workflows** enable you to manage business processes and the associated content. Workflow includes organization notifications, tracking, and transactions. SharePoint workflows include Approval, Collect Feedback, Collect Signatures, Three-State, and Publishing Approval. You can use SharePoint Designer or Visual Studio to create and deploy custom workflows. For example, your site may include a custom workflow for managing customer support issues, sales leads, or project tasks.

- **Web Part zones** are containers for Web Parts. As you customize your site, you can personalize, remove, and/or add more Web Parts.

- The **Recycle Bin** holds and enables you to restore deleted elements for a SharePoint site, such as files, lists, and libraries.

Be default, each template may have document libraries, form libraries, picture libraries, and Wiki libraries. Every template has a list of tools for announcements, calendars, contacts, discussion boards, issue tracking, links, surveys, and project tasks. Pages, sites, workspaces, and Web Parts pages are available in all the templates.

*Office Online* services include Web-based versions of Microsoft Word 2016, Excel 2016, PowerPoint 2016, and OneNote 2016. You can create these types of documents directly from your SharePoint site. These apps are focused on offering access to documents through any browser, across multiple platforms, and enabling creating and editing capabilities in standard formats.

The SharePoint document libraries store most file types and provide integration with Office products such as Word, Excel, PowerPoint, and OneNote. When you open an Office document in a document library, it will launch the associated Office Online app. When you click New in a document library, you can select the Office Online app that is appropriate for creating a new file, as shown in Figure 1.28. You can also upload existing files that you may have on your local computer, such as images, video, audio, or documents created in desktop applications such as AutoCAD, Photoshop, or Microsoft Office 2016. Documents can be organized into folders in the document library.

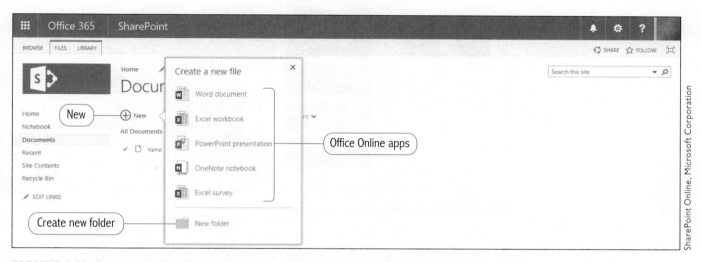

**FIGURE 1.28** Create New File Options Displayed in Classic SharePoint View

Office Online apps are supported by the following browsers:

- Microsoft Edge
- Internet Explorer 9 and later
- Chrome (latest version)
- Firefox (latest version)
- Safari (latest 2 versions)

---

**TIP: OFFICE ONLINE SUPPORT**
To find out if your mobile device is supported by Office Online, perform a search using the phrase *Office Online Browser Support*.

---

## Explore the Top-Level Team Site

Each SharePoint collection has a top-level site under which you can build subsites. The Team Site tile on the Sites page is the entry point into the top-level site. Top-level sites and subsites allow different levels of control over the features and settings for sites. Subsites can also contain other subsites. For instance, your organization may use a subsite for the Human Resources department. This site may have a subsite for employees and another for volunteers, with each site featuring different types of information focused on the needs of the members of the site. The infrastructure of a SharePoint site looks very similar to the tree-like hierarchy of folders in a file system (refer to Figure 1.4).

A *site hierarchy* is the complete hierarchical infrastructure including subsites and its own components, as shown in Figure 1.29. Because the subsites are contained within the top-level parent site, the complete hierarchical infrastructure of a SharePoint site includes its subsites.

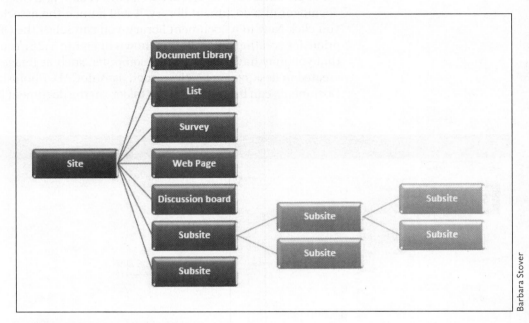

**FIGURE 1.29** SharePoint Site Hierarchy

Access to SharePoint sites is controlled through a system that uses permission levels. *Permission levels* are rights within a site and can be assigned to individual users or groups giving every group member the same rights within the same level in the site hierarchy. Rights to sites, lists, and libraries can be granted to SharePoint groups throughout the site hierarchy.

**To view a site's hierarchy, complete the following steps:**

1. Navigate to the top-level site for which you have the appropriate permission level within the collection.
2. Click Settings (the gear icon on the top navigation bar) and select Site settings from the menu.
3. Click Site hierarchy in the Site Collection Administration section.

Usually, top-level sites are created for an entire team and have many visitors (people who can only read the content), a few members (people who can create and update content), and one or two owners (people who can add, customize, or delete items within a site). Owners of a site have broad rights and can create and delete additional subsites or the current site, add additional users to one or more of the site groups, or create their own new custom groups of permissions. As subsites are created at different levels of the tree-like infrastructure, the total number of people with visitor's permissions usually decreases, whereas the number of people designated as members increases. These permissions determine what specific actions users can perform on the site. The default permission levels available in SharePoint Online are shown in Table 1.2.

**TABLE 1.2  SharePoint Online Permission Levels**

| Permission Level | Enables User to |
|---|---|
| Full Control | Access, edit, and delete all parts of the site. This permission level cannot be changed or deleted from SharePoint. |
| Design | Manage lists, libraries, and pages within a SharePoint site and approve content. |
| Edit | Add, edit, and delete lists, as well as view, add, update, and delete list items and documents. This is the default permission level assigned to the Members group. |
| Contribute | Read, create, and edit rights to existing lists and document libraries. |
| Read | View pages and items in existing lists and document libraries. |
| Limited Access | View a specific content item. Permission is not assigned to a user but rather to the item to which limited access is applied. This permission level cannot be changed or deleted from SharePoint. |
| Approve | Edit and approve pages, list items, and documents. |
| Manage Hierarchy | Create sites and edit pages, list items, and documents. |
| Restricted Read | View pages and documents, but not historical versions of documents. |
| View Only | View pages, items, and documents. |

Pearson Education, Inc.

When a new top-level site is created, three default Team Site group permission levels are created: Team Site Owners, Team Site Members, and Team Site Visitors, as shown in Figure 1.30. Owners have full control of all parts of the top-level site and subsites. Members have Edit permissions that enable them to collaborate by working in existing lists and document libraries. Visitors can only read pages within the site.

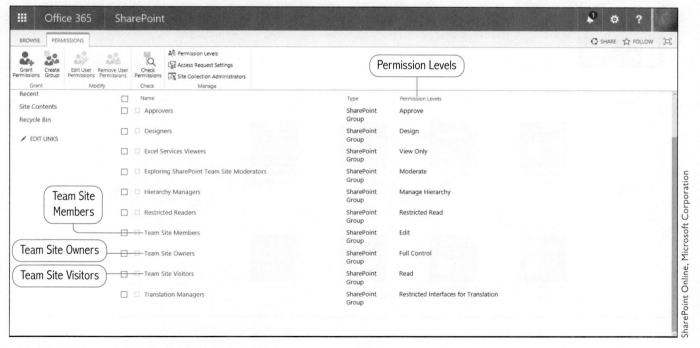

SharePoint Online, Microsoft Corporation

**FIGURE 1.30** SharePoint Online Permissions

Because SharePoint groups can be used across sites, having the ability to see all sites where a group has been assigned permissions can be very valuable. You can review the control each type of user has on the Site Permissions page. The permission levels for each group are displayed in the far right column.

## Get Started with SharePoint Sites

**STEP 1** ▶▶ The SharePoint Online interface automatically adds a team site template to your Sites page as your account is created. Other site templates, such as a public site, may also be available. The default template defines the site layout and provides a beginning set of components, such as a document library and a notebook in a team site. These tools are provided because they facilitate work and collaboration. The site components and other settings in the template can be modified as required by your organization. Sites that are created based on a template can be saved as a new template for use in the development of future sites.

> **TIP: SAVING A TEMPLATE**
> At the time this text was written, a site could only be saved as a template in a private, non-publishing site.

The team site enables teams to organize, create, and share information quickly. Apps can be added to the team site to increase the functionality using Site Contents on the Quick Launch. SharePoint lists, such as announcements, calendars, links, and tasks, are added as apps. You also have the option to create custom lists using the Custom List app. You can add libraries to contain certain types of files, such as documents, pictures, forms, and reports, by clicking Add lists, libraries, and other apps in the content area of your team site. The Discussion Board app enables members of the team to post and reply to forums. If your organization creates custom apps, they can also be added to your team site. Before you add an app to your site, you can review a description of the app by clicking App Details under the app icon, as shown in Figure 1.31. Click the app icon to add it to your team site.

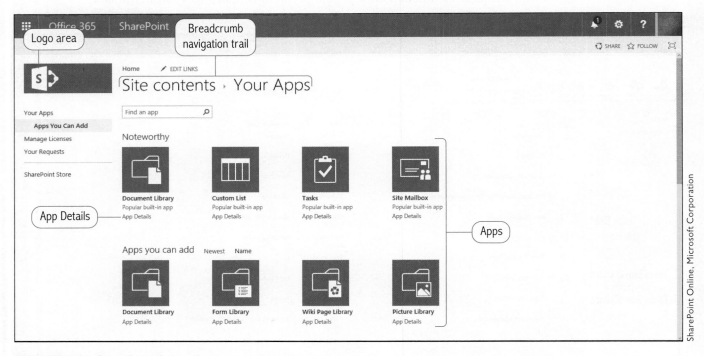

**FIGURE 1.31** SharePoint Online Apps

The team site layout includes tools and features that enable you to create new content and view the content on the site, as shown in Figure 1.32. The navigation bar, displayed across the top of the SharePoint Online window, enables you to use the tools in Office 365 and the SharePoint Online tools of Notifications, Settings, and Help. To the far right of the navigation bar, the photograph icon opens the User Info menu. The User Info menu displays the name of the user and a menu enabling you to update your personal profile and sign out of Office 365.

The **Ribbon** displays the tabs available for the page you are viewing. Keep in mind that the BROWSE tab does not display a Ribbon. **Contextual commands** change based on the page you are viewing. These commands are located on the far right side of the Ribbon control and enable you to share, follow, sync, edit, and focus on content. For instance, to hide the navigation for a site, click the Focus on Content button (see Figure 1.32). This is a toggle button, so you click it again to display the navigation.

The **top link bar** displays tab links to other sites and a Home link to enable you to return to the main page of the root site. You can customize the top link bar to include other links using the EDIT LINKS link. The search box on the right side of the top link bar enables you to search the current site. Depending on your location in the site, you may see the breadcrumb navigation trail available on the titles (as shown in Figure 1.31). The **breadcrumb navigation** trail enables you to see the path leading to the current page and to keep track of the current page location easily within the site, with clickable links to jump directly to a page.

The logo area (refer to Figure 1.31) is customizable and provides branding to your site. It also enables you to return to the home page of the current site with a single click.

The Quick Launch area is located in the left pane of the site; it provides easy access to elements that are available within the site, including libraries, lists, and sites, and includes a link to access all the site contents. Newly added components are featured under the Recent heading, notifying users that a new section has been added. The five newest links are displayed under the Recent heading. The Home button on the Quick Launch returns to the home page of the current site. Default links on a team site Quick Launch include Notebook, Documents, and Site Contents. The Notebook is a Web-based OneNote notebook where site members can share notes. The Documents link leads to the documents on the current site. The Site Contents link provides an overview of the installed apps, documents, and other site assets. You can add new links to the Quick Launch to make the interface more user friendly.

**Promoted links** are tiles that enable users to enter sites or add tools to a site. For instance, when you are viewing a site, the *Working on a deadline?* tile displays apps for Tasks and Calendar. The *What's your style?* tile enables you to select a different theme for your site.

The **content section**, located to the right of the Quick Launch, is the main body of the site page and includes all the elements you want to make available through the site (e.g., documents, lists, and Web Parts). Web Part zones and Wiki zones are used to house the content of the pages.

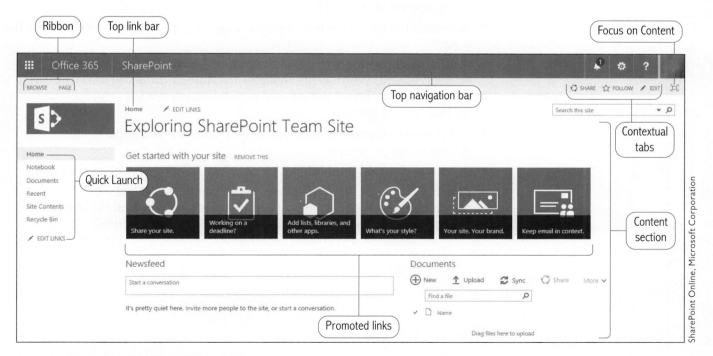

**FIGURE 1.32** SharePoint Team Site Layout

## Create a New SharePoint Site

 **STEP 2** ❯❯ Planning is an important step in creating a new site. You need to carefully analyze all the requirements related to the business or organizational processes you want to build, so you will be able to use the appropriate SharePoint tools and features in developing a new SharePoint site. You will need to take into consideration some core marketing, technical, usability, and social requirements while planning a SharePoint site.

- Determine the reasons for developing a new site. Are new business opportunities driving the need for a team site or public site? Do you need to provide more services or information to your users?

- Determine the short-term and long-term objectives for the website. Do you need to increase sales or build brand awareness? Will the site no longer be needed once a project is complete?

- Determine how often the site will be updated and who will be responsible for the content and updating of the site. If the site is informational, who will have permission to update it? Will team members collaborate by updating content and participating in discussions?

- Determine, in concrete numbers, how you will measure the success of the website. Will an increase in site visitors constitute success? How much money will the site have to generate to be considered successful?

- Determine the characteristics of the people using your website. How often are they online? Will they access the site using mobile devices? Are they familiar with using site tools, such as discussion boards and lists?

- What are the basic characteristics of users, such as age, occupation, educational level, income, and purchasing habits, and how will these impact the content or organization of the website? What is their level of technical proficiency?

- What is the corporate structure? What security is needed?

- Determine what site visitors should do on the site. Will they make a purchase, join a cause, collaborate on a project, or search for information that is important to them?

- Determine what value the users will derive from the site. Are they looking for specific information about a product or service? Will they actively participate within the site on a project?

- Determine the daily, weekly, or monthly usage of your site. How will you track the usage?

- Determine the source of the content and how it is organized. Will you use existing content? Who has the ability to add content? How will you ensure that the content is accurate? What visual elements, such as a logo, color scheme, and navigation, will you use?

- Determine the type of browser used by your potential audience. Will the users employ mobile browsers?

- Determine the need for third-party technologies, such as JavaScript or Flash.

- Determine the potential for database functionality. Will you allow personalization? Will site users be required to log in to the site? Will content be generated from a database, for example, for a catalog of products?

- Determine how your organization will be paid for products or services. Will you need to use secure online transactions?
- Determine other specific programming needs. Will personalization be a necessary part of the website experience for the users?

A team site contains the tools and features needed for successful communication and collaboration among the members of the group. After carefully considering the users of the site, you can create a new site in the team site collection.

**To create a new subsite in a team site collection, complete the following steps:**

1. Ensure the team site where you want to create the subsite is displayed in classic Sharepoint view.
2. Click Site Contents on the Quick Launch and click new subsite at the bottom of the window, as shown in Figure 1.33.
3. Type identifying information for the site into the form, as shown in Figure 1.34. Note that the URL name must be unique. In other words, you cannot have three subsites named *TeamSite*.
4. Click the Create button to finalize the selections you made. The site will be created and displayed in the SharePoint Online window.

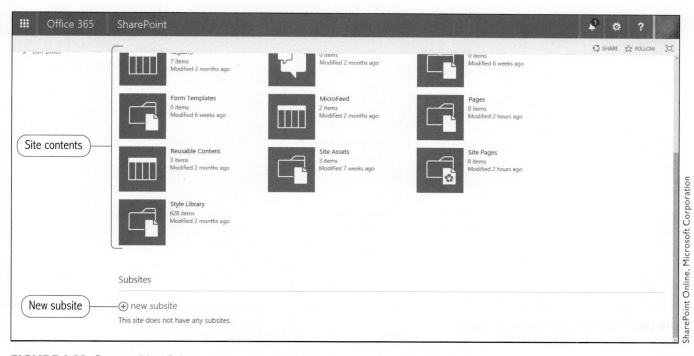

**FIGURE I.33** Create a New Subsite

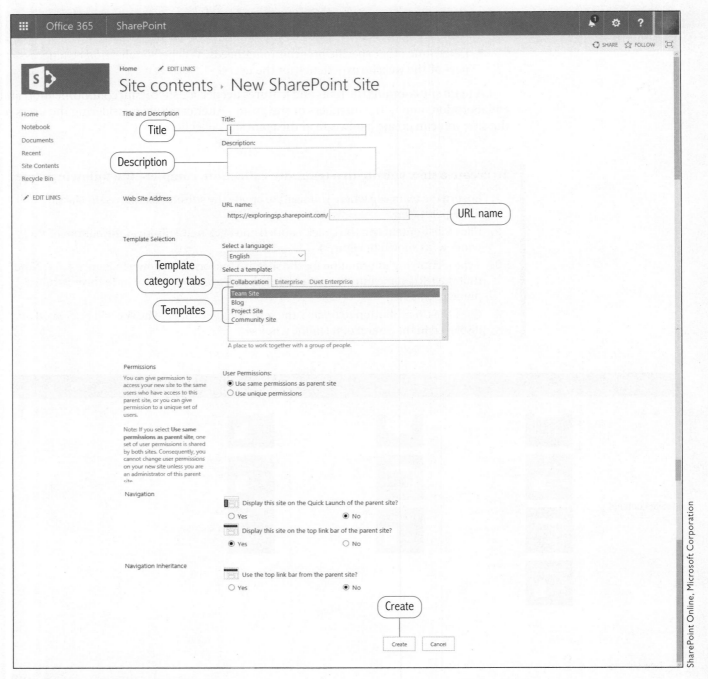

**FIGURE 1.34** New SharePoint Site Form

SharePoint Online, Microsoft Corporation

> **TIP: CREATING A URL**
> Best practices for creating a URL include using all lowercase letters and no spaces with the name. Some browsers do not handle blank spaces in a URL accurately, and that can cause your page not to be displayed.

A link to the new site will appear in the Following area on the Sites page. Click the link for the site to open it in the SharePoint Online window. You can add components to the site, apply a theme, or brand the site. It is a good practice to add the components that you think team members will use before you invite them to share the site. Additional components can be added as needed.

The new team site will have Newsfeed and Documents apps by default. Click Site Contents on the Quick Launch to review the apps installed on the site and to add additional apps, as shown in Figure 1.35.

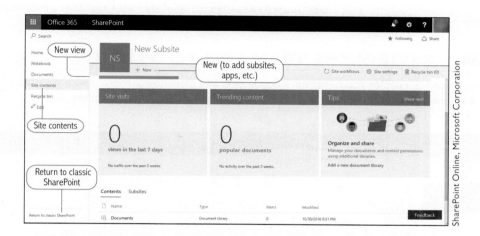

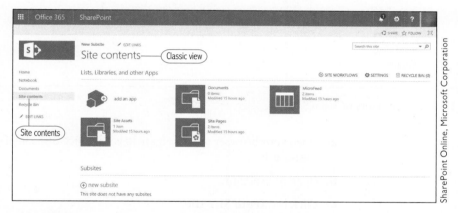

**FIGURE 1.35** Site Contents of Team Subsite (New View and Classic View)

---

**TIP: ACCESSING THE NEW SUBSITE**
You can also access the new subsite from the top-level team site. Depending on the selections you made as you created the site, links will appear on the Quick Launch or the top link bar.

---

**Quick Concept**

4. Describe the purpose of a SharePoint collection. *p. 29*

5. What four considerations you should make as you select tools for a new team site? *p. 32*

6. Describe the differences between the top link bar and the breadcrumb navigation. *p. 33*

# Hands-On Exercises

## 2 Explore SharePoint Online Sites

The team working on the Daniela's Table public website will use a top-level team site for collaboration activities. You will review the top-level team site capabilities and create a new team site with a subsite.

### STEP 1 ➤➤ REVIEW THE TEAM SITE TEMPLATE

The top-level team site enables you to organize documents and files and collaborate with your team. You will explore the default navigation and tools available on the top-level site. Refer to Figure 1.36 as you complete Step 1.

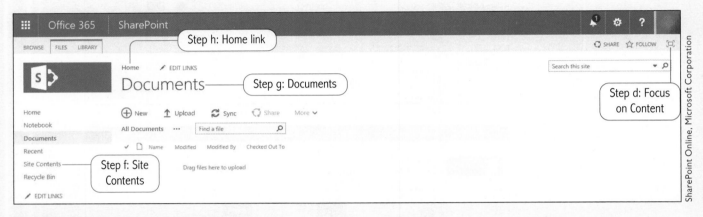

**FIGURE 1.36** Site Contents of Team Site

a. Open your browser and navigate to your Office 365 site if you closed it after Hands-On Exercise 1.

b. Open SharePoint.

c. Click the **Team Site tile**.

> **TROUBLESHOOTING:** The Team Site tile may have a different name, such as your university or college name followed by the words Team Site or your account name followed by Team Site. It is the only tile displayed in the content area of the screen when you first begin to use SharePoint Online. Other tiles will display as you add subsites to SharePoint.

The top-level team site opens.

d. Click **Focus on Content** below your name on the right side of the Ribbon.

Navigation buttons and links are removed from the page.

e. Click **Focus on Content** again to return the navigational controls to the display.

f. Click **Site Contents** on the Quick Launch. Click **Return to classic SharePoint** at the bottom of the Quick Launch.

The default apps are displayed.

**g.** Click the **Documents tile** in the Lists, Libraries, and other Apps section. Using the Snipping Tool, take a snip of the screen, and save it as **sp01h2Documents_LastFirst**.

The Documents page is displayed. Currently, there are no documents available.

**h.** Click the **SharePoint** on the top navigation bar.

The top-level team site page displays.

## STEP 2 ›› CREATE A NEW TEAM SITE AND SUBSITE USING A TEMPLATE

In preparation for collaboration with your colleagues, you will create a new team site and create a notebook to contain collaboration history notes. You will also create a subsite to enable people to use the discussion tool. You will work in classic SharePoint view. Refer to Figure 1.37 as you complete Step 2.

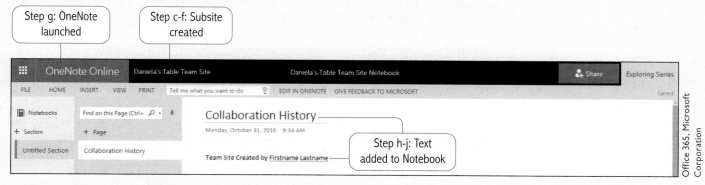

**FIGURE 1.37** Site Contents of Team Site

**a.** Click the **Team Site tile** and click **Site Contents** on the Quick Launch.

The new team site will be a subsite of the top-level team site.

**b.** Scroll to the Subsites section. Click **new subsite**.

The form for a New SharePoint Site is displayed.

**c.** Type **Daniela's Table Team Site** in the Title box. Type **This site supports the team designing the public website for Daniela's Table, a PBS show.** (include the period) in the Description box.

**d.** Type **danielastable** in the URL name box. Confirm that English is the selected language and that the Team Site template is selected.

**e.** Accept the default values for the User Permissions and Navigation Inheritance settings.

**f.** Click **Create**.

**g.** Click **Notebook** on the Quick Launch.

A notebook is opened in the Microsoft OneNote Online app.

**h.** Type the page title **Collaboration History** above today's date.

**i.** Click below the current date and type **Team Site Created by**, followed by **your first and last name**.

**j.** Click the **Daniela's Table Team Site link** on the top navigation bar.

The notebook entry is automatically saved and the team site is displayed.

**k.** Click **Notebook** in the Quick Launch. Review the notebook title and entry. Use the Snipping Tool to take a screen snip of the notebook. Name the file **sp01h2Notebook_LastFirst**.

**l.** Click the **Daniela's Table Team Site link** to return to the team site home page.

**m.** Click **Site contents** in the Quick Launch, scroll to the Subsites section, and then click **new subsite**.

You will create a subsite of Daniela's Table Team Site to enable people to have discussions using the tools available on the Community Site template.

**n.** Type **Daniela's Community Site** in the Title box. Type **The Community Site will be used for discussions.** (include the period) in the Description box. Type **community** in the URL name box. Click **Community Site** in the Select a template box. Accept all other defaults, and click **Create**.

After a few moments, the Community site is created. This site is a subsite to the Daniela's Table subsite.

**o.** Click the **SharePoint** on the top navigation bar, and click the **Daniela's Table Team Site tile**. Use the Snipping Tool to take a screen clip of the Daniela's Table Team Site. Name the file **sp01h2TeamSite_LastFirst**. You will submit the files you created at the end of the last Hands-On Exercise.

**p.** Click **SharePoint** on the top navigation bar to return to the SharePoint top-level page if you plan to continue to the next Hands-On Exercise. If not, click the photo icon on the right side of the top navigation bar and select **Sign out**.

---

**TROUBLESHOOTING:** Rather than a photo icon, your name may be displayed on the top navigation bar. Click your name and select Sign out.

# Get Started with Office 365 Tools

In today's business world, professionals are spending more time away from their desks, meeting with partners and customers, and collaborating with coworkers. Not only do they work from a distance, but busy professionals also use a variety of devices to stay in touch with their work, such as a PC, tablet, or smartphone. Office 365 tools enable the employees to stay connected in a reliable, secure environment regardless of their geographic location or the device they select.

Using Office Online apps, you can access and update Word documents, Excel spreadsheets, PowerPoint presentations, and OneNote notebooks without having Office programs installed on your computer or devices. Files stored in the cloud are accessible through OneDrive and can be synchronized to Office desktop applications. The SharePoint Newsfeed app enables you to post status messages, participate in conversations, and follow others. The People app places contact information at your fingertips and seamlessly coordinates the information with your Outlook.com account.

This section focuses on the Office 365 tools. You will learn about working with OneDrive, Newsfeed, People, Calendar, and Outlook. You will explore Office Online.

## Working with Office 365 Tools

Office 365 contains apps that connect you to your documents, email account, calendar, contacts, and team sites, using the cloud to sync your files so you are always up to date. There is no software learning curve for using Office 365 apps because they have the familiar interface of Office desktop applications.

There are many advantages to using cloud-based apps. You are relieved of the burden of applying new software updates, saving you time and money. There is a large amount of storage available as a part of your subscription price, and if you need more, you can arrange to purchase extra storage space in the cloud. From the business perspective, using cloud apps enables a business to scale up or down as its employee base changes. For instance, when a new employee is hired, a subscription for just that person is purchased, and the software does not have to be loaded on a computer for the new hire.

---

**TIP: EXPLORE OFFICE 365 SUBSCRIPTIONS**

You may be surprised by the variety of subscription offerings that are available for Office 365. You can tailor your subscription to the apps that you need to complete your work. Check out the subscription pricing options at https://products.office.com/en-us/buy/compare-microsoft-office-products

---

### Work with OneDrive for Business

**STEP 1 »** You may be familiar with OneDrive as a cloud storage location for your Office 2016 documents. With Office 365, you can access OneDrive for Business, which focuses on organizing your work documents and enables your company or organization to manage these documents. By storing your work documents in OneDrive for Business, you can easily share and collaborate with coworkers. A sync app enables you to synchronize your work between the desktop and mobile devices you use. For instance, you develop a PowerPoint presentation while at your desk in the office. You then ask your supervisor to review your facts and supply some additional figures for one of the slides. Your supervisor, who is working late, comments on and returns the presentation to OneDrive after you have left the office. The next morning, on your way to the conference, you access the presentation on your smartphone, complete a few minor edits, and store the presentation on OneDrive. When you arrive at the conference, you open the presentation on your tablet and deliver a successful speech.

The OneDrive for Business library enables you to store 1 TB of data in the cloud. Your library is integrated with SharePoint Online. You can follow documents on your newsfeed so that you are aware of when changes are made to them.

Access OneDrive for Business by clicking the OneDrive tile in Office 365. The left pane enables you to manage your folders, whereas the Files pane provides details about the files, as shown in Figure 1.38. Information about a file or folder is available by selecting the item and clicking the More options icon, and then selecting Details. The Details pane on the right side of the window displays information about the selected file or folder. Documents you save to OneDrive are private until you share them. The Sharing column, or the Share icon, enables you to share files or perform other actions using a dialog box. You can specify to share a document or folder with everyone in the organization by clicking Email Everyone on the Share dialog box. You can also share files with individuals you designate by clicking Invite people and adding email addresses to the dialog box along with a message.

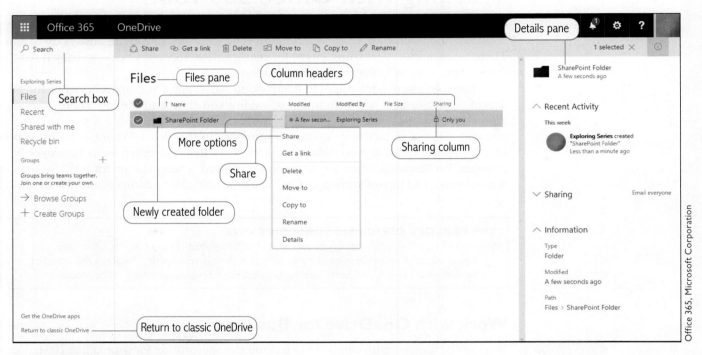

**FIGURE 1.38** OneDrive for Business

You can create files on OneDrive for Business with Office Online apps or you can upload existing files from your computer. Files and folders can be sorted in ascending or descending order and filtered by clicking the arrow next to the column headers of Name, Modified, and Modified By on the document list (refer to Figure 1.38). Type keyword search terms in the search box in the left pane to perform a search of the library.

# Work with Newsfeed

**STEP 2 >>** The Newsfeed page is a central location for following people, documents, sites, and tags and making microblog posts, called conversations or updates, in SharePoint Online. Click the Newsfeed tile in the Office 365 to open the Newsfeed. ***Microblog posts***, similar to tweets in Twitter, are short text messages that you type to inform others of your activities, opinions, or ideas. You can start a conversation with everyone in your organization or specify a SharePoint Online site with which to share the comment. An image can be added to the conversation by clicking the Picture icon below the text box. Different categories are available for viewing the ***Newsfeed streams*** (or updates) you are following, as shown in Figure 1.39, including Following, Everyone, Mentions (where you are mentioned), Activities, and Likes.

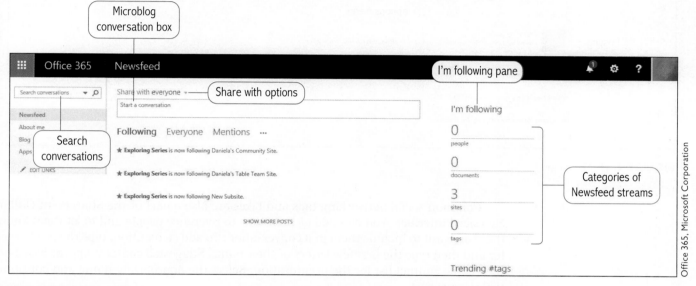

**FIGURE 1.39** Newsfeed

---

**TIP: REMOVING A SITE FROM FOLLOWING**

The SharePoint home page displays the sites that you are following in the left pane, as shown in Figure 1.40. If you do not want to follow something, click the star next to the name of the object to stop following it.

---

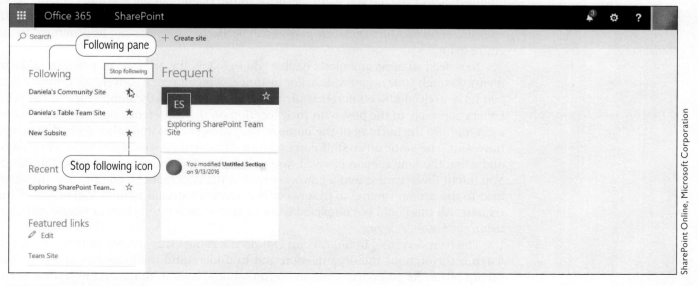

**FIGURE 1.40** SharePoint Online Following Pane

When you read a post that you wish to respond to, you have options to enable you to continue the conversation. Liking a Newsfeed post indicates your approval of the item or comment. It also promotes the post in importance. You can reply to a post by clicking Reply, as shown in Figure 1.41. More options for the conversation, available by clicking the More Options icon, include copying a link to the conversation and locking the conversation.

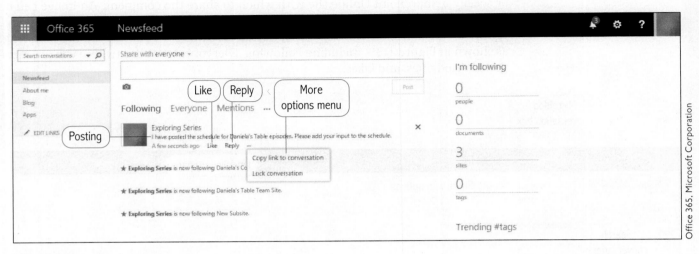

**FIGURE 1.41** Newsfeed

Common social networking tags and Likes are also a part of the SharePoint Online Newsfeed interface. You can add @ mentions to reference people and to let them know that you want to include them in a conversation. To add @ mention, type the @ character and then type the first few letters of their name. Suggested contacts appear based on the People contact list for the organization. Select the appropriate name and continue typing your post.

**Hashtags**, a common social networking tool, provide searchable categories of topics and help to organize posts. To tag a post with a category, type # followed by a keyword. You can include up to six tags in a single post. Later, to see all posts tagged with the category, click the keyword. You can also follow tags by clicking the tag in a posting and then clicking Follow.

Alerts enable you to mark documents, so that you are notified when they are changed. Select the file you want alerts for in the Document library, and click the More Options icon. Select Alert me and fill in the *Alert me when items change* dialog box with your preferences. More than one person can be alerted, so alerts can be generated to the entire team.

Newsfeed streams and alerts enable you to follow the progress of people and documents through your organization. For instance, you can post a conversation saying that you have arrived at a conference site and tag the name of the conference in the post. Others can reply to the post with their location on the conference floor so that you can meet and use the hashtag of the name of the conference to find other posts that people have sent. The home office staff can update a document on which you have set an alert, and when the new version is saved, you will receive an alert via email or text message. You might then request that a coworker review the document by adding an @ mention next to the person's name so that his or her newsfeed stream notifies him or her of the request. All this could be completed without face-to-face interaction or phone calls, but using your mobile device.

The Newsfeed tool in SharePoint Online is a robust way to keep in touch with colleagues throughout the organization and to understand the processes and activities taking place. As you participate in conversations, keep in mind that everyone in the organization might have access to the posts. Carefully consider whether people need the information you are thinking about posting. Be professional in the development of your conversations. Use full sentences and avoid acronyms unless you are sure that they are commonly known among your colleagues. Check your spelling and grammar before clicking the Post button.

## Work with Outlook

**STEP 3** ❯❯ As a component of Office 365, the Outlook app is a personal information manager that enables you to manage and collaborate by using email, contacts, calendars, and tasks. You can configure all your devices, from your desktop computer to your smartphone, to access your Outlook email account. This provides instant access to your personal information wherever and whenever you need it, using a browser.

The business world thrives on the use of email as a major communication tool. Outlook manages your incoming and outgoing email, providing the tools necessary to compose and reply to messages. From selecting only the recipients who need to see the message to adding a signature at the end, Outlook enables you to create professional correspondence.

The Outlook page displays your Inbox, as shown in Figure 1.42. The pane on the left side of the window enables you to navigate to the folders in your account. You can add more folders as needed to organize your workflow. Incoming messages are displayed in the Inbox pane of the window, and as you select a message, it displays in the Reading Pane on the right side of the window. Click New, next to the search box, to compose a new message. You can reply to the message or forward it to someone else by clicking Reply, Reply All, and Forward next to the message header. Click the More actions icon to display additional options, such as delete, categorize, mark as junk, and print. You can also use the toolbar above the message list to delete or archive messages, designate Junk, Sweep, move to a different folder, and assign categories. More commands include marking as read or unread, pinning or unpinning, flagging or clearing the flag, marking complete, ignoring, creating a rule, or printing the message.

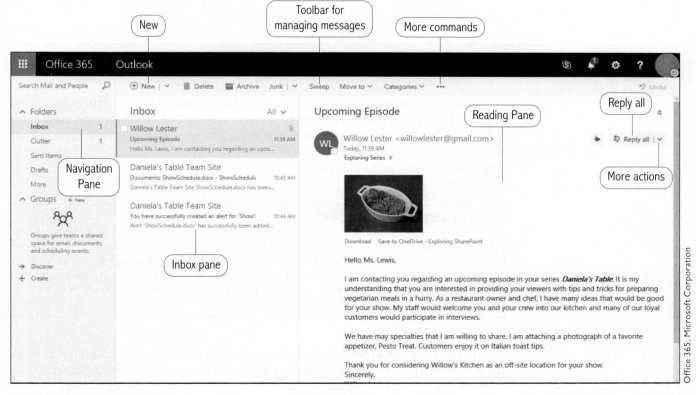

**FIGURE 1.42** Outlook App

When you reply to a message, the header area automatically includes the email contact information for the person who sent the message, as shown in Figure 1.43. If you use Reply All, everyone who was sent the original message will see your reply. You can include additional email addresses in the Cc: box to include other people to whom you want to send the message. As a professional consideration, carefully evaluate the list of people who are shown and determine if they really need to see your response before sending the message. After addressing the message, type the reply, adjust the formatting of the message, and add a signature or additional files, if desired.

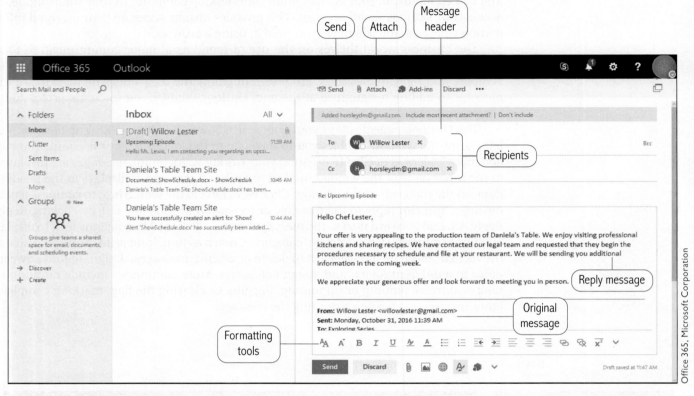

**FIGURE 1.43** Reply to Message

By default, messages that flow through Outlook are organized into conversations. You also have the option to view the messages as items. The **_Conversation view_** enables you to see your responses as a partial message. As you reply and your correspondent replies, you can reorganize your view of the messages by date, from, flagged, size, subject, type, attachments, and importance.

> **TIP: CREATE A SIGNATURE**
> To create a reusable signature in Outlook, click the Settings icon, and type Signature in the search box. Click Email Signature in the right pane, and type the information you will use in the email signature text box. Use the format tools as needed to create a professional signature. You can select to automatically include the signature on messages, or if you do not check that option, you can select to add it to specific messages as you compose them by clicking More Commands (above the header information), and then clicking Insert signature.

As you create and manage email, it is important to remain professional. Include only the people who need to see the message as recipients. Provide a descriptive subject that identifies the content of the message. Begin the message with a greeting, including the person's title if it is appropriate. Use complete sentences, and avoid jargon and acronyms unless you are sure the recipients will understand them. At the end of the message, provide your name and contact information (in the form of a signature). Be sure to attach the necessary files and reference them in the message so the recipient knows there are attachments. Check the spelling and grammar with a final proofreading before sending the message.

## Work with Tasks

An additional feature of Office 365 is Tasks. You can set up professional and personal tasks with reminders to keep you on track, as shown in Figure 1.44. Type a subject, select a due date, provide a short reminder message in the text box, and click Save. Click the Show more details button to display more options for tracking the completion of the task. You can even record the number of hours you spent on the task, mileage, billing, and company information. Charms, which are small icons, can be added to tasks to help to classify them. If you need specific documents for the task, you can attach them to the task so they are readily available.

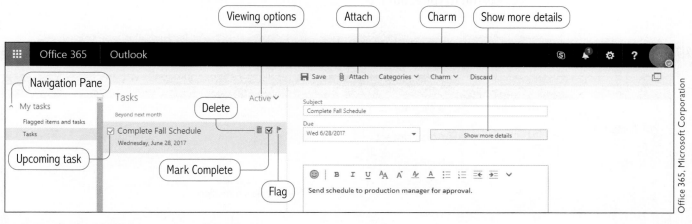

**FIGURE 1.44** Add a Task

As due dates arrive, you will be notified of the tasks you need to complete. You can mark the items as complete, flag them for follow up, or delete them from the list when you no longer need the reminder. Options above the task list enable you to view all the tasks, or active, overdue, or completed tasks. You can sort the tasks by due date, start date, status, subject, attachments, importance, and type.

Tasks can be added as an app to your SharePoint team site, where the team members can set up appropriate goals for completion of the project. Click Site contents on the Quick Launch, and then click add an app. Select the Tasks app from the Your Apps page, give it a unique name (you can add it to your team site multiple times with different names), and click Create. A timeline across the top of the page will help you identify both overdue and completed tasks, as well as future tasks.

> **TIP: FUNCTIONS OF OUTLOOK**
> Tasks, People, and Calendar are shown in the Outlook app, as they are functions of that application.

## Work with People

**STEP 4** ⟩⟩ In Office 365, contact information for your coworkers and other people is managed using the People page. Information can be displayed in a variety of ways, such as All contacts, People you may want to follow up with, Favorites, People on your calendar today, and People you frequently contact. You can add new contacts individually or import contacts from your Outlook.com account. People who have Office 365 accounts in your organization are likely to already be on your People page. You can also import people from the social networks to which you belong. You can create group contacts that enable you to contract everyone via email or to schedule a meeting. Contacts you add to the People page dynamically become available in other places in SharePoint Online and Office 365, such as Outlook and Calendar.

Contact information includes the name of the person, email addresses, phone numbers, instant message (IM) name, work information, addresses, notes that you might wish to include, and other facts such as webpage, spouse/partner, hobbies, and birthday information. By providing complete information, you can later use the search People box to find someone based on a piece of information. For instance, to search for someone who lives in a city you are about to visit on business, you can type the city name into the search People box. When you are in the Outlook application, you can display a miniature contact card by hovering over the name, To, or CC field of an email message.

Click New on the People page to begin the process of adding a new person to your contacts. Type information in the appropriate boxes and click a plus sign to access additional contact information entry boxes, as shown in Figure 1.45. Click Save to add the person to your contacts.

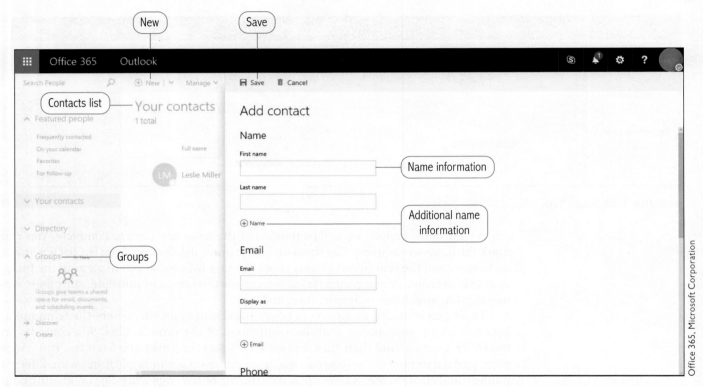

**FIGURE 1.45** Add a Contact

The accuracy of the information you store in People is important. Ensure the accuracy and completeness of the contact information. As you receive additional information, update the contact.

## Work with Calendar

STEP 5 ⟩⟩ A real advantage to using the Office 365 Calendar app is the ease with which it can be shared with others. You can create a number of calendars, for instance a personal calendar with appointments focusing on your private life, a team calendar, and a work calendar. The Calendar app can be added to your SharePoint team site to enable the whole team to collaborate using the Site contents page's add an app option.

To view calendars you manage, click the Calendar tile in Office 365. The left pane contains a monthly calendar, which you use to navigate to a specific day by clicking on the date, as shown in Figure 1.46. Below the calendar in the left pane is a list of the calendars you use. The central pane of the calendar is the calendar view you select. You can view the calendar by day, workweek, week, or month. The right pane of the window displays your upcoming events. As events approach, reminders appear letting you know that you have an appointment.

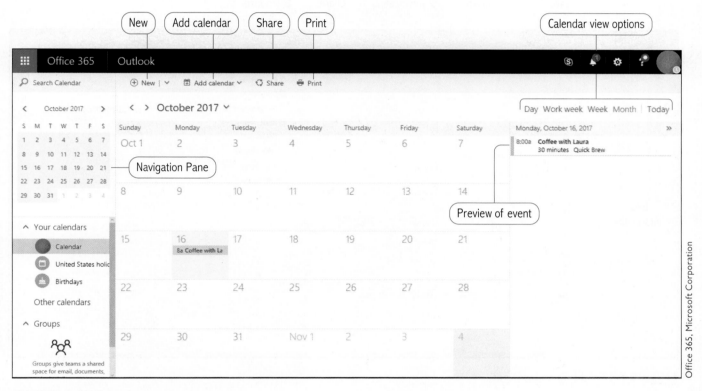

**FIGURE 1.46** Calendar

Office 365, Microsoft Corporation

Appointments are added to your calendar as events. Click New at the top of the calendar view pane to display the event form, as shown in Figure 1.47. You can also double-click on the date in the calendar view pane to open the event form. As you create the calendar event, attendees you type in the Add people box are cross-referenced with your contacts, and they will be notified when you create the event to help them prepare to attend. It is a good idea to add as much information as you can about the event, including how long you expect it to last, your status while you are attending the meeting (free, working elsewhere, tentative, busy, or away), and a complete description. Click Attach at the top of the form to insert a file attachment or picture. You can also categorize the calendar event, which color-codes the events on the calendar. Charms are another organizational method you can apply to the event. Skype meetings enable you to meet online, and you can add Skype information to the event message so that people can click to join in the meeting.

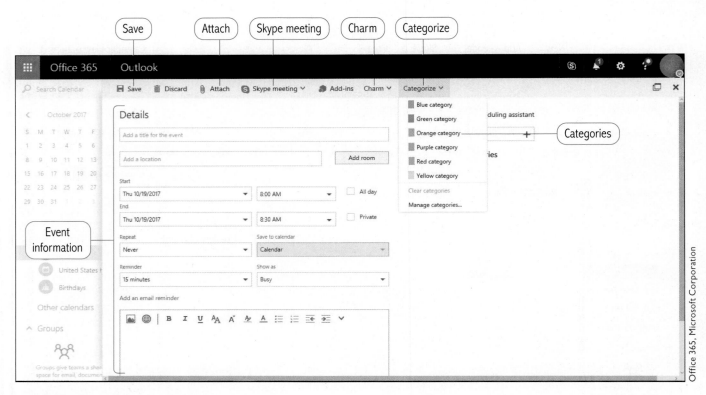

**FIGURE 1.47** Add Calendar Event

There is an important distinction between tasks and calendar events in Office 365. Tasks are date oriented but generally do not contain time or location information. Calendar events, however, provide this additional information. Set tasks for things that need to be completed, and use events for meetings and other date-driven items.

## Work with Office Online Apps

**STEP 6 ▶** Microsoft Office 365 tools include Office Online apps, which are app versions of popular Office 2016 desktop applications. The apps enable you to edit documents, spreadsheets, presentations, or notes using mobile devices. Desktop applications contain more features because the software applications are stored on your hard drive, where more storage space is available. Mobile devices use the cloud to access software applications. Mobile devices have less memory than a desktop computer and that limits the capabilities of apps. Therefore, online apps have fewer features than desktop software applications.

Accessed through OneDrive, the mobile Web apps include the following:

- **Word Online**—creates formatted documents that include text, pictures, tables, and links
- **Excel Online**—develops spreadsheets that include text, values, formulas, functions, tables, charts, and surveys
- **PowerPoint Online**—designs a presentation with text, illustrations, images, SmartArt, transitions, and animations
- **OneNote Online**—saves notes in the form of text, pictures, and links in notebooks

Office Online apps offer you many advantages. You can edit documents that you created in a desktop application and saved to your OneDrive on a mobile device. You can create new documents using the apps and later open them on your computer with an Office 2016 desktop application. The documents you create can be easily organized into folders and shared with people through your OneDrive, enabling collaboration. Further, the documents you create using Office Online apps can be placed onto your SharePoint team sites.

You access the Office Online apps using the OneDrive feature of Office 365 or open an app using the Office 365 tiles.

The Office Online apps will look familiar to you if you have used Office desktop applications. Although each app contains different commands, they all feature a Ribbon with tabs, groups, and commands. You can also invite people to share the document from the Office Online app. Documents you create in Office Online apps are automatically saved as you work within the document. When you view a document on a desktop computer using OneDrive, you have the option to edit the document using the full-featured desktop application. Click the Edit in *appname* tab to download the file to your computer and open the desktop application.

New apps are being added to Office 365 regularly. Sway is an app used to create websites with text, images, and interactive content to engage your audience. After you create the Sway, you can invite people to view your presentation much as you invite people to your team sites.

Another useful app is Planner, which enables you to manage and collaborate on plans in a visual way. After setting up your plans, you can track progress using the Planner hub. As with other Office 365 apps, Planner is fully integrated with Office 365 services, for instance, keeping Planner notes in a OneNote notebook, or important dates on the Outlook Calendar.

Within your organization, Yammer can enable you to communicate with your co-workers. You can gather your resources including photographs, video, and files, and share them seamlessly. Announcements, praise, polls, and updates upgrade your communications within your company.

**Quick Concept**

7. What types of files can be stored on OneDrive? *p. 41*

8. What is the difference between tasks and calendar events? *p. 50*

9. What are two advantages of using an Office Online app? *p. 50*

# Hands-On Exercises

**Skills covered:** Save a File to OneDrive for Business • Create a Newsfeed Post • Send Email • Create a Task • Add a People Contact • Add a Calendar Event • Use Office Online Apps

## 3 Get Started with Office 365 Tools

You decide to review the Office 365 tools so that you can advise others on the Daniela's Table team on how to use the tools. You will experiment with OneDrive for Business, Newsfeed, Outlook, Tasks, People, Calendar, and Office Online apps.

### STEP 1 ≫ SAVE A FILE TO ONEDRIVE FOR BUSINESS

You will create a folder and transfer a file to OneDrive for Business. Refer to Figure 1.48 as you complete Step 1.

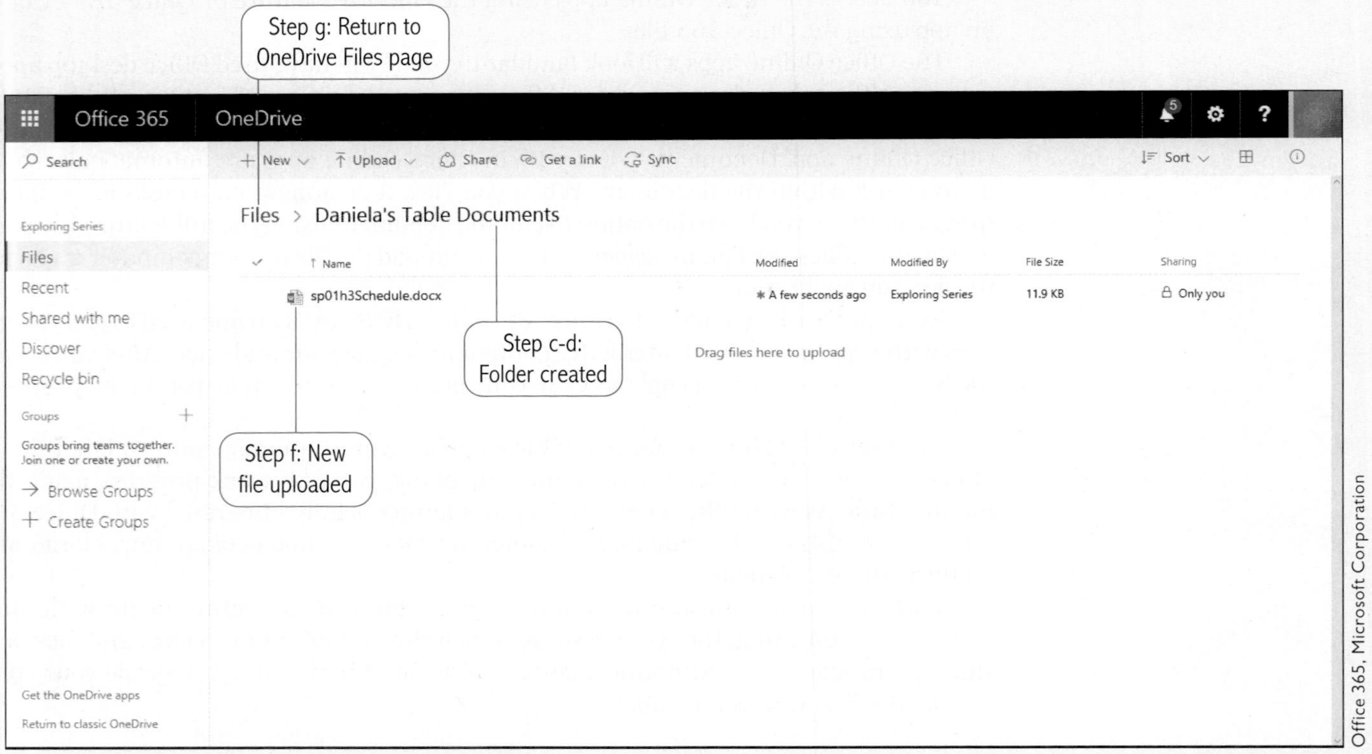

**Step g: Return to OneDrive Files page**

Office 365    OneDrive

🔍 Search

Exploring Series

Files
Recent
Shared with me
Discover
Recycle bin

Groups +
Groups bring teams together. Join one or create your own.
→ Browse Groups
+ Create Groups

Get the OneDrive apps
Return to classic OneDrive

+ New ∨   ⬆ Upload ∨   🔗 Share   🔗 Get a link   ⟳ Sync      ↓≡ Sort ∨   ⊞   ⓘ

Files > Daniela's Table Documents

| ✓ | ↑ Name | Modified | Modified By | File Size | Sharing |
|---|---|---|---|---|---|
| | sp01h3Schedule.docx | ✳ A few seconds ago | Exploring Series | 11.9 KB | 🔒 Only you |

**Step c-d: Folder created**

Drag files here to upload

**Step f: New file uploaded**

*Office 365, Microsoft Corporation*

**FIGURE 1.48** OneDrive Files and Folders

a. Open your browser and navigate to your Office 365 site, if you closed it after Hands-On Exercise 2.

b. Click the **Tiles icon** on the top navigation bar, and click the **OneDrive tile**.

The OneDrive for Business Files page displays.

c. Click **New**, and select **Folder** on the new file menu.

d. Type **Daniela's Table Documents** in the Name box, and click **Create**.

The folder appears in the OneDrive Files list in a few seconds.

> **TROUBLESHOOTING:** If a dialog box opens, close the dialog box to continue with the exercise.

**e.** Click the **Daniela's Table Documents folder** name you just created to open the folder. Click **Upload**, and select **Files**.

**f.** Navigate to the location where the student data files are stored, select the *sp01h3Schedule* file, and click **Open**. Use the Snipping Tool to take a screen snip that shows the contents of the Daniela's Table Documents folder. Name the snip file **sp01h3Folder_LastFirst**.

The file appears in the Daniela's Table Documents list.

**g.** Click **Files** in the breadcrumb navigation below the OneDrive for Business title to return to the OneDrive Files page.

STEP 2 ⟫ CREATE A NEWSFEED POST

You decide to create a Newsfeed post so that people in the organization will know that you are visiting with officials from PBS. Refer to Figure 1.49 as you complete Step 2.

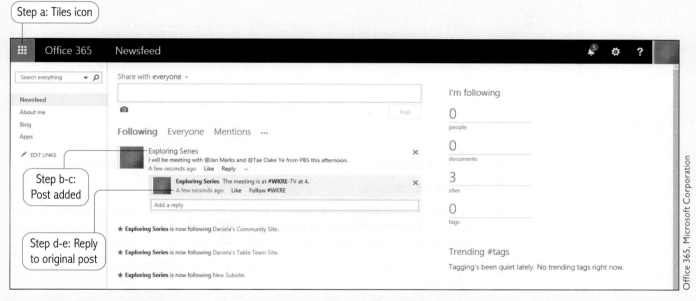

**FIGURE 1.49** Newsfeed Stream

**a.** Click the **Tiles icon** on the top navigation bar and click **Newsfeed** from the apps tiles.

The Newsfeed page displays. Depending on your previous activities on the site, the number of people, documents, sites, and tags in the Following section will vary.

**b.** Type **I will be meeting with @Jan Marks and @Tae Oake Ye from PBS this afternoon.** (include the period) in the Start a conversation box.

The post includes @ mentions for each person.

**c.** Click **Post**.

The Newsfeed stream is updated to include this microblog post.

**d.** Click **Reply** under the Newsfeed stream post that you just made.

A reply box opens enabling you to type a reply.

**e.** Type **The meeting is at #WKRE-TV at 4.** (include the period) in the reply box, and then click **Post**. Using the Snipping Tool, take a screen snip of the postings, and name the file **sp01h3Newsfeed_LastFirst**.

This post contains a hashtag for the PBS station name. The post is added to the Newsfeed stream and another reply box opens.

You will send an email message to Leslie Miller regarding your upcoming meeting. You will create a task to remind yourself to prepare a report for an upcoming meeting with Daniela. Refer to Figure 1.50 as you complete Step 3.

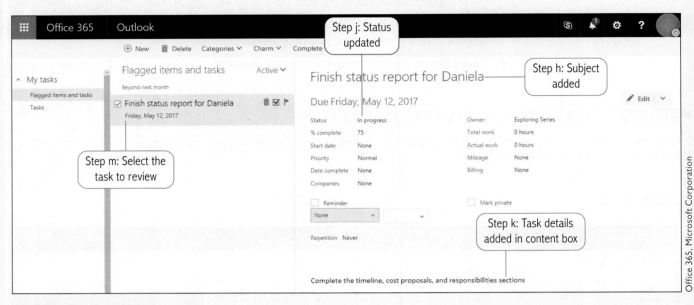

**FIGURE 1.50** Outlook Task List

a. Click the **Tiles icon** on the top navigation bar, and then click **Mail** from the apps tiles.

The Outlook app opens.

b. Click **New**. Type **lmillerpbs@gmail.com** on the To: line. Click **Cc** to open the Carbon copy line. Type **your college or university email address** on the Cc: line. Type a **semi-colon** and **your instructor's email address** on the Cc: line.

You will send a carbon copy of the message to your school email account and your instructor.

c. Type **sp01h3Email_LastFirst** on the Subject line.

d. Type the following message:

**Hello Leslie,**

**I am looking forward to our meeting. Please let me know of any documents that I should bring to our meeting this afternoon.**

**Thank you,**

**Firstname Lastname** (replace this with your actual name)

e. Select **your name** in the email message, and click **Italics** on the text formatting tools.

f. Review the message for correct spelling. Click **Send**.

A return message should come back to your Inbox in a few moments, as a reply from Leslie.

**TROUBLESHOOTING:** If you do not receive a reply from Leslie, your mail was possibly considered spam by the gmail.com server. The message was sent to your college or university email address as a confirmation that it was correctly sent.

**g.** Click the **Tiles icon** on the top navigation bar, and click **Tasks** from the apps tiles.

The Outlook Tasks page displays.

**h.** Click **New**, and type **Finish status report for Daniela** in the Subject box.

**i.** Click **Due arrow**, and select **tomorrow's date** on the calendar.

**j.** Click **Show more details**. Click the **Status arrow**, and select **In progress**. Select the **0** and type **75** in the % complete box.

**k.** Click **Show fewer details**, and type **Complete the timeline, cost proposals, and responsibilities sections** in the content box.

**l.** Click **Save** on the toolbar at the top of the message.

The task is saved to the Task list in Outlook.

**m.** Click the task in the Task list to review the information. Using the Snipping Tool, take a screen snip of the task, and name it **sp01h3Task_LastFirst**.

---

**STEP 4** ›› **ADD A PEOPLE CONTACT**

You will add Leslie Miller to your contact list using People because others on your team may need her contact information. Refer to Figure 1.51 as you complete Step 4.

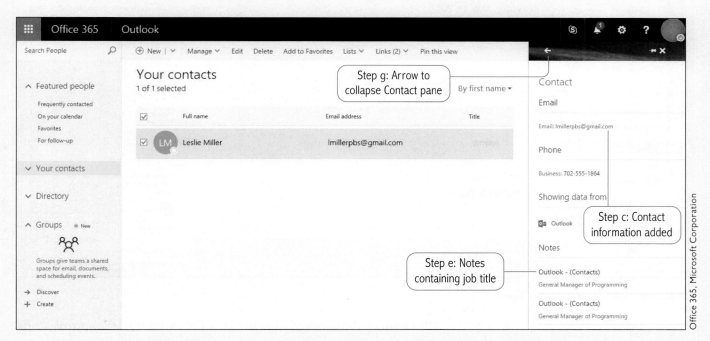

**FIGURE 1.51** Add a Contact to People

**a.** Click the **Tiles icon** on the top navigation bar, and click **People** from the apps tiles.

The People page is displayed.

**b.** Click **New**.

**c.** Type **Leslie** in the First name box and **Miller** in the Last name box. Type her email address **lmillerpbs@gmail.com**. Type **Leslie Miller** in the Display as box.

**d.** Type **702-555-1864** in the Phone Business box.

**e.** Click **Notes**, select **Notes**, and then type **General Manager of Programming** in the content box.

**f.** Click **Save**. Click **Your contacts** in the left pane.

The contact information is displayed in the Your contacts list. Additional contacts may be shown and you might have to scroll to see Leslie's information.

**g.** Select **Leslie Miller's entry** in the Your contact list. Click **See contact details** in the right pane to view Leslie's job title. Using the Snipping Tool, take a screen snip of the contact information, naming it **sp01h3People_LastFirst**.

> **TROUBLESHOOTING:** The contact details may be displayed without having to click the link in the right pane.

**h.** Click the **arrow** in the right pane above Contact to return to Leslie's contact information.

## STEP 5 ›› ADD A CALENDAR EVENT

You will add an event to the Calendar so that people can track you. Refer to Figure 1.52 as you complete Step 5.

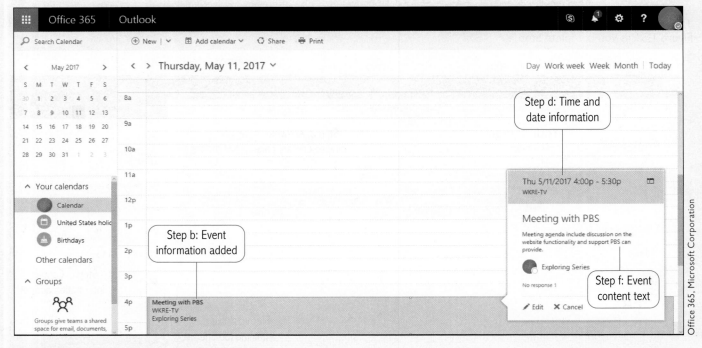

**FIGURE 1.52** Add Calendar Event

**a.** Click the **Tiles icon** on the top navigation bar, click **Calendar** from the apps tiles, and then click **New**.

The events form displays.

**b.** Type **Meeting with PBS** in the Add a title for the event box. Type **WKRE-TV** in the Add location box.

**c.** Type **Mill** in the Add people box, and click Leslie Miller's contact card to add her to the Attendees section.

> **TROUBLESHOOTING:** You may have to click Search Directory after typing a few letters of the person's name.

As you type names, Outlook searches People for possible matches, enabling you to select from a list of your contacts.

**d.** Click the **Start date arrow** and select **today's date**. Click the **Start time arrow** and select **4:00 PM**. Click the **End time arrow** and select **5:30 PM**. Click the **Reminder arrow** and select **1 hour**.

> **TROUBLESHOOTING:** If you are working on the weekend, or it is past 4:00 PM, select the next business day for the starting day.

**e.** Confirm that the Show as box contains Busy and the Repeat box contains Never.

**f.** Click the content box at the bottom of the event and type **Meeting agenda includes discussion on the website functionality and support PBS can provide.** (include the period).

**g.** Click **Send**.

The message is sent to the attendees if contact information is available and displayed on the Calendar page. If you do not list attendees, as you might for a personal appointment rather than a meeting, you would click Save to add the event to your Calendar page.

**h.** Select the **meeting** on the calendar, and click **Day** on the top right of the window to display the calendar in Day view. Click the **meeting** on the calendar to display the event information. Using the Snipping Tool, take a screen snip of the calendar displaying the details of the meeting. Name the file **sp01h3Calendar_LastFirst**.

## STEP 6 》 USE OFFICE ONLINE APPS

You will update a file that you added previously to your OneDrive using the Word Online app. You will also begin a OneNote notebook with notes about the meeting you had with Leslie and Tae. Refer to Figure 1.53 as you complete Step 6.

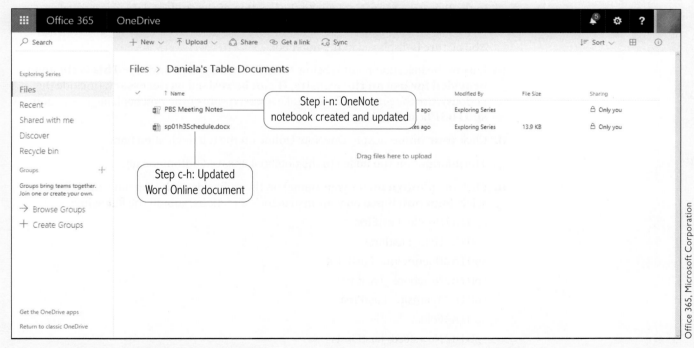

**FIGURE 1.53** Office Online Documents

**a.** Click the **Tiles icon** on the top navigation bar, click **OneDrive** from the apps tiles, and then click the **Daniela's Table Documents link**.

The Daniela's Table Documents folder opens, showing the *sp01h3Schedule* document.

**b.** Click the **sp01h3Schedule** document in the file list to open it.

**c.** Click **Edit Document** and select **Edit in Browser**.

You have just a few things to add to the schedule, so you will use Word Online. Word Online opens, displaying the Ribbon.

**d.** Click in the **Title column** for Episode 2, and type **Super Soups**.

**e.** Click in the **Title column** for Episode 3, and type **Veggie Delights**.

**f.** Click the **INSERT tab**, and click **Header & Footer** in the Header & Footer group.

**g.** Type your **first and last name** in the left header box.

**h.** Click **your name** on the top navigation bar. Click **sp01h3Schedule** in the file list to reopen the document. Using the Snipping Tool, take a screen snip of the document, naming the file **sp01h3Schedule_LastFirst**. Close the sp01h3Schedule browser tab.

When you use Word Online, changes you make are automatically saved. You do not have to perform a save operation before leaving a page. The Daniela's Table Documents folder contents are displayed.

**i.** Click **New** above Files in the Daniela's Table Documents folder, and select **OneNote notebook**.

> **TROUBLESHOOTING:** If you do not see New, you probably have a document selected in the files list. Click in the white space on the window to deselect the document.

**j.** Type **PBS Meeting Notes** in the Document Name box, and click **Create**.

**k.** Type **Planning Meeting** as the title for the notebook page.

**l.** Click in the content area below the date. Click the **INSERT tab**, and click **Picture** in the Pictures group. Navigate to the location of the student data files and select *sp01h3WKRE-TV_Logo*. Click **Open** and click **Insert**.

The picture is displayed in the notebook.

**m.** Ensure the insertion point is below the picture of the logo and type **This is the logo provided for use on the website. It can be resized as necessary.** (include the periods). Use the Snipping Tool to take a screen snip of the notebook page, and name it **sp01h3Planning_LastFirst**.

**n.** Click **your name** next to OneNote Online on the top navigation bar.

The information you added to the notebook is saved automatically.

**o.** Click the **photo icon** (or your name) on the right side of the top navigation bar, and select **Sign out**. Based on your instructor's directions, submit the following:

sp01h1Profile_LastFirst

sp01h1Help_LastFirst

sp01h2Documents_LastFirst

sp01h2Notebook_LastFirst

sp01h2Teamsite_LastFirst

sp01h3Folder_LastFirst

sp01h3Newsfeed_LastFirst

sp01h3Task_LastFirst

sp01h3People_LastFirst

sp01h3Calendar_LastFirst

sp01h3Schedule_LastFirst

sp01h3Planning_LastFirst

# Chapter Objectives Review

After reading this chapter, you have accomplished the following objectives:

1. **Explore Microsoft Office 365.**
   - Microsoft Office 365 contains business tools that enable you to collaborate online using cloud-based technologies.
   - SharePoint Online, a component of Office 365, is a cloud-based service that enables people and organizations to collaborate, store and manage documents, and provide a public website.

2. **Access and explore SharePoint Online.**
   - With the proper account, you access SharePoint Online by signing in to your Office 365 account. Areas of the SharePoint Online window include the Quick Launch with Following, Recent, and Featured Links, a search box, a navigation bar, and team site tiles.
   - Search SharePoint Online: You can search the SharePoint sites you have permission to access using the Search field.
   - Use the SharePoint Online Ribbon: The user-friendly interface of SharePoint Online contains a contextual Ribbon with tabs, groups of commands, and menus.

3. **View and edit SharePoint Online settings.**
   - The Site Settings page enables you to make changes to specific settings in SharePoint Online. You can add functionality to the SharePoint site by adding components on the Site contents page. While working on a site page, the editing features enable you to place and format components.
   - View and edit your SharePoint Online profile: Your profile is your professional information set that can be displayed to other members of your organization. You can add information to the profile and change your picture.

4. **Get Help.**
   - Help is available in SharePoint Online as topics or through keyword searches. The Help icon appears in the top-right corner of all Office 365 and SharePoint Online windows.

5. **Understand templates and the SharePoint top-level team site.**
   - Templates provide the basic tools and layout for a site or workspace. SharePoint includes a variety of site templates in the categories of Collaboration, Enterprise, and Duet Enterprise. As you create a new subsite, you select the template for the site.
   - Explore the top-level team site: A SharePoint collection is formed by a mandatory top-level site and one or more optional subsites, arranged in a tree-like hierarchy. The top-level site is usually a team site.
   - Get started with SharePoint sites: The default template of a site defines the site layout and provides components, or apps, which facilitate development of the site. A team site contains the tools and features needed for successful communication and collaboration among members of the group. You can edit the layout and pages prior to making the site available to others.
   - Create a new SharePoint site: Planning is an important part of creating any website, saving you time and effort. After creating a site, components can be added to increase the functionality of the site.

6. **Work with Office 365 tools.**
   - Office 365 apps enable you to communicate, collaborate, and create using cloud-based software applications.
   - Work with OneDrive for Business: OneDrive for Business enables you to sync your files among your computers.
   - Work with Newsfeed: Newsfeed provides a stream of information related to people and documents in the organization. You can add @ mentions and hashtags to postings in the Newsfeed.
   - Work with Outlook: Outlook enables you to manage your email. You can receive, reply, and send message. A folder hierarchy can be set up to manage the messages you want to keep. You can also delete messages that are not important.
   - Work with Tasks: You can set up professional and personal tasks with reminders to keep you on track. As due dates arrive, you will be notified of the tasks you need to complete.
   - Work with People: Contact information for your professional contacts is kept in People.
   - Work with Calendar: The calendars you create can be shared with others and enable you to keep a common schedule of events.
   - Work with Office Online Apps: Office Online apps are common business software applications that can be used on a desktop computer or mobile device.

# Key Terms Matching

Match the key terms with their definitions. Write the key term letter by the appropriate numbered definition.

a. Cloud computing
b. Content section
c. Library
d. Microblog post
e. Newsfeed stream
f. Notification area
g. OneNote Online
h. PowerPoint Online
i. Promoted link

j. Quick Launch
k. ScreenTip
l. SharePoint collection
m. SharePoint site
n. Status bar
o. Subsite
p. Team site
q. Template
r. Top-level site

1. _____ A parent site in a site collection. *p. 7*

2. _____ A beginning set of tools and a layout for a site or workspace. *p. 27*

3. _____ A collection of documents, pictures, or forms that can be shared with others. *p. 28*

4. _____ A collection of related webpages, apps, and other components that enables you to organize and manage documents and information, and to create workflows for the organization. *p. 7*

5. _____ A short text message that you type to inform others of your activities, opinions, or ideas. *p. 43*

6. _____ A site created within a top-level site. *p. 7*

7. _____ A small box with descriptive and helpful text displayed when you point to a command or control. *p. 19*

8. _____ A tile that enables users to enter sites or add tools to a site. *p. 33*

9. _____ Displays messages that communicate the progress of an operation for a few seconds. *p. 14*

10. _____ Displays updated information about people or sites that you are following. *p. 43*

11. _____ Enables you to design a presentation with text, illustrations, images, SmartArt, transitions, and animations. *p. 51*

12. _____ Enables you to save notes in the form of text, pictures, and links in notebooks. *p. 51*

13. _____ Facilitates collaboration among people in an organization by providing tools for information sharing and management. *p. 7*

14. _____ Feature that gives the user instant information in context, such as whether the page is checked out. *p. 14*

15. _____ Formed by a mandatory top-level site and one or more optional subsites. *p. 7*

16. _____ Pane that is common throughout all sites in SharePoint and provides easy access to elements within the site. *p. 8*

17. _____ Provides software applications through a Web browser and file storage on servers you connect to through the Internet. *p. 4*

18. _____ The main body of the site page that includes all the elements you want to make available through the site. *p. 33*

# Multiple Choice

1. SharePoint is a platform that includes:
   (a) Office 365 and SharePoint Online.
   (b) Outlook, Calendar, and People.
   (c) SharePoint Foundation, SharePoint Server, SharePoint Designer, SharePoint Online, and OneDrive for Business.
   (d) Word Online, Excel Online, PowerPoint Online, and OneNote Online.

2. A parent site is a(n) _____ site.
   (a) collection
   (b) enterprise
   (c) team
   (d) top-level

3. The Search field enables you to search:
   (a) everything on sites you have permission to access.
   (b) Microsoft help topics.
   (c) only the Office Online documents you create.
   (d) websites on the Internet.

4. Your SharePoint Online profile:
   (a) contains a link to your Documents page.
   (b) is available to everyone who has access to your organization's installation of SharePoint.
   (c) is created by default and contains no fields that you can update.
   (d) is used to access all the sites that contain your name.

5. A site hierarchy includes:
   (a) links to all the sites in your organization's SharePoint installation.
   (b) a listing of pages in a Document library.
   (c) rights to access sites in your organization's SharePoint installation.
   (d) subsites and components such as lists and document libraries.

6. You decide to change a user's permission level in the Daniela's Table site so the user can assist you in creating content. What page would you use to accomplish this task?
   (a) SharePoint Online Profile page
   (b) Share Your Site page
   (c) Site contents page
   (d) Site Settings page

7. The SharePoint Online _____ contains contextual commands, controls, and tools.
   (a) Notification bar
   (b) Ribbon
   (c) Site collection
   (d) Status bar

8. The Newsfeed stream of SharePoint Online contains:
   (a) formatting tools.
   (b) microblog posts from everyone in the organization.
   (c) posts about people and sites you are following.
   (d) site profiles.

9. To obtain information on the topic of deleting a file from a library, which tool or component of SharePoint Online would you use?
   (a) Help
   (b) ScreenTips
   (c) Search field
   (d) Site Settings

10. What is the SharePoint Online feature that enables you to share and collaborate on documents with others in your organization?
   (a) Newsfeed
   (b) Outlook
   (c) Office Online
   (d) OneDrive for Business

# Practice Exercises

## 1 Introduction to Management Information Systems Business Course

  Two years ago, as an undergraduate student in the Personal Computer Applications course, you learned about the SharePoint platform. As a result of your excellent work in this class, you have been hired as an undergraduate teaching assistant in the Introduction to Management Information Systems course and, as part of your new assignment, you will help students working on their assignments in the course laboratory. Your faculty supervisor has given you access to Office 365 and SharePoint Online. You will review the apps and become familiar with creating a subsite, which will be used to provide study tips and other information to the students as they complete the course using the classic SharePoint view. Keep in mind that your interface might display some of these items differently than shown in the steps. Refer to Figure 1.54 as you complete this exercise.

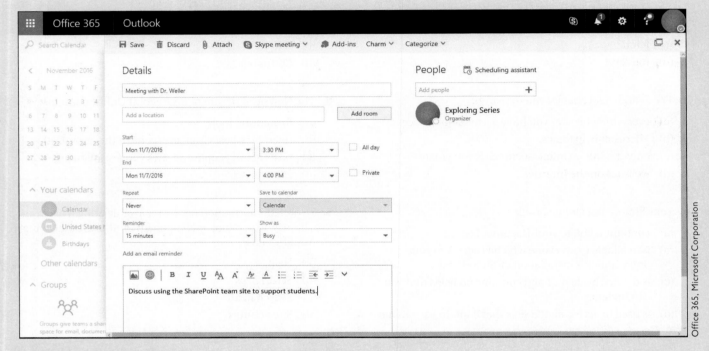

Office 365, Microsoft Corporation

**FIGURE 1.54** Calendar Event

a. Browse to **login.microsoftonline.com** and sign in to your Office 365 account.

b. Click the **photo icon** (or your name) on the top navigation bar. Click **About me** and click the **camera icon** in the Update profile pane. Click the **Change your photo link** in the Picture section.

c. Click **Upload photo**, navigate to a location on your computer that contains a picture of you (if you do not have a picture, use the file *sp01p1Picture* instead), and then click **Open**. Click **Save** once the picture is uploaded.

d. Click the **photo icon**, select **About me**, and then click **Update profile**. Click **Skills and expertise** in the Navigation Pane, and click in the **Here are some of my professional skills box**. Type **Undergraduate Teaching Assistant Intro to MIS**, and click **Add skill**. Click the **arrow** (next to the globe icon) and select **Only you can see this**. Take a screen snip, naming the file **sp01p1Details_LastFirst**.

e. Click the **Tiles icon** on the top navigation bar and click **SharePoint**. Click **Help** on the top navigation bar and click **Help** on the Help pane. Type **team site** in the Search Office help box and press **Enter**. Select the help topic **Plan the content for your SharePoint site** and read it carefully. You will be writing about the team site in a later step in this exercise. Close the SharePoint Help browser window when you have completed your review of the information. Close the SharePoint Help pane.

**f.** Click the **Team Site tile**. Click **Site contents** on the Quick Launch, and click **Return to classic SharePoint** at the bottom of the Quick Launch. Scroll to the Subsites section, and click **new subsite**.

> **TROUBLESHOOTING:** If you do not have a Team Site tile with your user name in the SharePoint window by default, click Create site, and type your user name followed by the words Team Site.

**g.** Type the title **MIS Course Site**. Type the description **This site will be used to support students taking Introduction to Management Information Systems.** Type the URL name **miscourse**. Ensure that the Team Site template is selected and that the user permissions are the same as the parent site. Click **Create**. Take a screen snip, naming the file **sp01p1MISCourse_LastFirst**.

**h.** Click the **Tiles icon** on the top navigation bar and click **OneDrive**.

**i.** Click **New** and select **Folder**. Type **MIS Course Documents** in the Name box, and click **Create**. Click the **MIS Course Documents folder** you just created.

**j.** Click **New**, and select **Word document**. Click **Document** in the top navigation bar, and type **sp01p1TeamSiteConsiderations_LastFirst** in the Document Name box, and then click in the blank document. Type the title **Team Site Considerations** at the top of the document. Format the title in font size 16, bold, with center alignment. Using the information you learned in step e, write at least five considerations you should make as you are creating a team site. Format the considerations in font size 11, not bold, with left alignment.

**k.** Click the **INSERT tab**, and click **Header & Footer**. Click the **right header placeholder** and type your name. Click the **left header placeholder** and type today's date. Close the document browser tab.

**l.** Right-click the **sp01p1TeamSiteConsiderations document file name** and select **Download**. Save the file to your local computer. Close the MIS Course Documents browser tab.

**m.** Click the **Tiles icon** on the top navigation bar and click **Tasks**. Click **New**, and type **Prepare for MIS course meeting** in the Subject box. Click the **Due arrow** and select the date for next Monday. Click **show more details**, and click the **Status arrow**. Click **In progress**, and type **25** in the % complete box. Click **show fewer details**. Click in the content box and type **Create site hierarchy chart and develop a document library permissions list**. Take a screen snip of the new task, naming it **sp01p1MISTask_LastFirst**. Click **Save** below the top navigation bar.

**n.** Click the **Tiles icon** on the top navigation bar and click **Calendar**. Click next Monday's date in the Navigation Pane and click **New**. Type **Meeting with Dr. Weller** on the event title line. Click the **Start time arrow** and select **3:30 PM**. Click in the **content box** and type **Discuss using the SharePoint team site to support students.** Take a screen snip of the event, naming it **sp01p1Event_LastFirst**. Click **Save** below the top navigation bar.

**o.** Sign out of your Office 365 account and close the browser. Based on your instructor's directions, submit the following:

sp01p1Details_LastFirst

sp01p1Event_LastFirst

sp01p1MISCourse_LastFirst

sp01p1MISTask_LastFirst

sp01p1TeamSiteConsiderations_LastFirst.docx

## 2 Class Reunion Team Site

**FROM**
**SCRATCH** As a former officer of your high school class, you are part of a committee planning for your next class reunion. After a Skype meeting with other committee members, you realize that the members are now living all across the country. You need a place to share documents and collaborate. You will create a Class Reunion Team Site in the new experience view of SharePoint Online and work with documents on the site. Remember that for some steps, the interface may use slightly different language to access tools. Refer to Figure 1.55 as you complete this exercise.

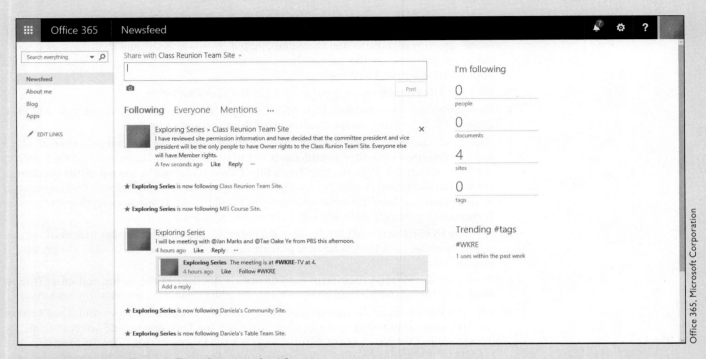

**FIGURE 1.55** Class Reunion Team Site Newsfeed Stream

a. Browse to **login.microsoftonline.com** and sign in to your Office 365 account.

b. Click the **photo icon** on the top navigation bar, and click **About me**.

c. Click **Update Profile**, and click **Schools and education** in the Navigation Pane. Add your high school name to the Schools box. Click **Add school**.

d. Click the **Tiles icon** on the top navigation bar and click **SharePoint**. Click **Help** on the top navigation bar and click **Help** in the Help pane. Type **site permissions** in the Search Office help box and press **Enter**. Select the help topic **Understanding permission levels in Share-Point** and read it carefully. You will be writing about permissions later in this exercise. Close the Understanding permissions levels in SharePoint window on the browser when you have completed your review of the information. Close the SharePoint Help pane.

e. Click the **Team Site tile**.

f. Click **Site Contents** on the Quick Launch, click **New**, and then click **Subsite**.

g. Type the title **Class Reunion Team Site**. Type the description **This site enables the planning committee to collaborate on our next class reunion.** Type the URL name **clsreunion**. Ensure that the Team Site template is selected and that the user permissions are the same as the parent site. Click **Create**.

**DISCOVER**

h. Click **Documents** in the Quick Launch of the Class Reunion Team Site, click **Upload**, and then select **Files**. Upload the workbook *sp01p2Budget* from the student data files. Open the workbook, and click **Edit Workbook** on the Excel Online Ribbon. Select **Edit in Browser**. Type **300** in cell B3. Type **75.00** in cell B5. Check the balance in cell C22. It should be as close to zero as possible. Adjust the Ticket Price per Person to create a zero or slightly above zero balance. Type your high school name in the title in place of the words High School. Move the insertion point to a blank cell. Click **Class Reunion Team Site** in the top navigation bar to return to the team site.

i. Right-click the **sp01p2Budget file** in the Documents library, and select **Rename**. Rename the file **sp01p2Budget_LastFirst** and click **Save**. Right-click the **file name** again, and select **Download**. Save the file to your local computer. Close the Documents browser tab.

j. Click the **Tiles icon** on the top navigation bar and click **Newsfeed**. Click the **Share with everyone arrow**, and select the **Class Reunion Team Site**. In the Newsfeed box type, **I have reviewed site permission information and have decided that the committee president and vice president will be the only people to have Owner rights to the Class Reunion Team Site. Everyone else will have Member rights.** Click **Post**.

k. Open the SharePoint site Class Reunion Team site. Take a full screen snip to show the name of the site, Newsfeed, and Documents. Name the file **sp01p2Class_LastFirst**.

l. Sign out of your Office 365 account. Based on your instructor's directions, submit the following:
sp01p2Budget_LastFirst.xlsx
sp01p2Class_LastFirst

# Mid-Level Exercises

## 1 Hope Hospital Business Office Management

FROM SCRATCH

The push toward electronic medical records requires a host of solutions to streamline and improve processes, that will take hospitals through the evolution from paper- and people-driven models to automated evidence-based and results-driven practices.

You work for the Hope Hospital, and your supervisor brought together a group of people to determine the best option for implementing a new system. He asked you to set up a new SharePoint Online site, based on the Project Site template, so that people could collaborate on this project.

a. Log in to your Office 365 account and create a new subsite under the top-level team site following these specifications:
   - Title: **Hope Hospital Project Site**
   - Description: **The project team will use this site to communicate regarding updating to electronic medical records.**
   - URL name: **hopehospital**
   - Select a template: **Project Site**
   - Accept all the other default values.

 **DISCOVER**

b. Explore the links to the components included in the Quick Launch, making note of how a Project Site is different from a Team Site in the available components. Compose an email message to your instructor using Outlook in Office 365 describing the differences. Use **sp01m1Hope_LastFirst** as the Subject of the message. Be sure to include the elements necessary in a business email message, such as a greeting and signature.

c. Add a note page to the Notebook, as follows:
   - Title: **Project Purpose**
   - Content: **This project will determine the best option for Hope Hospital in moving to electronic medical record management. Team members will review all of the options that fit within the budget and make a final recommendation to the director of Business Affairs.**

   Take a screen snip of the notebook, naming it **sp01m1Notes_LastFirst**. Return to the project site after reviewing the note for correct spelling and grammar.

d. Click **Calendar** on the Quick Launch of the Hope Hospital Project Site and add the following event to next Friday:
   - Title: **Planning Meeting**
   - Location: **Room 574**
   - Start: **Next Friday's date**
   - Time: **9:00 AM to 10:00 AM**
   - Description: **Meeting to review software options within the budget limits.**
   - Category: **Meeting**

**DISCOVER**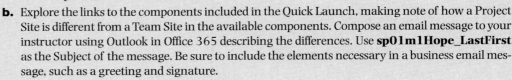

e. Click **Tasks** on the Quick Launch of the Hope Hospital Project Site and add the following task:
   - Task Name: **Meeting Agenda**
   - Due Date: Select next Thursday from the calendar menu.
   - Assigned to: Your name
   - Click **+** in the column headings for the task, and select **Text**. Click in the text column created and add: **Distribute via email**
   - Click **Stop editing this list** to save the task entry.

f. Click **Home** on the Quick Launch of the Hope Hospital Project Site and review the task. Click the arrow on the right side of the Project Summary page to display the calendar item. Take a full screen snip, showing the name of the site, the task, and the calendar item. Name the file **sp01m1Planning_LastFirst**.

**g.** Sign out of your Office 365 account. Based on your instructor's directions submit the following files:

sp01m1Planning_LastFirst

sp01m1Notes_LastFirst

## 2 Shelter Blog

FROM
SCRATCH

You have been an active volunteer at the local pet shelter for a few years. You decide to use your SharePoint Online skills to create a subsite where you can share photographs of pets in need of a new home and offer tips for bringing a new animal into your household. You have a lot of experience in working with shelter animals and you want to share it with everyone. You will add a blog subsite to this site for the tips. You will use the classic SharePoint view to work with these sites.

**a.** Log in to your Office 365 account, and create a new subsite under the top-level team site following these specifications:

- Title: **Shelter Pets Online**
- Description: **This site features tips and tricks for bringing home a new pet from our shelter.**
- URL name: **shelter**
- Select a template: **Team Site**
- Accept all the other default values.

DISCOVER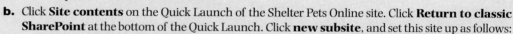

**b.** Click **Site contents** on the Quick Launch of the Shelter Pets Online site. Click **Return to classic SharePoint** at the bottom of the Quick Launch. Click **new subsite**, and set this site up as follows:

- Title: **Shelter Pets Online Blog**
- Description: **This is a blog for postings about new animals seeking homes.**
- URL name: **shelterblog**
- Select a template: **Blog**
- Accept all the other default values.

**c.** Explore the links on the Quick Launch of the blog and compare them to what you have seen on Team Sites and Project Sites you have created.

**d.** Click **Events** on the Quick Launch of the Shelter Pets Online Blog. Click **Create a post** in the right pane, and create an event following these specifications:

- Title: **Adoption Event**
- Body: **Shelter Pets will be holding their monthly adoption event at Elmo Park from 4-6 PM on Saturday. We hope you will join us and consider adopting a kitten or puppy. We have lots!**
- Format the words *Shelter Pets* in the body of the message in bold, font size 13. Format the words *Elmo Park* in bold, red font.
- In the Category list box, select Events, and click **Add**.
- Click **Publish**.

**e.** Click **Home** on the top link bar. Two posts are shown. You decide to focus the reader's attention on the Adoption Event by removing the Welcome to my blog! post. Click the **More Options icon** in the Welcome to my blog! post, and select **Edit**. Click **Delete Item** in the Actions group on the EDIT tab. Click **OK** on the Message from webpage box. Click **Home** on the top link bar to display the Event post.

**f.** Click **SharePoint** on the top navigation bar, and open the Shelter Pets Online team site. Note that both the team site and the blog site are shown on the top link bar. Click **Site contents** and locate the Shelter Pets Online Blog in the Subsites section at the bottom of the page. Click the link to display the blog subsite. Click **0 comments** and type **We have a litter of poodle puppies!** in the Add a comment box and then click **Post**.

**g.** Take a screen snip showing the Shelter Pets Online Blog posting and comment. Name the file **sp01m2Blog_LastFirst**.

**h.** Sign out of your Office 365 account. Based on your instructor's directions, submit sp01m2Blog_LastFirst.

# Beyond the Classroom

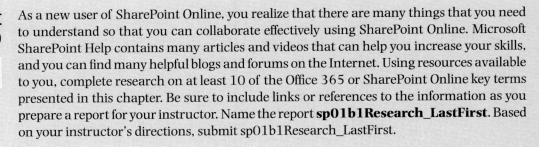

## SharePoint Help

**GENERAL CASE**

As a new user of SharePoint Online, you realize that there are many things that you need to understand so that you can collaborate effectively using SharePoint Online. Microsoft SharePoint Help contains many articles and videos that can help you increase your skills, and you can find many helpful blogs and forums on the Internet. Using resources available to you, complete research on at least 10 of the Office 365 or SharePoint Online key terms presented in this chapter. Be sure to include links or references to the information as you prepare a report for your instructor. Name the report **sp01b1Research_LastFirst**. Based on your instructor's directions, submit sp01b1Research_LastFirst.

## Using OneDrive for Business

**DISASTER RECOVERY**

As a recently hired employee, you have been reviewing your predecessor's files and realize that many of his documents are missing. You surmise that the former employee stored his documents on OneDrive, rather than on OneDrive for Business. Review information in Help or from other online resources on using OneDrive for Business at the organizational level to store documents. Create a memo with a list of guidelines that all employees should follow as they store documents. Name your completed document **sp01b2OneDrive_LastFirst**. Based on your instructor's directions, submit sp01b2OneDrive_LastFirst.

# Capstone Exercise

You work for a major financial management advisory company, Wellington Finances, and your supervisor asked you to get acquainted with Office 365 and SharePoint Online and see how your company can use the applications to enhance key business processes and meet company objectives. You will create a subsite from the top-level site and add a subsite for a project and a Basic Search Center. The Basic Search Center will enable users to find information located anywhere on the site.

## Create a Subsite

Using your top-level SharePoint Online team site, you create a subsite based on a Team Site template.

**a.** Open Office 365 in Internet Explorer and sign in to your account.

**b.** Create a new subsite with the following specifications:
- Title: **Wellington Finances**
- Description: **Wellington Finances specializes in small investor mutual funds and bonds.**
- URL name: **wellington**
- Template: **Team Site**

## Create Subsites

You will add two subsites to the Wellington Finances team site, using the Project template and the Basic Search Center. The project will focus on developing a class in investing for high school students. The search center will be used to find information about the company.

**a.** Create a new subsite to the Wellington Finances team site with the following specifications:
- Title: **Project Investor**
- Description: **This collaboration site is used to create a course for high school students in investing wisely.**
- URL name: **prjinvestor**
- Template: **Project Site**

**b.** Create a subsite to the Wellington Finances team site (not the project site) that follows these specifications:
- Title: **Search Wellington**
- Description: **This is an internal search site.**
- URL name: **searchwellington**
- Template: **Enterprise tab, Basic Search Center**

## Explore Subsites

You explore the subsites you created to determine their purposes and how they apply to the task you were given by your supervisor.

**a.** Return to the Wellington Finances site. Add a Newsfeed post: **Wellington Finances focuses on the young investor. Be a part of Project Investor!**

**b.** Take a full screen snip of the Wellington Finances site, naming the file **sp01c1Wellington_LastFirst**.

**c.** Access the Project Investor subsite. Add a calendar event for next Tuesday: **Focus Group, Lindenville High School, 3:00 PM to 4:00 PM, Mr. Flander's Marketing Class**, **Meeting** category.

**d.** Return to the Wellington Finances site. Enter the Search Wellington subsite. Complete a search using the term **Focus**. Point to the first link in the results list and review the information. Open the Calendar event and review the information. Take a screen snip of the event, naming the file **sp01c1Focus_LastFirst**.

## Report Your Findings

After reviewing the subsites you created, you are ready to contact your supervisor with a report.

**a.** Use the Outlook app to create a professional looking email message to send to your instructor following these specifications:
- Subject: **sp01c1Subsites_LastFirst**
- Focus the body of the message on the differences between the three subsites you created for Wellington Finances.
- Apply font formatting to at least one element in the message.
- Include a professional signature.

**b.** Send the email to your instructor.

## Return to New View

After completing the project set-up, you reset the classic view to display the new view throughout your entire team site.

**a.** Click **SharePoint** on the top navigation bar and click the **top-level team site tile**.

**b.** Click the **PAGE tab**, click **Library Settings** in the Page Library group, and then click **Advanced settings** in the General Settings section.

**c.** Scroll to the **List experience section**, and select **New experience**. Click **OK**.

**d.** Click the **photo icon** on the top navigation bar and select **Sign out**. Close the browser window.

**e.** Based on your instructor's directions, submit the following:

sp01c1Focus_LastFirst

sp01c1Wellington_LastFirst

# SharePoint

# SharePoint Sites

**LEARNING OUTCOME**

• You will customize a site template and add apps, lists, and libraries.

**OBJECTIVES & SKILLS:** After you read this chapter, you will be able to:

# CASE STUDY | Daniela's Table Site Customization

As a media specialist for Daniela's Table, a PBS cooking show, you are leading a team of people in the development of the website that will support the show with recipes, tips, and show schedules. Your team members are located across the country and outside of the United States. The geographically diverse team members collaborate using a SharePoint Online team site.

Initially, you reviewed the options available in SharePoint Online and Office 365. You now focus on customizing the team site to fit the needs of the project and team members. You will add SharePoint Online apps to the team site to increase the functionality of the site and enable the team members to work in partnership. The team is beginning to develop documents and other media files that should be organized so that everyone can easily find what he or she needs. You will explore lists and libraries in SharePoint to enable your team to effectively create and update documents on the team site. Document management is a focus of your job as team leader, so you will review how to control files in SharePoint Online.

*Designates skills that require an account that enables you to complete the steps.

## CHAPTER 2

## Working with SharePoint Online Sites

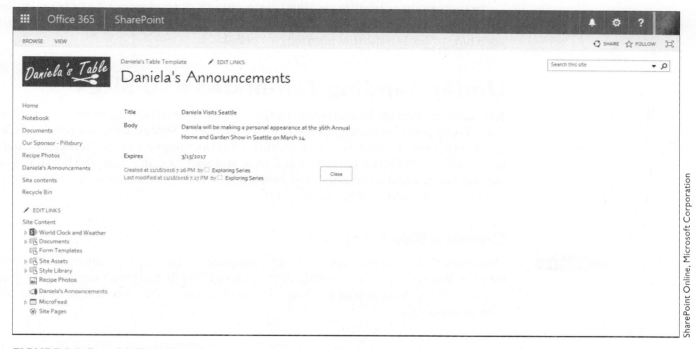

**FIGURE 2.1** Daniela's Table Team Site

SharePoint Online, Microsoft Corporation

## CASE STUDY | Daniela's Table Site Customization

| Starting Files | Files to be Submitted |
|---|---|
| sp02h1Logo | sp02h1French_LastFirst |
| sp02h1Table | sp02h1Site_LastFirst |
| sp02h2Bruschetta | sp02h1Layout_LastFirst |
| sp02h3Budget | sp02h1Home_LastFirst |
| sp02h3Logo | sp02h1SiteInvitation_LastFirst (email) |
| sp02h3Pesto | sp02h1SiteTemplate_LastFirst.wsp* |
| sp02h3Table | sp02h2Apps_LastFirst |
|  | sp02h2Announce_LastFirst |
|  | sp02h2Photo_LastFirst |
|  | sp02h2EpisodeCalendar_LastFirst |
|  | sp02h2QuickLaunch_LastFirst |
|  | sp02h3Folder_LastFirst |
|  | sp02h3FolderView_LastFirst |
|  | sp02h3Photos_LastFirst |

# Tools to Customize a Site

SharePoint sites foster and encourage team collaboration through the use of discussions, shared documents, files, contacts, events, calendars, tasks, blogging, knowledge bases (such as Wikis), and surveys. SharePoint site templates are the starting point in the design and development of a variety of sites. As you select the template for a site or subsite, consider the layout, structure, and capabilities of the template and how it fits the needs identified in the planning stage. In addition to selecting from the built-in templates in SharePoint Online, you can develop your own custom templates and implement them on your sites.

In this section, you will learn about customizing a site and saving it as a template for future use. You will share a site so that others can view it using a browser. You will also learn how to delete a site that is no longer needed.

## Understanding Templates and Sites

Templates can provide several design features for a site, and they can be reused for other sites. Basing a site on a template saves time and money. Default template types include Team Site, Blog, Project Site, Community Site, Documents Center, Records Center, Enterprise Search Center, Basic Search Center, and SAP Workflow Site. The layout of the site is defined, and a beginning set of components, such as a discussion board or document library, are provided by the template.

### Create a Site Template

**STEP 1** ▶▶ SharePoint Online enables you to create a template to your own specifications as a private site. You must have access to the Admin tile in Office 365 to create a private site. You will use a SharePoint default template to set up the basics of the site and make alternations to the design.

**To create a private site, complete the following steps:**

1. Click the Tiles icon and select the Admin tile.
2. Click Resources on the left pane and select Sites.
3. Click Add a site and fill out the Create Site Collection page. Click OK.
4. Open the site by clicking the URL link on the SharePoint admin center page, and clicking *Go to this site* on the site window.

As you save the template, it will be stored in the top-level site's Solutions Gallery as a custom template that you can install as you create a new subsite. For instance, you create a new team site using the default Team Site template and modify it with your organization's logo, images, and welcome text. You then save your customized template into the Custom collection for use in creating other customized team sites. This saves you time and effort as you create new sites for your organization.

A ***solution*** is a site template that can be distributed to others or archived on your local computer. It can contain just the framework for the site, or it can also contain site content. For instance, saving a template after applying a new layout or a theme is an example of a solution. If you develop the site by adding lists, libraries, Web Parts, or pages, these items can also be saved as part of the solution. It is important to note that your site collection resources are limited in size based on the type of account you have. Adding additional content to a template can cause it to exceed the resource limit. The site collection administrator can generally increase the limit.

**To save a site template based on a site, complete the following steps:**

1. Navigate to the site that will serve as the template.
2. Click the Settings icon and select Site settings from the menu.
3. Click Save site as template in the Site Actions section.
4. Type a file name, template name, and description, as shown in Figure 2.2. Click Include Content to place the lists and document libraries from the site on the template.
5. Click OK.

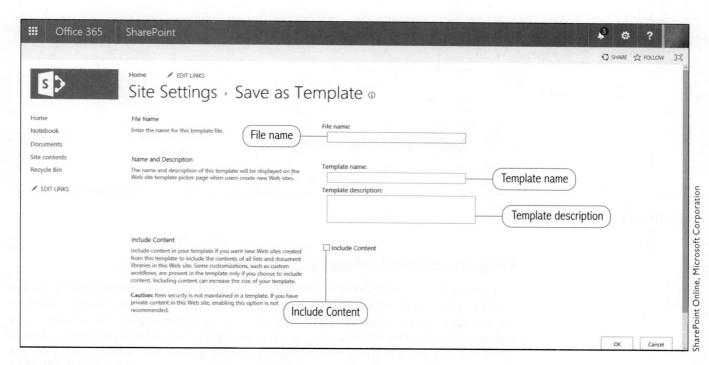

**FIGURE 2.2** Save a Template

---

**TIP: SUBSITES ARE NOT SAVED IN THE TEMPLATE**
As you save a site solution, any subsites to the top-level site of the collection are not saved. Each subsite must be saved as a solution separately.

## Use a Custom Template

The templates you create are available when a new subsite is created either from the top-level site or from other subsites. Click Site Contents on the Quick Launch, and click *new subsite* to open the New SharePoint Site page, as shown in Figure 2.3. Click the Custom tab in the Template Selection section and select the custom template solution you want to use. It is important to note that the Custom tab appears only if you have created a template and activated it. Complete the other necessary steps to create the subsite.

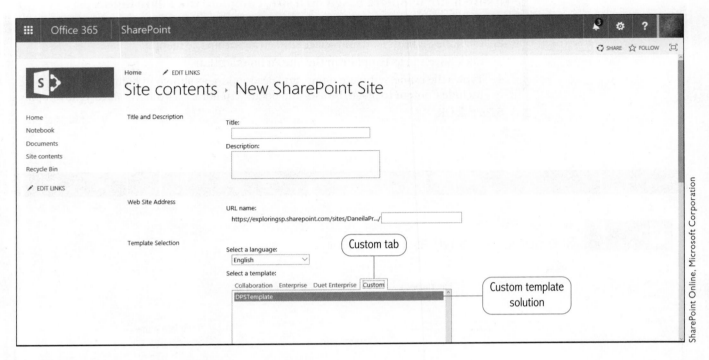

**FIGURE 2.3** Use a Custom Template Solution

## Download and Upload a Site Template

A **solution file** is a template file that has a .wsp (Web Solution Packet) extension. The solution file is what you transfer to someone else when they need to use your template. For instance, you may be the Web designer for your organization and serving many departments. You can create a custom template for the Human Resources (HR) department and transfer it to the person who manages the SharePoint Online sites for the HR department. Solutions are stored in the Solutions Gallery and must be activated on the server (after uploading) before they can be used to create new sites.

---

**To download a template solution file, complete the following steps:**

1. Navigate to the top-level site.
2. Click the Settings icon and select Site settings from the menu.
3. Click Solutions in the Web Designer Galleries section.
4. Right-click the template file name and click Save target as from the menu. The Save As dialog box displays, as shown in Figure 2.4.
5. Navigate to the location on your local computer where you want to save the file, and then click Save.

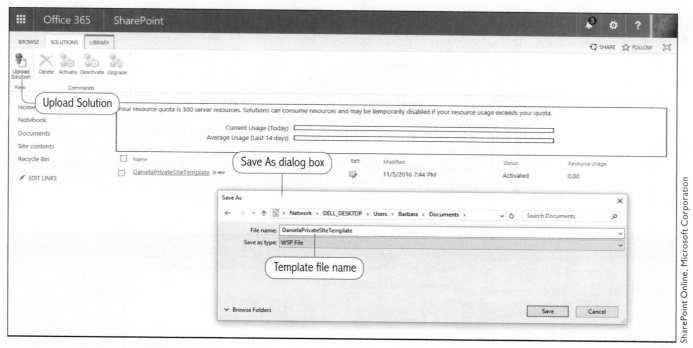

**FIGURE 2.4** Download a Template

With the .wsp file saved on your local computer or flash drive, you can upload the custom template to a new collection. Just as solutions are stored in the top-level site, when you want to upload a custom template solution file, you must be on the top-level site.

**To upload a template solution file, complete the following steps:**

1. Navigate to the top-level site.
2. Click the Settings icon and select Site settings.
3. Click Solutions in the Web Designer Galleries section.
4. Click Upload Solution in the New group on the SOLUTIONS tab (refer to Figure 2.4).
5. Click Browse, navigate to the location where the file is stored on your local computer, and select the file name. Click Open.
6. Click OK.

---

**TIP: UPLOADING A TEMPLATE FROM ANOTHER ACCOUNT**
You may have trouble if you upload a template from another account into your SharePoint Online site.

---

## Activate and Deactivate Site Templates

Site templates can be activated or deactivated as necessary. For instance, when you upload a new template to the Solutions Gallery, it is deactivated by default and you will activate it so others can use it. For example, you might deactivate a custom template when you are proposing or designing a new template for a department in your organization, but do not yet have the authorization from the department manager to make the template available to the users.

**To activate or deactivate a custom site template, complete the following steps:**

1. Navigate to the top-level site.
2. Click the Settings icon and select Site settings.
3. Click Solutions in the Web Designer Galleries section.
4. Click the check box next to the file name of the template you want to activate to select it.
5. Click Activate or Deactivate in the Commands group on the SOLUTIONS tab, as appropriate.
6. Click the appropriate Activate or Deactivate command in the Solution Gallery dialog box that opens, as shown in Figure 2.5.

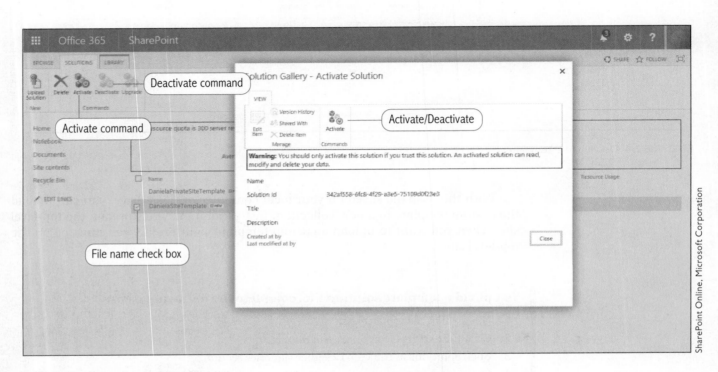

**FIGURE 2.5** Deactivate a Template

---

**TIP: ACTIVATE OR DEACTIVATE A TEMPLATE**
You can activate or deactivate a template by clicking the menu arrow next to the Edit icon and then selecting the appropriate action.

---

## Edit or Delete a Template

Inevitably, whenever you create a template, someone will suggest some changes to improve it. You can edit templates by editing the site you used to create a template. You also have the option to use the template to create a new site, which you then edit. In either case, a best practice is to save the original template to your local computer prior to making adjustments to it, as discussed previously.

Templates you no longer need can be deleted, with the exception of the default site templates of SharePoint Online, which cannot be deleted. To delete a template, it must first be deactivated, as described earlier. After deactivation, click the menu arrow and select Delete, as shown in Figure 2.6. Click OK in the Message from webpage dialog box to confirm your intention to delete the site template to the Recycle Bin.

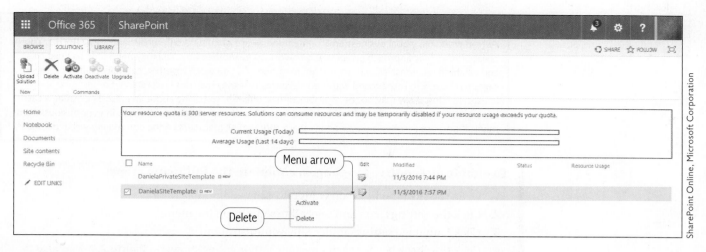

**FIGURE 2.6** Delete a Template

# Customizing a Site

As you plan for sites that you will provide to teams or the public, you carefully consider their needs and preferences. If you are working with an international audience, you should consider changing the language and regional settings to enable them to view the site based on settings they have selected in their browser.

SharePoint Online enables you to customize many site page elements to change the look and feel of the site. As a site designer, you can create a custom brand using site themes, color themes, and font themes that reflect the organization. You can use the organization's logo on the site, further branding the site.

Within the site, the navigation links and navigation aids are altered to improve the user experience as they move from one page to another throughout the site. Links can be added or removed from the top link bar and the Quick Launch. Additional navigation is implemented by adding Tree view below the Quick Launch.

New pages are added to the SharePoint Online site to fit the needs of your organization. The pages can be customized by adding content and adjusting the layout. Elements such as tables, pictures, video, audio, apps, and web parts can be added to the custom pages. You can delete site pages that are no longer needed by the users. The home page of a site can be changed to control where site visitors enter the site, enabling you to provide introductory information for the site and a customized screen layout. For instance, you may want to display announcements on a site home page so that everyone sees them as they come into the site, without having to click an announcement link. The customizations to pages and to the site can be reset to the original site definition if you decide that this is a necessary action.

## Change Language and Regional Settings

**STEP 2** ⟫ SharePoint Online supports a ***Multilingual User Interface (MUI)*** that enables you to specify support for various languages in the sites that you create. This is important because less than 10% of the world's population speaks English as a first or second language. Global business is becoming more commonplace, and as you develop sites, you must be aware of and prepare for this trend.

By specifying alternative languages as you design a site, you enable people to access the site interface in the language they select. It is important to note that MUI is not translation of the site contents, but rather a display of the user interface elements in different languages. For example, the default menus and actions, columns, navigation bar links, and site title and description are displayed in the alternative languages, whereas announcements or documents remain in their original language. The advantage of specifying alternative languages is that it relieves you from having to develop multiple sites with the same content for business associates or customers.

**To enable alternative languages, complete the following steps:**

1. Open the site for which you want to specify additional languages.
2. Click the Settings icon and select Site settings on the menu.
3. Click Language settings under Site Administration.
4. Click the check box for each alternate language, as shown in Figure 2.7. You also select whether to enable translation of user-specified text, such as the site title and description, to automatically overwrite the existing text in all alternate languages.
5. Click OK to apply the alternate languages to the site.

SharePoint Online, Microsoft Corporation

**FIGURE 2.7** Additional Languages

In addition to specifying alternative languages, you can select regional settings that affect the way numbers, dates, and time appear on a site, as shown in Table 2.1. The time zone setting is important when team members are working in different time zones and trying to coordinate their schedules for meetings and other events. For instance, if someone on the East Coast sets a meeting for 3:00 PM, another person on the West Coast will arrive for the meeting 3 hours late. To compensate for the difference in time zones, the site time zone is set for the local time, and each team member then sets his or her regional setting to his or her own location. As team members upload items or schedule events, the correct times will be reflected on the site.

Another worthwhile setting to consider in the regional settings is the time format of 12 versus 24 hours. Many organizations use the 24-hour clock to standardize time. For instance, 1:00 PM on a 12-hour clock is 13:00 on a 24-hour clock.

**TABLE 2.1 Regional Settings**

| Option | Use |
| --- | --- |
| Time Zone | Standard time zone for the site |
| Locale | Language used to display numbers, dates, and time |
| Sort Order | Language used to control the sort order |
| Set Your Calendar | Type of calendar |
| Enable an Alternate Calendar | Secondary calendar to provide extra information on calendar features |
| Define Your Work Week | Sets time and days that make up the work week and the first week of the year |
| Time Format | 12-hour or 24-hour time format |

Pearson Education, Inc.

**To access the regional settings, complete the following steps:**

1. Open the site for which you want to make regional settings.
2. Click the Settings icon and select Site settings on the menu.
3. Click Regional settings under Site Administration.
4. Select the settings that are appropriate, as shown in Figure 2.8, and click OK to apply the settings to the site.

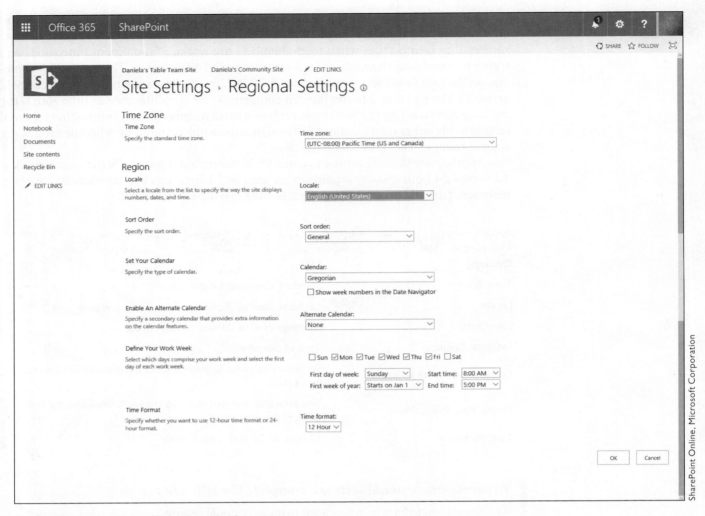

**FIGURE 2.8** SharePoint Online Regional Settings

## Change a Site Title and Logo

As you create a new site, you provide a title that appears throughout the site. When you have the site displayed, the title is shown across the top of the home page and in numerous pages on the top link bar. The title is also shown when search results are reported. You can change the title after creating the site. For example, the focus of a site might change and you want to reflect the new focal point in the site title, or the title might contain a spelling error. The title and description can be changed using the Site Settings page.

**To change the title of a site, complete the following steps:**

1. Open the site for which you want to change the title.
2. Click the Settings icon and then select Site settings on the menu.
3. Click Title, description, and logo under Look and Feel.
4. Change the title or description, as shown in Figure 2.9, and click OK.

SharePoint Online, Microsoft Corporation

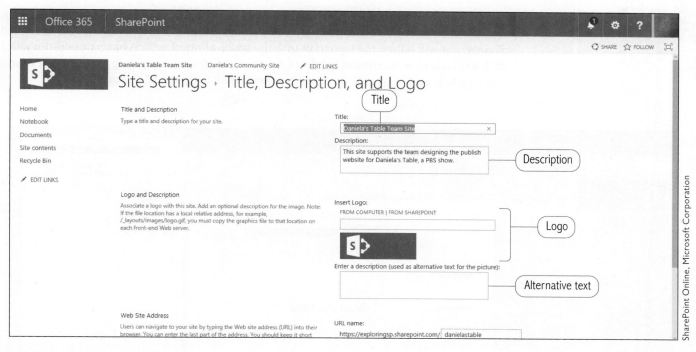

**FIGURE 2.9** Title Site Settings

As you plan for a site, consider the look and feel of the site and how you might brand it to reflect your organization. You can use the company logo or another graphic you have developed to brand a team site. This extra step dresses up the site, while enabling the team members to identify it quickly and ensure they are completing their work in the correct site. For instance, you may create a quick graphic in Paint with the team name or project name and use that as a logo. Photographs can also be used as a logo, so if your team is working on a project for a new product, a picture of the product or prototype might be a good logo for the site. A veterinary clinic might use a picture of a dog or cat as a logo on its site. An electronics distributor could use a circuit board graphic as a logo. To help brand the whole site, it is a good idea to keep the logo consistent throughout a site collection. In other words, if a team site contains a subsite, then that subsite should have the same logo as the team site so that users will understand that they are still within the same site.

The Site Settings page enables you to add a logo to the site (refer to Figure 2.9). The source of the logo can be a file from your computer or from the SharePoint site folder.

If you are selecting a file from your computer, as shown in Figure 2.10, the file will be uploaded to the site and you will select a destination folder where it will be stored. SharePoint will adjust the logo to fit into the space allotted, which has a maximum width of 180 pixels by a maximum height of 64 pixels. If you are designing a logo, it will render more clearly on the page if you use these settings for the size of the graphic.

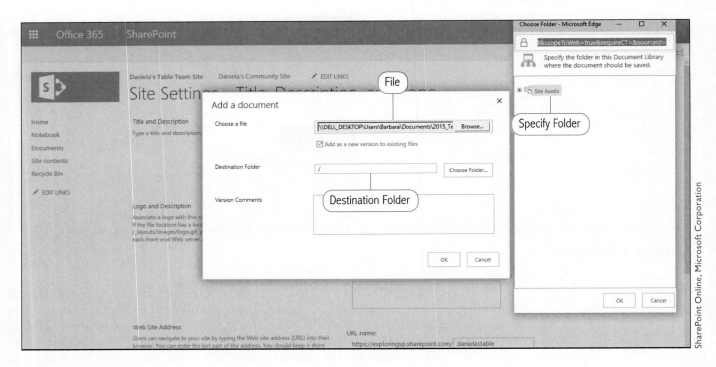

**FIGURE 2.10** Site Logo Insertion

Whenever you add graphics or pictures to a website, you should include an alternative text description for the picture (refer to Figure 2.9). This enables accessibility by people who use adaptive technologies such as screen readers. This text is also visible when a user points to the logo for a few seconds, as a ScreenTip. If you do not specify alternative text, the name of the site is the default value displayed.

## Work with Navigation Links and Aids

**STEP 3** ▸▸ One of your main goals as a site designer is to make sites as user friendly as possible. Carefully consider the navigation of the site as you create it. SharePoint Online provides two main areas for navigation, the Quick Launch and the top link bar. The top link bar contains links to the top-level site in the site collection and to the subsites within the collection. The Quick Launch provides access to the home page of the site using Home and to other sites in the collection by using Site contents. In addition, the site logo acts as a link to return to the home page of a site.

You can modify the top link bar and Quick Launch to add or remove navigational links. If you want to modify the top link bar, click EDIT LINKS on that navigation bar. Likewise, to edit the links on the Quick Launch, click EDIT LINKS on the Quick Launch, as shown in Figure 2.11. For instance, you may wish to add a link directly to a subsite on the Quick Launch so the user does not have to click Site contents and then find the link at the bottom of the Site contents page. You can also add links to sources outside of the site, such as websites, by adding a URL as a link. This is useful if a particular website contains information that the team will regularly need to access, such as government regulations or product information.

**FIGURE 2.11** Site Navigation

> ### To add a navigational link, complete the following steps:
>
> 1. Open the site on which you want to add a navigational link.
> 2. Click EDIT LINKS on either the top link bar or Quick Launch.
> 3. Click link and type the text that will be used for the link and the address of the page or site in the dialog box and click OK, or if the classic view is displayed, you can drag and drop a link to a file, page, or list, as shown in Figure 2.12.

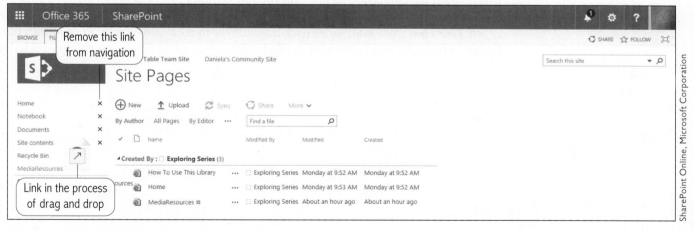

**FIGURE 2.12** Quick Launch Edit in Classic View

Links can be removed from the top link bar or Quick Launch using EDIT LINKS. Click the X (Remove this link from navigation) to the right of the link name on the top link bar or Quick Launch to delete the link (refer to Figure 2.12). This does not delete the actual page or site but rather just removes the link from the view of the user.

The order of the links on the navigation bar can be changed to improve the user experience. For instance, you may want to provide a link to the top-level site and have it appear at the top of the Quick Launch. Click EDIT LINKS and then drag the links into the proper order on the Quick Launch.

In some cases, you may need to edit a link by changing the name or the link itself. Website URLs change, documents get moved, or a link is incorrectly typed, all of which necessitate an edit. To change a link, click EDIT LINKS and click the link on the navigation bar, as shown in Figure 2.13. Click Edit a link next to the link name to display the Edit link dialog box where you can adjust the name or the address of the link.

**FIGURE 2.13** Edit an Existing Link

The Site Settings page can also be used to change the links on the top link bar and the Quick Launch. Click the Settings icon, click Site settings, and then select the navigation bar you want to change in the Look and Feel section of the Site Settings page. You can use this method to rearrange the links on the navigation bar by clicking Change Order and then using the arrows to select a different numerical order.

A *Tree view* adds additional user-friendliness to your site by providing hierarchical navigation similar to a Folders list in File Explorer. Users can expand or collapse folders to quickly locate and open documents, pages, and other site assets, as shown in Figure 2.14. A white arrow next to the item indicates it can be expanded, with a black arrow used to collapse the item.

**To display the Tree view on the Quick Launch, complete the following steps:**

1. Open the site on which you want to add the Tree view.
2. Click the Settings icon, select Site settings on the menu, and then click Navigation Elements under the Look and Feel section (refer to Figure 2.14).
3. Click the Enable Tree View check box to select it, and click OK.

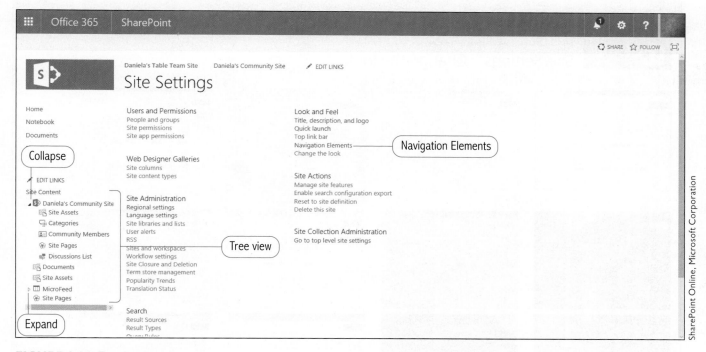

**FIGURE 2.14** Tree View

## Change the Look of a Site

STEP 4 >> As you design sites, consider the look and feel of the site as an important part of user-friendliness. Everyone likes to work in an attractive work environment, and the same consideration should be made for the sites in which they work. A ***site theme***, similar to other Microsoft themes, defines the layout, and font and color schemes for a site. SharePoint Online provides professionally designed site themes with various backgrounds and colors, as shown in Figure 2.15.

**FIGURE 2.15** SharePoint Online Themes

Themes enable you to make color and font selections for page elements that you can quickly apply to the complete site. If you make modifications to the theme, they will be reflected on all pages of the site. This provides a consistent look and feel to all of the pages in the site. **Color themes** affect page elements such as backgrounds, text, and hyperlinks and some graphic elements such as bullets and horizontal rules (or lines). **Font themes** dictate the fonts used for heading and body text.

Themes can be used to help brand your site. For example, if you are planning a university website, you will probably use the school's colors as a basis for selecting theme colors for the site. Using a site theme as a starting point, you can further modify the settings to customize the theme to the branding required by your organization or your tastes.

---

**TIP: CONSIDER YOUR AUDIENCE**

As you apply themes to sites, consider audience characteristics and the purpose for your site. Provide adequate contrast in color choices so that the site text is easy to read. Dark backgrounds can cause problems with reading text for some older users, but they can provide a dramatic environment for displaying art work. Strive to balance the theme with the needs of the audience and the site purpose.

---

To apply a new theme to a site, click the Settings icon, select Site settings on the menu, and then click Change the look in the Look and Feel section of the Site Settings page. Select the theme (refer to Figure 2.15) you want to use as the starting point for the design of the site. After a few moments, the Change the look page displays a preview of the page with options for modifications in the left pane, as shown in Figure 2.16. You can change the background picture by adding, replacing, or removing the picture. Click the Colors arrow to select a different color theme. The Site layout dictates the location of the menus on the site, with two default layouts available. Click the Fonts arrow to select a different font theme. Each font theme includes a font for the headings and another for the content text.

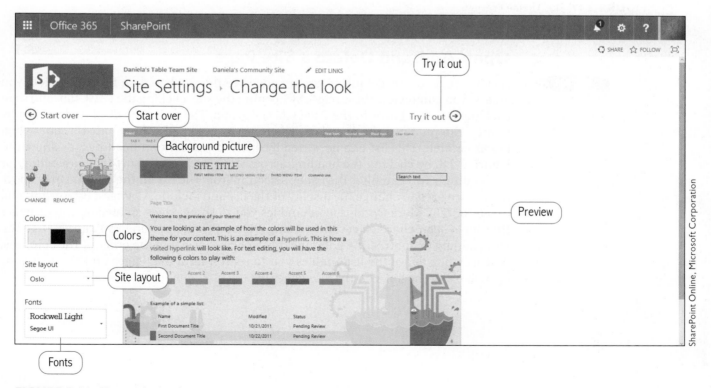

**FIGURE 2.16** Change the Look

When you have completed your selections in the left pane, click Try it out at the top of the preview. In a few moments, your site is displayed with the new theme settings, as shown in Figure 2.17. Using the arrows on the top right of the display, you can return to the Change the look page or accept the changes and apply them to your site. To return to the theme selection page that displays all of the available themes, click Start over in the left pane of the Change the look page.

Return to theme selection page

Accept theme settings

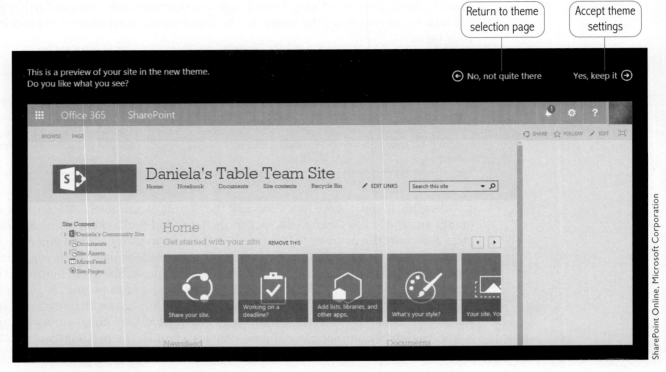

**FIGURE 2.17** Site Theme Preview

## Open, Add, and Delete a Site Page

**STEP 5** ⟩⟩ As you create a site, default pages are added to the site based on the type of site you create. You can review these pages by opening the site, clicking the PAGE tab, and then clicking View All Pages in the Page Library group. The pages are displayed in a list by name, who modified the page last, when it was modified, who created it, and when it was created. This list can be sorted by each of the column headings, as shown in Figure 2.18, by clicking the heading arrow and selecting the sort type (ascending or descending). You can filter the list by selecting from the list on the menu. Links above the list are used to change the display of the list and include All Pages, By Author, and By Editor. The More Options icon enables you to show pages created by you or pages that have been changed recently. Using the additional options you can change the view, adding or subtracting columns that are displayed and the order of the columns. A search box above the list enables you to search for a file. Pages on the site can be opened using the links on the Site Pages list.

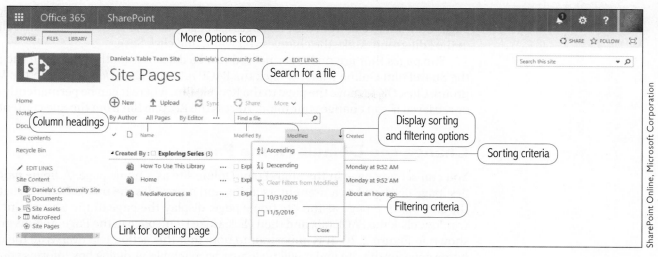

**FIGURE 2.18** Site Pages List

SharePoint Online, Microsoft Corporation

---

**TIP: ACCESSING THE SITE PAGES LIST PAGE**
The Site Pages list page can be accessed in a number of ways. You can click Site contents on the Quick Launch and click the Site Pages tile. You can also click the Settings icon, click Site contents, and then click the Site Pages tile.

---

You can add new pages to the SharePoint Online site to fit the needs of your organization or team. The easiest way to add a new page is to click the Settings icon, and then select Add a page from the menu. This method works regardless of what page you are viewing. Another option for creating a new page is to open the Site Pages, as previously discussed, and click New above the page list. Provide a name for the new page, and click Create.

The new page appears as a blank page with a frame in which you add and format content, as shown in Figure 2.19. The Ribbon contains tabs for formatting the text and inserting objects such as tables, media, links, app, web parts, and embedded code. When you have completed your work on the page, click Save to place the new page on the site.

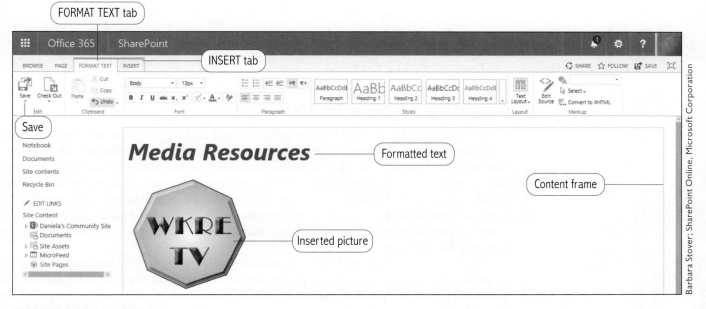

**FIGURE 2.19** New Page Layout

Barbara Stover; SharePoint Online, Microsoft Corporation

As you might expect, you can edit pages that have previously been created. Open the page you want to edit from the Site Pages list page, click the PAGE tab, and then click Edit in the Edit group. Make the changes you want, and click Save.

Site pages that are no longer needed can be deleted from the site. Open the page in the SharePoint Online window. Click the PAGE tab, and click Delete Page in the Manage group. Click OK to move the page to the Recycle Bin, where it can be permanently deleted or retrieved if you change your mind. Access the Recycle Bin from the Site contents page.

## Change the Default Home Page

You can set any page in the SharePoint Online site as a home page. A **home page** is the first page displayed as a user enters a site, and it provides the navigational structure for the site. To set a page as the site home page, display the page in the SharePoint Online window, click the PAGE tab, and then click Make Homepage in the Page Actions group, as shown in Figure 2.20. It is important to note that this action will overwrite the original home page for the site and it will no longer be available. A dialog box informs you of this consequence before you complete the process of assigning a new home page for a site. Click OK to continue with the new home page.

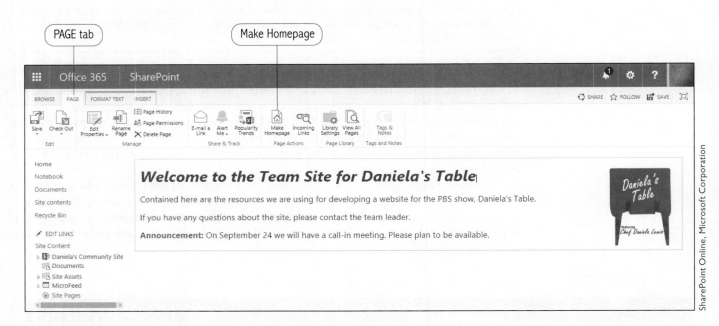

**FIGURE 2.20** Set the Default Home Page

## Resetting a Site at Its Definition

As you use your SharePoint Online sites, you will make changes to the look, feel, and functionalities to customize the pages for your organization. Pages are built on templates that have a site definition. The site definition, and therefore the template page, is shared across all of the pages with the site collection in a concept called *ghosting*. As you customize site pages, only the differences between the original site definition and the changes you made are saved into the content libraries. This improves the loading performance of your webpage because the template page loads from the cache memory and the changes are added to the page.

As you use SharePoint Online to update the site pages, they become unghosted. **Unghosted** pages are customized pages that do not contain the characteristics of the standard configuration and layout of the site definition. These unghosted pages are stored in the content libraries of the site and loaded from the libraries when requested by a browser. This slows the performance of the website. To regain the advantage of the ghosting concept, you can reghost all or part of the pages within a site back to the original site definition. **_Reghost_** means to reset the pages to the original site definition, removing all customization and reverting the page back to the configuration and layout of the template.

---

**To reset a page or an entire site, complete the following steps:**

1. Open the home page of the site.
2. Click the Settings icon and select Site settings on the Settings menu.
3. Click Reset to site definition in the Site Actions section of the Site Settings page.
4. Click Reset specific page to site definition version if you only want to reset one page and type the URL for the page in the box, as shown in Figure 2.21. If you want to reset the entire site, click Reset all pages in this site to site definition version.
5. Click Reset to complete the action.

---

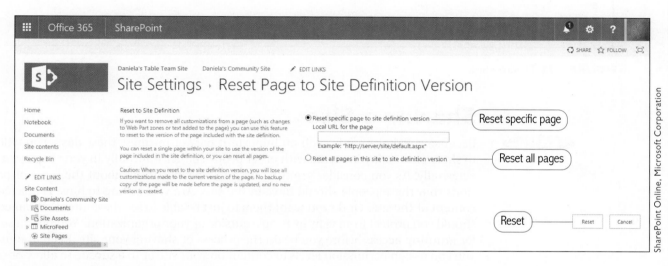

**FIGURE 2.21** Reset to Site Definition

## Delete a Site

After some time, you may decide you want to delete a site from SharePoint Online. Consider this action carefully, because it is permanent, and all content, pages, and the site itself are deleted. A deleted site will not be stored in the Recycle Bin; hence, you will not be able to recover it. If a site contains subsites, you will not be able to delete the parent site until you have deleted the subsites.

You have two options for site deletion. You can use the Site Settings page when you have opened the site you want to delete, as shown in Figure 2.22, or you can use the Sites and Workspaces page from the top-level site. You should always make backups of your sites to avoid the loss of hours and hours of work.

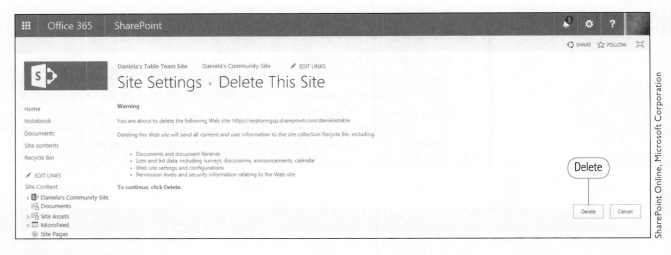

**FIGURE 2.22** Delete a Site

# Sharing a Site

 Because collaboration is such an important part of business these days, you will want to share sites that you create with other people, either internally in your organization or externally. As you consider granting access to people, think about the types of permissions that these people should have in the site. Are you willing to have people edit the content of the site? Or do you want them to just be able to see the content? What content should you protect from view by people outside of your organization? You need a strategy for granting access before you begin the process of sharing your site. Keep in mind that you can assign permission levels to content on your site or to a subsite to allow or restrict access or actions, such as editing.

**To share a site, complete the following steps:**

1. Navigate to the site you want to share in SharePoint Online.
2. Click Share on the contextual toolbar below the Notification and Settings icons.
3. Click Invite people, as shown in Figure 2.23, to type names or email addresses in the Enter names or email addresses box. You can also include an optional message that will be part of the email invitation.
4. Click the SHOW OPTIONS/HIDE OPTIONS link below the text boxes (SHOW OPTIONS was clicked in Figure 2.23) to select a group or permission level to assign to the person or persons to whom you are granting access.
5. Click Share to send the email message.

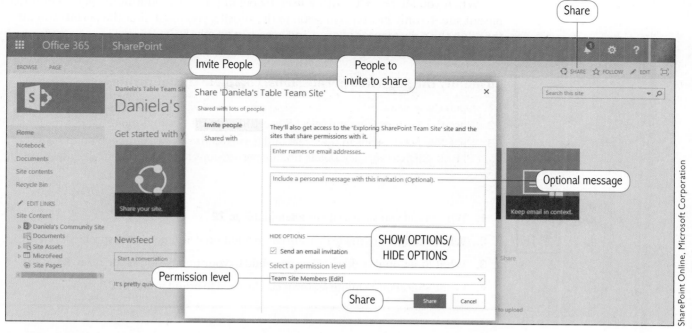

**FIGURE 2.23** Share a Site

When the person you invited checks his or her email, a message with a link to your SharePoint Online site appears. After the person clicks the link, he or she will be asked to sign in using a Microsoft account or with an organizational account for Office 365.

You can also use Share on the contextual toolbar to display a list of the people who have access to the site, as shown in Figure 2.24. Click *Shared with* in the left pane of the Share dialog box to display a list of people with access. Click Advanced to view the Permissions page and select a group to view the members of that group. For instance, in the example shown in Figure 2.24, Leslie Miller, an external user, is in the Team Site Members group, enabling her to edit the content of the site.

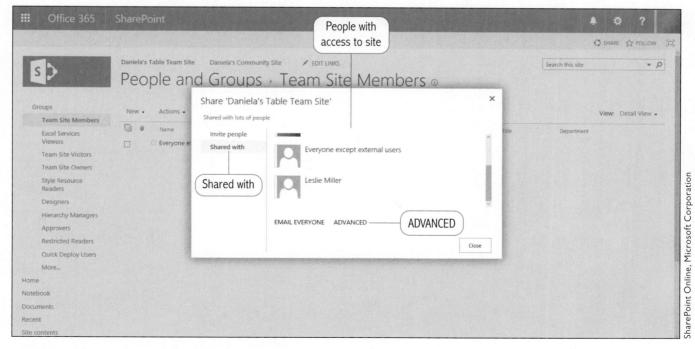

**FIGURE 2.24** Review with Whom the Site is Shared

When you share a site with a user, by default, the person inherits permission to the parent site. To only grant permission to the subsite, you must alter the permission inheritance on the subsite prior to granting access to people.

**To modify the inherited permissions, complete the following steps:**

1. Open the subsite.
2. Click the Settings icon and select Site settings on the Settings menu.
3. Click Site permissions in the Users and Permissions section, and then on the PERMISSIONS tab, click Delete unique permissions in the Inheritance group.

*Quick Concept*

1. Why would you save a site as a template? *p. 72*
2. What changes are made to a site when additional languages are specified? *p. 77*
3. What functionality does a Tree view add to your navigation strategy? *p. 84*
4. What SharePoint Online features can be used to brand a site? *p. 87*

# Hands-On Exercises

**Skills covered:** Create a Private Site* • Create a Site Template • Use a Custom Template • Download and Upload a Site Template* • Activate and Deactivate Site Templates* • Edit or Delete a Template* • Change the Language and Regional Settings • Change a Site Title and Logo • Work with Navigation Links and Aids • Change the Look of a Site • Open, Add, and Delete a Site Page • Change the Default Home Page • Share a Site

## 1 Tools to Customize a Site

As the team leader for the Daniela's Table website project, you are responsible for guiding the team and ultimately determining the look and feel of the website. Using the tools available for customizing a site, you will create a sample site that the team will use as a starting point.

---

**STEP 1 》》 CHANGE THE LANGUAGE AND REGIONAL SETTINGS**

You will begin by creating a private site in which you will store the template. (Note: Depending on your Office 365 account, you may not be able to set up a private site, but you can still create a template.) You will then make sure that your website is accessible to people who speak French and Spanish, as well as English. You will also check the regional settings for the site to ensure they are set to your current location. Refer to Figure 2.25 as you complete Step 1.

**FIGURE 2.25** Site Displayed in French

a. Open your browser and navigate to your Office 365 site.

b. Note whether you have access to the Admin tile, and follow the appropriate set of instructions below:

| If you have an Admin tile: | If you do not have an Admin tile available: |
|---|---|
| • Click the **Admin tile**. | • Click the **SharePoint tile**, and click the **Team Site tile**. |
| • Click **Resources** in the left pane and select **Sites**. | • Click **Site Contents** on the Quick Launch. |
| • Click **Add a site**. | • Click **Return to classic SharePoint** at the bottom of the Quick Launch. |
| | • Click **new subsite** at the bottom of the page. |

**TROUBLESHOOTING:** If you do not have an Admin tile, you will not be able to create a private site, but you can complete the creation of a site template.

**c.** Type **Daniela's Table Site Example** in the title box and follow the remaining steps based on whether you have access to the Admin tile:

| If you have an Admin tile: | If you do not have an Admin tile available: |
|---|---|
| • Type **daniela_template** in the empty box following Web Site Address (the third box in the section; it does not contain an arrow). | • Type **daniela_template** in the URL box. |
| • Ensure Team Site is the selected template. | • Ensure Team Site is the selected template. |
| • Type your **user name** in the Administrator box and click the **Check Names box** on the right side of the box to confirm that the correct name is selected for the administrator of the account. Your name will have an underscore when it is confirmed. | • Click **Create**. |
| • Click **OK**. Click **Allow**. It can take a few moments for the site to build. *New* displays next to the URL on the Admin page when the process is complete. | |
| • Click the **URL** to the new site and click the **URL** a second time in the site collection properties dialog box to open it. | |

> **TROUBLESHOOTING:** To return to the private site, you must open the Admin center, click Resources in the left pane, and then select Sites. Click the URL to the site, and click Go to this site on the dialog box to open the site.

**d.** Click **Settings** on the top navigation bar, and select **Site settings** on the menu.

The Site Settings page contains the settings for language and regional settings in the Site Administration section.

**e.** Click **Language settings** in the Site Administration section of the Site Settings page. Select **French** and **Spanish** in the Alternate languages section. Accept the default value (No) for Overwrite Translations. Click **OK**.

The site user interface will now be available to users who speak English, French, or Spanish. The Site Settings page displays so you can make additional adjustments.

**f.** Click **Regional settings** in the Site Administration section of the Site Settings page. Click the **Time zone arrow**, and select the time zone for your current location. Click the **Locale arrow** and select **English (United States)**. Click the **Time format arrow** and select **24 Hour**. Click **OK**.

You will test the language settings to ensure they are working.

**g.** Click the **photo icon** (or your name) on the top navigation bar, and select **About me**. Click **Update profile**, scroll to and then click **How can I change language and regional settings**. Click the link **here**, click the **ellipses** (...) next to Details, and then select **Language and Region**. Click the arrow in the *Pick a new language box*, select **French (France)**, and then click **Add**. Click the **up arrow** next to French (France) in the My Display Languages list to move French to the top of the list. Scroll to the bottom of the page and click **Save all and close**. Click **OK** on the Profile Changes dialog box.

> **TROUBLESHOOTING:** It can take several minutes for the language settings to take effect after you have changed them.

**h.** Close all browser tabs, wait a few moments, and then sign back into Office 365. Follow the appropriate steps below based on whether you could create a private site:

| **If you have an Admin tile:** | **If you do not have an Admin tile available:** |
|---|---|
| • Click the **Admin tile**.<br>• Click **Resources** in the left pane and select **Sites**.<br>• Click the **URL** for the site you create which ends with Daniela_template.<br>• Click **Go to this site**. | • Click the **SharePoint tile**.<br>• Click the **Team site tile**.<br>• Click **Site Contents** on the Quick Launch.<br>• Click **return to classic SharePoint** at the bottom of the Quick Launch.<br>• Click **Daniela's Table Site Example** in the Subsites section. |

The subsite template displays in French. It can sometimes take quite a while to change the display. Review the left pane and the global navigation bar to see the changes.

**i.** Open the Snipping Tool and take a full-screen snip showing the site in French. Save the file as **sp02h1French_LastFirst**.

You will now return your profile settings to English.

**j.** Click the **photo icon** (or your name) on the top navigation bar, and click the top menu item **À propos de moi** (About me). Click **Mettre à jour le profil** (Update profile), click the **More Options icon**, and then click **Comment puis-je modifier les paramètres de langue et de région** (How can I change language and regional settings). Click **ici**, click the **ellipses** (...), and select **langue et région**. Select **Français (France)** in the My Display Languages list, and click the **X** on the far right of the selection. Scroll to the bottom of the page and click **Enregistrer tout et fermer** (Save and close). Click **OK** in the Profile Changes dialog box. Sign out of Office 365 and close your browser.

After changing the language settings, you sign out of Office 365 so the interface can reset to the new language settings. Again, this may take some time to change back to English.

## STEP 2 ›› CUSTOMIZE THE TITLE, LOGO, AND NAVIGATION

As you plan the template, you want to add customization to help brand the site and make it more user friendly. You will change the title and logo and add some navigation links to the site. Refer to Figure 2.26 as you complete Step 2.

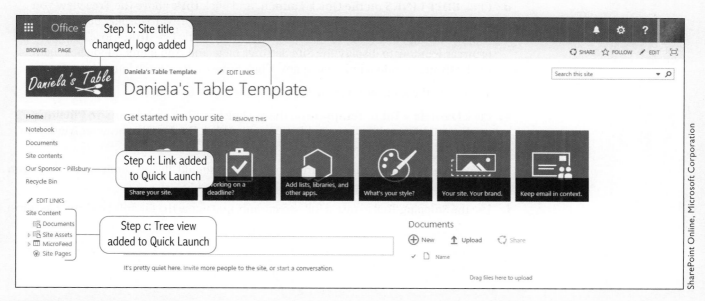

**FIGURE 2.26** Site Customization

SharePoint Online, Microsoft Corporation

**a.** Open your browser and navigate to your Office 365 site. Open the Daniela's Table Site Example based on whether you were able to access the Admin tile:

| If you have an Admin tile: | If you do not have an Admin tile available: |
|---|---|
| • Click the **Admin tile**.<br>• Click **Resources** in the left pane and select **Sites**.<br>• Click the **URL** for the site you create which ends with Daniela_template.<br>• Click **Go to this site**. | • Click the **SharePoint tile**.<br>• Click the **Team site tile**.<br>• Click **Site Contents** on the Quick Launch.<br>• Click **return to classic SharePoint** at the bottom of the Quick Launch.<br>• Select **Daniela's Table Site Example** in the Subsites section. |

You will continue to work on the template team site you created in Step 1.

> **TROUBLESHOOTING:** If the site is still displayed in French, click the Refresh icon on the browser. Keep in mind that it may take some time for the changes to take effect.

**b.** Click **Settings** on the top navigation bar, and select **Site settings** from the menu. Click **Title, description, and logo** in the Look and Feel section of the Site Settings page. Make the following adjustments to the settings:

- Type the title **Daniela's Table Template**.

- Click **FROM COMPUTER** in the Insert Logo section. Click **Browse** and navigate to *sp02h1Logo* in the student data files. Select the file, and click **Open**. Click **OK**.

- Click in the **Enter a description box** below the logo, and type **Daniela's Table Logo**.

- Click **OK**.

The title of the site changes and the logo is displayed in the upper left corner of the window.

**c.** Click **Navigation Elements** in the Look and Feel section. Select the **Enable Tree View checkbox**, and click **OK**.

The Tree view navigation is displayed on the Quick Launch.

**d.** Click **EDIT LINKS** on the Quick Launch, and click **link** above the Tree view you added in step c. Type **Our Sponsor-Pillsbury** in the Text to display box. Type **http://www.pillsbury.com** in the Address box. Click **Try link**. Close the Pillsbury browser window to display the Site Settings page and Add a link dialog box again. Click **OK** in the Add a link dialog box. Click **Save** on the Quick Launch.

The link to the sponsor's website is added to the Quick Launch.

**e.** Click **Daniela's Table Template** on the top link bar. Click **Our Sponsor-Pillsbury** on the Quick Launch and ensure the site opens. Click **Back** on the browser window to return to Daniela's Table Template.

As you add links and other resources to a site, you should always confirm that they open correctly.

**f.** Use the Snipping Tool to take a full-screen snip, and name the file **sp02h1Site_LastFirst**.

You decide to experiment with the custom color and font themes available in SharePoint Online to further brand the site. Refer to Figure 2.27 as you complete Step 3.

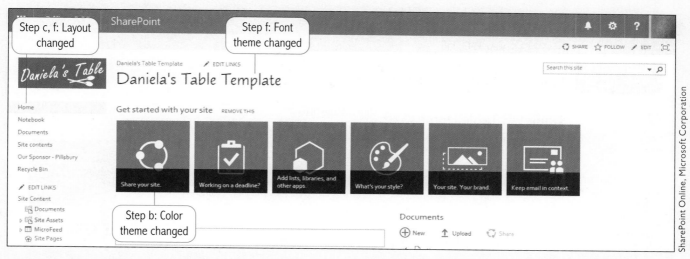

**FIGURE 2.27** Site Theme Customization

**a.** Click **Settings** on the top navigation bar, and select **Site settings** from the menu. Click **Change the look** in the Look and Feel section of the Site Settings page. Click **Green**.

Although you want the site to ultimately contain blue elements, you will begin your experimentation with the Green theme. The background of the Green theme does not contain an image, which presents a clean look and feel to the site.

**b.** Click the **Colors arrow**. Point to the various color themes and observe the preview. Click the color theme at the top of the list **This palette is primarily White with Gray-80% and Dark Blue.**

The preview displays the site using the selected theme colors.

**c.** Click the **Site layout arrow**. Select **Oslo**.

The Quick Launch is removed and the links are moved across the top of the page in the preview.

**d.** Click the **Fonts arrow** and select the font theme **Blueprint MT Pro/Corbel**.

**e.** Click **Try it out** and review the elements you changed on the page.

You decide that you would like the Quick Launch to display on the left side of the site, with the Tree view you added earlier. It may take some time for the changes to display.

**f.** Click **No, not quite there**. Click the **Site layout arrow** and select **Seattle**. Click **Try it out** and review the new layout. Click **Yes, keep it**.

**g.** Click **Home** on the Quick Launch. Take a full-screen snip, and name the file **sp02h1Layout_LastFirst**.

Your template team site will feature a customized page that you will set as the home page for the site. Refer to Figure 2.28 as you complete Step 4.

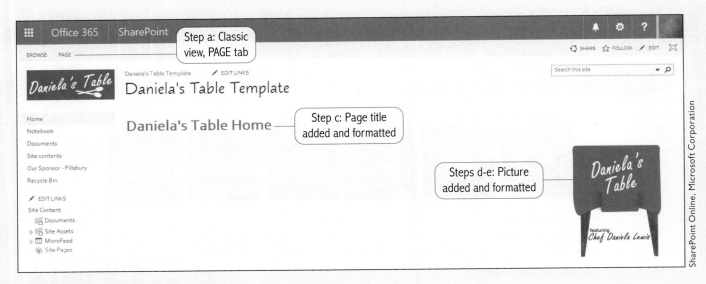

**FIGURE 2.28** Home Page Customization

a. Click the **PAGE tab**, and click **View All Pages** in the Page Library group. Click **Return to classic SharePoint** at the bottom of the Quick Launch.

All of the default pages for the site are displayed.

b. Click **New,** and type the page name **site_home**. Click **Create**.

A blank page appears with a content box for customization.

c. Type **Daniela's Table Home**, and press **Enter**. Select the text you typed and apply the **Heading** font, size **24pt**, **bold**, and color **Dark Blue, Accent 1** (top row, fifth column).

d. Click below the text. Click the **INSERT tab**, click the **Picture arrow**, and then select **From Computer**. Click **Browse**, navigate to the student data files, select *sp02h1Table*, and then click **Open**. Click **OK**.

The image appears on the page but is quite large and not in a good location.

e. Click **Position** in the Arrange group on the IMAGE tab, and select **Right**. Click in the **Horizontal Size box** in the Size group, type **200**, and then press **Enter**.

> **TROUBLESHOOTING:** The image must be selected before the IMAGE tab is available on the Ribbon.

f. Click the **PAGE tab**, and click **Make Homepage** in the Page Actions group. Click **OK** in the Message from webpage dialog box.

g. Click the **Save arrow** in the Edit group, and then click **Save**.

The new home page is displayed with the customizations you made.

h. Click the **PAGE tab**, and click **View All Pages** in the Page Library group. Click the **More Options icon** next to How To Use This Library, and click the **More Options icon** on the menu. Select **Delete**, and click **OK** in the dialog box.

The default page created when the site was created is moved to the Recycle Bin.

i. Click **Site contents** on the Quick Launch, and click **Recycle Bin** on the top right of the window and confirm that the file is in the Recycle Bin.

You will leave this file in the Recycle Bin for now.

j. Click **Home** on the Quick Launch. Use the Snipping Tool to make a full-screen snip of the home page for the site. Name the file **sp02h1Home_LastFirst**.

**STEP 5 ⟩⟩ SHARE A SITE**

Your template team site is ready to share with other people, so you will invite them to view the site. Once again, a private site is handled a little differently than a SharePoint site. Refer to Figure 2.29 as you complete Step 5.

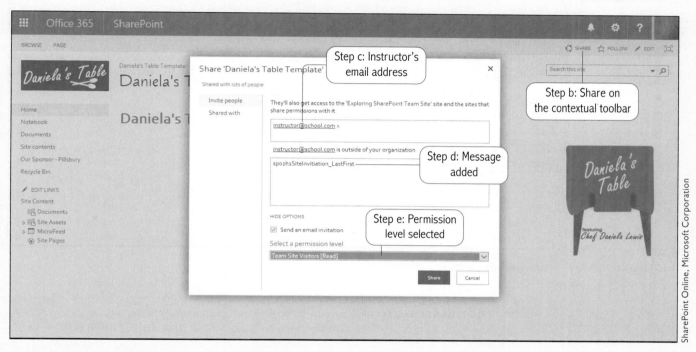

**FIGURE 2.29** Share a Site

a. **Set up the private site for sharing (skip to Step b if you are not working with a private site):** Click **Office 365** and click the **Admin tile**. Click **Resources** in the left pane, and select **Sites**. Click the **link** that contains the URL to your site (it contains the words daniela_template). Click **Edit** in the Sharing status section. Click **Off** to change it to On. Click **Save**. Click **Go to this site** in the dialog box.

b. Click **SHARE** on the contextual toolbar on the right side of the window. Click **Invite people** in the left pane.

c. Type **your instructor's email address** in the *Enter names or email addresses* box.

d. Type **sp02h1SiteInvitation_LastFirst** (using your name in place of LastFirst) in the *Include a personal message with this invitation* box.

e. Click **SHOW OPTIONS**, and click the **Select a permission level arrow**. Select **Team Site Example Visitors [Read]**.

f. Click **Share**.

You are satisfied with the template you have created, so you will save the site as a template and download it as a backup file on your local computer. You will also create a new site with the template to test the file and then delete it after you have reviewed it. You will not be able to complete this step if you have not been building the template on a private site. Refer to Figure 2.30 as you complete Step 6.

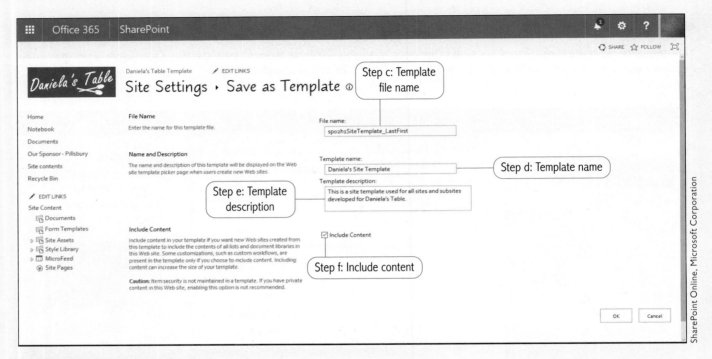

**FIGURE 2.30** Work with a Template

> **TROUBLESHOOTING:** You must be working with a private site in order to save a template. If your account did not enable you to create a private site in Step 1, skip Step 6 completely.

**a.** Click **Settings** on the top navigation bar, and select **Site settings** on the menu.

**b.** Click **Save site as template** in the Site Actions section of the Site Settings page.

**c.** Type **sp02h1SiteTemplate_LastFirst** (using your name in place of LastFirst) in the File name box.

**d.** Type **Daniela's Site Template** in the Template name box.

**e.** Type **This is the site template used for all sites and subsites developed for Daniela's Table.** (include the period) in the Template description box.

**f.** Click the **Include Content check box** to select it, and click **OK**. Click **solution gallery** in the Operation Completed Successfully window.

> **TROUBLESHOOTING:** If you do not see *solution gallery*, click Settings on the top navigation bar, select Site settings, and then click Solutions under the Web Designer Galleries on the Site Settings page.

**g.** Right-click the file **sp02h1SiteTemplate_LastFirst**, and select **Save target as** from the menu. Navigate to the location where you save your work, and click **Save**. Close any pop-up windows (probably at the bottom of the screen) that open after the save function is complete.

The .wsp file is downloaded to your local computer. You will upload it to SharePoint Online for practice, but you must first deactivate and delete the template on SharePoint.

**h.** Click **Settings** on the top navigation bar, and select **Site settings** from the menu.

**i.** Click **Solutions** in the Web Designer Galleries section. Click the **check box** for the template file sp02h1SiteTemplate_LastFirst to select the template, and then click the **arrow** to the right of the file name. Select **Deactivate**. Click **Deactivate** in the Commands group on the VIEW tab in the dialog box.

Templates must be deactivated before you can delete them.

**j.** Click the template file **sp02h1SiteTemplate_LastFirst check box**, and click the **arrow** to the right of the file name. Select **Delete** and click **OK** in the Message from webpage box.

The template is removed from the solutions list.

**k.** Click **Upload Solution** in the New group on the SOLUTIONS tab. Browse to and select the file **sp02h1SiteTemplate_LastFirst**. Click **Open**. Click **OK**. Click **Activate** in the Commands group on the VIEW tab in the Add a document dialog box.

**l.** Click **Settings** on the top navigation bar, select **Site contents** from the menu. Ensure that the classic SharePoint view is displayed.

**m.** Click **new subsite**, and type the following information into the form:

- Title: **Daniela's Template Test**
- Description: **Template Test**
- URL name: **daniela_test**

**n.** Click the **Custom tab** under Select a template, and select **Daniela's Site Template**. Scroll to the bottom of the screen and click **Create**.

You accepted the defaults and created a site based on your template for review. Notice that the site looks like the template you created, including the title, image, and link to the sponsor on the Quick Launch.

**o.** Click **Settings** on the top navigation bar, and select **Site settings** from the menu. Click **Delete this site** in the Site Actions section of the Site Settings page. Review the warning, and then click **Delete**. Click **OK** in the dialog box.

**p.** Click **GO BACK TO SITE** to return to the top-level team site, if you plan to continue to the next Hands-On Exercise. If not, sign out of Office 365 and close all browser windows. Files you created during this exercise will be submitted at the end of the last Hands-On Exercise.

# SharePoint Online Apps

The creation of team sites for collaboration is all about customizing the sites to enable people to communicate and be productive. You can customize sites by adding apps. **Apps** are small, easy-to-use Web applications that have a specific purpose. Although some default apps are available on the various SharePoint Online site templates, you can add new apps to increase the functionality of the site. For instance, you can create a site using the Team Site template, and then add a Discussion Board app, which is not in the original template, to the site.

SharePoint Online apps also enable you to work with lists and libraries. A **list** is a collection of announcements, links, survey questions, groups of discussions, or tasks. It contains information arranged as records. For instance, a contact list would contain names, addresses, and phone numbers stored in common fields in each record. A **library** is a collection of documents, pictures, or forms that can be shared with others. Files, such as Word documents, Excel workbooks, JPG files, and Adobe PDF files, are stored in libraries.

In normal business operations, documents can be difficult to collaborate on as a group. One person may make changes that do not filter out to other people who are simultaneously making changes to their copies of the same document. Using SharePoint Online apps, you can collaborate in real time with other team members to create and update documents stored and accessed from lists and in libraries within sites. The Web-based interface reflects changes made to documents while maintaining a single centralized copy in the lists or libraries.

In this section, you will learn how to manage apps on a site. You will view information about apps and explore the SharePoint Store. You will add and remove apps from a site. You will learn about lists and libraries and how they are managed in SharePoint apps.

## Using SharePoint Apps

Apps that you can add to your sites are available built-in to SharePoint Online, or you can download an app from the Microsoft online SharePoint Store. Some apps are available for free in the SharePoint Store, whereas others must be purchased. Custom apps, developed by your organization, can also be added to your site. Using Access 2016, you can create your own custom apps.

SharePoint apps can be lists, libraries, site templates, and custom solutions (as discussed in the previous section). You can create a new list or library based on built-in list and library app templates. When you create a new site using a SharePoint Online template, template-specific lists, libraries, pages, and apps necessary to support the use of the list or library are created by default. The apps enable you to create, review, update, and delete documents in the list or library. New lists or libraries can be created if you have a sufficient permission level on the site. The availability of types of lists and library apps is controlled by the features activated on the site.

> **TIP: MAKE YOUR SHAREPOINT SITE A TRUSTED SITE**
> It is advisable to setup your SharePoint Online site as a Trusted Site in Internet Explorer. Click the Tools gear icon on the browser window, and then click Internet options. Click the Security tab, and then click Trusted sites. Click Sites, and type the URL of your top-level site. Click Add. Click Close, and click OK.

### View Apps

 The Site contents page of every site provides a view of the apps already installed on the site, as shown in Figure 2.31 in classic view. The apps are displayed by name, with the number of stored items, and modification information, such as when the app was

installed. Point to an app to display the More Options icon and click an option such as Settings or About on the option menu to review the properties of the app.

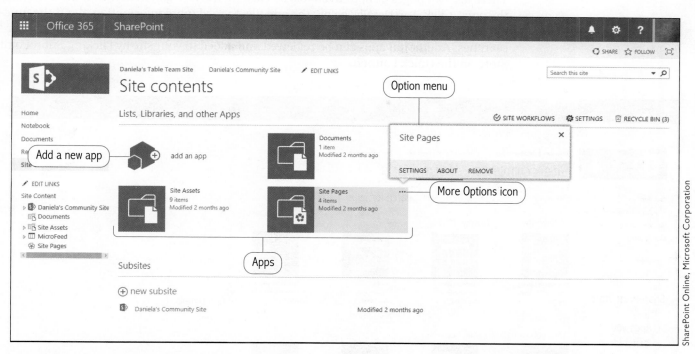

**FIGURE 2.31** Apps Available on Site Contents Page (Classic View)

The apps include the list and library templates that enable you to create specific types of lists, such as calendars or contacts, and libraries, such as asset or picture libraries. Table 2.2 shows the list and library templates and apps available by default in SharePoint Online.

| TABLE 2.2 List and Library Templates and Apps | |
|---|---|
| **List Templates** | **Library Templates** |
| Custom List | Document Library |
| Links | Form Library |
| Contacts | Wiki Page Library |
| Calendar | Picture Library |
| Promoted Links | Asset Library |
| Tasks | Data Connection Library |
| Issue Tracking | Report Library |
| External List | Site Mailbox |
| Discussion Board | |
| Custom List in Datasheet View | |
| Survey | |
| Access App | |
| Import Spreadsheet | |

Apps can be added to the site you are viewing by clicking *add an app* in the content section of the Site contents page and selecting Apps. The Your Apps page arranges the available apps in the categories of Noteworthy and Apps you can add. These are the default apps from SharePoint Online, as shown in Figure 2.32. The Noteworthy apps are suggestions for popular apps that are often added to the type of site you are using. There are two pages of apps available by clicking the navigation arrow at the bottom of the page. Click App Details, below the app tile, to read more information about the functionality of the app. A search box on the page enables you to find apps based on keyword searches. Additional apps can be reviewed and added to your site by clicking SharePoint Store on the Quick Launch.

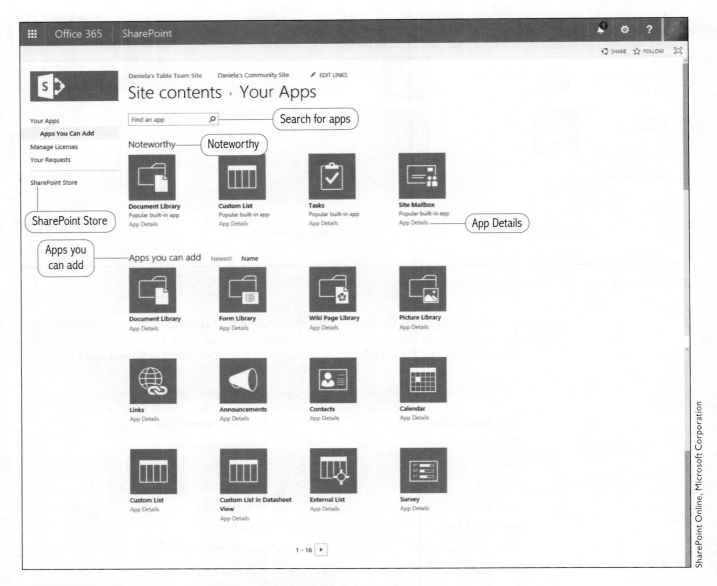

**FIGURE 2.32** Default Apps Available in SharePoint Online

---

**TIP: SPECIALTY APPS**

Some apps enable you to import or create files directly in SharePoint Online. For instance, the Import Spreadsheet app imports the columns and data of an existing spreadsheet into a list. The Access app provides the tools needed to create tables in a database in SharePoint.

---

The SharePoint Store features apps in many different categories, including Content Management, Financial Management, Lifestyle and Fun, and Project Management. These apps were built by people to solve specific problems or to add functions to their sites, and they have made them available in the SharePoint Store for purchase or free.

A rating system of stars indicates how the community of SharePoint designers feels about the apps, with five stars indicating the highest recommendations. You can display the SharePoint Store apps using filters such as Most Relevant, Highest Rating, Most Downloaded, Lowest Price, Name, and Newest. As you review the apps, point to the app tile to see a description of the purpose of the app, as shown in Figure 2.33. You may notice some grayed-out tiles, which indicate that the app cannot be added to the type of site from which you are browsing.

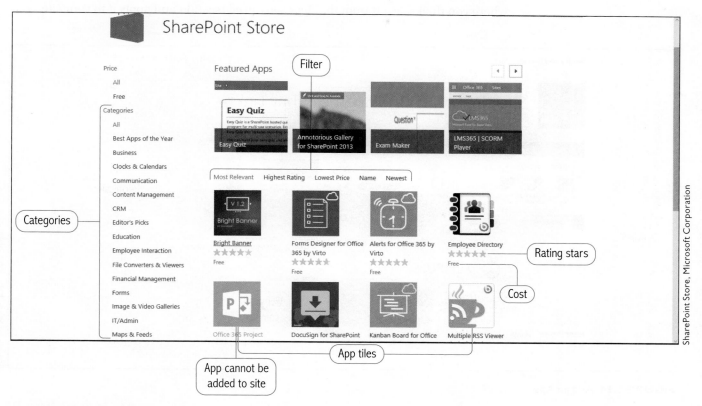

**FIGURE 2.33** SharePoint Store Apps

---

**TIP: PERMISSIONS FOR ADDING APPS**

You need to have Site Owner or Full Control permissions to add apps from the SharePoint Store to your sites.

---

## Add and Remove Apps

As you have seen, apps are available from within SharePoint Online and through the SharePoint Store.

When you decide to add a new app from the SharePoint Store to your SharePoint site, click the app tile. A page opens displaying more information about the app, as shown in

Figure 2.34. Review the information carefully and consider any screen previews that are available, along with costs and other information. Most apps are offered for download by agreeing to accept the terms that are given for permissions. Click the permissions link and review the requirements prior to installing the app. You can generally visit the website of the company offering the app for additional information. When you are ready to download the app to your site, click ADD IT, and confirm that you wish to add the app. After a short download period, you are notified you have received the app, and a check box indicates the site to which it will be added. The app downloads to the Your Apps page, where you then select it from the *Apps you can add* section and apply it to your site.

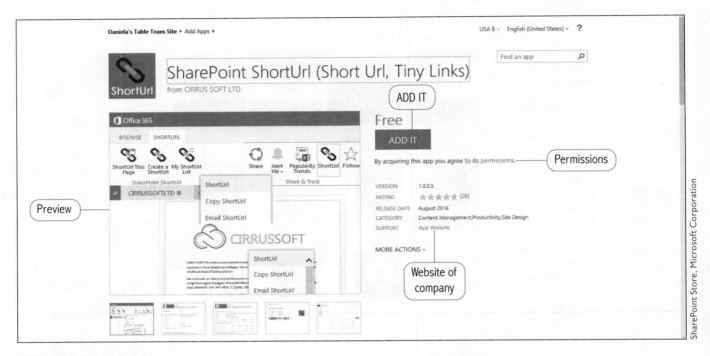

**FIGURE 2.34** Add an App

---

**TIP: SHAREPOINT STORE APPS**
When you add SharePoint Store apps to a site, you will not be able to save the app as a part of the solution template. The best practice is to add the apps after you have created a new site with the solution template.

---

Installing a list or library template app usually only requires that you provide a name for the app, as shown in Figure 2.35. Additional options for creating the list or library are available by clicking the Advanced Options link. These options vary depending on the type of list or library you are creating, and include items such as Description, Version History, or Document Template. By default, new libraries do not support versions. Hence, when you make changes to documents in the library, the changes replace the previous copy stored in the library. If you select to not include version histories, it minimizes the storage space, but it leaves you unable to retrieve a previous document version to compare changes or to revert back to a previous version should you accidentally delete a section of the text and need to retrieve it.

---

**TIP: NAMING LISTS OR LIBRARIES**
Because the name of the list or library becomes part of the URL for the list or library, it is a good idea to use an underscore, rather than a blank space, as you type the name.

---

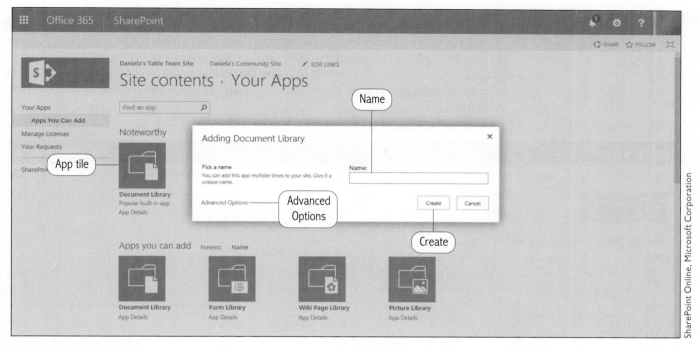

**FIGURE 2.35** Add a Library

If after a period of use, you decide that an app no longer fits the needs of the users of a site, it can be removed. This removes clutter from the site, making it easier for people to navigate and find the tools they really want to use. From the Site contents page, point to the app tile, click the More Options icon, and then click Remove, as shown in Figure 2.36. Confirm that you want to remove the app by clicking OK. When you remove an app from a site, it is moved to the Recycle Bin, in case you change your mind. Some apps remain on the Site contents Your Apps page for future installation but are removed from the site where you originally loaded them.

> **TIP: MORE OPTIONS SELECTION**
> Some apps require an additional selection of the More Options icon on the menu that opens before the Remove option is displayed (see Figure 2.36).

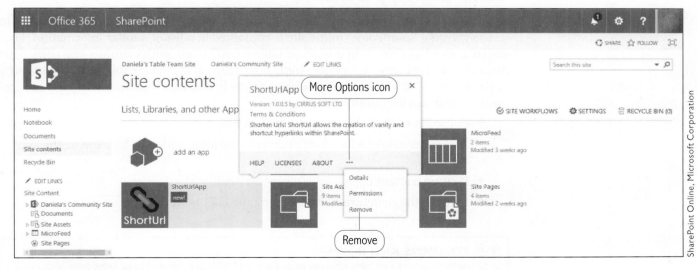

**FIGURE 2.36** Remove an App

## Open Apps

STEP 2 >> Apps serve as containers for files, documents, and lists. To see the information, you open the app by clicking the app tile on the Site contents page or by clicking the link on the Quick Launch. When you open an app, you can edit the content or add new information. When you are using classic view, the Ribbon contains additional commands, as shown in Figure 2.37.

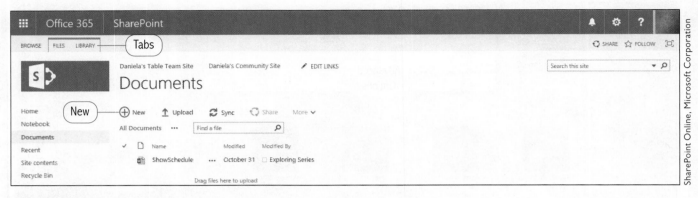

**FIGURE 2.37** Documents App (in Classic View)

**To open an app, complete the following steps:**

1. Navigate to the site where you want to display the app.
2. Click Settings on the top navigation bar and select Site contents on the menu. An alternative is to click Site contents on the Quick Launch.
3. Click the app tile that you want to open.

Depending on the app you select to open, you will have different options. For example, you can open documents, view pictures, or review tasks contained in the app. On the Documents app opened in Figure 2.37, there is an option for adding a new document and commands available on the FILES and LIBRARY tabs. If you open a list app, such as a Tasks app, you can add new data to the list, as well as browse through the items on the list.

## Work with App Content

Apps can hold data records (in lists) or files (in libraries). Almost all data that you create or use within a SharePoint Online site is contained in a list of similar information. Lists are structured as records in a familiar table-based layout, with columns and rows. This makes it easy for everyone to understand how items on the list are related. Each list has a particular set of attributes that describe an item in the list, based on the app used to create it. SharePoint lists enable you to:

- Control how the information is displayed.
- Assign permissions for modifications to the information or for viewing the list content.
- Require content approval for a new list item.
- Manage the structure and data using the LIST tab.

---

**TIP: COLUMNS AND ROWS**

In SharePoint, columns are also referred to as *fields*, and rows are referred to as *items* or *records*.

---

In SharePoint Online, document management is based on libraries. Libraries are built on the same philosophy as lists; hence, they enable you to customize the way in which they store and present information to the user. The main difference between a library and a list is that an item in a library must contain a file and the accompanying metadata to the file. *Metadata* is information about the file, such as who created it and when. Document management has some unique requirements but includes some list features such as column views, versioning, and content approval. Fortunately, after learning about lists, you will be very comfortable working with libraries because they are very similar.

After you open an app, you can view or modify the contents of the app. For instance, in Figure 2.38, the Site Assets include a file that you may want to update. You can open it from the Site Assets app, by clicking on the file name link. Click the More Options icon next to the file name to view properties of the file and options for editing, sharing, and more. Select Open (or Edit) to modify the contents of the file. You can also click the More Options icon on the menu for other options such as properties, rename, share, and delete. When you delete an app content item, it is moved to the Recycle Bin, where you can restore it later if you want, or you can permanently delete it from the site.

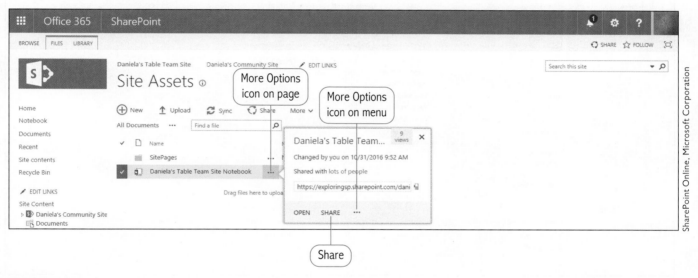

**FIGURE 2.38** Edit App Content

The options you have for working with app content depend on the type of element and are therefore contextual. For instance, for library content items, the options might include Edit, enabling you to edit a document by opening it in an Office Web app, such as Word Online. Generally, you can open or view a content item, as well as edit it using Web apps in the browser or local computer applications such as Office 2016 applications. Depending on the content item, you may have the option to delete it. Some content types enable you to follow them, or you can view who is sharing them and invite more people to share them.

## Change App Settings

STEP 3  The app settings in SharePoint Online enable you to manage the content items and apply permissions for the specific app. For instance, the Document library settings contain three categories of settings you can alter: General Settings, Permissions and Management, and

Communications, as shown in Figure 2.39. Additional options for adding columns and altering the view are available on this page. Lists contain similar categories.

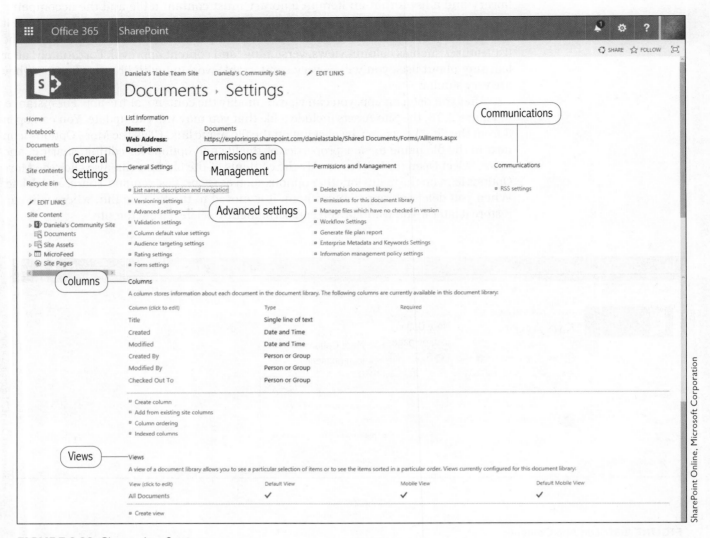

**FIGURE 2.39** Change App Settings

General Settings enable you to name and describe the list or library so that users can understand the purpose and apply version, validation, audience targeting, rating, and form settings. The Permissions and Management category enables you to delete a list or library, save it as a template, modify the permissions, alter the Workflow settings, and more. In the Communications category, you can configure the list to enable advanced information integration through RSS settings. Columns determine how the information is stored and enable you to require certain types of information about the list or library. You can also alter the format of the types of information; for instance, specifying single lines of text or multiple lines. Through the Views category, you can give access to the information to users with different devices, such as smartphones, and you can create new views to customize the way information is displayed to users.

**To change the app settings, complete the following steps:**

1. Navigate to the site where you want to change the app settings.
2. Click Settings on the top navigation bar and select Site contents on the menu. An alternative is to click Site contents on the Quick Launch.
3. Point to the app tile you want to change, click the More Options icon, and then select Settings on the menu.
4. Select the link for the item you want to alter, make the changes, and then click OK, or Save. An example for changing the Documents app Name and Description is shown in Figure 2.40.

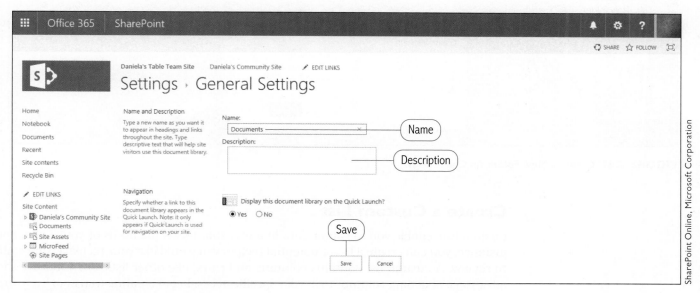

**FIGURE 2.40** Change General Settings

---

**TIP: ADVANCED APP SETTINGS**
With the proper permissions on a site, you may have access to advanced settings (refer to Figure 2.39), which enable you to further customize the app. Descriptions next to each option provide you with the purpose for the setting.

---

## Use Folders to Organize Lists and Libraries

Just as folders help you to organize files in your computer system, SharePoint Online enables you to create a hierarchy of folders and manage lists or libraries. Folders can contain up to 5,000 items. Lists and libraries are initially created without folders, and folders must be enabled on the Advanced Settings page of the list or library to create the folders. Once you have enabled folders on a site, you create new folders by opening the list or library from the site in classic view, clicking the ITEMS tab (for a list folder) or the FILES tab (for a library folder), clicking New Folder in the New group, and providing a folder name, as shown in Figure 2.41. You can also create a new folder in the new experience view by opening the site, clicking New, selecting Folder, and providing a folder name. The resulting folder will appear as a folder icon that you normally see in Windows. Open the folder and add new items to the folder.

**FIGURE 2.41** Create a New Folder (in Classic View)

## Create a Custom List

Custom lists enable you to gather data in a way that meets the needs of your team. For instance, you can create a list of potential recipes you would like your recipe testing staff to review. A custom list contains columns and rows, like other lists, but you have the advantage of adding columns to fit your specific needs. Begin creating a custom list using the *add an app* link in classic view on the Site contents page. Click the Custom List tile, and provide a name for the list. In the new experience view, create a custom list by clicking the New button and selecting List. Provide a name and description for the list, and click Create. Click the More Options icon on the Site contents page to open the Settings page for the list. From the Settings page, add columns that are needed by clicking Create column in the Columns section. Additional columns can be added while viewing the list page by clicking + to the right of the last column and selecting the type of data to be stored in the column. Click More Column Types at the bottom of the menu to display all of the types of columns you can add to the list. The Create Column page, as shown in Figure 2.42, also enables you to name the column, provide a description of the type of data to be stored in the column, and set an option to require or not require that the column contain information.

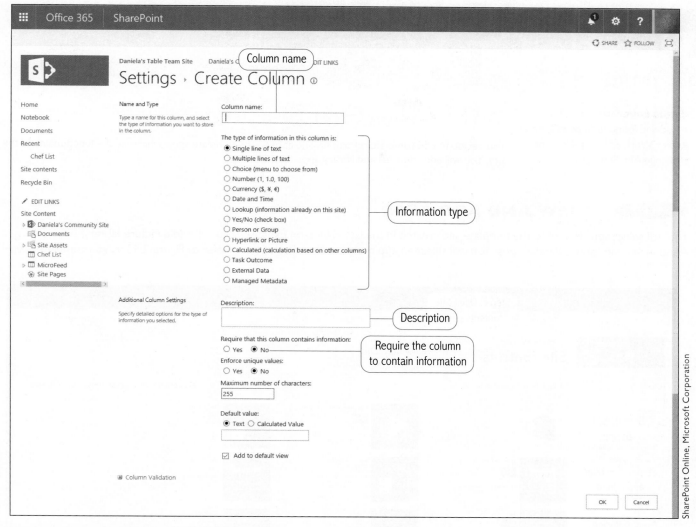

**FIGURE 2.42** Add Columns to a Custom List

---

**TIP: IMPORT A SPREADSHEET AS A LIST**

If the data you want on a list is kept on an Excel spreadsheet, you can import it into SharePoint Online as a list, enabling you to use the SharePoint tools to manage the list. Use the Import Spreadsheet app to complete the import process.

---

**Quick Concept**

5. Describe the sources of apps that you can use in your SharePoint Online sites. *p. 104*

6. Describe the major difference between lists and libraries. *p. 104*

7. What is the advantage of using folders? *p. 113*

8. Describe the purpose of metadata in libraries. *p. 111*

# Hands-On Exercises

**Skills covered:** View Apps
• Add and Remove Apps • Open
Apps • Work with App Content
• Change App Settings

## 2 SharePoint Online Apps

You decide to add some SharePoint Online apps to the template site to increase the functionality of the site. You will add some list and library apps.

---

**STEP 1 ›› VIEW AND ADD APPS**

You will select apps to add to the template site created in the last Hands-On Exercise. You will add a Picture Library, Announcements, and Calendar apps. You will select an app from the SharePoint Store. Refer to Figure 2.43 as you complete Step 1.

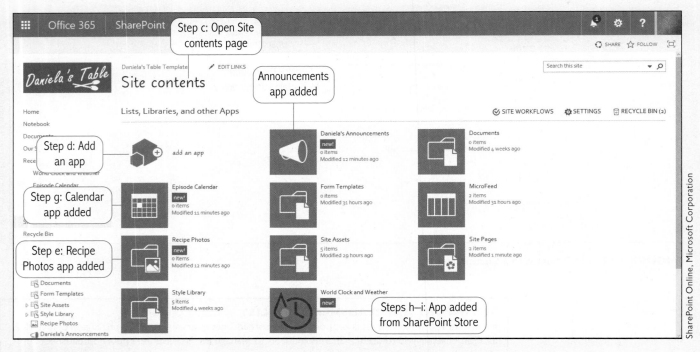

**FIGURE 2.43** Add Apps

**a.** Open your browser and navigate to your Office 365 site, if you exited after the previous Hands-On Exercise.

**b.** Open the Daniela's Table Template site, either by accessing it through the Admin app if you made a private site, or through the Subsites section of the Site contents page from the Team Site.

You will add the apps by editing the template.

**c.** Click **Settings** on the top navigation bar, and select **Site contents** on the menu. Ensure that the classic view is displayed, and click Return to classic view at the bottom of the Quick Launch if not.

**d.** Click **add an app** on the Site contents page.

The default apps are shown on the Your Apps page.

**e.** Scroll to locate the Picture Library app, and click the **Picture Library app tile**. Type **Recipe Photos** for the name of the Picture Library. Click **Create**.

You can have multiple Picture Library apps with different names for different purposes on a site.

**f.** Click **add an app**, scroll to and click the **Announcements app tile**. Type **Daniela's Announcements** for the name. Click **Create**.

**g.** Click **add an app**, scroll to and then click the **Calendar app tile**. Type **Episode Calendar** for the name. Click **Create**.

**h.** Click **add an app**, click **SharePoint Store** on the Quick Launch, and then click **Clocks & Calendars** in the Categories displayed in the left pane of the SharePoint Store page. Locate and click the **World Clock and Weather tile** (click Next at the bottom of the page to view additional pages or type the name of the app into the search box). Click the **permissions link** in the right pane and review the permissions. Close the permissions dialog box to return to the World Clock and Weather tile page. Click **ADD IT**, click **Continue**, click **Return to site**, and then click **Trust It**.

> **TROUBLESHOOTING:** You may have to log in to your Microsoft account to complete the download.

The app takes a few moments to load onto the Site contents page. You will now add the app to the Home page.

**i.** Click **Home** on the Quick Launch, and click the **PAGE tab**. Click **Edit** in the Edit group, and click below the title Daniela's Table Home. Click the **INSERT tab**, and then click **App Part** in the Parts group. Click **World Clock and Weather** in the Parts middle pane, and then click **Add** below the right pane.

The weather displays on the page after a few moments. Do not be concerned about any spacing issues.

**j.** Click the **Settings icon** on the Weather app, and type the **name of your state** in the Search Location box. Click **Search**, select a **location** in the Search Results, and click **Add**. Click the **close button** next to the default location in the Saved Locations box to remove it from the list. Click **Save**.

**k.** Click **Save** in the Edit group of the FORMAT TEXT tab. Take a screen clip displaying the entire window, naming it **sp02h2Apps_LastFirst**. Click **Site contents** on the Quick Launch.

After adding the apps to the site, you will experiment with them to review their capabilities. Refer to Figure 2.44 as you complete Step 2.

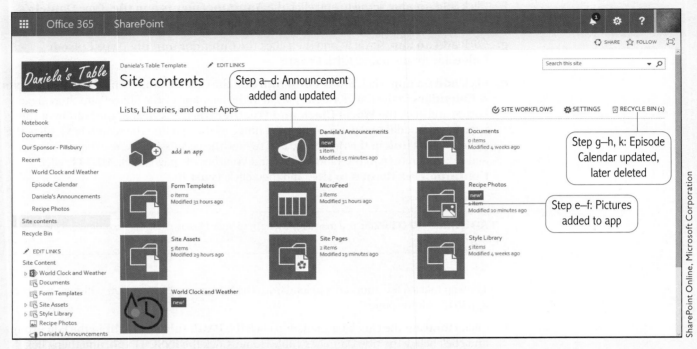

**FIGURE 2.44** Information Added to Apps and an App Removed

a. Click the **Daniela's Announcements tile** (be sure to click the tile and not the area to the right of the tile), and click **new announcement**.

b. Type the following information:

- Title: **Daniela Visits Seattle**
- Body: **Daniela will be making a personal appearance at the Home and Garden Show in Seattle on March 14.**
- Expires: **3/15/2018**
- Click **Save**.

The announcement appears on the Daniela's Announcements list with an icon to indicate it is a new item.

c. Click the **Daniela Visits Seattle link** to open the list item. Review the announcement.

The announcement list item opens with a Ribbon for managing it.

d. Click **Edit Item** in the Manage group. Click in front of the word Home and type **36th Annual**. Click **Save**. Click the link to the announcement again to display it, and take a screen shot showing the announcement. Name the file **sp02h2Announce_LastFirst**.

e. Click **Recipe Photos** on the Quick Launch. Click **Upload**, and click **Browse**. Navigate to the location of your student data files, and click *sp02h2Bruschetta*. Click **Open**, and click **OK**.

The photograph loads. You will add information about the photograph.

f. Point to the picture, and click the **More Options icon** when it displays. Click **More actions** (...) on the menu and select **Properties**. Scroll down and type the following information:

- Title: **Daniela's Hurry-Up Bruschetta**
- Description: **This photograph supports the June 14 episode.**

- Keywords: **bruschetta, tomato, basil**
- Click **Save**.

Take a screen shot displaying the entire window, naming it **sp02h2Photo_LastFirst**.

This library stores photographs and enables you to manage the pictures.

**g.** Click **Episode Calendar** on the Quick Launch. Click **Mar** of next year on the calendar displayed on the Quick Launch, and click **14** on the calendar for March 14. Click the **EVENTS tab**, and click **New Event**.

The New Item dialog box opens with March 14 selected as the date for the starting and ending time.

**h.** Type the following information into the New Item dialog box:

- Title: **Live Show Taping**
- Location: **Seattle Home and Garden Show**
- Start Time: **8 AM**
- End Time: **3:30 PM**
- Description: **Episode 14 feature clip**
- Click **Save**.

The calendar displays the time frame in blue and displays the title.

**i.** Make a screen shot of the Episode Calendar showing the date in March. Name the file **sp02h2EpisodeCalendar_LastFirst**.

**j.** Click **Home** on the Quick Launch to return to the home page of the site.

After reviewing the Site contents, you decide that you will remove the Episode Calendar, which is kept as a document.

**k.** Click **Site contents** on the Quick Launch, point to the **Episode Calendar tile**, and then click the **More Options icon**. Click **REMOVE**, and click **OK** on the dialog box.

The Episode Calendar is removed from the site and placed in the Recycle Bin.

---

**STEP 3** >> **CHANGE APP SETTINGS**

After reviewing the results of your work with apps, you decide that you should add the Recipe Photos app and the Daniela's Announcements app to the Quick Launch. You will also change the Quick Launch to not display the Recent category. Refer to Figure 2.45 as you complete Step 3.

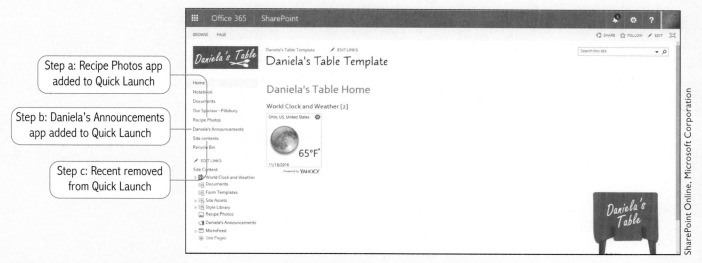

**FIGURE 2.45** App Settings Changed

**a.** *Point to the* **Recipe Photos tile** on the Site contents page, and click the **More Options icon**. Click **SETTINGS**, and click **List name, description and navigation** in the General Settings options. In the Navigation area, click **Yes**, and click **Save**.

Recipe Photos is displayed on the Quick Launch.

**b.** Click **Site contents** on the Quick Launch, point to the **Daniela's Announcements tile**, and click the **More Options icon**. Click **SETTINGS**, and click **List name, description and navigation** in the General Settings options. In the Navigation area, click **Yes**, and click **Save**.

Daniela's Announcements is displayed on the Quick Launch.

**c.** Click **EDIT LINKS** on the Quick Launch. Click **X** (Remove this link from navigation) next to Recent on the Quick Launch, and click **OK** on the Just checking dialog box. Click **Save** on the Quick Launch.

The Recent category is removed from the Quick Launch.

**d.** Click **Home** on the Quick Launch. Make a screen clip showing the entire screen. Name the file **sp02h2QuickLaunch_LastFirst**.

**e.** Leave the site open, if you plan to continue to the next Hands-On Exercise. If not, sign out of Office 365 and close the browser window. The files you created in this exercise will be submitted at the end of the last Hands-On Exercise.

# Work with Documents

SharePoint Online provides you with a set of user-friendly tools for working with documents. You can upload documents and move them within the site. You can edit the document properties. Documents can be checked in or out. You can also delete and restore documents as needed. SharePoint Online enables you to work with documents using the FILES tab on the Ribbon. Keep in mind that documents are files, and they are stored in libraries in SharePoint. You can have multiple libraries for different types of documents, or you can store all of your documents in one library, with multiple folders for organization.

In this section, you will learn how to upload documents and edit their properties within a SharePoint site. You will also learn to use the check-in and check-out options. You will then learn about deleting, restoring, and exchanging documents between SharePoint sites.

## Using SharePoint Lists and Libraries

Providing accurate data and documents is crucial to productivity when working with a team. You will need to be able to find the information you need easily, make updates, and then distribute it to others. SharePoint Online enables you to manage all of the documents on the site to accomplish your team's goals.

> **TIP: OPEN THE DOCUMENTS FOLDER**
> You can access the Documents folder by clicking Documents on the Quick Launch or clicking Settings, selecting Site contents, and then clicking the Documents tile in classic view or the Documents link in the new experience view.

The Document Library app enables you to upload documents from your local computer hard drive, a network server, or other SharePoint site. New documents can be created using the app. In a fashion similar to how you manage files on your local computer, you can find, select, and move the documents into folders or other site locations. Documents can be deleted and, if necessary, restored if you need the file again. Metadata identifies the file and is used in searches to help you find the document for which you are searching.

SharePoint Online has built-in protection that keeps people from opening and editing the document at the same time, which protects the integrity of the document. You can check out a document for editing and effectively remove it from view of others until it is checked back in to the document library. Documents are available to other people within the organization (if not checked out) and can be made available to external users by email invitation, much as you share a site with external users.

### Upload Documents

**STEP 1** ›› Using Upload on the Documents list FILES tab in SharePoint Online, you can upload a single document or multiple documents at one time.

**To access the FILES tab and upload a single file using classic view, complete the following steps:**

1. Navigate to the site to which you want to add a document.
2. Click Settings, and click Site contents on the menu. An alternative is to click Site contents on the Quick Launch.
3. Click the tile of the document library app to which you want to upload files.
4. Select the folder where you want to store the document, if appropriate.
5. Click Upload, and click Files.
6. Click Browse, select the file you want to upload, and then click Open.
7. Select the Overwrite existing files check box if a file with the same name and type already exists in the library and you want to replace it with the new file you are uploading. Click OK.

Multiple document uploads are handled using both SharePoint Online and Windows File Explorer. Follow the previous steps to display the Document folder, and open a File Explorer window. Navigate to the location of the files you want to upload, and then select and drag them onto the SharePoint Online page to the *drag files here* location. A progress bar informs you of the stages of the upload above the file list, as shown in Figure 2.46. When the process is complete, you will see *Upload completed* followed by the number of files that were uploaded. Click Dismiss to return to the normal view of the Documents page. The file names will appear in the library listing.

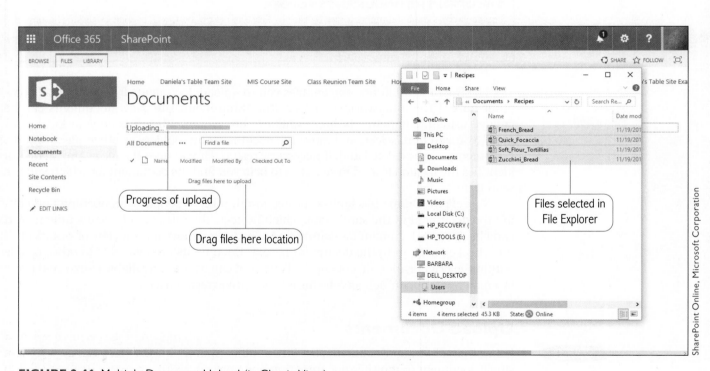

**FIGURE 2.46** Multiple Document Upload (in Classic View)

---

**TIP: OPEN A LIBRARY IN FILE EXPLORER**
You can open the currently selected SharePoint library with File Explorer from the LIBRARY tab by clicking Open with Explorer in the Connect & Export group. You may find it more convenient to work in the File Explorer window because you have access to your local computer file structure in the left pane while viewing the SharePoint library in the right pane. After you make adjustments to the files in File Explorer, close the window, and then refresh the SharePoint Online browser window to review the updates.

## Edit Document Properties

**STEP 2** ▶▶ After you finish uploading a document to a library, you can perform further actions on that document. For each document, you can open a pane that enables you to review the document properties, recent activity, who it is shared with, and file information, such as the type of file and when it was last modified. To display these options, click the More Options icon next to the file name and select Details. You can also view and edit the properties, view and edit the file in the browser, check it in or out, review compliance details and workflows, download a copy, review who the file is shared with, and delete the file, using the More Options menu as shown in Figure 2.47.

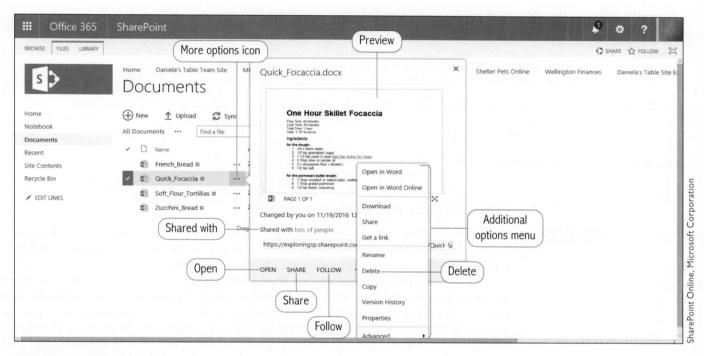

**FIGURE 2.47** File Options

---

**TIP: MORE ABOUT DOCUMENT PROPERTIES**

As a site owner, you can add more properties to describe a document. Each property of a document corresponds to a column in the Document library or list.

---

In classic view, you can display the properties of files included in your site using View Properties option in the Manage group on the FILES tab, as shown in Figure 2.48. You can edit the properties, view version history (if available), manage permissions, and manage check-in/check-out options. Select the file in the library by clicking the Select or Deselect column to the left of the file name, click the FILES tab, and then click View Properties in the Manage group. You can also select Edit Properties in the Manage group, also shown in Figure 2.48, which enables you to change properties such as the file name and title.

As you edit the properties for a file in a library, you can provide a new name for the file, much as you would rename a file in other applications, and provide a descriptive title for the file. Keep in mind that file names should not contain spaces, but rather underscores, to ensure that they are easily found within the server. The title can contain spaces and makes it easier for the user to determine the content of the file. For instance, the file name *eps2_tortillas* is not as easy to understand as *Soft Flour Tortillas*. By default the file name is shown in the Documents listing, but you can modify the view of the library to display the title column to provide a more user-friendly listing, as shown in Figure 2.48.

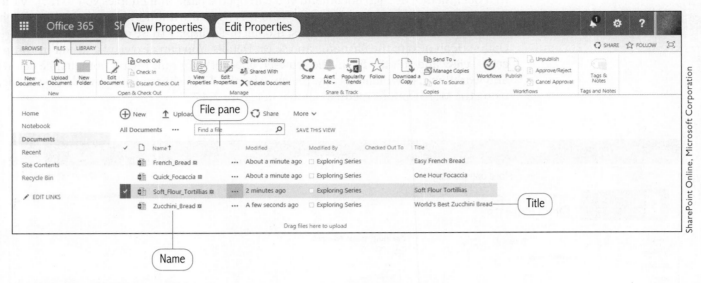

**FIGURE 2.48** File Name and Title

## Check Documents In and Out

STEP 3 ›› SharePoint Online enables you to check out documents that you need to work on for a longer period of time. Other users will not be able to work on that document, and they will not see your changes until you check in the document.

When you check out a document, the Check Out flag is set to Yes and the user name of the person who checked out the document is stored. A green arrow next to the file icon indicates the file is checked out, and by pointing to the file icon, you can see who has the document checked out, as shown in Figure 2.49. A column can be added to the library view to display this information on the Documents listing to help your users to know who is working on a document. You should always remember to check in a document when you finish editing it, so that others can access it.

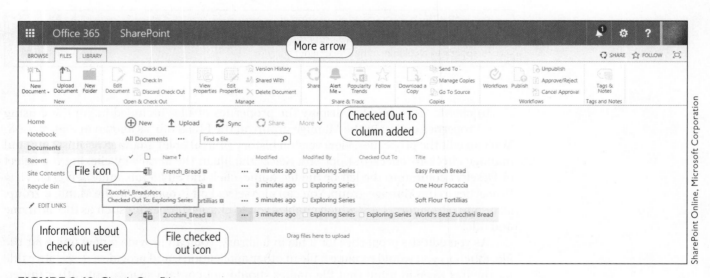

**FIGURE 2.49** Check Out File

**To check out (or check in) a document in classic SharePoint view, complete the following steps:**

1. Navigate to and select the document in the Documents library, by clicking the Select or Deselect column to the left of the file name.
2. Click the More arrow above the file list and select Advanced.
3. Click Check Out. A small green icon with an arrow pointing to the right on the file icon indicates the file is checked out.
4. Edit and save the document, and click Check In to make it available to other users.

If you check in the document in classic view, the Check in dialog box enables you to retain the check out and add comments on the changes made to the document, as shown in Figure 2.50. When you retain the check out by clicking Yes in the dialog box, you make the document changes available for others to view, but they cannot modify the document because it will still be checked out to you.

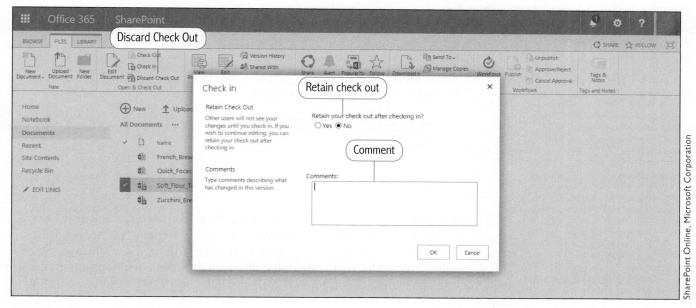

**FIGURE 2.50** Check In Options

---

**TIP: MULTIPLE DOCUMENT CHECK OUT**
If you find yourself with multiple documents checked out to you, you can select the ones you want to check in using the Documents listing, click the FILES tab, and then click Check In.

---

If, after checking out a document, you decide to return the document without the changes you have made, click Discard Check Out in the Open & Check Out group on the FILES tab in classic view. This discards the changes and checks the file back into the Documents listing.

---

**TIP: OVERWRITING CHECKED OUT DOCUMENT SETTING**
Imagine, for example, a scenario where your team needs to make a time-sensitive modification to a document, and the team member who has the document checked out is not immediately available. If you are the site owner, you can check in documents that other users have checked out. As you check in the document, a warning will be displayed naming the user who has the document checked out, with the checkout date and time. Click Yes on the warning. The document status will change to checked in, and other users can view and modify the most recent version.

---

## Delete Documents and Recover Deleted Documents

Every time you delete a document from a list or library, you are not losing it forever. Documents that you delete are stored in the Recycle Bin of your site, which functions in a similar way to the Recycle Bin in Windows. The Recycle Bin enables you to either restore a deleted document to its original location or remove it permanently from the Recycle Bin.

You can delete a document from a library after selecting it, either by clicking Delete Document in the Manage group on the FILES tab in classic view or by clicking the More Options icon next to the file name, and then clicking the More Options icon in the menu to display the Delete command. Click OK in the message dialog box to move the file to the Recycle Bin, as shown in Figure 2.51.

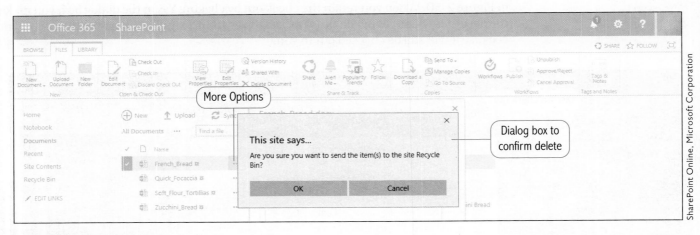

**FIGURE 2.51** Delete a File

It is sometimes necessary to undelete a file that was deleted. Click Settings on the top navigation bar, and then click Site contents on the menu. Click Recycle Bin, select the check box for the file or files you wish to restore, and then click Restore Selection on the toolbar under the Team Site name. If you want to delete files permanently from the Recycle Bin, select them, and click Delete Selection on the toolbar, as shown in Figure 2.52.

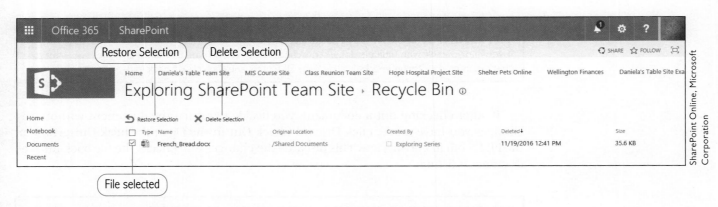

**FIGURE 2.52** Recycle Bin

---

**TIP: BACKUP BEFORE YOU DELETE**

It is a good idea to create a backup version of a file on your local computer or flash drive before you delete it from a site.

---

## Exchange Documents between Websites

The commands included in the Copies group, on the FILES tab in classic view, enable you to create and manage copies of the documents included in a library. This fosters collaboration across the organization and saves time because multiple documents can be created based on a single document.

The **Send To** command is used to distribute documents to other libraries, making them available for other teams or in a centralized location. Using Send To, you copy the original file, called the *source file*, into a different library. The copy can be edited independently of the source file, but you have the option to send updates from the source to the copies. For example, you have a budget template that departments across the company must complete. You can copy it to multiple libraries, and each department can fill in the data on their own library copy. If a formula is changed in the source document, the update can be sent to the other copies throughout the company.

Select the file you want to copy in the library Documents listing, and click the FILES tab in classic view. Click Send To in the Copies group and select Copy to display the Copy dialog box, as shown in Figure 2.53. Type the full URL of the SharePoint library where the copy will be stored. You can specify a new name for the copy if desired. Selections relating to updating the copies include whether a prompt will be displayed when an updated source file is checked in and whether an alert will be issued when the source file is updated. Click OK to copy the file to the destination library or folder.

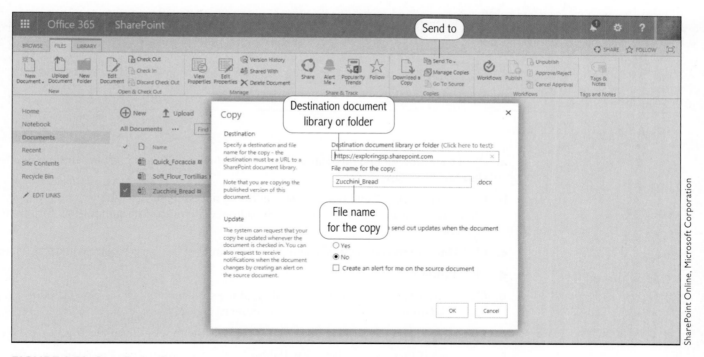

**FIGURE 2.53** Copy Dialog Box

**Quick Concept**

9. Describe the differences in the way you upload a single file and the way you upload multiple files at one time. *p. 122*

10. What are four options you have available for editing document properties? *p. 123*

11. Why is it important to check in a document after you have checked it out and completed your edits? *p. 124*

# Hands-On Exercises

## 3 Work with Documents

After some consideration and discussion with team members, you decide to add a few documents to the template so that they will be available in any site that is created from the template. For instance, you believe that everyone should have access to the budget for the website.

### STEP 1 》》 UPLOAD AND ORGANIZE DOCUMENTS

You will add the budget for Daniela's Table to the template. You will also upload logo files so they are on hand for anyone who needs them. Refer to Figure 2.54 as you complete Step 1.

**FIGURE 2.54** Upload a Document

a. Open your browser and navigate to your Office 365 site, if you exited after the previous Hands-On Exercise.

b. Open the Daniela's Table Template site, either by accessing it through the Admin app if you made a private site or through the Subsites section of the Site contents page from the Team Site.

c. Click **Documents** on the Quick Launch and ensure that the site is displayed in classic view.

d. Click **Upload**.

e. Click **Browse** and navigate to the location of the student data files. Click *sp02h3Budget*, and click **Open**. Click **OK** in the Add a document dialog box.

After a few moments, the document appears in the Documents library listing.

f. Click the **FILES tab**, and click **New Folder** in the New group. Type **Logo Folder** in the Name box, and click **Create**.

The folder is created and appears on the Documents library listing.

g. Click the **Logo Folder link** to open the folder. Open **File Explorer** using the Windows task bar, and navigate to the location of the student data files. Select the files *sp02h3Logo*, *sp02h3Pesto*, and *sp02h3Table*. Drag these three files onto the SharePoint Online window where you see the words *Drag files here to upload*.

After a few moments, all three documents appear in the Documents library listing.

h. Close File Explorer. Take a screen snip showing the Logo Folder and contents. Name the file **sp02h3Folder_LastFirst**.

After adding the logos to the Documents library, you realize that it would be better to have descriptive titles displayed for the files. You will edit the properties and display a new column with the titles. Refer to Figure 2.55 as you complete Step 2.

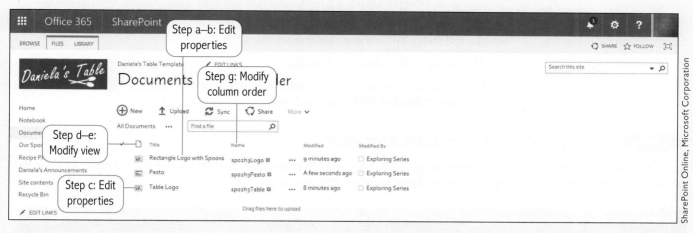

**FIGURE 2.55** Edit File Properties

a. Select **sp02h3Logo** in the Documents library listing (click to the left of the file name). Click the **More Options icon** next to the file name, and click **More Options**. Select **Properties** from the menu.

> **TROUBLESHOOTING:** If you do not see sp02h3Logo, it is possible that you moved out of the folder where you uploaded it. Click the Logo Folder link on the Documents page to open the folder.

b. Type **Rectangle Logo with Spoons** in the Title box. Click **Save**.

The title is now stored with the file name for the file.

c. Select **sp02h3Table** on the Documents library listing. Click the **More Options icon**, and click the **More Options icon** in the dialog box. Select **Properties** from the menu. Type **Table Logo** in the Title box, and click **Save**.

d. Click the **More options icon** next to All Documents, and select **Modify this View**. Select **Title** in the Columns section. Click **Name (linked to document with edit menu)** to deselect it so that it will not display. Click **OK** at the top of the page.

The main Documents library page is displayed with the updated view. Changes you make in a folder view affect all of the library's views. The columns include the Type icon, Modified, Modified By, and Title, in that order. This is not a well-organized column structure. You will move the Title to appear next to the Type icon.

e. Click **More Options** next to All Documents in the Documents library listing, and then select **Modify this View**. Click the **number arrow** next to Title in the Columns section, and then select **2**. Click **OK** at the top of the page.

The columns are arranged in an order that makes more sense.

f. Click the **Logo Folder link** and review the folder contents.

One file appears to have no name, when in reality it has no title. You realize that the More Options icon that enables you to change the properties is also missing from the file listing. You will add the file name back to the listing to solve this problem.

**g.** Click the **More Options icon** next to All Documents in the Documents library listing, and then select **Modify this View**. Click **Name (linked to document with edit menu)** in the Columns section to select it. Click the number arrow and then select **3**. Click **OK** at the bottom of the page.

The main Documents library listing is displayed with the Title and Name columns.

**h.** Click the **Logo Folder link** to display the contents of the folder. Add the title **Pesto** to the sp02h3Pestofile using Step c as an example.

The title is displayed for the Pesto file.

**i.** Make a screen snip of the Logo Folder displaying the files with the Title and Name. Name the file **sp02h3FolderView_LastFirst**.

### STEP 3 ›› WORK WITH A DOCUMENT

You will update the budget spreadsheet by checking it out and making an adjustment. You will then check it back in. You will also delete an unnecessary document from the library. Refer to Figure 2.56 as you complete Step 3.

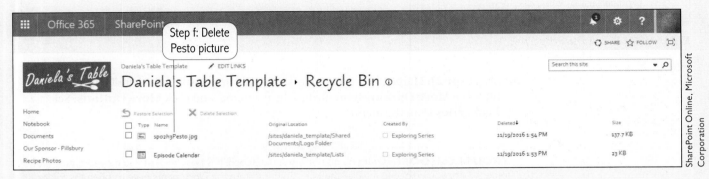

**FIGURE 2.56** App Settings Changed

**a.** Click **Documents** in the breadcrumb trail at the top of the page.

The budget file and the Logo Folder are displayed.

**b.** Select the **sp02h3Budget file** by clicking to the left of the icon. Click the **FILES tab**, and click **Check Out** in the Open & Check Out group.

A green arrow on the icon lets you know the file is checked out.

**c.** Click the **sp02h3Budget name link** to open the file in Excel Online. Click **Edit Workbook**, and select **Edit in Browser**.

The Excel Online app opens, enabling you to make changes to the document.

**d.** Click **cell C5** (it contains 10%), and type **8**. Click cell **A1**.

The value in cell C5 is formatted as 8%. The change is automatically saved.

**e.** Click **Daniela's Table Template** in the top navigation bar. Select the *sp02h3Budget* file by clicking to the left of the icon. Click the **FILES tab**, and click **Check In**. Type **Updated** and today's date in the Comments box. Click **OK**.

You have checked the file back in so others can use it.

**f.** Click the **Logo Folder** icon to open the folder. Select the *sp02h3Pesto* file by clicking to the left of the icon. Click the **More Options icon** for the file, and click **More Options** in the menu. Select **Delete**, and click **OK** to send the item to the Recycle Bin.

**g.** Click **Site contents** on the Quick Launch. Click **Recycle Bin** and click the **check box** next to sp02h3Pesto.jpg to select it. Click **Restore Selection**, and click **OK**.

You realize that the Pesto photograph should not be in the Logo Folder. You will move it to the Recipe Photos library.

**h.** Click **Documents** on the Quick Launch, and click the **Logo Folder icon** to open the folder. Select the **sp02h3Pesto file**, and drag the **picture icon** to Recipe Photos on the Quick Launch.

> **TROUBLESHOOTING:** Be sure to drag the picture icon, not the link. If the sp02h3Pesto file will not move, delete it from the Logo Folder, and then add it to the Recipe Photos document library from the student data files and edit the properties to change the title to Pesto.

The file is moved to the Recipe Photos document library.

**i.** Click **Recipe Photos** on the Quick Launch, and take a screen snip of the folder showing the photographs. Name the file **sp02h3Photos_LastFirst**.

**j.** Sign out of Office 365 and close any browser windows. Based on your instructor's directions, submit the following:

sp02h1French_LastFirst

sp02h1Site_LastFirst

sp02h1Layout_LastFirst

sp02h1Home_LastFirst

sp02h1SiteInvitation_LastFirst (email)

sp02h1SiteTemplate_LastFirst.wsp*

sp02h2Apps_LastFirst

sp02h2Announce_LastFirst

sp02h2Photo_LastFirst

sp02h2EpisodeCalendar_LastFirst

sp02h2QuickLaunch_LastFirst

sp02h3Folder_LastFirst

sp02h3FolderView_LastFirst

sp02h3Photos_LastFirst

* Note: you will only have this file if you completed the steps for a private site.

# Chapter Objectives Review

After reading this chapter, you have accomplished the following objectives:

1. **Understand templates and sites.**
   - Templates can provide several design features for a site, and they can be reused for other sites. Site templates are activated or deactivated as necessary, and they can be edited or deleted.
   - Create a site template: SharePoint Online enables you to create a site from a template and save a site as a template.
   - Use a custom template: The templates you create are available on the Custom tab when a new subsite is created either from the top-level site or from other subsites.
   - Download and upload a site template: As solution files, templates can be used throughout SharePoint Online, or they can be downloaded and transferred to other people.
   - Activate and deactivate site templates: You must activate a newly uploaded solution file to use it.
   - Edit or delete a template: Templates are edited using site editing tools. Templates that are no longer necessary can be deleted after deactivating them.

2. **Customize a site.**
   - SharePoint Online enables you to customize many site page elements to change the look and feel of a site.
   - Change language and regional settings: Sites can support multiple languages through the use of the Multilingual User Interface, which displays site navigation in the user's preferred language.
   - Change a site title and logo: You can brand the site to the specifications of your organization, including using the organization's logo.
   - Work with navigation links and aids: The navigation within the site can be changed with custom links and navigational aids, such as the Tree view.
   - Change the look of a site: The look of the site can be changed with the use of themes, color themes, font themes, and site layouts.
   - Open, add, and delete a site page: Pages can be added or deleted in a site. Deleted pages are stored in the Recycle Bin until they are restored or permanently deleted.
   - Change the default home page: A page within the site can be designated as the default home page and opens when the site is accessed.
   - Resetting a site at its definition: Ghosting is the concept of sharing the site definition across all pages in a site collection. As changes are made to the pages, they become unghosted. You can reghost the pages to the original site definition by resetting a site at its definition.
   - Delete a site: Unneeded sites can be deleted. They are not stored in the Recycle Bin when deleted.

3. **Share a site.**
   - Using the Share features in SharePoint Online, you can invite people to view your site. Different permission levels can be assigned to the people with whom you share the site.

4. **Use SharePoint apps.**
   - Apps are small, easy-to-use Web applications that have a specific purpose and that you can add to your site. List and library apps are available by default in SharePoint Online, and additional apps are available in the Microsoft SharePoint Store. List apps contain data that you create or use within SharePoint Online, whereas library apps store files such as documents or pictures. You can organize lists and libraries using folders.
   - View apps: The Site contents page contains a view of the apps available on the site.
   - Add and remove apps: More apps are added to the site using the Site contents page. You can remove apps that you no longer need.
   - Open apps: Click the app tile to open an app. You can edit the content or add new information after opening the app.
   - Work with app content: Apps can hold data records (in lists) or files (in libraries). You can alter the view of the information, assign permissions, require content approval for a new item, and manage the structure and data of apps.
   - Change app settings: There are three categories of settings you can alter in apps, General Settings, Permissions and Management, and Communications.
   - Use folders to organize lists and libraries: Folders help you organize site information. A hierarchy of folders enables you to find the information you need.
   - Create a custom list: Custom lists enable you to gather data in a way that meets the needs of your team. Custom lists contain rows and columns that organize information.

5. **Use SharePoint lists and libraries.**
   - Documents can be uploaded to a SharePoint Online site, and Microsoft Office documents can be edited within SharePoint Online.
   - Upload documents: Much like the File Explorer that you use in Windows, you can upload a single document or multiple documents at once to a library in SharePoint Online.
   - Edit document properties: You can edit the document properties to make the information more user friendly.
   - Check documents in and out: You can check documents in and out as you reserve them for your personal editing.
   - Delete documents and recover deleted documents: Documents can be deleted and recovered from the Recycle Bin.
   - Exchange documents between websites: You can create and manage copies of the documents and send them to other libraries.

# Key Terms Matching

Match the key terms with their definitions. Write the key term letter by the appropriate numbered definition.

a. App
b. Color theme
c. Font theme
d. Home page
e. Library
f. List
g. Metadata
h. Multilingual User Interface (MUI)

i. Reghost
j. Send To
k. Site theme
l. Solution
m. Solution file
n. Tree view
o. Unghosted

1. _____ A collection of announcements, links, surveys, discussion boards, or tasks that contains information arranged as records. *p. 104*

2. _____ A collection of documents, pictures, or forms that can be shared with others. *p. 104*

3. _____ A site template that can be distributed to others or archived on your local computer. *p. 72*

4. _____ A template file that has a .wsp (Web Solution Packet) extension. *p. 74*

5. _____ Customized pages that do not contain the characteristics of the standard configuration and layout of the site definition. *p. 90*

6. _____ Defines the layout, font, and color schemes for a site. *p. 86*

7. _____ Dictates the fonts used for heading and body text. *p. 87*

8. _____ Enables you to specify support for various languages in the sites that you create and enables people to access the site interface in the language they select. *p. 77*

9. _____ Information about the file, such as who created it and when. *p. 111*

10. _____ Provides for hierarchical navigation similar to a Folders list in File Explorer. *p. 84*

11. _____ Reset the pages to the original site definition, removing all customization, and revert the page back to the configuration and layout of the template. *p. 91*

12. _____ Affects page elements such as backgrounds, text, hyperlinks, and some graphic elements, such as bullets and horizontal rules (or lines). *p. 87*

13. _____ Small, easy-to-use Web application that has a specific purpose. *p. 104*

14. _____ The first page displayed as user enters a site and provides the navigational structure for the site. *p. 90*

15. _____ Command used to distribute documents to other libraries, making them available for other teams or in a centralized location. *p. 127*

# Multiple Choice

1. The Multilingual User Interface (MUI) enables you to:

   (a) allow any language to be used on the site.

   (b) specify the language people must use to view your site.

   (c) translate site documents into other languages.

   (d) translate the site interface elements into the specified languages.

2. The display of 13:30 for time is controlled by the:

   (a) language settings.

   (b) location of the SharePoint server.

   (c) regional settings.

   (d) top-level site settings.

3. An alternative text description enables:

   (a) accessibility by people using adaptive technologies.

   (b) links to other pages in the site.

   (c) searches of your site.

   (d) a display of help topics.

4. To provide users with additional links to external URLs, you:

   (a) add links on the Quick Launch or top link bar.

   (b) change site settings.

   (c) display Tree view navigation.

   (d) enable top-level navigation.

5. When you create a site theme, you can select:

   (a) site icon themes.

   (b) site color themes, font themes, languages, and regional settings.

   (c) site layout, colors, and fonts.

   (d) site layout, display languages.

6. You decide to change the color theme of your site. What page would you use to accomplish this task?

   (a) Change the look page

   (b) Color theme page

   (c) Site contents page

   (d) Site theme page

7. A site template is a _____ that can be distributed to others.

   (a) collection

   (b) solution

   (c) top-level site

   (d) workflow

8. To specify the home page for a site, you use the _____ tab.

   (a) HOME

   (b) INSERT

   (c) PAGE

   (d) SITE

9. To view or modify app contents, you must first:

   (a) change the app settings.

   (b) declare permissions to the app.

   (c) edit the app.

   (d) open the app.

10. To upload multiple documents to a SharePoint site at one time, which application(s) do you use?

    (a) File Explorer

    (b) A browser

    (c) SharePoint Online and File Explorer

    (d) SharePoint Online and a browser

# Practice Exercises

## 1    Introduction to Management Information Systems Course

As an undergraduate teaching assistant in the Introduction to Management Information Systems course you will help students working on their assignments in the course laboratory. Your faculty supervisor has given you access to Office 365 and SharePoint Online so that you can develop an online presence that the students can use to ask questions and support each other. You will utilize a template, themes, and apps to develop a subsite for the students. You will add some important documents to the subsite. Refer to Figure 2.57 as you complete this exercise.

**FIGURE 2.57** Introduction to Management Information Systems Course Template

a. Sign into your Office 365 account.

b. Click the **SharePoint tile** and click the **Team Site tile**. Click **Site contents** on the Quick Launch, ensure that the classic SharePoint view is displayed, and click **new subsite**.

c. Type **MIS Course Site Template** for the title, **Management Information Systems Course Template** for the description, and **mis_course** for the URL name. Accept the default for a Team Site template, Permissions, and Navigation Inheritance. Click **Create**.

d. Click **Settings** on the top navigation bar, and select **Change the look** on the menu. Click **Immerse**. Click the **Colors arrow**, and click **This palette is primarily Gray-25% with Gray-80% and Black** (seventh option on the list). Click the **Fonts arrow**, and then click **Century Gothic**. Click **Try it out**. Review the site design, and then click **Yes, keep it**.

e. Click **Language settings** in the Site Administration section of the Site Settings page, and click **Spanish**. Click **OK**.

f. Click **Regional settings** in the Site Administration section of the Site Settings page, and select your current time zone. Click **OK**.

g. Click **Title, description, and logo** in the Look and Feel section of the Site Settings page. Click **FROM COMPUTER** in the Insert Logo section, and click **Browse**. Navigate to the location of your student data files, select *sp02p1Logo*, and then click **Open**. Click **OK**. Type **MIS Study Site Logo** for the description. Click **OK**.

h. Click **EDIT LINKS** on the top link bar, and click **link**(next to Save) on the top link bar. Type your college or university name in the Text to display box. Type the URL to your school's website; be sure to include http:// in front of www in the URL. Click **OK**. Click **Save**.

i. Click **Home** on the Quick Launch at the top of the window. Click the **PAGE tab**, and click **Edit** in the Edit group. Click the **REMOVE THIS link** next to the Get started with your site Web part to select it. Click **OK**. Click **Save** in the Edit group.

**j.** Click **Settings** on the top navigation bar, and select **Site contents**. Click **add an app**, and click the **Links tile**. Type **Important Links for Research** in the Name box, and click **Create**.

**k.** Click **add an app**, and click **SharePoint Store** on the Quick Launch. Type **Poll** in the Find an app box, press **Enter**, locate and then click **Gimmal Quick Poll**. (If the Gimmal Quick Poll app is not available, click another free poll app.) Click **ADD IT** (you may have to log in to your Microsoft account), click **Continue**, and then click **Return to site**. Click **Trust It**. You may have to wait a few moments for the app to load.

**l.** Click **Home** on the Quick Launch, and click the **PAGE tab**. Click **Edit**, and click in the empty top Web Part box under Edit Item. Click the **INSERT tab**, and click **App Part** in the Parts group. Select **Quick Poll** in the left pane, and click **Add** below the right pane. Click **Save** in the Edit group on the FORMAT TEXT tab.

**m.** Click **Site contents** on the Quick Launch at the top of the window, and click the **Quick Poll tile**. Click the **Manage Quick Polls tile**, click the **ITEMS tab**, and click **New Item**. Type **When can you meet for study group?** in the Question box. Click in the **Answer choice 1 box** and type **Saturday morning**. Click in the **Answer choice 2 box** and type **Saturday afternoon**. Click the **Answer choice 3 box**, and add **Monday evening**. Click **Save**. Click the MIS Course Site Template link on the top navigation bar to return to the course site template.

**n.** Select a time to test the app and click **Vote**. Make a screen shot that shows the home page with the question and graph. Name the file **sp02p1Poll_LastFirst**.

**o.** Click **Site contents** on the Quick Launch. Click the **Important Links for Research tile** on the Site contents page, and click **new link**. Click after http://, and then type **www.microsoft.com**. Type **Microsoft** in the Type the description box. Type **Use this site for product support** in the Notes box. Click **Save**. Click the link to test it, and click **Back** on the browser window to return to your SharePoint site. Take a screen snip of the Important Links for Research page and name it **sp02p1Links_LastFirst**.

**p.** Click **Documents** in the Quick Launch, and click **Upload**. Click **Browse**, and navigate to the location of the student data files. Click *sp02p1StudyGroups*, click **Open**, and then click **OK**.

**q.** Click the **More Options icon** next to the file you just uploaded, and click the **More Options icon** on the dialog box. Select **Properties**. Type the title **Study Groups**, and click **Save**. Click the **More Options icon** next to All Documents, and select **Modify this View**. Select **Title** from the Columns list, and change the number to **2**. Change the number for Name to **5**. Click **OK**.

**r.** Click the **sp02p1StudyGroups** link in the Name column. Click **Edit Document**, and select **Edit in Browser**. Add your name to Group 1. Click **sp02p1StudyGroups** on the top navigation bar, and type **_LastFirst** (using your last and first names) at the end of the file name. Click in the document window to automatically save the file. Click **MIS Course Site Template** on the top navigation bar. Right-click the file name **sp02p1StudyGroups_LastFirst** in the Name column and select **Download**. Click **Save As**, navigate to the location where you store your files, and click **Save**.

**s.** Sign out of your Office 365 account and close the browser. Based on your instructor's directions, submit the following:

sp02p1Poll_LastFirst

sp02p1Links_LastFirst

sp02p1StudyGroups_LastFirst

## 2 Class Reunion Team Site

As a former officer of your high school class, you are part of a committee planning for your next class reunion. You will create a Class Reunion site that reflects your school colors and is easy to navigate. You will work with documents on the site and create a template to back up your work. You will complete the exercise using Internet Explorer, rather than Microsoft Edge, because to add a Spreadsheet app you must have access to Active X controls through the browser. Refer to Figure 2.58 as you complete this exercise.

**FIGURE 2.58** Class Reunion Template

a. Open Internet Explorer (not Microsoft Edge). Hint: Type Internet Explorer in the Windows search box. Sign on to your Office 365 account and click the **SharePoint tile**.

b. Click the **Team Site tile**. Click **Site Contents** on the Quick Launch, ensure that the classic view of SharePoint is displayed, and then click **new subsite**.

c. Type **Class Reunion Template** for the title, **This is the template for the class reunion site** for the description, and **cls_reunion** for the URL name. Click **Team Site** on the Collaboration template tab. Accept all other defaults. Click **Create**.

d. Click **Settings** on the top navigation bar, and select **Site settings**. Click **Regional settings**, click the **Time zone arrow**, and then select your local time zone. Click **OK**.

e. Click **Change the look** on the Site Settings page. Click **Green**. Click the **Colors arrow**, and then select **This palette is primarily Dark Teal with White and Turquoise** (10th option on the list). Click the **Fonts arrow**, and select **Century Gothic**. Click **Try it out**. Review the site design, and click **Yes, keep it**.

f. Click **Title, description, and logo** on the Site Settings page. Click **FROM COMPUTER** in the Insert Logo section. Navigate to the location of the student data files, select *sp02p2Logo*, and then click **Open**. Click **OK**. Type **Go Tigers Logo** for the description for alternative text for the picture. Click **OK**.

g. Click **Home** on the Quick Launch. Click the **PAGE tab**, click **Check Out** in the Edit group, and then click **Edit** in the Edit group. Click the **REMOVE THIS link** next to Get started with your site, and click **OK**. In the top Web Part box, type **5th Class Reunion**. Select the words you just typed, and then change the font color to **Gold** on the Standard Colors palette. Change the font to **Heading**, and increase the size to **24 pt**. Apply **Bold** formatting. Click **Save** in the Edit group. Click the **PAGE tab** again, and click **Check In**. In the Comments box, type **Updated by, your name**, and **today's date**. Click **Continue**. Click the **PAGE tab**, and click **Make Home-page** in the Page Actions group. Click **OK**, and click the **BROWSE tab**.

h. Click the **Address bar** on the browser, right-click and select **Copy** to copy the URL to the clipboard. Click the **Tools icon** (gear) on the Internet Explorer window, and then click **Internet options**.

Click the **Security tab**, and then click **Trusted sites**. Click **Sites**, right-click in the **Add this website to the zone box**, and then select **Paste** to paste the URL from the clipboard. Click **Add**. Click **Close**, and then click **OK**.

**i.** Click **Site contents** on the Quick Launch, and click **add an app**. Click the **Import Spreadsheet app tile** on the second page of apps. Type **RSVPs** for the Name. For the Description, type **These people sent in their RSVPs and will attend the reunion.** Click **Browse**, and navigate to the location of your student data files. Select *sp02p2RSVP*, click **Open**. Click **Import**. Select **Range of Cells** for the Range Type in the Import to Windows SharePoint Services list dialog box. Click the **Select Range collapse dialog box icon**, and select all cells with data on the spreadsheet. Click the **expand dialog box icon** on the dialog box window to display the full dialog box, and click **Import**.

**j.** Click **Site contents** on the Quick Launch, and click the **RSVPs tile**. Click **edit this list**, scroll to the bottom of the list, and add your last and first name. Scroll back to the top of the RSVPs list and click **Stop editing this list**.

**k.** Click **Site contents** on the Quick Launch, and click **EDIT LINKS** on the Quick Launch. Drag the **RSVPs tile** to the Quick Launch, placing it just below the Home link, left-aligning it with the other menu items. Click **Save**.

**l.** Click **Documents** on the Quick Launch, and click **New**. Select **New folder**, and type **Planning Committee Documents**. Click **Create**. Click the folder link you just created, click **Upload**, and then click **Browse**. Navigate to the location of the student data files, and select *sp02p2Budget*. Click **Open**, and click **OK**. Click the **More Options icon** next to the file name you just uploaded, and click the **More Options icon** on the dialog box. Select **Properties**, and type **Class Reunion Budget** in the Title box. Click **Save**.

**m.** Click the **More Options icon** next to All Documents, and select **Modify this View**. Select **Title** in the Columns section, and change the number to **2**. Change the number for **Name** to **5**. Click **OK**.

**n.** Open the **Planning Committee Documents folder**. Make a screen shot of the Documents page showing the Class Reunion Budget document. Name the file **sp02p2Budget_LastFirst**. Click **Home** on the Quick Launch, and make a second screen shot. Name the file **sp02p2Home_ LastFirst**.

**o.** Sign out of your Office 365 account and close the browser. Based on your instructor's directions, submit the following:

sp02p2Budget_LastFirst

sp02p2Home_LastFirst

# Mid-Level Exercises

## 1 Hope Hospital Business Office Management

As the Web designer for Hope Hospital, you have been working with a group of people who are implementing a new Electronic Medical Records system. You will create a project site. The site will be attractively formatted with a theme, and you will implement navigational strategies to make the site more user friendly. You will add a new Document library with some folders for organizing the work. You will upload an Excel document into the folder and make modifications using Excel Online. Internet Explorer is used for this exercise so that you can use the Import Spreadsheet app.

**a.** Open Internet Explorer. Log in to your Office 365 account, ensure you are viewing the classic SharePoint display, and create a new subsite under the top-level team site following these specifications:

- Title: **Hope Hospital Template**
- Description: **This template site enables people to collaborate on projects.**
- URL name: **hh_template**
- Select a template: **Project Site**
- Accept all of the other default values.

**b.** Change the language settings to enable people who prefer **Spanish** to view the site navigation in Spanish. Apply the **local time zone** to the site.

**c.** Change the theme of the site as follows:

- Theme: **Blossom**
- Colors: **This palette is primarily White with Gray-80% and Orange.**
- Site Layout: **Oslo**
- Fonts: **Bodoni Book Segoe UI**

**d.** Enable the **Tree view** navigational element on the site. Add a link to the top link bar to **http://www.cms.gov**, displaying the text **Centers for Medicare and Medicaid Services**.

**e.** Add the **Import Spreadsheet app** to the site, with these specifications:

- Name: **EHR Software Options**
- Description: **This is a list of software options the team will study for possible implementation.**
- File: *sp02m1Software*
- Range Type: **Range of Cells**
- Select Range: **Sheet1!$A$2:$C$15**
- Make a screen shot showing the imported spreadsheet. Name the file **sp02m1Software_LastFirst**.

**f.** Add a Document library named **Project Documents** to the site. Add Project Documents to the top link bar. Create two new folders in Project Documents named **Electronic Records** and **Nutrition Counseling**.

**g.** Open the Electronics Records folder and upload the file *sp02m1AgingAccounts*. Open the file **sp02m1AgingAccounts** in Excel Online and add **your name** as a patient to the bottom of the list. Your account number is **746358**. Leave all other columns empty. Change the file name to **sp02m1AgingAccounts_LastFirst**. Return to the Hope Hospital Template, Electronics Record folder. Download the sp02m1AgingAccounts_LastFirst file to your storage location.

**h.** Click **Home** on the top link bar, and expand the Project Documents folder in the Quick Launch. Take a screen shot, naming the file **sp02m1HopeTemplate_LastFirst**.

**i.** Sign out of your Office 365 account and close the browser. Based on your instructor's directions, submit the following:

sp02m1Software_LastFirst

sp02m1AgingAccounts_LastFirst

sp02m1HopeTemplate_LastFirst

As a volunteer at Shelter Pets Online, you developed ideas for a site where you can share photographs of pets in need of a new home and offer tips for bringing a new animal into your household. You will create a Team Site and a Blog subsite. You will improve the looks of the site and add some pictures to the site.

a. Log in to your Office 365 account, open SharePoint, ensure you are viewing the site in classic view, and then create a new subsite under the top-level team site following these specifications:
   • Title: **Shelter Pets Online Template**
   • Description: **This is the template for the Shelter Pets Online site.**
   • URL name: **shelter_template**
   • Template: **Team Site**
   • Accept all other default values

b. Create a new subsite to the Shelter Pets Online Template, and set this site up as follows:
   • Title: **Shelter Pets Online Blog Template**
   • Description: **This is a template for the blog site.**
   • URL name: **shelterblog_template**
   • Template: **Blog**
   • Accept all of the other default values.

c. Navigate to the Shelter Pets Online Template top-level site. Change the theme of the site to **Characters**. Change the colors to **This palette is primarily White, with Gray-80% and Red.** Click **REMOVE** below the background picture to remove it from the page. Change the fonts to **Impact** and **Segoe UI**. Add the logo *sp02m2Logo* to the site. Enter a description for the logo of **Shelter Pets Online logo** for the graphic.

d. Navigate to the Shelter Pets Online Blog Template and add the logo *sp02m2Logo* to the site. Enter a description of **Shelter Pets Online logo** for the graphic. Change the theme of the site to **Characters**. Change the colors to **This palette is primarily White, with Gray-80% and Red.** Remove the background picture. Change the fonts to **Impact** and **Segoe UI**.

e. Use the Site Settings page to change the navigation, by selecting **Display the same navigation items as the parent site** in the Global Navigation section.

f. Navigate to the Shelter Pets Online Template parent site. Add a Picture Library app to the Shelter Pets Online Template parent site named **Adorable Dogs**. Add a second Picture Library app to the Shelter Pets Online Template parent site named **Cuddly Cats**. Add an Announcements app to the Shelter Pets Online Template parent site named **Shelter Pets Online Announcements**.

g. Edit the Quick Launch links to remove the **Recent link**. Remove the **Notebook link** from the Quick Launch. Drag the **Adorable Dogs Picture Library link** to a position just under Home on the Quick Launch. Drag the **Cuddly Cats Picture Library link** to a position under the Adorable Dogs link on the Quick Launch.

h. Remove the **Get started with your site tiles** from the Home page of the Shelter Pets Online Template. Edit the Home page to place the **Shelter Pets Online Announcements app** above the Newsfeed and Documents Web Parts.

i. Add an announcement to the Shelter Pets Online Announcement app, as follows:
   • Title: **Pet Fair Coming in June!**
   • Body: **Our annual Pet Fair will feature the newest pet products, nutritious foods, and the top trainers in our area. We invite you to visit us for a day of fun. You can even adopt a new pet during the Pet Fair.**
   • Expires: **July 1**

j. Take a screen snip of the Shelter Pets Online Template home page, naming it **sp02m2Shelter_LastFirst**.

**k.** Upload the file *sp02m2Lucy* to the Adorable Dogs Picture Library, editing the file name property to **Lucy**. Upload the following files to the Cuddly Cats Picture Library.

- *sp02m2Kiki*
- *sp02m2Lydia*
- *sp02m2Reggie*
- *sp02m2Sam*
- *sp02m2Sugar*

Edit the file name property for each picture, removing the sp02m2 portion of the name. Add keywords for each picture of **cat, adoption**.

**l.** Take a full screen snip showing the Cuddly Cats Picture Library. Name the file **sp02m2Pictures_LastFirst**.

**m.** Sign out of your Office 365 account. Based on your instructor's directions, submit the following:

sp02m2Shelter_LastFirst

sp02m2Pictures_LastFirst

# Beyond the Classroom

**SharePoint Help**

SharePoint is used by a large international community of companies for developing their portals. One of the most professional and helpful sites where you can find examples of how SharePoint is used by companies is created by Microsoft. Use a browser to open the Microsoft Case Studies page (www.microsoft.com/casestudies/default.aspx), and type **SharePoint** in the Search box. Select two case studies, and then create a report, using Word Online, on your findings about how SharePoint helped the organizations. Be sure to include links or references to the information as you prepare a report for your instructor. Name the report **sp02b1CaseStudies_LastFirst**. Based on your instructor's directions, submit sp02b1CaseStudies_LastFirst.

**Site Backup Experience**

Your direct supervisor, Mary McMillian, sent you the memo *sp02b2Memo*. Review the memo, and write a policy, using Word Online, to your instructor describing steps the company can take to ensure that it does not lose important documents in the future. Name the file**sp02b2SiteBackUp_LastFirst** and download it from Office 365. Based on your instructor's directions, submit sp02b2SiteBackUp_LastFirst.

# Capstone Exercise

As the Web designer for Wellington Finances, you have been asked to prepare a template for the Wellington Finance Project Investor site. Your goal is to make the site interesting for high school students, who will participate in the educational experience.

## Create a Subsite

Using your top-level SharePoint Online team site, you create a subsite that will be used to create the template.

**a.** Sign in to your Office 365 account and create a new subsite with the following specifications:
  - Title: **Project Investor Template**
  - Description: **Updated by**, your name, and today's date
  - URL name: **project_investor**
  - Template: **Team Site**

## Customize a Site

You will customize the site to make it user-friendly to students.

**a.** Change the regional settings so that the time zone matches your local time zone. Change the language settings to enable the display of the navigational structure in **Spanish**.

**b.** Add the logo *sp02c1Logo* to the site, with the description of **Project Investor logo**.

**c.** Change the theme to **Green**. Change the colors to **This palette is primarily White with Gray-80% and Green.** Change the site layout to **Oslo**. Change the font to **Blueprint MT Pro** and **Corbel**.

**d.** Add a new page with the name **project_investor_home**. Make the following adjustments to the page:
  - Add the picture *sp02c1Investors* to the placeholder. Add the alternative text **Successful investors** to the picture. Change the vertical size of the picture to **150 px**.
  - Add the following text to the right of the picture, formatting with the **Heading 1, 13pt** style:
    **Project Investor will help you meet your savings goals through education, collaboration, and experience**.
  - Make the page the Home page for the site and save it.
  - Edit the properties of the site home page to change the title to **Project Investor Home**.

## Add and Work with Apps

To help organize the students you will add a calendar app to the site. An announcement app will alert them to special events.

**a.** Add the Calendar app to the site, with the name of **Course Calendar**. Add the Announcements app, with the name of **Project Investor Announcements**.

**b.** Set up an event on the Calendar two weeks from today's date based on the following specifications:
  - Title: **Project Investor Team Meeting**
  - Location: **Wellington Finances, Room 465**
  - Start time: **4:15 PM**
  - End time **6:15 PM**
  - Description: **The first team meeting will focus on getting to know the members of your investing team.**
  - Display the calendar showing the event and take a screenshot. Name the file **sp02c1Calendar_LastFirst**.

**c.** Create an announcement with the following specifications:
  - Title: **Lindsey Wolloqit to Speak!**
  - Body: **Lindsey Wolloqit, president of Wellington Finances, will join us via video conferencing during our next Project Investor session. You do not want to miss this opportunity to ask questions**!
  - Expires: **Two weeks from today's date**
  - Open the announcement item, and take a screen shot. Name the file **sp02c1Announcement_LastFirst**.

## Update the Navigation

To make the site more user friendly, you will add the calendar and announcements to the top link bar.

**a.** Remove the **Recent** link and the **Notebook** link from the Quick Launch.

**b.** Place a link to the **Course Calendar** to the right side of the Documents link.

**c.** Place a link to the **Project Investor Announcements** to the right side of the Course Calendar link.

## Work with Documents

To provide the students with materials for study, you will create folders, add a document, and update the properties for the folder and document.

**a.** Create a folder in the Documents app named **Investing Tips**.

**b.** Upload the document *sp02c1InvestingTips* to the Investing Tips folder.

**c.** Edit the properties for the *sp02c1InvestingTips* file to include a title of **Investing Tips for Students**.

**d.** Modify the view of the Investing Tips folder to include the **Title** in the second column, moving the **Name** to the third column. Remove the **Modified** and **Modified By** columns.

**e.** Open the Investing Tips folder, and take a screen shot showing the page. Name the file **sp02c1Investing_LastFirst**.

## Save and Share the Template Site

You are now ready to ask for your supervisor's feedback.

**a.** Share the site with your instructor, via an email invitation. Type **sp02c1Share_LastFirst** in the personal message box of the invitation. Be sure to sign the email invitation with your name and today's date. Provide **Team Site Visitors [Read]** permissions.

**b.** Sign out of your Office 365 account. Based on your instructor's directions, submit the following:

sp02c1Calendar_LastFirst

sp02c1Announcement_LastFirst

sp02c1Investing_LastFirst

# SharePoint

# Customize a Webpage

## LEARNING OUTCOME

• You will customize and update a SharePoint Online page.

## OBJECTIVES & SKILLS: After you read this chapter, you will be able to:

## CASE STUDY | Daniela's Table Webpages

As the team leader and Web designer for Daniela's Table, you are responsible for the appearance of the website that supports the PBS show. You have been collecting the recipes that will be featured in the upcoming show, and now it is time to develop a page that will contain a recipe. You will use SharePoint Online to create and edit a new Wiki page. You are excited about designing the page that will be used as the basis for all other recipe pages in the site. Not only do you get to work with text, but there are photographs and other media assets to use on the pages.

You decide to add a web part to the site to increase the functionality. You will create a second page devoted to upcoming episodes and the recipes that will be featured. You will add a Picture Library Slideshow Web Part to display a series of photographs of food. A list of upcoming episodes will be uploaded as an app part. You will then add a Text Filter Web Part to enable the site users to filter the list app part based on the type of food they want.

Fotolia/Burlingham

# Working with SharePoint Webpages

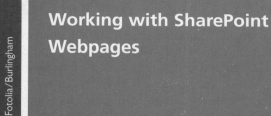

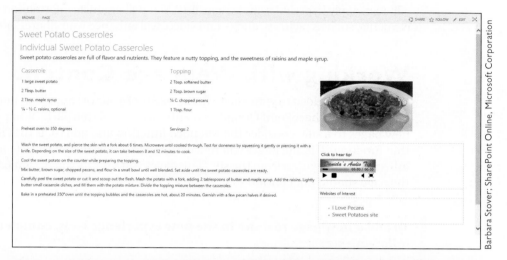

## CHAPTER 3

Barbara Stover; SharePoint Online, Microsoft Corporation

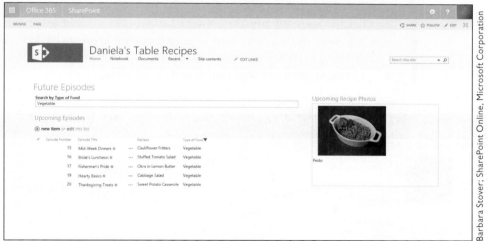

Barbara Stover; SharePoint Online, Microsoft Corporation

**FIGURE 3.1** Daniela's Table Webpages

## CASE STUDY | Daniela's Table Webpages

| Starting Files | Files to be Submitted |
|---|---|
| sp03h1SweetRecipe.docx<br>sp03h1Casserole.jpg<br>sp03h1AudioTip.mp3<br>sp03h1TipGraphic.png<br>sp03h2Pesto.jpg<br>sp03h2UpcomingEpisodes.xlsx<br>sp03h2Casserole.jpg<br>sp03h2Bruschetta.jpg | sp03h1Recipe_LastFirst<br>sp03h2Episodes_LastFirst |

# Tools to Customize a Webpage

After setting up a website with apps, lists, libraries, pages, and documents, you are ready to turn your attention to working with SharePoint Online page content. Each page in the site can have its own individual design and functionality. All the pages use a combination of generic webpage elements, such as text, images, hyperlinks, lists, tables, and forms. SharePoint Online pages also have some specific elements such as SharePoint Controls. These user-friendly tools enable you to create pages that function and display the way you want by inserting elements into a page and modifying their characteristics.

In this section you will learn about editing SharePoint Online pages. You will format and edit text, apply hyperlinks, and create lists. You will organize information into tables. Media elements, such as pictures, audio, and video, will enhance your SharePoint Online pages.

## Working with Webpage Content

Webpages are added to your site to fit the needs of your organization and can be fully customized using SharePoint Online, text entry tools, and web parts or app parts. As you add new pages to a site, consider the intended function and add tools that focus the users on that function. The site pages will reflect the theme selected for the site and automatically inherit the navigation from the site. This saves you time as you design pages. The name of the page should not contain spaces.

> **To add a new page to a site in the new experience view, complete the following steps:**
>
> 1. Open the site where you want to add a new page.
> 2. Click the Site contents on the Quick Launch, and click Pages on the Quick Launch.
> 3. Click New, and select the type of page you want to create (Wiki Page, Web Part Page, Site Page) as shown in Figure 3.2.
> 4. Type an appropriate page name, and click Create.

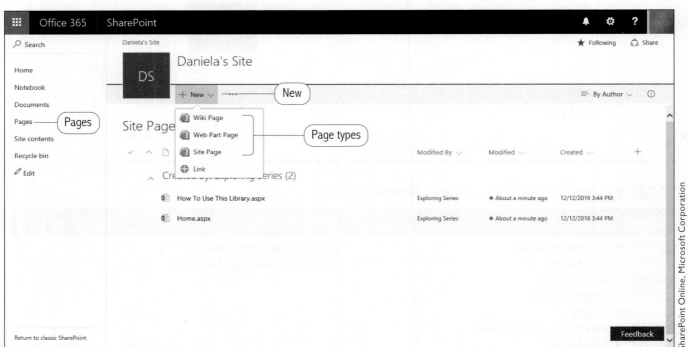

**FIGURE 3.2** Add a Page (New Experience View)

In SharePoint Online, pages that you create are stored in the Site Pages library. Media content is stored in a Site Assets library. The Team Site template contains these libraries by default.

The SharePoint Online browser interface provides a comprehensive set of user-friendly page-editing functionalities. If you have permission to edit a page and the page is not checked out by another user, you can edit the contents of the page. You begin editing a page by opening the page, clicking the PAGE tab, and then clicking Edit in the Edit group. You can also click EDIT on the contextual toolbar below the photograph icon to open the page in Edit mode, as shown in Figure 3.3. Yet another alternative is to click the Settings icon and click Edit page.

---

**TIP: VIEW ALL PAGES**

If you do not see the page you wish to view, click All Pages on the Sites Pages page (under New), and then select the page from the displayed list.

---

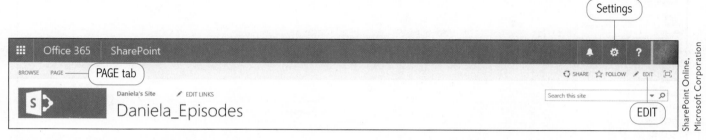

**FIGURE 3.3** Edit Page Content (Classic View)

Depending on the type of page you are editing, each page displayed in editing mode will look different. On the *Wiki page*, you can only type in the page body content area, as shown in Figure 3.4, whereas in the *Web Part page*, you can add new web parts using Web Part zones and edit the existing web parts.

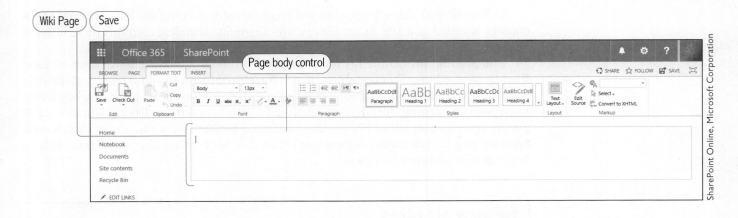

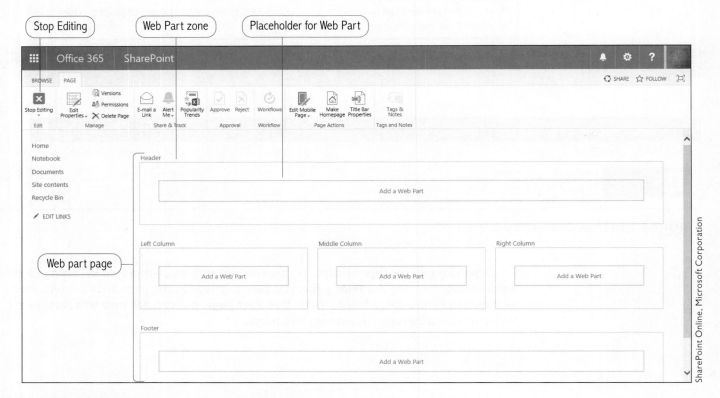

**FIGURE 3.4** Wiki Page and Web Part Page (Classic View)

The method used for saving the changes depends on the type of page you are viewing. You click Stop Editing in the Edit group when editing a Web Part page. On a Wiki page, you have different options for saving the page. Click Save, as shown in Figure 3.4, and the page edits are saved and you are returned to the page view. Click Save and Keep Editing (click the Save arrow in the Save group, as shown in Figure 3.5), and the edits are saved but you remain in Edit mode so you can make more changes. Click Stop Editing on the Save menu to exit the Edit mode, with a prompt to save or discard changes you have made to the page.

> **TIP: ANOTHER WAY TO SAVE**
> Click SAVE on the contextual toolbar below your name to save your edits and display the page.

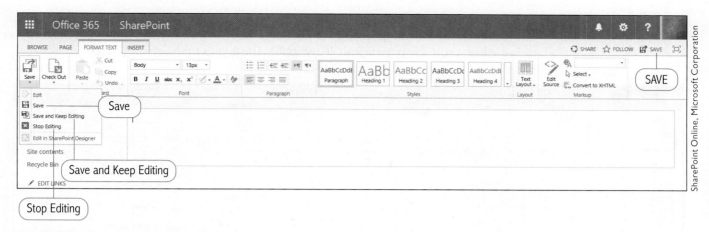

**FIGURE 3.5** Save Menu (Classic View)

As you work on a page in a site that other people can access, it is a good practice to check out the page while you are working on it, just as you do with documents in a SharePoint library. Click Check Out in the Edit group to reserve your editing rights. Be sure to check in the page after you have completed your edits. Click the Check In arrow to display a menu of options, as shown in Figure 3.6. If you click the Discard Check Out option on the Check In menu, any changes you have made while editing will be discarded. If someone fails to check in a page after editing, the site administrator can override the check out to make the page available to others.

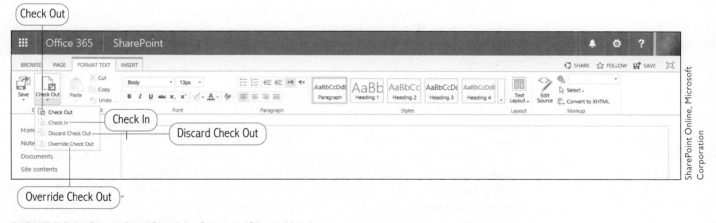

**FIGURE 3.6** Check Out/Check In Options (Classic View)

The SharePoint Online editing workspace in classic view includes the Ribbon with tabs and the editing window. A status bar at the top of the page indicates that you have the page checked out and that it is editable.

## Add Text to a Webpage

**STEP 1** » The most common type of webpage content is text. Text appears in many different ways on a webpage, including normal body text, headings, links, and formatted as ordered or unordered lists. You can type text directly onto the page, import the content of a text file, or copy and paste text from another file. It can also be edited and formatted to emphasize the purpose of the webpage and enhance its appearance.

Designers begin the process of editing pages by selecting a layout. The Text Layout gallery in the Layout group on the FORMAT TEXT tab, shown in Figure 3.7, enables you to select a suitable page layout. This applies the layout to the current page.

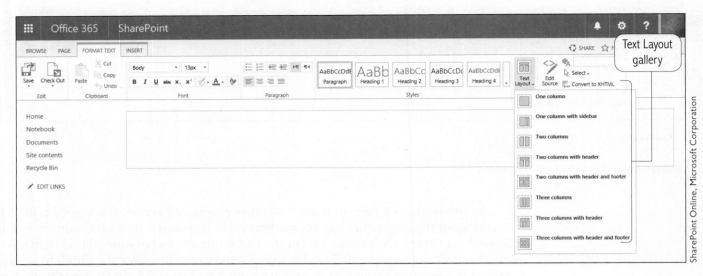

**FIGURE 3.7** Text Layout Gallery (Classic View)

Whether you type text, or copy and paste it, it is entered in the page body content areas of the layout. Text formatting is similar to other Microsoft Office applications, using the Font, Paragraph, and Styles groups on the FORMAT TEXT tab. When you type text directly on a webpage, position the insertion point where you want the text to appear and begin typing the text. When you reach the end of the line, the insertion point is automatically positioned at the beginning of the next line. Press Enter when you want to start a new paragraph.

You can copy and paste (or move) text from one document to another or within the same page using the Copy and Paste commands in the Clipboard group on the FORMAT TEXT tab. To copy text from another application, open the source file, select the desired text, and then copy it. To paste the copied text on the webpage, open the webpage, click to position the insertion point where you want the new text, and paste it.

When you paste text onto a SharePoint Online page, you can use alternative Paste commands while displaying the page in Internet Explorer to control how the text is pasted. Click the Paste arrow in the Clipboard group of the FORMAT TEXT tab to select between Paste, Paste Clean, and Paste Plaintext, as shown in Figure 3.8. Paste Clean removes any styles that are applied to the copied text before placing it on the webpage, but retains any formatting, such as bold or italic. Paste Plaintext places the contents of the Clipboard on the page as plain text with no formatting or styles at all. To paste while using Microsoft Edge, either use Ctrl+V or right-click and select Paste.

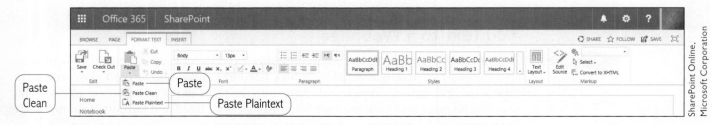

**FIGURE 3.8** Paste Options in Internet Explorer (Classic View)

When you paste text onto webpages, an excess of tags generated by the Office application are included within the text, which increases the risk of creating a webpage with compatibility and accessibility errors. For this reason, it is a good idea to use Paste Plaintext to place copied text onto a page.

## Edit and Format Text on a Webpage

After you have placed text on the webpage, you might want to edit and format it. SharePoint Online enables you to move, replace, or delete text and change its appearance. Using techniques familiar to you through using Microsoft Office, you select the text and then click the command for the action you want.

To move text, select the text, cut it from the current location, place the insertion point in the new location, and then paste it into the new location. To replace text, select it, and then type the new text. To delete text, select it, and press Delete.

The font can be changed in two ways, using the Font group on the FORMAT TEXT tab:

- Select the text where the font changes will be applied, and then click the Font arrow in the Font group to select a font, and then use the Font group options to change the properties such as size, color, text styles (bold, italic), and text effects (underline, strikethrough, subscript, or superscript).

- Position the insertion point where you want to insert text, and then make selections in the Font group prior to typing the text.

The text size can be specified on webpages using a rather wide selection of units: keywords, ems, exs, pixels, percentages, picas, points, inches, centimeters, and millimeters. Only pixels, keywords, ems, and percentages are commonly used to size text for a computer monitor. When using these four measurement units, the text size is set either by adding to or subtracting from the text size already set on the viewer's browser screen. Hence, if you do not specify a size for text using Cascading Style Sheets (CSS), browsers apply their base font size, which is 16 pixels for most browsers. CSS is discussed in detail in Appendix A.

The font types available include the theme fonts and thirteen additional fonts, which include serif, sans serif, and decorative fonts. Arial, Calibri, Lucida Console, Segoe UI, Tahoma, and Trebuchet MS are sans serif fonts. Courier, Garamond, Georgia, Palatino Linotype, and Times New Roman are popular serif fonts. Comic Sans and Impact are in the decorative font category, and they can be a little difficult to read on a webpage.

Font styles can be used to enhance text and emphasize the message. The most frequently used font styles are bold and italic. You can apply more than one font style to selected text, for example a combination of bold and italic.

The default font color for text on a webpage is black. You can alter the font color to emphasize a word or an entire paragraph. You can select colors from a wide range using the More Colors option on the Font Color menu. You can also select a highlight color to emphasize text as if it were marked with a highlighter pen. You have the same highlight color options that are available for applying a font color.

Some of the better known text effects, in addition to underline, are superscript and subscript. The Strikethrough option enables you to mark text that is under discussion for deletion.

Styles are SharePoint Online features that enable Web designers to format text using built-in HTML styles. Among the styles included in the Styles gallery in the Styles group, as shown in Figure 3.9, are page elements and text styles. Page elements include paragraphs, headings, and alternative heading styles. Text styles include normal, quote, emphasis, reference, and accent styles. The heading styles range from Heading 1, which is the largest heading font, to Heading 4, which is the smallest. As you point to styles in the gallery, a live preview displays the effects on the selected text.

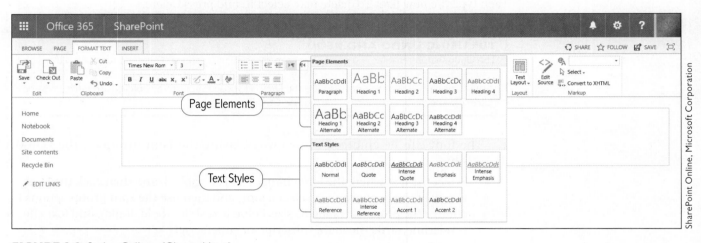

SharePoint Online, Microsoft Corporation

**FIGURE 3.9** Styles Gallery (Classic View)

---

**TIP: KEEP IT SIMPLE**

With all the choices you can make to format the text on a page, it is a good idea to exercise restraint. Emphasize the important parts, such as headings, but avoid overdoing the formatting with bold, italic, and colored fonts. Avoid using underlined fonts, because on webpages, underlines indicate hyperlinks and people will try to click them as they navigate through the page.

---

It is always important to check your webpage for spelling errors. The Spelling command is in the Spelling group on the FORMAT TEXT tab. Click the button to check the spelling of the words on the entire page. A dialog box indicates the number of errors found, and when you click OK, the words are underlined with the familiar red wavy line. Click a marked spelling error and select the correct spelling, or click Ignore or Ignore All to ignore the spelling error message.

---

**TIP: MISSING SPELLING COMMAND**

If the Spelling command is not available on your FORMAT TEXT tab, you must activate it on the top-level site. Click the Settings icon, and then select Site settings from the menu. Click Site collection features in the Site Collection Administration section, and then scroll down and next to SharePoint Server Publishing Infrastructure, click the Activate button. It may take a few moments before it is activated. Once it is activated, click the Settings icon again, and then select Site settings from the menu. Click Manage site features in the Site Actions group, and then click the SharePoint Server Publishing Activate button. The Spelling command is now available on the FORMAT TEXT tab when you edit pages in the site.

---

## Add Hyperlinks

STEP 2 » Nobody likes to explore cluttered and confusing webpages. Most people instinctively prefer clear, well-organized, and easy-to-navigate pages. Keeping your webpages clean and organized is an important design consideration. Hyperlinks and lists are two features that can help Web designers achieve these goals.

Hyperlinks can help designers break the content of a large, difficult-to-navigate webpage into a set of webpages that are connected. You can create hyperlinks to your SharePoint documents and pages on your current site, or you can add a link to a URL on the Web.

Hyperlinks are not just colored, underlined words that magically open another webpage. The HTML code contains a tag with the URL of the linked page, which the browser requests from the server when you click the link. A URL can include an address for a webpage or file on the Internet, on your computer, on a local network, a bookmark within a webpage, or an email address.

Two different kinds of URLs exist: absolute and relative. An ***absolute URL*** provides a full path to a webpage or file, whereas a ***relative URL*** provides the path to a webpage or a file in relation to another file. The HTML code in Figure 3.10 shows how typical absolute and relative URLs look. Notice that the relative URLs are often shorter than absolute URLs.

Absolute URL → http://www.eng.auburn.edu/users/Daniela/recipes.aspx

Relative URL → /images/recipes/bruschetta.jpg

**FIGURE 3.10** Absolute and Relative URLs

Absolute URLs are required to access webpages or files outside of your SharePoint installation. When websites include multiple webpages and many folders and subfolders, the URLs can be confusing and difficult to remember and type correctly; you should use relative URLs in these situations. In addition to being shorter, there are significant advantages to using relative URLs when relocating a website to another place on the same Web server or on another Web server. Using relative URLs cuts down on the time required to adjust links from the previous location.

Links to URLs commonly begin with http://, https://, mailto:, ftp://, and file://, as shown in Table 3.1. These protocols determine how a browser communicates with the server where the page is stored. As you use the Link command on the INSERT tab, you type the appropriate prefix as a part of the absolute URL. When you are creating a relative link, the prefix automatically appears as a part of the URL as you select the Web asset from the SharePoint site.

| TABLE 3.1 Protocols | |
|---|---|
| **Protocol** | **Protocol Type** |
| http:// | Hypertext Transfer Protocol |
| https:// | Hypertext Transfer Protocol Secure |
| mailto: | Email |
| ftp:// | File Transfer Protocol |
| file:// | Local computer file |

Pearson Education, Inc.

**To create hyperlinks, complete the following steps:**

1. Open the webpage in Edit mode.
2. Position the insertion point where you want the link to display.
3. Click the INSERT tab, and click Link in the Links group.
4. Select the type of link: From SharePoint (which uses a page from your SharePoint site) or From Address (which uses a URL to an external site).
5. Select the Web asset for a SharePoint link, as shown in Figure 3.11, and click Insert. For a From Address link, type the text to display and the URL, and then click Try link to test the link prior to clicking OK.

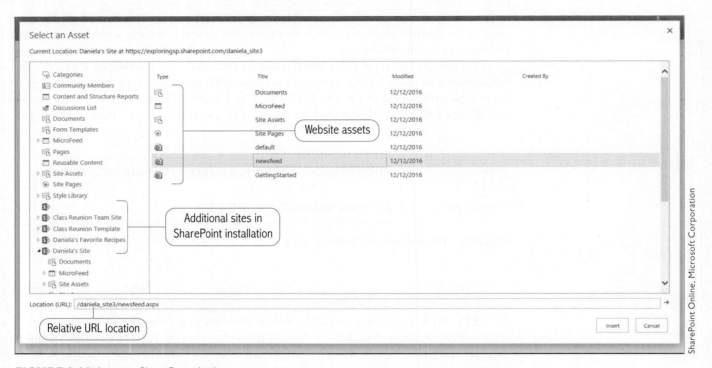

**FIGURE 3.11** Insert a SharePoint Link

---

**TIP: DISPLAYING LINK TEXT**
When you select a SharePoint hyperlink, the name of the Web asset appears as the link. For instance, if the file *danielas_contact.docx* is selected, this is the text that appears. To create more user-friendly link text, such as *Daniela's Contact Information*, type the text you want to display, select it, and then insert the SharePoint link as described in the steps.

---

After creating a link, you can further modify it using the LINK tab, which appears when the link is selected. You can specify that the hyperlink target opens in a new tab in the browser window. The file that opens when a hyperlink is clicked is called the ***hyperlink target***.

**To open the hyperlink target on a new browser tab, complete the following steps:**

1. Create the link on the SharePoint page.
2. Select the link in Edit mode, and click the LINK tab.
3. Select Open in new tab in the Behavior group, as shown in Figure 3.12.

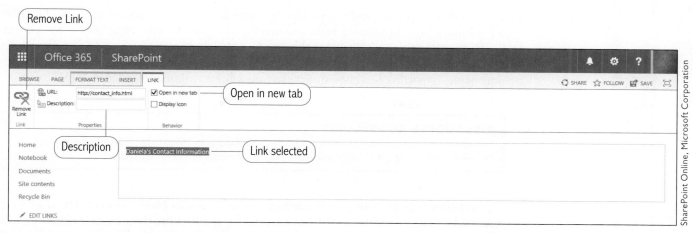

**FIGURE 3.12** Modify a Hyperlink (Classic View)

When you move the pointer over a hyperlink in Browse mode or when viewing the webpage in a browser, the hyperlink target URL displays in a box at the bottom of the screen. Although this is helpful information to some users, a ScreenTip display can be much more descriptive, as shown in Figure 3.13. A *ScreenTip* is text that displays in the body of the webpage whenever the pointer is moved over the hyperlink in Browse mode, or when viewing the webpage in a browser. Designers use ScreenTip text to provide users with more information about the related hyperlink. You can add ScreenTip text to links created within the site or external to the site.

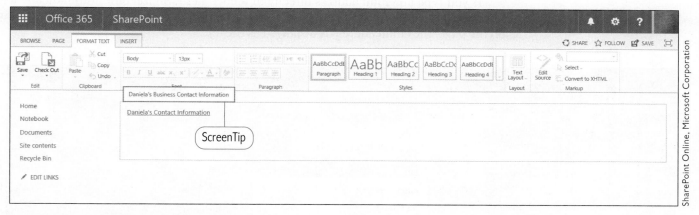

**FIGURE 3.13** ScreenTip Display (Classic View)

**To create ScreenTip text, complete the following steps:**

1. Create the link on the SharePoint page.
2. Select the link in Edit mode, and click the LINK tab.
3. Type the ScreenTip text you want to display in the Description box in the Properties group (refer to Figure 3.12).

You can remove a hyperlink in two ways: by deleting the text and the associated link from the page or by keeping the text on the page but removing the associated link. To delete a hyperlink and its text completely from the page, select the hyperlink in Edit mode, right-click, and then click Cut. Alternatively, you can select the linked text, and then press Delete. To preserve the hyperlink text on the page but delete the link associated with it, select the linked text, click the LINK tab, and then click Remove Link in the Link group, as shown in Figure 3.12.

A link to a specific position within the same document or another document is called a bookmark link. Bookmark links are helpful navigation tools, especially when you are dealing with long pages, because they replace the slower scrolling using the scroll bars. Bookmark targets are placed within the page, and bookmark links use the targets as a part of the hyperlink text. Bookmarks in SharePoint Online are coded in HTML.

---

**TIP: ADDING BOOKMARKS**
You can create a document in Word, set up the bookmarks, and then copy and paste the content of the Word document onto a page to easily set up bookmarks in SharePoint Online.

---

Another type of common hyperlink, called a ***mailto link***, connects the user to an email address on a webpage. When users click a mailto link, their default email application opens or they are presented with a menu of applications they can use to send email.

---

**To create a mailto link, complete the following steps:**

1. Click the INSERT tab on the page where you want to insert the link.
2. Click Link in the Links group, and select From Address.
3. Type the text you want to display as the hyperlink.
4. Type mailto: followed by the email address (with no space after the colon) in the Address box, as shown in Figure 3.14.

---

If you type an email address directly in a document, SharePoint automatically formats it as a mailto link, but you do not have the option to provide the link text to display on the page; the email address is displayed as the link.

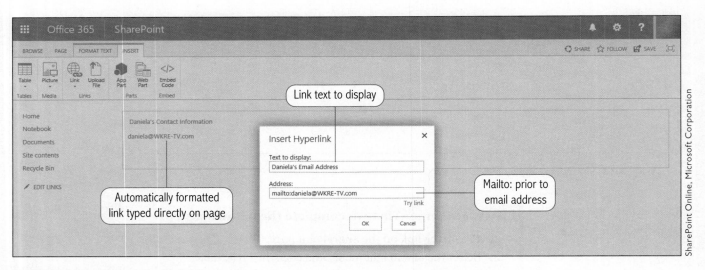

**FIGURE 3.14** Add a Mailto Link (Classic View)

In SharePoint Online, you cannot set page properties to change the color of hyperlinks. Color options are selected as a part of the overall theme applied to the site. You can view hyperlink color options by clicking the Settings icon, selecting Site settings from the menu, and then clicking Change the look in the Look and Feel section. A visited link has a different color than an unvisited link. A rollover effect is automatically added to an active hyperlink (a link as it is pointed to or clicked by a user) and displays an underline when a website visitor moves the pointer over the hyperlink.

## Format Lists

Lists are great tools for organizing webpage content in a concise and consistent fashion. The SharePoint Online list styles are numbered and bulleted. Use a numbered list when the order in which elements appear is important, such as a list of meetings scheduled for the day, or a list of instructions included in a software application tutorial. If the order of the elements is not important use a bulleted list.

The ***list format*** is a common format seen on almost any webpage. Lists help you organize and present your content in a consistent and concise fashion. Figure 3.15 shows examples of text formatted as numbered and bulleted lists. To apply a list format to text, select the text in Edit mode, and then click the appropriate list format in the Paragraph group on the FORMAT TEXT tab. You can also select the list format before you type the list items.

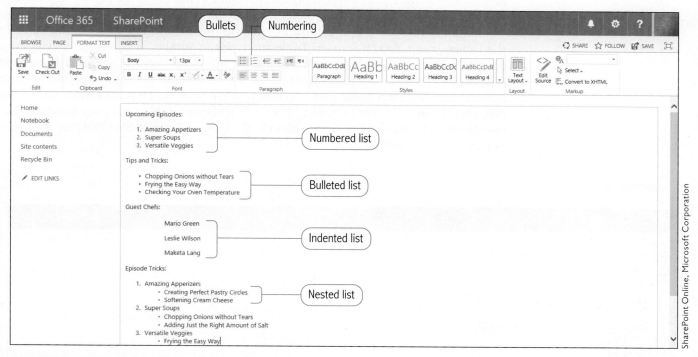

**FIGURE 3.15** List Formats (Classic View)

Although not technically a list format, you can use the Paragraph group Indent and Outdent commands to create a list with neither numbers nor bullets. The text was selected and the Indent command clicked twice to create the list shown in Figure 3.15.

Nested lists are popular features used by Web designers to emphasize text categories and subcategories. Using SharePoint, you can create nested lists including the same list format (numbered or bulleted) or use a different format, as shown in Figure 3.15. To set the subcategories, type them into the list, select the text that you want to be in a subcategory, click Indent in the Paragraph group, and then click Bullets or Numbering for the format to apply to the subcategory.

## Work with Tables

**STEP 3** ❯❯ Tables have always played an important role in Web design. The fact that tables are supported by all browsers and are similar to the tables used in many other desktop applications makes them attractive to Web designers from beginners to professionals. SharePoint Online has a comprehensive set of tools for inserting and formatting tables.

A **table** is a collection of rows having one or more columns. A **cell** is the intersection of a column and a row. A **nested table** is a table inserted within the cell of another table. Because you can hide the table grid lines, the underlying structure of the table may not be apparent to your website users.

> **TIP: SETTING THE DIMENSIONS OF A TABLE**
> Setting the dimensions of a table as a percentage of the browser window size is highly recommended, because it ensures the proper display of all elements included in the table regardless of the size of the browser window.

Before creating a table, consider how many rows and columns you need, the elements that will be placed in the table cells, and the total width and height of the tables. SharePoint Online enables Web designers to establish the height and width of a table in pixels or as a percentage of the browser window size.

In Edit mode, you create a table by clicking the INSERT tab and clicking Table in the Tables group. You click Insert Table and type the number of columns and rows you want to include in the table, or you can use the Insert Table grid. The **Insert Table grid** is a graphical table that enables you to select the number of rows and columns for your table. Using the Insert Table grid, you can create a table that is a maximum size of ten columns by ten rows. For example, to create a three-row table with three columns, display the Insert Table grid, and then point to the third column of the third row, as shown in Figure 3.16, and click.

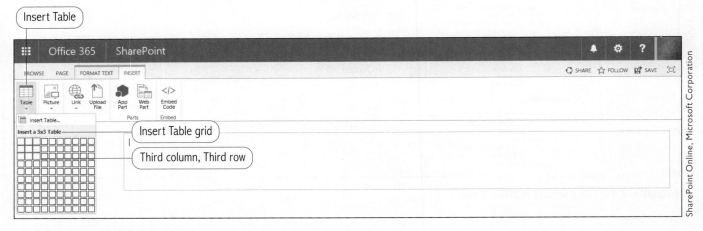

**FIGURE 3.16** Create a Table (Classic View)

Just as you create alternative text for graphics that you insert on webpages, you should create a summary that displays when the table is not visible because of the use of adaptive technologies. Click the TABLE LAYOUT tab, and type summary information in the Summary box in the Properties group (see Figure 3.17).

After inserting a table in a webpage, you can always add more rows or columns. Position the insertion point in the last column of the last row, and press Tab to add another row. You can add more rows and columns anywhere in the table by positioning the insertion point in the desired location, and clicking one of the four buttons in the Rows & Columns group on the TABLE LAYOUT tab: Insert Above, Insert Below, Insert Left, or Insert Right, as shown in Figure 3.17.

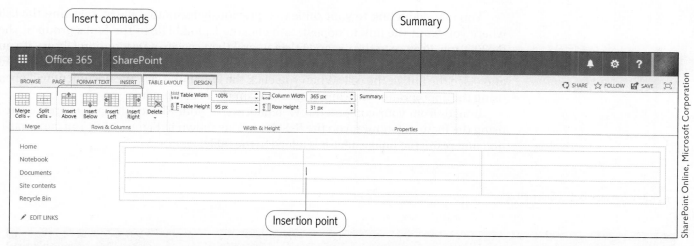

**FIGURE 3.17** Add Table Rows or Columns (Classic View)

As careful as you might be when creating a table or inserting rows or columns into a table, it is only human to make mistakes or to change your mind. Fortunately, you can delete a row or column from a table at any time. To delete a row, select a cell on the row you want to delete, click the Delete arrow in the Rows & Columns group on the TABLE LAYOUT tab, and then select Delete Row. To delete a column, select a cell in the column you want to delete, click the Delete arrow in the Rows & Columns group, and then select Delete Column. Likewise, you can also delete a cell or the entire table using the Delete commands, as shown in Figure 3.18.

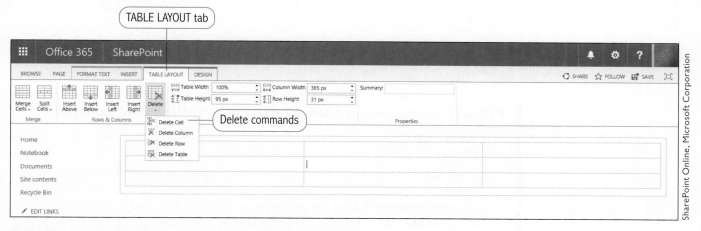

**FIGURE 3.18** Delete Table Rows or Columns (Classic View)

As previously discussed in this chapter, you can add text to a webpage in three ways: type directly in the page, copy and paste text into the page, or insert a link to a previously formatted file into the page. You can use these same methods for entering text into a table.

When you want to enter text directly in the cell of a table, you first position the insertion point where you want the text to appear, and type the text. Press Enter to start a new paragraph in the same cell, or press and hold Shift while pressing Enter to add a line break.

To copy and paste text into a table cell, copy the text from the original source location, position the insertion point in the cell where you want text to appear, and then click Paste in the Clipboard group of the FORMAT TEXT tab.

You can add a link to your table to a previously formatted file by selecting the cell where you want the link to appear, and clicking Upload File in the Links group of the INSERT tab. Browse to the file and select it, and then specify a Destination Library if you want to use something other than the Site Assets library. Click OK to complete the upload and place the link in the cell. When you click the link in the cell, the document will open using the appropriate Office application on your local computer.

Images from your computer, a Web address, or your SharePoint assets are inserted using the Picture command on the INSERT tab, as shown in Figure 3.19. You can reposition and resize the image after it is added to the table.

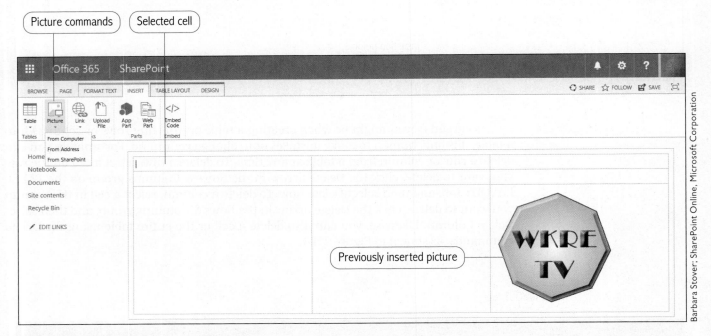

**FIGURE 3.19** Insert an Image (Classic View)

**To insert an image into a cell in a table, complete the following steps:**

1. Select the cell.
2. Click Picture in the Media group on the INSERT tab.
3. Select the source type (From Computer, From Address, or From SharePoint) from the menu.
4. Navigate to the location of the picture, select it, click Open, and then click OK. If you are using a picture from your SharePoint assets, select the file and click Insert. If you are adding a picture from an address, type the address and provide alternative text, and then click OK.

After inserting a picture, it is important to remember to provide alternative text to describe the picture so people using adaptive technologies will be able to understand what the picture is.

Using tools available on the DESIGN tab, you can format the table. Select the options from the Table Style Options group, as shown in Figure 3.20, which include Header Row, Footer Row, First Column, and Last Column. You can toggle the grid lines off and on using Show Grid Lines on the DESIGN tab to help you visualize the table. These grid lines are not displayed when the page is viewed using the BROWSE tab.

Based on the theme of the site, you can style the table using options on the Styles menu in the Table Styles group on the DESIGN tab. As you move the pointer over each option, a live preview displays the style on the selected table, as shown in Figure 3.20. Click when you locate the one you want to use. The table style includes settings for the border color, cell color, and header or footer color. The header or footer is only changed if you selected the Table Style Options for Header Row or Footer Row.

> **TIP: WHAT HAPPENED TO THE TABLE STYLE OPTIONS?**
> The results of including the Table Style Options may not be evident if you use the Light or Clear table style.

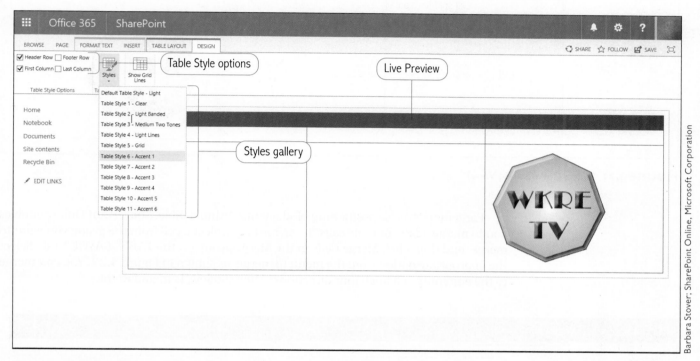

**FIGURE 3.20** Use Table Styles (Classic View)

To further format a table, you can change the size of the table, a row, or a column using the options in the Width & Height group on the TABLE LAYOUT tab. The table width is represented as a percentage, but you can also type the width in pixels, such as 700 px for a table to fit the width of the page. Likewise, you can set the height of the table using percentages and pixels. The number of paragraphs in a table also affects the height of the table. The column width or row height is adjusted by clicking in a cell, and then making the adjustment in the Column Width or Row Height box in the Width & Height group.

Web designers commonly choose to split or merge cells to position elements within a table. Theoretically, you can split a cell into as many distinct cells as needed. Likewise, you can merge as many distinct cells as needed into one merged cell.

To split a cell, click anywhere inside it, and click Split Cells in the Merge group on the TABLE LAYOUT tab. Select whether you want to split the cell into columns, with Split

Horizontal, or rows, with Split Vertical, as shown in Figure 3.21. Repeat the process to create additional splits in the cell.

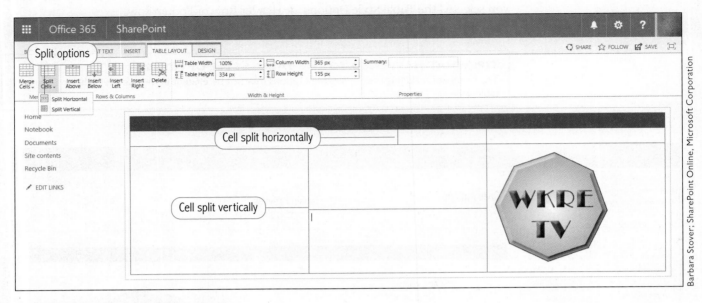

**FIGURE 3.21** Split a Cell (Classic View)

For a more precise positioning of elements within a table, SharePoint Online enables you to merge adjacent table cells. To merge cells, select a cell from the group you want to merge, and then click Merge Cells in the Merge group on the TABLE LAYOUT tab. Select the appropriate option from the menu to merge, as shown in Figure 3.22. You can merge to the adjoining cell in all four directions: Above, Below, Left, and Right.

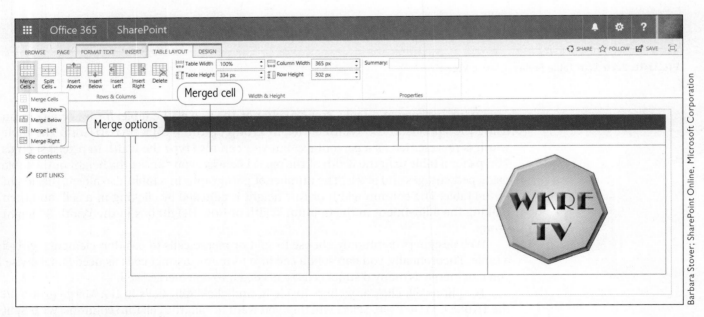

**FIGURE 3.22** Merge Cells (Classic View)

Nested tables are used by Web designers to further refine the position of elements within a webpage. Theoretically, you can insert a nested table in any cell of a table, but in reality, you should not add more than one or two nested tables. To insert a nested table, first position the insertion point in the desired cell location, and follow the regular procedure for creating a table, using the INSERT tab. You can use the same table features on a nested table to format it, as shown in Figure 3.23.

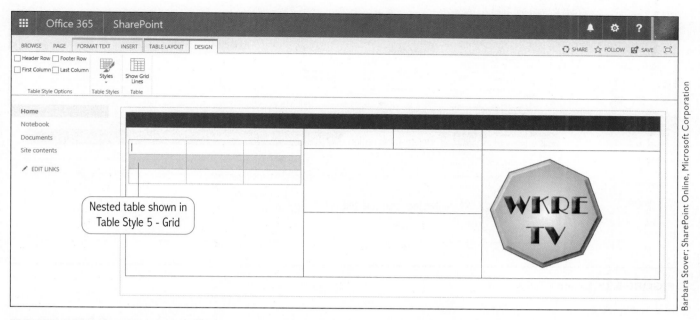

**FIGURE 3.23** Nested Table (Classic View)

By selecting a table, you can apply formatting to the entire table at one time. Select a whole table by clicking in the table, and on the FORMAT TEXT tab, clicking Select in the Markup group. Red dotted lines surround the table or portion of the table as you move the pointer over the menu options. Figure 3.24 shows how a nested table looks when selected. Select a cell in a nested table to apply formatting to just that table.

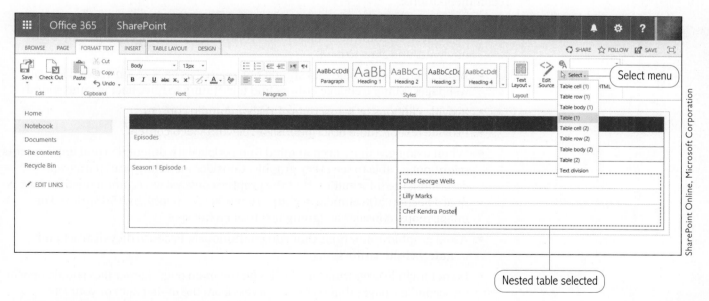

**FIGURE 3.24** Select a Table (Classic View)

---

**TIP: DRAGGING A TABLE**

After a table is selected, point to the outside left border to display a four-pointed arrow, and then drag it anywhere you want it on the webpage.

---

If you want to delete a table, click inside the table, click Delete in the Row & Columns group on the TABLE LAYOUT tab, and then click Delete Table. The nested table is being deleted in Figure 3.25.

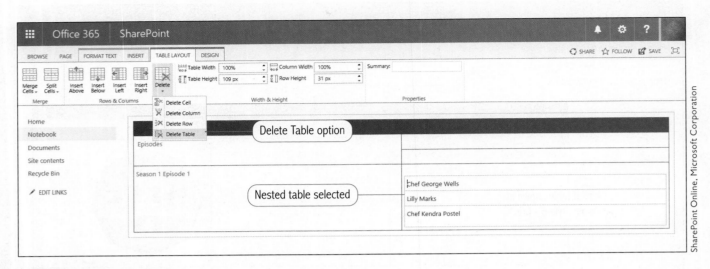

**FIGURE 3.25** Delete a Table

# Working with Asset and Picture Libraries

SharePoint empowers Web designers to increase the attractiveness of their websites by using graphics and multimedia elements. Web designers need to balance the demanding requirements of developing highly technical, usable, accessible, and attractive webpages. (Appendix A includes the top 10 do's and don'ts of Web design, along with references to a few great websites that synthesize these tips.) When combining these elements, Web designers follow a set of Web style guidelines including, but not limited to, the following recommendations:

- Use graphic, audio, and video files only when they support your webpage's message. Overusing such files makes your webpages cumbersome, difficult to navigate, and slow to load.

- As a general rule, audio files should not be used as background sound for your webpages. Many webpage visitors find it irritating to have background sound.

- Provide captions or transcripts of relevant audio content.

- Provide text or audio descriptions for relevant video content.

- When using graphics, keep in mind that people with different visual impairments might not be able to see every graphic. Consider including brief paragraphs describing the information that the graphic conveys, as recommended by Access Board Section 508 standards (http://www.access-board.gov/508.htm). For image maps, consider assigning text to each hot spot.

- Avoid graphic animations that run continuously, because they distract and irritate website visitors.

- Do not include large multimedia files on the main page. Larger files should appear on secondary pages that users can access from the main pages of your site.

- Give users a clear idea about the content of multimedia files before they begin to download them. Include descriptive information about the multimedia files on the main page, with previews such as still shots from the video. List the run time for media, and the file size for downloadable materials.

- Clearly explain the software requirements for accessing the multimedia files, such as media players needed, and provide a download link to the player software.

- Store audio and video files on a streaming media server, which is a server that ensures high quality when delivering audio and video files via the Internet. Such servers enable users to quickly load and play these files in a browser.

In SharePoint Online, multimedia assets are stored in libraries. You can upload the multimedia assets prior to inserting them, or they will automatically be uploaded as you complete the insert process. You can insert media assets from your computer, a URL address, or from a SharePoint library.

Media assets include pictures, audio, and video, in the form of files that are stored as site assets on SharePoint. The advantages of storing these files in an asset library are numerous; files can be tagged, organized, and shared across the organization. As you upload media files to the asset library, you can specify keywords and metadata to describe the file. Common metadata types include content type, name, title, comments, author, date picture was taken, and copyright information. Metadata enables you to search for and find files in SharePoint.

You can create a site asset library by adding the Asset Library app to your site. This app enables you to upload, tag, and organize the files you will use in SharePoint. Click the Settings icon, and click Site contents on the menu. Click New, and App. Select the Asset Library app, type a name for the library, and then click Create, as shown in Figure 3.26. You can have multiple asset libraries with different names on a site, which enables you to place specific types of media in specific libraries. For instance, a Picture Asset Library might contain only photographs, whereas a Video Asset Library might hold only video.

**FIGURE 3.26** Add an Asset Library App (Classic View)

Files are added to the library by clicking new item or dragging files from File Explorer to the SharePoint Online library. To change the properties of a previously uploaded media file, point to the tile that represents the media, click the More Options icon, click the More Options icon on the menu, and select Properties to open a dialog box where you can update the metadata by adding keywords, comments, the author's name, the date and time the photograph was taken, copyright information as shown in Figure 3.27.

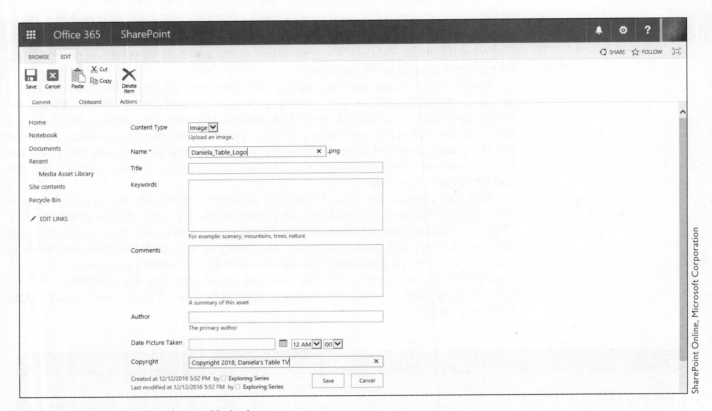

**FIGURE 3.27** Update Metadata on Media Asset

## Insert Pictures on a Webpage

 Pictures you select to display on your webpage should be in a file format that is supported by most browsers. Images affect the content, style, and online performance of your webpage. When choosing images that you want to add to a webpage, never forget that each image you add increases the amount of time required for the webpage to display on your visitors' browsers. Common formats for webpage images include GIF, JPEG, and PNG.

- **GIF (Graphics Interchange Format)** GIF files are most often used for drawn graphics and are the preferred standard for line art and limited-color graphics. GIFs are often used for animated images. You can create animated GIFs by combining several images and displaying them one after another in rapid succession. You can create these animations using most graphic applications, including many of the graphic and animation programs that can be downloaded from the Internet for free. GIFs support transparent colors. There are some drawbacks to using GIFs. They can display only 256 colors and tend to have large file sizes. The large file size can increase the time required to display GIFs in a browser.

- **JPEG (Joint Photographic Experts Group)** JPEGs (also known as JPGs) can display all 16.7 million colors that are available, and JPEG is the format most often used for photographs. JPEGs use a lossy image compression algorithm. Although increasing the degree of compression can considerably reduce the file size, it often reduces the quality of the image. Another drawback of JPEGs is that they do not support animation or transparent colors.

- **PNG (Portable Network Graphics)** PNG is a popular format that might eventually replace the GIF file format. PNGs can be used for animated graphics.

They support transparent colors, and can display all 16.7 million colors available. PNG is a newer file format, and unfortunately, some older browsers do not support the format, which causes some compatibility problems.

*Interlacing* is a technology used for displaying images in stages. This process randomly displays lines of the image as it builds it on the page. For example, every third line of the image is displayed, then every fifth line, followed by every sixth line, and so on until the whole image is displayed. This technology can be used with GIF, JPEG, and PNG files on the Internet, which enables users (especially those with a slow connection) to get a general idea of what the image is going to look like before it is fully displayed.

*Adobe Flash* (or simply Flash) is used for displaying multimedia content, usually for animated graphics. Adobe Flash is a popular application used to create Flash-animated graphics. To view a Flash-animated graphic, the user needs the Flash player, which can be downloaded free from the Adobe website (www.adobe.com). SharePoint supports Flash files.

You have the option of uploading pictures to a SharePoint Online asset library prior to placing them on a webpage or uploading them as you place them on the webpage. To add a photograph from an asset library to a webpage in Edit mode, click the INSERT tab, click Picture in the Media group, and then select From SharePoint. Navigate to the asset library that contains the picture, select the picture, and then click Insert, as shown in Figure 3.28. You can sort and filter large lists of graphics using the options for Content Type, Name, Modified, Modified By, and Length.

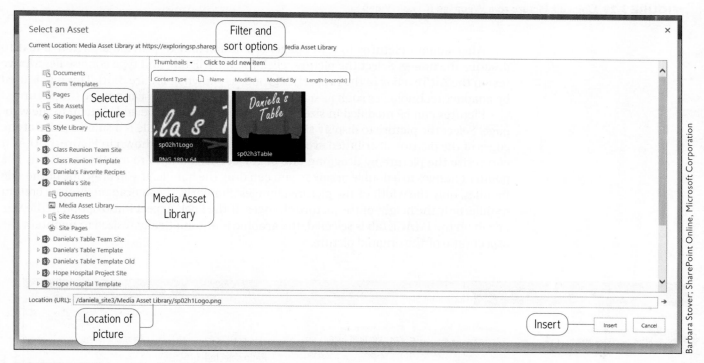

**FIGURE 3.28** Select a Picture from an Asset Library

Barbara Stover; SharePoint Online, Microsoft Corporation

To upload a picture from your local computer, click Picture in the Media group on the INSERT tab, and select From Computer. Browse to the location of the picture, select it, and then click Open. Select the Destination Library, as shown in Figure 3.29, and click OK. After successfully uploading the document, SharePoint Online displays a form where you can update the properties and metadata for the file.

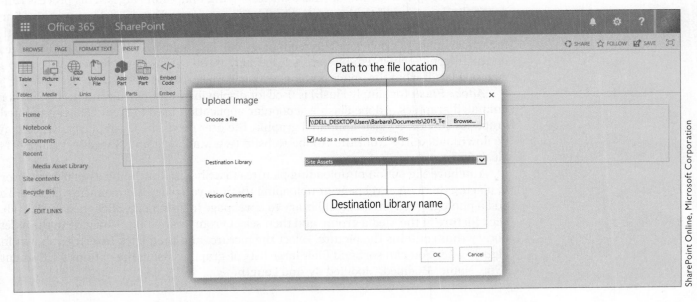

**FIGURE 3.29** Upload a Picture to a Webpage (Classic View)

After adding pictures to a webpage, it is important to provide alternative text to describe the image. Select the picture, click the IMAGE tab, and type concise descriptive text in the Alt Text box in the Properties group, as shown in Figure 3.30. This text is used by adaptive technologies such as screen readers, when the user cannot see the picture.

Pictures can be modified in size and position once you have added them to the webpage. Select the picture to display sizing handles. A sizing handle is a small square at the edges of the picture, distributed evenly around the picture, as shown in Figure 3.30. You can resize the picture by dragging one of the corner handles to another position. The pointer changes to a double arrow so you can drag the handle. If you drag one of the side handles, only the width of the picture changes. Similarly, if you drag on a top or bottom handle, only the height of the picture changes. If the Lock Aspect Ratio option in the Size group on the IMAGE tab is selected, the graphic is automatically resized to maintain the aspect ratio of the original picture.

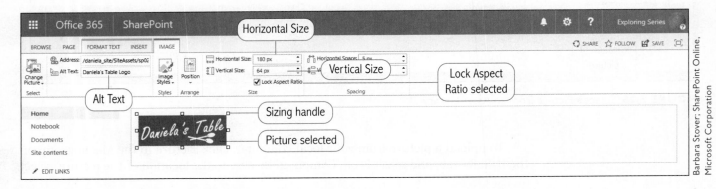

**FIGURE 3.30** Resize a Picture (Classic View)

You can also resize a picture using the Horizontal Size and Vertical Size commands (refer to Figure 3.30) in the Size group on the IMAGE tab. Again, the Lock Aspect Ratio option is important to maintain the aspect ratio of the picture, so select it before you begin to change the sizes.

You can adjust the position of an image in a page layout by floating the image to the right or left side of the content, or you can set the inline wrapping of the text to the top, middle, or bottom, as described in Table 3.2. Select the picture, and then click Position in the Arrange group on the IMAGE tab. Select the appropriate position. Figure 3.31 shows the words *Guest Chefs* wrapped inline to the middle of the image.

| TABLE 3.2 | Positioning an Image | |
|---|---|---|
| Setting | | Position |
| Float | Right | Moves image to far right side of page, with text to the left |
| | Left | Moves image to far left side of page, with text to the right |
| Inline | Top | Wraps text to a position even with the top of the image |
| | Middle | Wraps text to a position halfway between the top and bottom of the image |
| | Bottom | Wraps text to a position even with the bottom of the image |

Pearson Education, Inc.

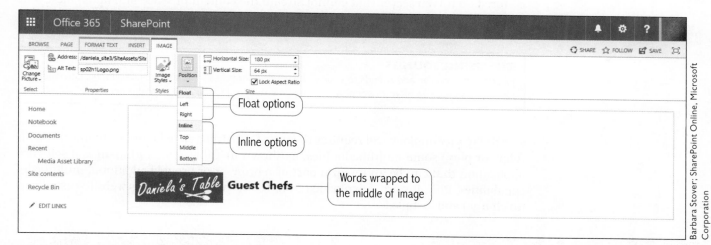

**FIGURE 3.31** Position a Picture (Classic View)

Barbara Stover; SharePoint Online, Microsoft Corporation

Image Styles, available on the IMAGE tab, enable you to add borders ranging from a thin line border to a dark border. Select the picture, click the IMAGE tab, and then click Image Styles to select the border you want, as shown in Figure 3.32.

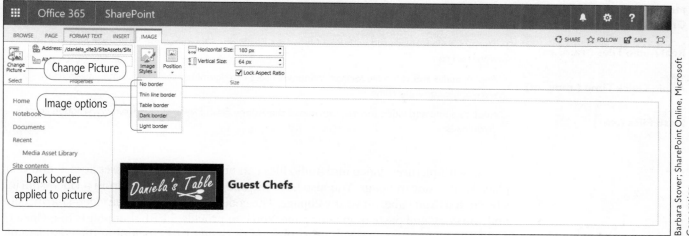

**FIGURE 3.32** Add an Image Style (Classic View)

Barbara Stover; SharePoint Online, Microsoft Corporation

If at a later time you decide to replace the picture with another, you can use the Change Picture command on the IMAGE tab. Select the picture, and click Change Picture (refer to Figure 3.32). Select the new picture from your computer, an address, or a SharePoint asset library. The newly inserted picture will retain the settings for Image Style and Position.

> **TIP: UNDO SETTINGS**
> You can use Undo on the FORMAT TEXT tab to undo picture settings.

## Insert Video and Audio on a Webpage

Using sound and video is another way Web designers enhance their webpages. If you choose to add audio and video elements to your websites, you can make the multimedia available in two formats. You can incorporate sound and video files that can be downloaded and played, or create streaming audio and video files that enable users to hear and view these files while they are downloading. A streaming video file is sent in compressed form to the browser and displayed as a sequence of images as it arrives. If your webpage is stored on a Web server that cannot stream the content of video and audio files, your visitors must completely download them before they can see or listen to them.

> **TIP: USING SOUNDS**
> Just because you can add sounds to your webpage does not mean you should. Like graphic files, audio files increase the size of your webpage and the time required to load the page in a browser.

Today's technology still requires the use of programs called plug-ins to interact with (view or play) some multimedia files, as shown in Table 3.3. A **_plug-in_** is a software application that can be an integral part of a browser or provide additional multimedia capabilities. Plug-ins are downloaded from the software developer's website (usually at no charge) and installed.

**TABLE 3.3   Audio and Video File Types Supported by SharePoint**

| File Type | Description |
|---|---|
| **Windows Video Files (.avi)** | The standard audio and video file format for Microsoft Windows |
| **Windows Media Files (.wmv, .wma, .asf)** | The file formats supported by Windows Media Player. Download the Windows Media Player plug-in from http://windows.microsoft.com/en-us/windows/windows-media-player |
| **Motion Picture Experts Group (.mpg, .mpeg)** | The audio and video format used with Windows Media Player and Real Networks RealPlayer. Download the Windows Media player, or the RealPlayer plug-in from www.real.com |
| **Real Audio Files (.ram, .ra)** | The audio file format used with Real Networks RealPlayer. Download the RealPlayer plug-in from www.real.com |
| **Apple Quick Time (.mov, .qt)** | Apple's audio and video file format. Windows users can download the QuickTime plug-in from www.apple.com/quicktime |
| **Flash Files (.swf)** | Adobe's audio and video format. Download the Adobe Flash Player plug-in from www.adobe.com/downloads |

As with pictures, video and audio files can be uploaded to an asset library and then placed onto your webpage. You also have the option to embed code from a video-sharing site, such as YouTube, on your webpage. The code is generated on the video-sharing site, and you copy and paste it on your page. You can provide a URL that points to a video or audio file on another site. You must provide the exact URL, including the complete file name, in order for the file to play.

Video and audio media appear on your webpage as a Media Web Part, which provides the controls for playing the media. You have the option to change the title of the Media Web Part using the Properties group on the MEDIA tab, as shown in Figure 3.33. You can also select to start the media automatically and loop it until stopped using the Properties group. The style of media player can be changed from a Dark style to a Light style using the Styles command in the Player Styles group. The size of the media player is changed using the Size group on the MEDIA tab. You can also change the background picture of the media player to something that corresponds to your site branding. Click Change Image in the Preview group of the MEDIA tab, navigate to the location of the picture, and then select the one you want to use.

**FIGURE 3.33** Insert Video or Audio on Webpage (Classic View)

In addition to adding the media files to a webpage using the Media Web Part, you can create a hyperlink to the audio or video file that a user clicks to display the media. This media will play on the media player installed on the user's computer, rather than from within the webpage. To insert a link to a media file, click the INSERT tab, click Link in the Links group, and then select the source, either From SharePoint or From Address. Select the file for which you want to provide a link or type the URL. The link displays a file name (refer to Figure 3.33), so be sure to change the Description to something that provides details about the content of the file using the Properties on the LINK tab. You might also select the Display Icon option to place an icon that indicates the type of file it is next to the file name.

For the past few years, the technology of video streaming has developed and improved. Powerful companies, such as Microsoft and Real Media, are investing in research dedicated to improving the performance standards for web-based video. The popularity of Web-based video is also driven by the reduction in the prices of digital video cameras and the popularity of smartphones, which enables more people and businesses to create their own video clips and post them on the Web. However, the size of video files is still rather large and the quality of delivery is not always the best.

> **TIP: LIVE BROADCAST**
> Streaming video is usually sent from preexisting video files. However, it can be distributed as part of a live broadcast in which the video signal is converted into a compressed digital signal and transmitted from a special Web server that can multicast (send the same file to multiple users at the same time).

**Quick Concept**

1. As you create webpages on your site, what is a general goal you should always strive to achieve? *p. 148*

2. Describe an example of how an absolute URL is used, and how a relative URL is used. *p. 155*

3. Describe the considerations you should make in deciding the type of list format to apply to a list. *p. 159*

# Hands-On Exercises

## 1 Tools to Customize a Webpage

As the Web designer in the Daniela's Table project, you make many decisions, including how to format and style pages within the website. You will experiment with a SharePoint Online Wiki page (all pages in SharePoint Online are Wiki pages) to develop the general template that will be used for the recipe pages in the site.

### STEP 1 ▶▶ ADD AND FORMAT TEXT

You will add text and format it on a newly created page in a new site. Refer to Figure 3.34 as you complete Step 1.

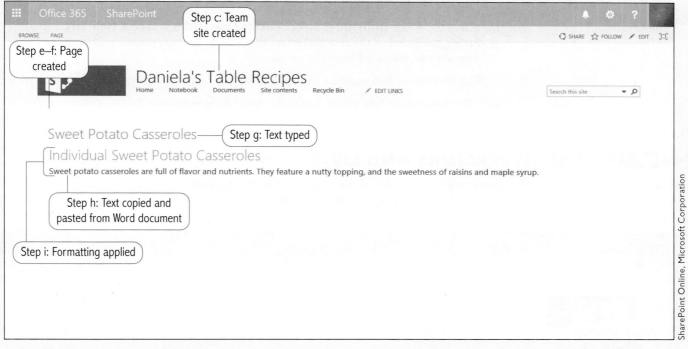

**FIGURE 3.34** Site with Formatted Text

SharePoint Online, Microsoft Corporation

**a.** Open **Internet Explorer** (not Microsoft Edge) and navigate to your Office 365 site.

**b.** Open SharePoint. Click the **Team Site tile**. Click **Site Contents** on the Quick Launch.

The default apps tiles are displayed.

**c.** Click **Return to classic SharePoint** at the bottom of the Quick Launch. Scroll down the page, and click **new subsite**. Type **Daniela's Table Recipes** in the Title box. Type **This site contains the recipes for Daniela's Table** in the Description box. Type **daniela_recipes** in the URL name box. Confirm that **English** is the selected language and that the **Team Site** template is selected. Accept the default values for the User Permissions and Navigation settings. Click **Create**.

You are creating a subsite so you can work out your design before showing it to the team members.

**d.** Click the **Settings icon**, select **Site settings**, and then click **Change the look** in the Look and Feel section of the Site Settings page. Scroll down and select **Breeze** for the theme. Click **REMOVE** under the picture in the left pane to remove the background picture, and click **OK**. Click the **Site layout arrow** and select **Oslo**. Click **Try it out**, and click **Yes, keep it**.

**e.** Click **Site contents** on the top Quick Launch, and click the **Site Pages tile**.

You will work on a new Wiki page.

**f.** Click **New** on the Site Pages page. Type **Sweet Potato Casseroles** in the New page name box. Click **Create**.

The blank page opens with a content frame displayed.

**g.** Type **Individual Sweet Potato Casseroles** in the content frame and press **Enter**.

**h.** Open the Word document file *sp03h1SweetRecipe* from the student data files in Word. Select the **second paragraph**, beginning with *Sweet potato* and ending with *maple syrup*. Click **Copy** in the Clipboard group. Return to the Recipes page in SharePoint, and click below the title in the content frame. Click the **Paste arrow**, and select **Paste Clean**. Click **Allow access** if a dialog box opens with this option.

You used text from a file to save time and increase accuracy.

**i.** Select the words **Individual Sweet Potato Casseroles** and click **Heading 1** in the Styles group. Select the rest of the text that you copied and pasted, and click the **Font size arrow**. Select **13** from the menu.

The text is now formatted in 13 pt rather than 13 px font.

**j.** Click **Save** in the Edit group. Leave the Word document open for steps later in the exercise.

---

**STEP 2** ⟩⟩ **USE HYPERLINKS AND LISTS**

Knowing that the site users will want to explore other sites about cooking, you add a hyperlink to an absolute URL. You also will arrange the links into a bulleted list. Refer to Figure 3.35 as you complete Step 2.

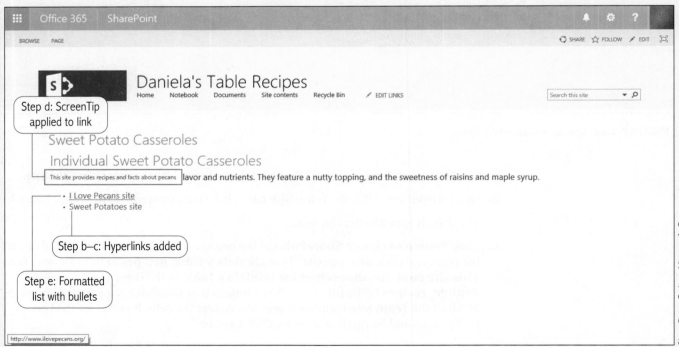

**FIGURE 3.35** Links and Bulleted List

a. Click the **PAGE tab**, and click **Edit** in the Edit group. In the content frame, click after the period following *maple syrup* and press **Enter**.

You will continue to work on the page you created in step 1 by inserting a hyperlink.

b. Click the **INSERT tab**, and click **Link** in the Links group. Select **From Address**. Type **I Love Pecans site** in the Text to display box. Type **http://www.ilovepecans.org** in the Address box. Click **Try link** to confirm the site loads. Close the site's tab in the browser window. Click **OK** in the Insert Hyperlink dialog box. Press **Enter**.

c. Create a link to the Sweet Potato site **http://www.sweetpotatoes.com** with the text **Sweet Potatoes site**, using the skills learned in step b.

d. Click within the first hyperlink, and ensure the LINK tab is displayed. Select **Open in new tab** in the Behavior group. Type **This site provides recipes and facts about pecans** in the Description box in the Properties group.

e. Repeat step d with the second hyperlink. Type **This site provides information about sweet potatoes** in the Description box.

You set the hyperlinks to open in a new tab so that the user will be able to return easily to the Recipes page.

f. Select both hyperlinks, and click the **FORMAT TEXT tab**. Click **Bullets** in the Paragraph group.

Bullets help to organize the links and make them stand out.

g. Click **Save** in the Edit group. Point to each link and review the ScreenTip text. Click each link to ensure the site opens correctly. Close the tab on the browser for the link after reviewing the site.

> **TROUBLESHOOTING:** If a link does not open on a new tab, click the PAGE tab, click Edit, click the link on the page, and then correct the settings on the LINK tab.

## STEP 3 ›› WORK WITH A TABLE

Tables enable you to organize many elements on the page. You will use a table to format the recipe portion of the page. Refer to Figure 3.36 as you complete Step 3.

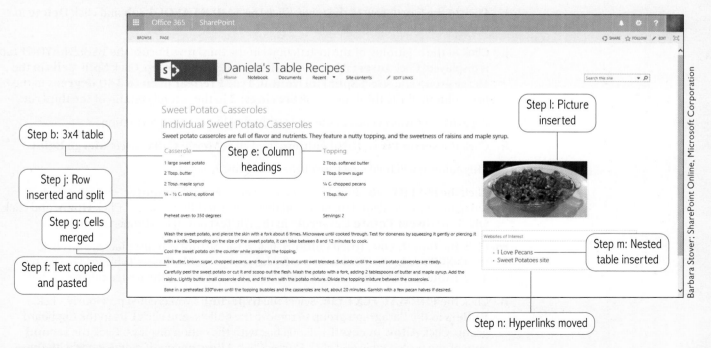

**FIGURE 3.36** Table Inserted on Page

**a.** Click the **PAGE tab**, and click **Edit**. Place the insertion point after the Sweet Potatoes site link.

**b.** Click the **INSERT tab**, and click **Table** in the Tables group. Use the Insert Table grid to create a **3×4 Table**.

The table appears on the page. You want to reduce the impact of the borders, so you will select a different table style.

**c.** Click the **DESIGN tab**, and click **Styles**. Click **Table Style 1 - Clear**.

The table appears to have disappeared, so you will turn on the grid lines to assist you as you add information to the table.

**d.** Click **Show Grid Lines** in the Table group.

**e.** Type **Casserole** in the first row, first column of the table. Press **Tab** and type **Topping** in the first row, second column of the table. Select both column headings, and click the **FORMAT TEXT tab**. Click **Heading 2** in the Styles group.

The column headings are now attractively placed and formatted.

**f.** Open the Word document *sp03h1SweetRecipe* by clicking the Word icon on the taskbar. Select the four ingredients in the left column, and click **Copy** in the Clipboard group. Paste the ingredients into the **second row**, **second column** of the table on the SharePoint page. Click **Allow access** if a dialog box displays with the option. Repeat this step to copy the ingredients in the right column into the **second row**, **first column** of the table.

**g.** Click in the **third row, first column**. Click the **TABLE LAYOUT tab** and click **Merge Cells** in the Merge group. Select **Merge Right**.

The first and second columns of the third row are merged.

**h.** Display the Word window that contains the file *sp03h1SweetRecipe* by clicking the Word icon on the taskbar. Select the instructions for the recipe, and copy and paste them into the merged cell you just created. Click **Allow access** if a dialog box displays with this option. Close the Word document.

The recipe is organized under the two lists of ingredients. You realize there is an extra row in the table, so you will delete it.

**i.** Click in the fourth row of the table. Click the **TABLE LAYOUT tab** and click **Delete** in the Rows & Columns group. Click **Delete Row**.

**j.** Click at the beginning of the instructions in the third row. Ensure the TABLE LAYOUT tab is displayed. Click **Insert Above** in the Rows & Columns group. Click **Split Cells** in the Merge group and select **Split Horizontal**. Type **Preheat oven to 350 degrees** in the first column of the third row. Type **Servings: 2** in the second column of the third row.

An extra row was needed in the table to display important information.

**k.** Click the **second row, third column**, and click **Merge Cells**. Select **Merge Below**.

This column will hold a picture of the baked casserole.

**l.** Click the **INSERT tab**, and click **Picture**. Select **From Computer**, click **Browse**, navigate to the student data files, and then select *sp03h1Casserole*. Click **Open**, and click **OK**. Type **Sweet Potato Casserole** in the Alt Text box in the Properties group.

**m.** Click the **fourth row, third column**, below the picture you just placed, and click the **INSERT tab**. Click **Table** in the Tables group. Use the Insert Table grid to create a **1×2 Table**. Type **Websites of Interest** in the first row of the nested table.

**n.** Click the **FORMAT TEXT tab**. Select the **hyperlinks** you created previously, click **Bullets** in the Paragraph group to remove the bullets, and click **Cut** in the Clipboard group. Click **Allow access** if a dialog box with the option displays. Click the **second row** of the nested table and click **Paste**. Click **Allow access** if a dialog box with the option displays. Click **Bullets** in the Paragraph group to add the bullets back to the hyperlink list. Delete any extra lines where you cut the text or in the table.

**o.** Click **Save**.

## STEP 4 ›› INSERT A MEDIA ASSET

Daniela records short audio tips to include with each recipe. You will add an Asset Library app to store the media, and add the media asset to the page. Refer to Figure 3.37 as you complete Step 4.

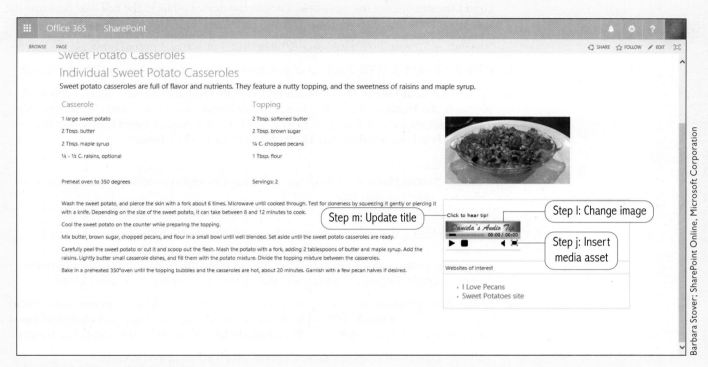

**FIGURE 3.37** Insert Media Asset

**a.** Click **Site contents** on the top Quick Launch, click **add an app**.

> **TROUBLESHOOTING:** If you cannot open the Site contents page, you may have omitted the save action in the last step. Save the page, and then access Site contents.

**b.** Navigate to the Asset Library tile (you may have to use the navigation at the bottom of the page). Click the **Asset Library tile**, and type **Audio Asset Library**. Click **Create**.

The new library app appears in the Site contents list. You will add a media asset to the library.

**c.** Create another Asset Library, named **Graphic Asset Library**, using steps a and b.

This library will hold graphic elements such as logos.

**d.** Click the **Audio Asset Library tile**, and click **Upload**. Click **Browse**, navigate to the student data files, and then select *sp03h1AudioTip*. Click **Open**, and click **OK**.

A properties box opens enabling you to apply a Title, Keywords, Comments, and Author properties.

**e.** Type **Toasted Pecan Tip** as the Title. Type **pecans, sweet potato casserole** for Keywords. Click **Save**.

**f.** Click **Site contents** on the top Quick Launch, and click the **Graphic Asset Library tile**. Upload the *sp03h1TipGraphic* file to the Graphic Asset Library, using step d as an example. Type the Title **Tip Graphic** and the Keywords **tip graphic, Daniela's Audio Tip**. Click **Save**.

With the audio file and graphic file uploaded, you are ready to add them to the page.

**g.** Click **Site contents** on the top Quick Launch, and click the **Site Pages tile**. Click the **Sweet Potato Casseroles link** to open the page. Click the **PAGE tab**, and click **Edit**.

**h.** Click in the table where the recipe is located. Click the **DESIGN tab**, and click **Show Grid Lines** to display the table grid. Click in the nested table, in the cell that contains the text Websites of Interest.

You will add the audio file just above the Websites of Interest nested table.

**i.** Click the **TABLE LAYOUT tab**, and click **Insert Above** in the Rows & Columns group.

**j.** Click in the **first row** of the nested table. Click the **INSERT tab**, and click **Video and Audio** in the Media group. Select **From SharePoint**. Scroll down and click **Daniela's Table Recipes** in the left pane to expand the list. Click **Audio Asset Library** in the left pane, and click **Toasted Pecan Tip** in the right pane. Click **Insert**.

> **TROUBLESHOOTING:** If a message saying Microsoft Silverlight should be installed, complete the installation and then complete step j.

**k.** Select the Media Web Part by clicking the words **Media Web Part** above the graphic of the Media Web Part you just inserted into the table. Ensure **Lock Aspect Ratio** in the Size group on the MEDIA tab is selected. Type **180** in the Horizontal Size box in the Size group and press **Enter**. Click **Styles** in the Player Styles group, and select **Light**.

**l.** Click **Change Image** in the Preview group on the MEDIA tab. Select **From SharePoint**. Scroll to and select **Daniela's Table Recipes** in the left pane, and select **Graphic Asset Library** in the left pane. Click the **Tip Graphic tile** in the right pane, and click **Insert**.

You add a standard graphic that will appear on all audio tips on the site.

**m.** Type **Click to hear tip!** in the Title box in the Properties group to replace the words *Media Web Part*. Click the **Play arrow** on the player to listen to the audio tip. Click the **PAGE tab**, and click **Save**.

After placing media on a page, you should always review the entire media file.

**n.** Take a screen shot of the webpage and name it **sp03h1Recipe_LastFirst**. You will submit this file after the last Hands-On Exercise.

**o.** Click **SharePoint** on the top navigation bar to return to the top-level team site if you plan to continue to the next Hands-On Exercise. If not, sign out of Office 365 and close the browser window.

# Work with Web Parts and App Parts

Web Part pages are SharePoint webpages that contain one or more web parts. The default home page for a top-level team site contains Get started with your site, Newsfeed, and Documents web parts, for example. Web parts are important SharePoint components, especially when deciding how information is presented to SharePoint users. This technology enables SharePoint sites to be flexible and highly customizable. An app part is a web part that provides access to a list or library on the page.

In this section, you learn how to work with web parts and app parts. You will work with the Web Part Gallery, and add, modify, and remove web parts and app parts. You will also connect and customize web parts and app parts.

## Using Default Web Parts and App Parts

A Web Part page displays Web Part zones with blue borders in a grid pattern. Web Part zones are containers for web parts. For instance, in the Hands-On Exercise 1, you used a Web Part zone to display the audio media player. Web parts are components that can be reused. They can contain any type of web-based information, including analytical, collaborative, and database information. Web parts can be used to search and manage data in external databases and file systems. Web parts can be exported and uploaded on different sites for reuse. You can also develop custom web parts to provide functions found in other applications, enabling you to integrate your SharePoint environment with other existing systems within the organization.

SharePoint Online comes with a number of built-in web parts that are available for you to add to your pages. The built-in web parts, as well as ones you might create and upload, are organized into categories. Some web parts are specific to certain types of sites. App parts are lists and libraries, and are a category of web parts.

SharePoint Online contains numerous web parts, with just one page shown in Figure 3.38. From this page you can preview the web part, edit the properties, and sort or filter the list.

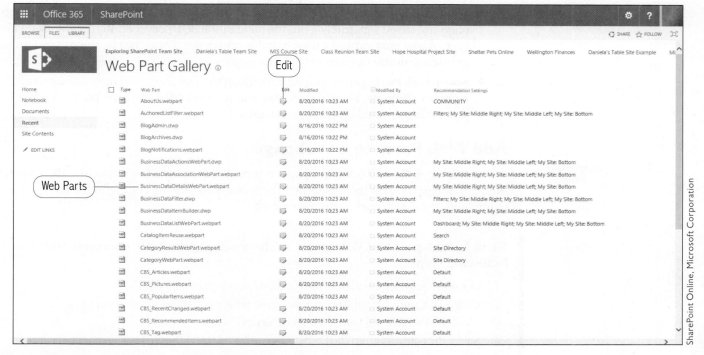

**FIGURE 3.38** Web Part Gallery (Classic View)

The **Web Part Gallery** contains all the web parts available to the top-level site and its subsites. To preview a web part and see additional information about the purpose, click the web part link. The Media Web Part you used in the previous Hands-On Exercise is shown as a preview in Figure 3.39.

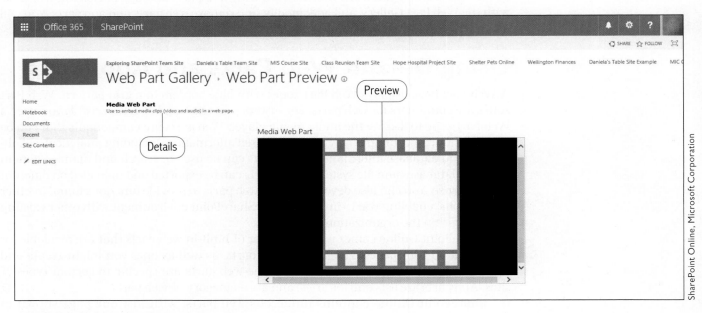

**FIGURE 3.39** Web Part Preview

Web Parts can also be classified by their specific location within a page.

- **Dynamic Web Parts** can be placed on a Wiki page in a Web Part zone. These web parts are saved separately from the page in the SQL Server content database. This type of web part contains user-editable properties. For example, the user might be able to minimize the web part on the page.

- **Static Web Parts** can be placed directly on the webpage, and they are saved as a part of the page. These web parts cannot be edited by the user, but rather the properties are fixed by the page designer.

## Add Web Parts to a Webpage

After creating a site and adding a page, you may want to further customize the page by utilizing web parts. This increases the functionality by placing coding in the background to implement the web part as the user sees it.

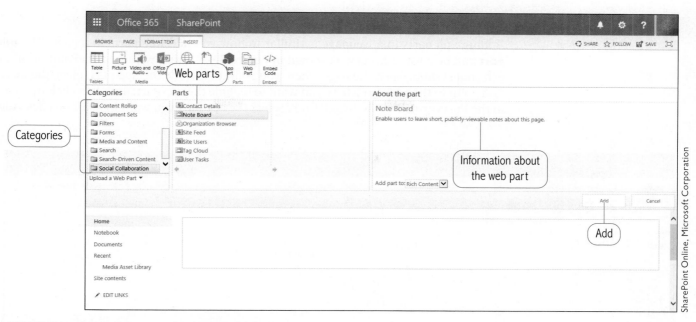

**FIGURE 3.40** Insert Web Part on Page (Classic View)

The web parts are arranged in 10 categories, with varying numbers of web parts available in each category. The About the part pane displays a description of the web part. The bottom pane displays the webpage, so you can have an idea of what you are adding to the page.

Although all pages in SharePoint Online are Wiki pages, some contain Web Part zones, and are known as Web Part pages. Web Part zones contain only web parts; thus, you cannot insert other elements such as text or an image into a Web Part zone. A border surrounds the Web Part zone, and the name of the zone appears in the top-left corner, as shown in Figure 3.41. The borders and zone name are not visible on the completed webpage.

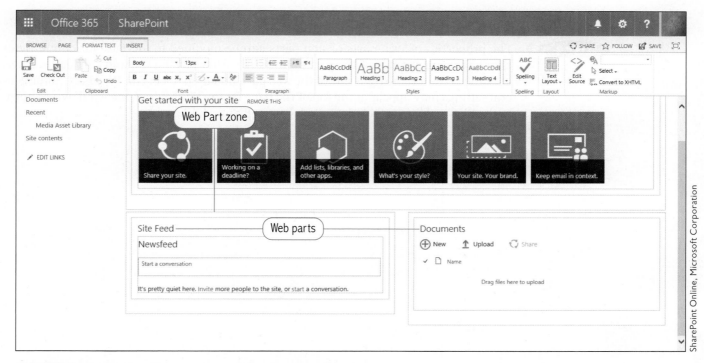

**FIGURE 3.41** Web Part Zones and Web Parts (Classic View)

## Add App Parts to a Webpage

Adding app parts to a webpage is similar to how you add web parts to a page. The **app part** can be a list or library, as shown in Figure 3.42, either within SharePoint or on an external system. Open the page where you want to include the app part, place the insertion point in the position where you want to include the app part, and then click App Part in the Parts group on the INSERT tab. Select the app part you want to use, and click Add.

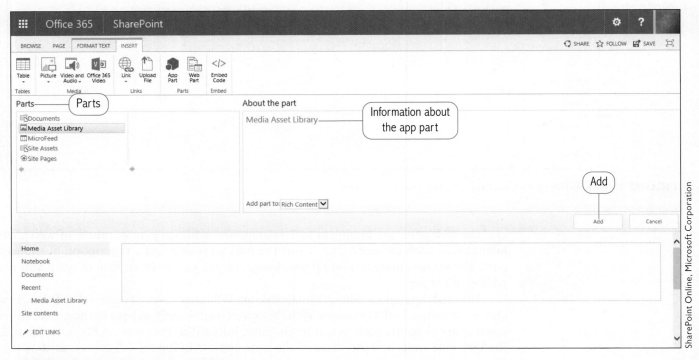

**FIGURE 3.42** Insert an App Part (Classic View)

## Modify a Web Part or App Part

**STEP 2 ▶▶** The properties of web parts or app parts can be modified to increase functionality or change the appearance of the part on the page. After placing the web part on the page, click the arrow on the right side of the web part, and then select Edit Web Part. Some general settings may appear at the top of the pane on the right side of the window, as shown in the Picture Library Slideshow Web Part in Figure 3.43.

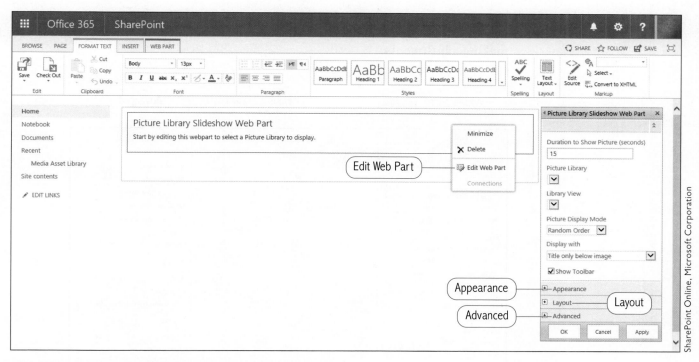

**FIGURE 3.43** Modify Web Part Properties (Classic View)

You can modify three major categories of a web part: Appearance, Layout, and Advanced. Depending on the type of web part, additional categories may display. Click the plus icon next to the category to expand the options. In the Appearance category, you can display or change the title, alter the height or width, change whether the web part appears minimized (Chrome State), and whether the title or border are displayed (Chrome Type). The Layout category enables you to hide the web part, change the direction of the text and data in the web part, and determine which zone the web part is in and its relationship to other web parts in the zone (Zone Index). The Advanced category contains settings for enabling the user to adjust the layout, the display properties of the title, the Help options, the display of icon images on the title bar and catalog, and the error messages provided to the user as he or she works on the page.

Each of the category options are displayed in Figure 3.44. Click Apply to display the web part with the properties you have selected, and click OK when you are finished making adjustments.

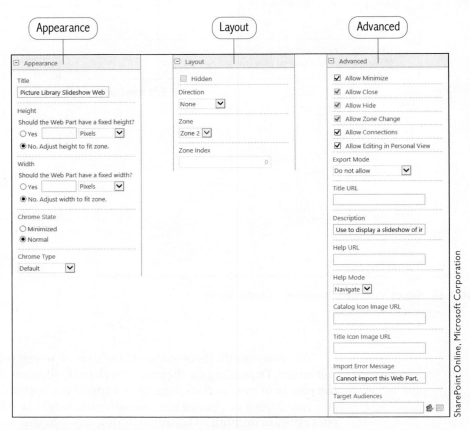

**FIGURE 3.44** Modify Options: Appearance, Layout, Advanced

The List Views pane, displayed when you edit a list web part or app part, contains the same property panels of Appearance, Layout, and Advanced, but displays AJAX Options and Miscellaneous as well. At the top of the pane, you can customize the list view of the web part by clicking Edit the current view below the selection box, as shown in Figure 3.45. This option is used to add or delete columns from the view. The Toolbar Type property controls the display of functional links on the web part. For example, the Summary Toolbar displays a link to add a new document or item below the title, whereas the No Toolbar option removes the links from the Web Part Display. Click Apply to view the changes you made on the web part, and click OK when you are satisfied with the changes.

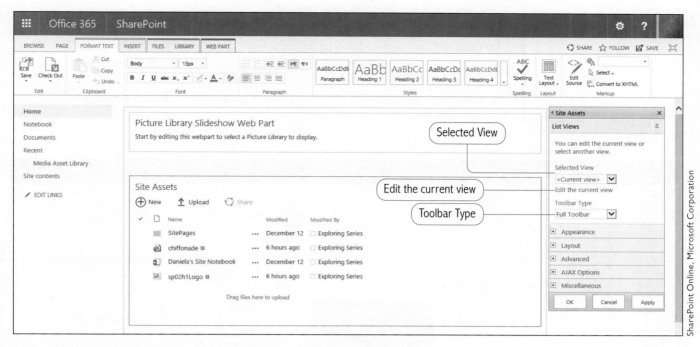

**FIGURE 3.45** Modify List View Properties (Classic View)

You might find it convenient to minimize a web part so you can display more of the page as you work on it. Click the arrow on the right side of the web part, and click Minimize. You can restore the web part to full size in the same manner, as shown in Figure 3.46. Commands on the WEB PART tab also enable you to minimize and restore web parts. If you leave the web part minimized, it will appear the same way on the page after you save it.

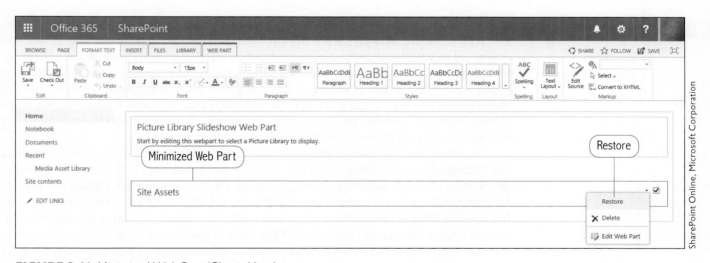

**FIGURE 3.46** Minimized Web Part (Classic View)

## Export and Upload a Web Part or App Part

**STEP 3** ⟫ Once you finish configuring a web part, including both common and unique properties, you may want to reuse the web part, with the same settings, in other sites or pages. SharePoint enables you to export and import most web parts. This means you can share the web part or app part with other people, or archive it for future use.

When you export a web part, an XML file is created. The XML file extension for exported files is .webpart or .dwp.

**To export a web part, complete the following steps:**

1. Click the arrow on the web part, and select Export, as shown in Figure 3.47.
2. Click the arrow on the Internet Explorer message bar (usually at the bottom of the window) and select Save as.
3. Navigate to the location where you want to store the file and click Save. Close the message bar.

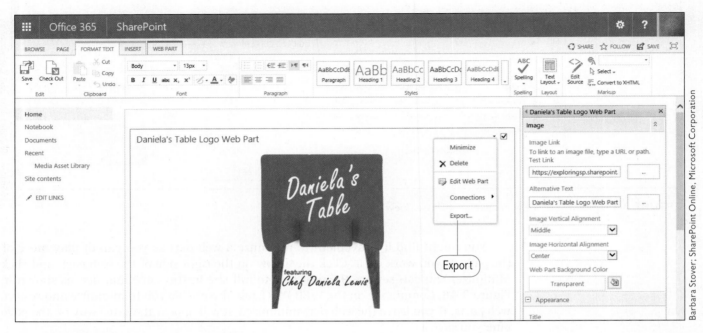

**FIGURE 3.47** Export a Web Part (Classic View)

Web parts are available from the Internet, in addition to the ones you create and download to your local computer. Some must be purchased and others are available for free. There are two ways to upload a web part. You can place the web part in the Web Part Gallery, described in the beginning of this section, or you can upload the web part as you insert it onto the page. By uploading to the Web Part Gallery, the web part is available for other people to use on site pages they edit. If you upload the web part by inserting it, you will have to reinsert it (and upload it) each time you want to use it.

To upload the web part to the Web Part Gallery, navigate to the top-level site, click the Settings icon, and then select Site settings on the menu. Click the Web Parts link in the Web Designer Galleries section. Click the FILES tab, and click Upload Document. Navigate to the web part, click Open, and then click OK. After a few moments, a dialog box opens enabling you to change the name, title, description, group, and recommendation settings, as shown in Figure 3.48. Click Save to place the web part in the gallery. You will find the web part in a new category named Miscellaneous when you want to insert the web part onto a page.

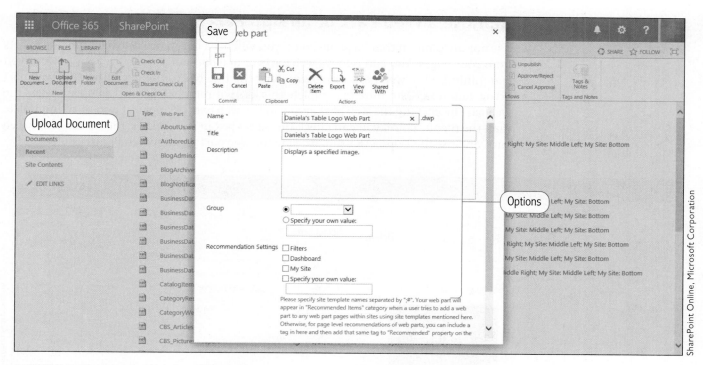

**FIGURE 3.48** Upload a Web Part (Classic View)

You also have the option to upload the web part as you insert it onto a page. Open the page you want to contain the web part for editing. Click Web Part in the Parts group on the INSERT tab. Click the Upload a Web Part arrow, and browse to the location of the web part. Select the file, and click Open. Click Upload. After a few moments, the web part will display in the Imported Web Parts category for insertion onto a page, as shown in Figure 3.49.

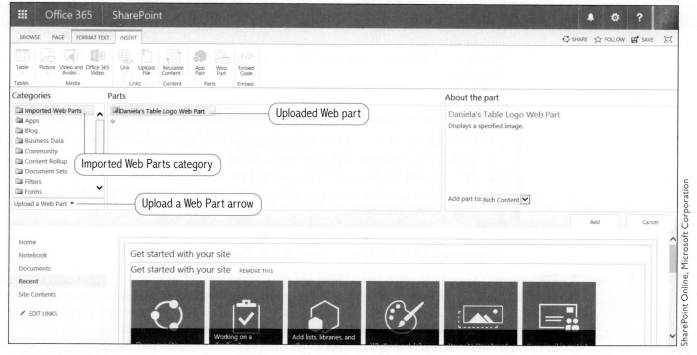

**FIGURE 3.49** Import a Web Part (Classic View)

## Remove a Web Part or an App Part

It is not uncommon that, at some point, you will need to remove web parts and app parts from your pages. You can remove web parts or app parts in one of three ways. First, you can minimize the web part, displaying only the title bar to the user. Click the web part arrow and select Minimize to complete this form of removal. Second, you can delete the web part by clicking the web part arrow in the web part or app part and selecting Delete from the menu. Third, you can check the Select box in the upper-right corner of the web part, and use the WEB PART tab to delete the web part, as shown in Figure 3.50.

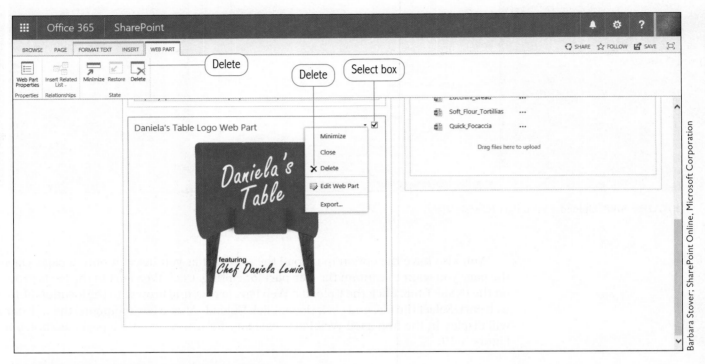

**FIGURE 3.50** Delete a Web Part (Classic View)

It is important to note that these deletion methods affect only the page, and the web part or app part is still available via the Web Part Gallery or the INSERT tab. To completely remove the web part from the site, you must delete it from the Web Part Gallery on the top-level site.

> **To delete the web part from the top-level site, complete these steps:**
>
> 1. Open the top-level site. Click the Settings icon and select Site settings from the menu.
> 2. Click Web parts in the Web Designer Galleries section.
> 3. Click the Edit icon next to the file name of the web part you want to delete.
> 4. Click Delete Item in the Actions group of the EDIT tab, and click OK in the Message from webpage dialog box.

## Connect Web Parts and App Parts

 Once you have added web parts or app parts to a page, you can connect them to create data-driven pages. For instance, you can import data using the Import Spreadsheet app in SharePoint Online, and use the INSERT tab to add the list as an app part to a page. To assist users in finding data on the list, you can connect a web part app, such as the Text Filter, that filters the list and displays information that matches the user's criterion. You can even add multiple filters to further define the list, as shown in Figure 3.51.

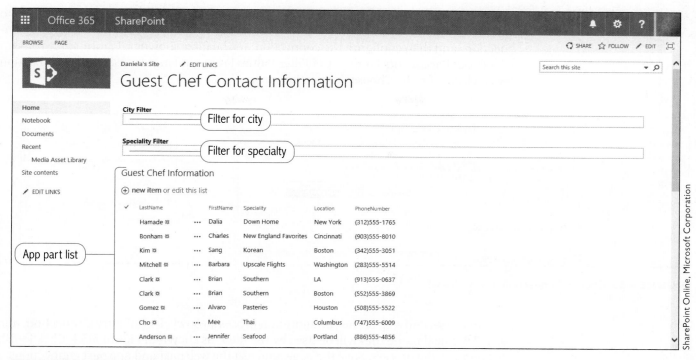

**FIGURE 3.51** Filtering of an App Part List

Businesses and organizations connect web parts and app parts to provide information to their customers and clients. Some web parts, such as the Picture Library Slideshow Web Part, require a connection with a library or list to function. Other connections can be made between other web parts and app parts. You may connect a filter web part, such as a Text Filter, and a list. For instance, a list might contain stock market symbols, with a full name and description of each company's symbol. The Text Filter Web Part can be connected to the stock market symbol field, which enables the user to look up information about the company. By connecting web parts and app parts, you can display only the information relevant to the user.

After opening the page for editing and adding the web parts or app parts you want to connect on the page, you may have to edit the properties of the web part to Allow Connections in the Advanced category in the Edit pane. Click the arrow for the web part that you want to connect and click Connections. Select the web part or app part you want to connect with, as shown in Figure 3.52.

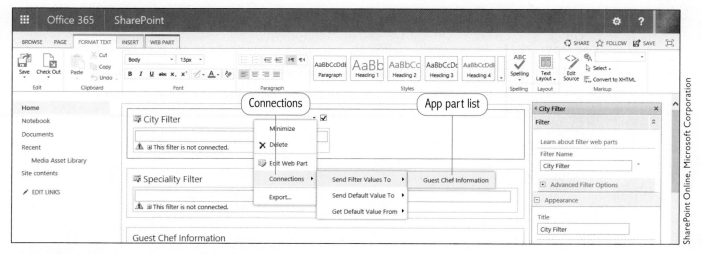

**FIGURE 3.52** Make a Connection (Classic View)

After selecting the web part or app part connection, a dialog box may display to further refine the connection parameters. In this two-step process, you choose the connection, and then configure the connection. In the filter shown in Figure 3.53, you can select Get Parameters From or Get Filter Values From, and in this case, the second option was selected for the Choose Connection step.

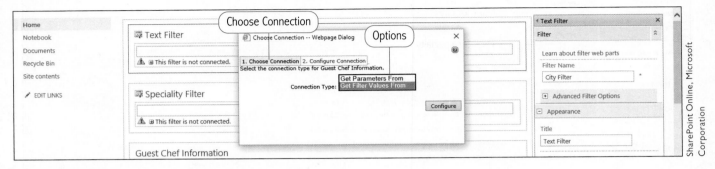

**FIGURE 3.53** Choose Connection (Classic View)

In the second step of the configuration process, you click Configure Connection, and select the field name that will be used by the filter, as shown in Figure 3.54. Click Finish to complete the process. Save the page, and test the web part and app part connections.

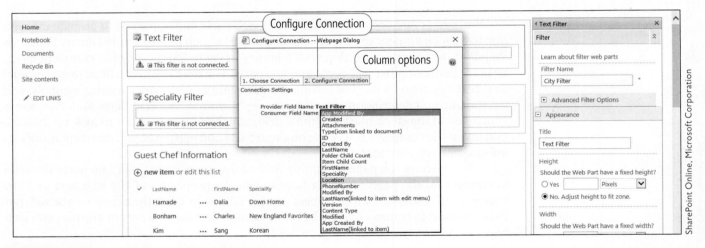

**FIGURE 3.54** Configure Connection (Classic View)

**Quick Concept**

4. Describe the differences between a web part and an app part. ***pp. 181, 184***

5. Describe the types of modifications you can make to web parts. ***p. 185***

6. What is the purpose of connecting web parts and app parts? ***p. 190***

# Hands-On Exercises

**Skills covered:** Add Web Parts • Modify a Web Part • Add App Parts • Modify an App Part • Connect Web Parts and App Parts

## 2 Work with Web Parts and App Parts

You decide to increase the functionality of the Recipes site to include web parts and app parts. You will add these elements, modify their properties, and export and upload a web part. You will also make a connection between a web part and an app part.

### STEP 1 ►► ADD A WEB PART

To prepare for using a web part, you will begin by uploading photographs to a Picture Library. You will then create a new page and add a web part to the page. Refer to Figure 3.55 as you complete Step 1.

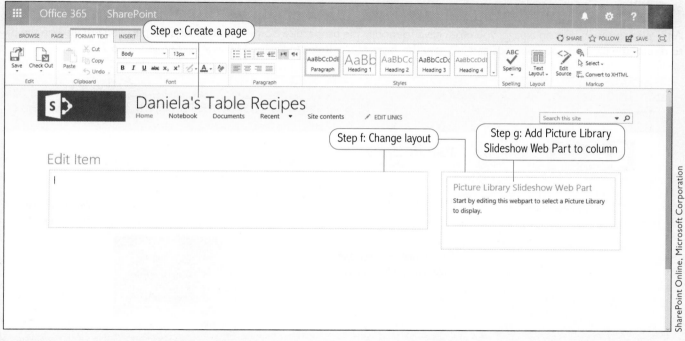

**FIGURE 3.55** Add a Web Part (Classic View)

SharePoint Online, Microsoft Corporation

a. Open **Internet Explorer** (not Microsoft Edge) and navigate to your Office 365 site (if you exited after the previous Hands-On Exercise). Click **Team Site tile**.

b. Click **Site Contents** on the Quick Launch, ensure that the classic SharePoint view is displayed, and click the subsite link to **Daniela's Table Recipes**.

You will create a library on this site to contain photographs.

c. Click **Site contents** on the top Quick Launch, and click **add an app**. Click the **Picture Library tile**, and type **Recipe Picture Library**. Click **Create**. When the tile displays, click the new **Recipe Picture Library tile**.

The Recipe Picture Library will contain pictures of the recipes.

d. Open **File Explorer** and navigate to the student data files. Arrange the windows so you can see both SharePoint Online and File Explorer. Select *sp03h2Bruschetta*, *sp03h2Casserole*, and *sp03h2Pesto*, and then drag them to the SharePoint Online **Recipe**

**Picture Library**, where it says *Drag files here to upload*. Drop the files when you see the words *Drop here* in the box. Close File Explorer and return SharePoint Online to full screen.

**e.** Click **Site contents** on the top Quick Launch, click the **Site Pages tile**, and click **New**. Type **Future Episodes** in the New page name box, and click **Create**.

You will create a new page for the web parts. The purpose of the page will be to display a preview picture of upcoming recipes, as well as provide a method of filtering an app part list.

**f.** Click **Text Layout** in the Layout group on the FORMAT TEXT tab, and select **One column with sidebar**.

There are now two-page content frames displayed. You will add a Web Part to the right-hand frame.

**g.** Click in the frame in the right-hand column, click the **INSERT tab**, and then click **Web Part** in the Parts group. Click **Media and Content** in the Categories pane. Click **Picture Library Slideshow Web Part** in the Parts pane. Click **Add**.

The Web Part is displayed on the page.

**STEP 2 ⟩⟩ MODIFY A WEB PART**

After placing a web part on a page, you often have to modify the properties. You will modify the web part you installed on the page to display the pictures you uploaded and improve the appearance. Refer to Figure 3.56 as you complete Step 2.

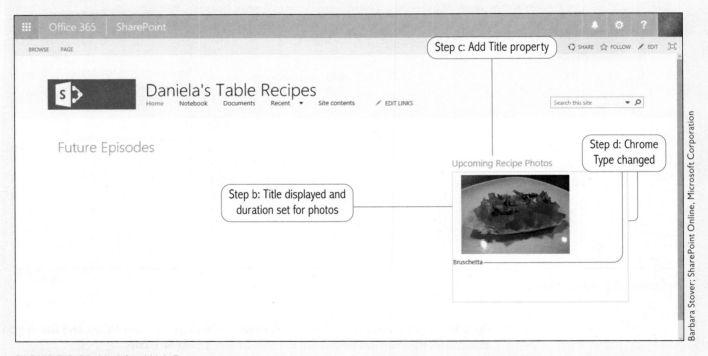

**FIGURE 3.56** Modify a Web Part

**a.** Click the title Picture Library Slideshow Web Part to select the web part, click the **arrow** to the right of the title bar of the Picture Library Slideshow Web Part, and then select **Edit Web Part**.

The Web Part Properties pane opens.

**b.** Change the Duration to Show Picture to **10**. Confirm that the **Recipe Picture Library** is selected in the Picture Library box. Confirm that **Title only below image** is selected in the Display with box. Click **Show Toolbar check box** to deselect it.

**c.** Replace the text in the Title box in the Appearance section by typing **Upcoming Recipe Photos**.

**d.** Scroll down the Edit Web Part pane, click the **Chrome Type arrow**, and then select **Title and Border**.

The Chrome Type you selected will add a border to the photographs and display the title of the photograph underneath it.

**e.** Click **OK**.

**f.** Click **Save** in the Edit group on the FORMAT TEXT tab.

The photographs will change every 10 seconds in the Web Part.

**STEP 3 ›› UPLOAD AN APP PART**

You will upload a listing of upcoming episodes as an app part and install it on the page. You will also add a Text Filter Web Part to the page. Refer to Figure 3.57 as you complete step 3.

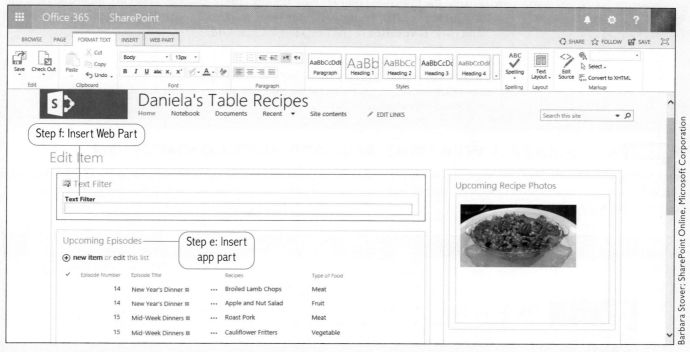

**FIGURE 3.57** Upload an App Part (Classic View)

**a.** Click **Site contents** on the top Quick Launch, and click **add an app**. Click the **Import Spreadsheet tile** (you may have to navigate to another page). Type the name **Upcoming Episodes**, and type the description **These are some of the recipes that will be featured in upcoming episodes.** Click **Browse** in the File location box, navigate to the student data files, and then select *sp03h2UpcomingEpisodes*. Click **Open**, and click **Import**.

> **TROUBLESHOOTING:** If you receive an error message as you upload the file, you should make sure your main SharePoint Online site is a trusted site in Internet Explorer, and that you are using Internet Explorer for this exercise. Click the browser Tools icon, click Internet options, and then click the Security tab. Click the Trusted Sites icon, and click Sites. Type the URL of the top-level site into the Add this website to the zone, and click Close. Click OK to close the Internet Options dialog box. Close and reopen the browser for the setting to take effect.

**b.** Click the **Range Type arrow** and select **Range of Cells**. Click **Select Range Minimize** on the right side of the Select Range box, and select all the cells with data in the spreadsheet. Click **Range Expand** on the right side of the dialog box, and click **Import**.

The list of upcoming episodes appears as a list. You will install the app part on the Upcoming Episodes page.

   **c.** Click **Site contents** on the top link bar. Click the **Site Pages tile**, and click the **Future Episodes link**.

   **d.** Click the **PAGE tab**, and click **Edit** in the Edit group. Click in the left-hand column page content frame.

   **e.** Click the **INSERT tab**, and click **App Part**. Select **Upcoming Episodes** in the Parts pane, and then click **Add**.

   **f.** Ensure the insertion point is above the Upcoming Episodes Web Part zone, and click the **INSERT tab**. Click **Web Part** in the Parts group. Click **Filters** in the Categories pane, and click **Text Filter** in the Parts pane. Click **Add**.

## STEP 4 ⟫ CREATE A WEB PART AND APP PART CONNECTION

After adding a filter web part to the page, you will make a connection between the web part and the app part you uploaded earlier. This will enable the page viewers to look for recipes that feature a kind of food, like bread or meat. Refer to Figure 3.58 as you complete step 4.

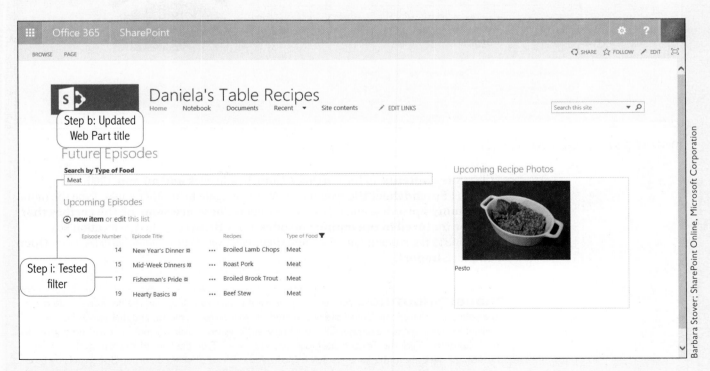

**FIGURE 3.58** Connect a Web Part and App Part

   **a.** Point to the **Text Filter Web Part title**, click the **arrow** on the title bar of the Text Filter Web Part, and then select **Edit Web Part**.

You will edit this web part before you make the connection to the app part.

**b.** Replace the text in the Filter Name box and the Title box in the Text Filter pane with **Search by Type of Food**. Click **Apply** at the bottom of the Web Part Properties pane.

The web part contains the new title. You will now connect it to the app part you installed earlier.

**c.** Point to the **Search by Type of Food Web Part title**, click the **arrow** on the title bar of the Search by Type of Food web part, and then select **Connections**.

> **TROUBLESHOOTING:** The Web Part Properties pane must be open to see Connections on the menu. If you do not see Connections, select Edit Web Part, click the arrow on the title bar again, and then select Connections.

**d.** Select **Send Filter Values To** and select **Upcoming Episodes**.

The Choose Connection Webpage Dialog box opens.

**e.** Click the **Connection Type arrow** and select **Get Filter Values From**.

**f.** Click **2. Configure Connection** and click the **Consumer Field Name arrow**. Select **Type of Food** on the menu. Click **Finish**.

**g.** Click **OK** on the Web Part Properties pane. Click **Save** in the Edit group on the FORMAT TEXT tab.

After installing the web part and app part, you will test the Text Filter.

**h.** Type **bread** in the Search by Type of Food box, and press **Enter**.

The app list is filtered to show only breads. Note that capitalization of the Type of Food is not considered in the filtering process.

**i.** Type **Meat** in the Search by Type of Food box, and press **Enter**.

You have tested two of the types, so you are confident that the connection is working correctly.

**j.** Take a screen shot of the webpage displaying the Meat search results. Name the file **sp03h2Episodes_LastFirst**.

**k.** Click in the **Search by Type of Food box**, and click the **X** on the far-right side to remove the search term. Press **Enter**.

The Upcoming Episode list returns to a full view of the information.

**l.** Sign out of your Office 365 account. Based on your instructor's directions, submit the following:

sp03h1Recipe_LastFirst

sp03h2Episodes_LastFirst

# Chapter Objectives Review

After reading this chapter, you have accomplished the following objectives:

1. **Work with webpage content.**
   - Webpage content is added to new Wiki pages that you create in SharePoint Online. All pages in SharePoint Online are Wiki pages. These pages are stored in the Site Pages Document Library. Web Part pages are Wiki pages that enable you to add web parts to a page using Web Part zones.
   - Add text to a webpage: You can add text and media assets, such as pictures, audio, and video, to a webpage.
   - Edit and format text on a webpage: Text elements can be formatted and modified using tools in SharePoint Online.
   - Add hyperlinks: Hyperlinks enable you to provide navigation to other SharePoint documents and pages on your current site or to a URL on the Web. They are composed of HTML code that contains a tag with the URL of the linked page. An absolute URL provides the full path to a webpage or file, whereas a relative URL provides a path to a webpage or a file in relation to another file.
   - Format lists: Lists, whether bulleted or numbered, help to organize the page. Numbered lists are used when a specific order is required, such as in a step-by-step process. Bulleted lists are used when no specific order is needed for the list elements.
   - Work with tables: Tables organize data and information on a webpage. Tables are a collection of rows and columns. Nested tables can be added to cells in a table. Working with SharePoint Online, you can modify the layout of the table by adding, deleting, merging, and splitting rows, columns, or cells. Data can be typed directly in the cells of a table, copied and pasted from another document, or inserted as a previously formatted file. Media assets can also be added to a table.

2. **Work with asset and picture libraries.**
   - Media assets, such as pictures, audio, and video, are stored as site assets in SharePoint Online. You create asset libraries and upload media to the library, so that you can use it throughout your site and have organization of the media assets. Using asset libraries enables you to include metadata with the files. If you do not upload media assets to a library, they are uploaded to the Site Assets Library as you add them to your page.
   - Insert pictures on a webpage: The most common picture formats used on the Web include GIF, JPEG, and PNG.

   - Insert video and audio on a webpage: Media assets include pictures, audio, and video, in the form of files that are stored as site assets on SharePoint. Some media requires the use of a plug-in player to view, which is usually available as a free download. After adding media assets to a webpage, you can modify the properties.

3. **Use default web parts and app parts.**
   - Web parts are SharePoint components that can contain any type of web-based information, including analytical, collaborative, and database information. Web parts can be used to search and manage data in external databases and file systems. There are more than 70 built-in default web parts in SharePoint Online, and you can upload additional web parts that you write or purchase from Internet sources. App parts enable you to place a view of a library or list on a webpage.
   - Add web parts to a webpage: The Web Part Gallery contains all the web parts available to the top-level site and its subsites. Web parts are added to a webpage using the gallery. Dynamic Web Parts are placed in a Web Part zone on the Wiki page. Static Web Parts are placed directly on the webpage, and saved as a part of the webpage.
   - Add app parts to a webpage: App parts can be a list or a library, within SharePoint or on an external system. They are added to webpages similarly to how web parts are added.
   - Modify a web part or app part: SharePoint Online provides options for adding and removing web parts or app parts. Modifying the properties of a web part or app part enables you to change the appearance or layout of the component on the page.
   - Export and upload a web part or an app part: You can reuse web parts that you have uniquely configured by exporting and importing them. You can also share the exported web parts with other people.
   - Remove a web part or app part: You can remove web parts or app parts by minimizing them on the page, or deleting them using tools on the Web Part menu or the WEB PART tab.
   - Connect web parts and app parts: By connecting web parts and app parts, you can create data-driven pages. For instance, you can filter an app part list using a web part for the filter. Add the components to the webpage first, and then connect them and set up the properties so the web part and app part communicate.

# Key Terms Matching

Match the key terms with their definitions. Write the key term letter by the appropriate numbered definition.

| | | | |
|---|---|---|---|
| **a.** | Absolute URL | **k.** | List format |
| **b.** | Adobe Flash | **l.** | Nested table |
| **c.** | App part | **m.** | PNG (Portable Network Graphics) |
| **d.** | Cell | **n.** | Relative URL |
| **e.** | Dynamic Web Parts | **o.** | ScreenTip |
| **f.** | GIF (Graphics Interchange Format) | **p.** | Static Web Parts |
| **g.** | Hyperlink target | **q.** | Table |
| **h.** | Insert Table grid | **r.** | Web Part Gallery |
| **i.** | Interlacing | **s.** | Web Part page |
| **j.** | JPEG (Joint Photographic Experts Group) | **t.** | Wiki page |

**1.** _____ A collection of rows having one or more columns. *p. 160*

**2.** _____ A common format seen on almost any webpage, usually as a numbered or bulleted list. *p. 159*

**3.** _____ A graphical table that enables you to select the number of rows and columns for your table. *p. 160*

**4.** _____ A popular application used to create animated graphics, which requires a free downloadable plug-in to view. *p. 169*

**5.** _____ A table inserted within a cell of another table. *p. 160*

**6.** _____ A technology used for displaying images in stages. *p. 169*

**7.** _____ A web part used to display the contents of a list or library on a webpage. *p. 184*

**8.** _____ Contain user-editable properties, and the web parts are saved separately from the page in the SQL Server content database. *p. 182*

**9.** _____ Contains all the web parts available to the top-level site and its subsites. *p. 182*

**10.** _____ Contains only a page content control into which you can insert text, media assets, web parts, and app parts. *p. 149*

**11.** _____ Contains Web Part zones, which are containers for web parts and app parts. *p. 150*

**12.** _____ File format that can display all 16.7 million colors that are available and is the format most often used for photographs. *p. 168*

**13.** _____ File format that supports transparent colors, can display all 16.7 million colors available, and can contain animated images. *p. 168*

**14.** _____ Provides a full path to a webpage or file. *p. 155*

**15.** _____ Provides the path to a webpage or a file in relation to another file. *p. 155*

**16.** _____ Text that displays in the body of the webpage whenever the pointer is moved over the hyperlink in Browse mode or when viewing the webpage in a browser. *p. 157*

**17.** _____ The file or page that opens when a hyperlink is clicked. *p. 156*

**18.** _____ The intersection of a column and a row in a table. *p. 160*

**19.** _____ The format used most often for drawn graphics and animated images. *p. 168*

**20.** _____ Web parts placed directly on the webpage, and saved as a part of the page. *p. 182*

# Multiple Choice

**1.** Which type of page contains only a body control when you first create the page?

(a) App page

(b) Editing page

(c) Web Part page

(d) Wiki page

**2.** While in Edit mode on a page in SharePoint Online, the Undo and Redo commands are located on the:

(a) FORMAT TEXT tab.

(b) top navigation bar.

(c) Quick Launch.

(d) PAGE tab.

**3.** Which one of the following is an example of an absolute URL that is used to create a hyperlink in SharePoint Online?

(a) /danielaskitchen/recipes.html

(b) http://home.pearsonhighered.com/what-we-do.html

(c) /products-services/course-resources/mylab.html

(d) www.pearsonhighered.com/what-we-do.html

**4.** You have created a list of ingredients for a recipe. Which type of list format should you use to display the list?

(a) Bulleted

(b) Lettered

(c) Nested

(d) Numbered

**5.** After creating a table on a SharePoint page, you decide that one cell actually needs to be two cells. Which command do you use to accomplish this goal?

(a) Column Width

(b) Insert Left

(c) Merge Cells

(d) Split Cells

**6.** Which of the following picture formats uses a lossy image compression algorithm?

(a) GIF

(b) Interlaced

(c) JPEG

(d) PNG

**7.** Alternative text:

(a) is a metatag.

(b) is used for headings.

(c) helps place photographs accurately on the page.

(d) is used by adaptive technologies, such as screen readers.

**8.** When you insert an audio or video clip on a webpage, it appears:

(a) as a hyperlink.

(b) as an asset file.

(c) as a Media Web Part.

(d) with embed code.

**9.** App parts include:

(a) Dynamic Web Parts.

(b) lists and libraries.

(c) Static Web Parts.

(d) Web Parts.

**10.** When you export a web part, a file is created with which extension?

(a) .app or .webapp

(b) .html or .htm

(c) .webpart or .dwp

(d) .xml or .xlsx

# Practice Exercises

## 1 Introduction to Management Information Systems Course

As an undergraduate teaching assistant, you have been working on creating an online presence for the Management Information Systems Course using SharePoint Online. You have decided that students should know about a new program that identifies a mentor in each residence hall. Students will be able to call on a mentor when they need assistance with writing papers, studying for tests, and working on projects. You begin by creating a new page on a site, adding information about the program and some web parts. You will then connect a web part to an app part list to enable the students to search for a mentor. Refer to Figure 3.59 as you complete this exercise.

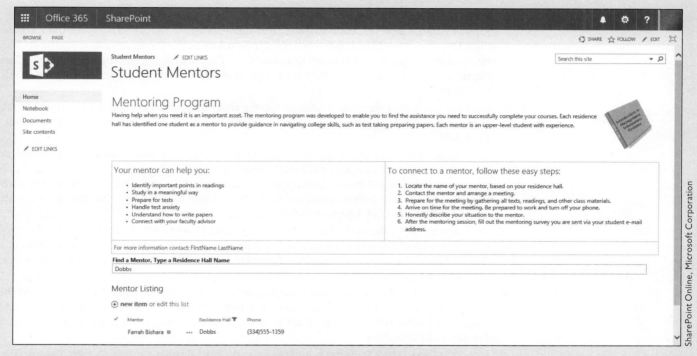

**FIGURE 3.59** Management Information System Course Page

a. Open **Internet Explorer**. Navigate to and sign into your Office 365 account.

b. Click the **SharePoint tile** and click the **Team Site tile**. Click **Site Contents** on the Quick Launch, ensure that the classic SharePoint view is displayed, and then click **new subsite** to add a new subsite.

c. Type **Student Mentors** in the Title box. Type **This site enables students to look up mentors** for the Description. Type **mentor** for the URL name. Accept all the remaining default values, and click **Create**.

d. Click **Site contents** on the Quick Launch, click the **Site Pages tile**, and then click **New**. Type **Student Mentors** for the New page name, and click **Create**.

e. Open the Word document *sp03p1Mentor* and copy all the text in the file. Paste the text on the SharePoint Online page, allowing access if prompted. Close Word.

f. Click the **FORMAT TEXT tab**. Select the first line of text, and click **Heading 1** in the Styles group. Select the line *Your mentor can help you*, and click **Heading 2** in the Styles group. Apply the **Heading 2** style to the line *To connect to a mentor, follow these easy steps*.

g. Select the six lines of text under *Your mentor can help you*, and click **Bullets** in the Paragraph group. Select the six lines of text under *To connect to a mentor, follow these easy steps*, and then click **Numbering**.

h. Click below the last item on the last list. Click the **INSERT tab**, and click **Table**. Use the Insert Table grid to insert a **2×1 Table**. Click the **DESIGN tab**, and click **Show Grid Lines**.

i. Select the heading and text in the first list (*Your mentor can help you*), and click **Cut**. Position the insertion point in the first column of the table, and click **Paste**. Repeat this step to cut and paste the second list (*To connect to a mentor, follow these easy steps*) into the second column of the table. Delete any extra spaces that occur and make sure the headings for each list remain styled as Heading 2.

j. Click in the second column, click the **TABLE LAYOUT tab**, and then click **Insert Below**. Click **Merge Cells** in the Merge group, and click **Merge Right**. Type **For more information contact:**, and press the **Spacebar** once. Click the **INSERT tab**, and click **Link**. Select **From Address**. Type your name in the Text to display box, and type **mailto:** followed by your email address. Click **OK**.

k. Click to the right of the heading *Mentoring Program*. Click the **INSERT tab**, and click **Picture**. Select **From Computer**, click **Browse,** and navigate to the file *sp03p1Graphic*. Click **Open**. Click **OK**. Click the **IMAGE tab**, click the **Alt Text box** in the Properties group on the IMAGE tab, and then type **MIS 100 book graphic**. Click **Position** in the Arrange group, and select **Right**. Make sure the Lock Aspect Ratio option is selected, and change the Horizontal Size to **120 px**.

l. Click the last row of the table, and press the **down arrow** on the keyboard. Click the **INSERT tab** and click **Web Part** in the Parts group. Click the **Filters** category and select **Text Filter**. Click **Add**.

m. Click **Save** in the Edit group on the FORMAT TEXT tab. Click **Site Contents** on the Quick Launch, and click **add an app**. Click the **Import Spreadsheet tile** (you may have to navigate to another page), type **Mentor Listing** in the Name box, and then type **List of mentors with residence hall and phone number** in the Description box. Navigate to and select the file *sp03p1MentorInfo*. Click **Open**, and click **Import**.

n. Click **Range of Cells** for the Range Type. Click **Select Range Minimize** button on the right side of the Select Range box, select all the cells with data in the spreadsheet, and then click **Range Expand** on the right side of the Import to Windows SharePoint Services list dialog box. Click **Import**.

o. Click **Site contents** on the Quick Launch, and click the **Site Pages tile**. Click the **Student Mentors link**. Click the **PAGE tab**, and click **Edit**. Click below the Text Filter Web Part, and click the **INSERT tab**. Click **App Part** in the Parts group, click **Mentor Listing** in the Parts list, and then click **Add**.

p. Select the **Text Filter Web Part**, and click the **WEB PART tab**. Click **Web Part Properties**. Change the Filter Name and Title to **Find a Mentor, Type a Residence Hall Name**. Apply the changes in the Web Part properties pane. Click the arrow next to the title of the web part, and point to **Connections**. Select **Send Filter Values To**, and select **Mentor Listing**. Click the **Connection Type arrow**, and select **Get Filter Values From**. Click the **2. Configure Connection tab**, and click the arrow for the Consumer Field Name. Select **Residence Hall**. Click **Finish**. Click **OK** at the bottom of the Web Part Properties pane.

q. Click **Save**. Test the Text Filter by typing **Dobbs** in the filter box. Press **Enter**, and scroll to display the filtered list.

r. Take a screen shot of the Student Mentors page displaying the filtered Mentor Listing. Name the file **sp03p1Mentor_LastFirst**.

s. Sign out of your Office 365 account. Based on your instructor's directions, submit sp03p1Mentor_LastFirst.

## 2 Class Reunion Search Page

FROM SCRATCH     As a member of the class reunion committee, you have created a website for sharing information with your classmates and the planning team. The team asked you to create a page on the site to enable classmates to search for people they know, find out about where they currently live and other family information. You will create a sample page for the team to review. Refer to Figure 3.60 as you complete this exercise.

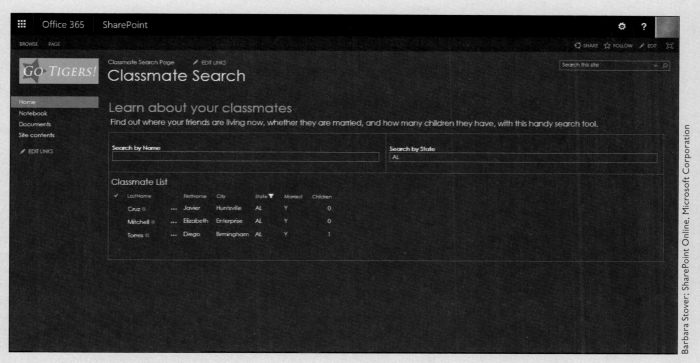

**FIGURE 3.60** Class Reunion Search Page

a. Open **Internet Explorer**. Navigate to and sign into your Office 365 account.

b. Click the **SharePoint tile** and click the **Team Site tile**. Click **Site Contents** on the Quick Launch, ensure that the classic SharePoint view is displayed, and then click **new subsite** to add a new subsite.

c. Type the title **Classmate Search Page**, the description of **Page designed to help classmates connect**, and the URL name **classmate_search**. Accept the remaining defaults, and click **Create**.

d. Click the **Settings icon** and select **Change the look** on the menu. Click **Green**. Click the **Colors arrow**, and click **This palette is primarily Dark Teal with White and Turquoise** (10th option on the list). Click the **Fonts arrow** and click **Century Gothic**. Click **Try it out**. Review the site design, and click **Yes, keep it**.

e. Click **Title, description, and logo** in the Look and Feel section on the Site Settings page. Click **From Computer** in the Logo and Description section. Navigate to the location of the student data files, select *sp03p2Logo*, and click **Open**. Click **OK**. Type **Go Tigers Logo** for the description for alternative text for the picture. Click **OK**.

f. Click **Site contents** on the Quick Launch, and click **add an app**. Click the **Import Spreadsheet app tile** (you may have to navigate to another page). Type **Classmate List** in the Name box, **Listing of classmate information** in the Description box, and then navigate to and select the file *sp03p2Class*. Click **Open**, and click **Import**.

g. Click the **Range Type arrow** and select **Range of Cells**. Click the **Select Range Minimize** button on the right side of the Select Range box, select all the cells with data in the spreadsheet, click **Range Expand** on the right side of the Import to Windows SharePoint Services list dialog box, and then click **Import**.

h. Click **Site contents** on the Quick Launch, click the **Site Pages tile**, and click **New**. Type **Classmate Search** in the New page name box and click **Create**. Type **Learn about your classmates** in the page content box, and press **Enter**. Select the text you typed and click **Heading 1** in the Styles group. Click below the text you typed and type **Find out where your friends are living now, whether they are married, and how many children they have, with this handy search tool.** Press **Enter**. Select the text you just typed, and change the font size to **13 pt**.

**i.** Click below the text you typed in step h. Click the **INSERT tab** and click **Table**. Use the Insert Table grid to place a **2×2 Table** on the page.

**j.** Click in the **first row**, **first column**, click the **INSERT tab**, and then click **Web Part** in the Parts group. Click **Filters** in the Categories pane, and select **Text Filter** in the Parts pane. Click **Add**.

**k.** Click the **first row**, **second column**, and insert a second **Text Filter** using step j as an example.

**l.** Click in the **second row**, **first column**, and click the **TABLE LAYOUT tab**. Click **Merge Cells**, and click **Merge Right**.

**m.** Click in the **second row** of the table to select it. Click the **INSERT tab**, and click **App Part** in the Parts group. Click **Classmate List** in the Parts pane and click **Add**. Click the arrow on the title bar of the Classmate List and select **Edit Web Part**. Click the **Toolbar Type arrow** and select **No Toolbar**. Click **OK** at the bottom of the Web Part Properties pane.

**n.** Click the **arrow** on the right side of the Text Filter [1] Web Part title in the first row, first column, and select **Edit Web Part**. Type **Search by Name** for the Filter Name and the Title. Click the arrow next to the filter title Text Filter [1], and point to **Connections**. Point to **Send Filter Values To**, and select **Classmate List**. Click the **Connection Type arrow** and select **Get Filter Values From**. Click the **2. Configure Connection tab**, and select **LastName**. Click **Finish**. Click **OK** at the bottom of the Web Part Properties pane.

**o.** Click the arrow on the right side of the Text Filter Web Part in the first row, second column, and select **Edit Web Part**. Type **Search by State** for the Filter Name and Title. Expand the Advanced Filter Options in the Filter Name section in the Web Part Properties pane, and then type **2** for the Maximum number of characters. Click the **arrow** on the right side of the Text Filter Web Part again and point to **Connections**. Point to **Send Filter Values To** and click **Classmate List**. Click the **Connection Type arrow** and select **Get Filter Values From**. Click the **2. Configure Connection** and select **State**. Click **Finish**. Click **OK** at the bottom of the Web Part Properties pane.

**p.** Click **Save**. Type **Seo** in the Search by Name box and press **Enter** to test this feature. One record should be displayed in the Classmate List. Take a screen shot of the webpage, naming the file **sp03p2NameSearch_LastFirst**.

**q.** Clear the Search by Name box by clicking the **X** in the box. Type **AL** in the Search by State box to test this feature. Three records should be displayed in the Classmate List. Take a screen shot of the webpage, naming the file **sp03p2StateSearch_LastFirst**. Clear the Search by State box.

**r.** Sign out of your Office 365 account. Based on your instructor's directions, submit the following:
sp03p2NameSearch_LastFirst
sp03p2StateSearch_LastFirst

# Mid-Level Exercises

## 1 Hope Hospital Contact Page

FROM SCRATCH

As the Web designer for Hope Hospital, you have the responsibility of developing all the webpages on the site. These pages are later approved by the Communications Director for publication. Your most recent assignment is to create a News page. You will use the Image Viewer Web Part and format text attractively before submitting the page to the Communications Director.

a. Log in to your Office 365 account and SharePoint, and create a new subsite under the top-level team site following these specifications:
   - Title: **Hope Hospital News Page**
   - Description: **This page provides information to our community.**
   - URL: **hope_page**
   - Template: **Team Site**

b. Create a Picture Library named **HopePhotos**. Upload the file *sp03m1HopeMain* to the Hope Photos library.

c. Add a new page to the site named **Hope News**. Change the text layout to **One column with sidebar**.

d. Insert an **Image Viewer Web Part** from the Media and Content category. Link to the *sp03m1HopeMain* picture that you uploaded to the Hope Photos Picture Library, as follows:
   - Image Link: replace *http://* with **../HopePhotos/sp03m1HopeMain.jpg**
   - Alternative Text: **Hope Hospital Central Building**
   - Title (in Appearance section): **Hope Hospital**
   - Chrome Type (in Appearance section): **Title Only**
   - Click **OK**.

e. Open the Word document *sp03m1HopeText*, copy the first seven paragraphs, and paste them into the right column. Format the first paragraph with **Heading 2**. Format the remaining items as a **bulleted** list, change the font size to **11 pt**, and the color to **Light Turquoise, Accent 1 Lighter**.

f. Copy the remaining four paragraphs from the *sp03m1HopeText* document and paste them under the photograph. Remove any extra space that might occur between the heading and the photograph. Format the heading as **Heading 1**. Check the spelling of the page, and proofread it carefully, correcting any errors (*IQHealth* is spelled correctly).

g. Insert a hyperlink to your email address at the end of the last sentence (after *by contacting*), with your name displayed. Save the page.

h. Take a screen shot of the completed page, naming it **sp03m1HopeNews_LastFirst**. Sign out of your Office 365 account. Based on your instructor's directions, submit sp03m1HopeNews_LastFirst.

## 2 Shelter Pets Online

FROM SCRATCH

As a volunteer Web designer for the organization Shelter Pets Online, you have been experimenting with a website to advertise the pets that are available for adoption. You decide to use your skills to create an attractive page to bring together a searchable list of available dogs and a slide show of some photographs of pets that are available.

a. Open Internet Explorer, and log in to your Office 365 account and SharePoint. Create a new subsite under the top-level site following these specifications:
   - Title: **Shelter Pets Online Page**
   - Description: **This is a page example for Shelter Pets Online.**
   - URL name: **shelter_page**
   - Template: **Team Site**
   - Accept all the other default values.

**b.** Change the theme of the site to **Characters**. Change the colors to **This palette is primarily White, with Gray-80% and Red**. Remove the background picture. Change the fonts to **Impact** and **Segoe UI**. Add the logo *sp03m2Logo* to the site. Enter a description for the logo of **Shelter Pets Online logo** for the graphic.

**c.** Import the Excel file *sp03m2DogData* using the Import a Spreadsheet app following these specifications:

- Name: **Available Dogs**
- Description: **Updated by**, followed by your name and today's date

**d.** Create a Picture Library named **Cuddly_Cats**. Upload the images *sp03m2Sam*, *sp03m2Kiki*, *sp03m2Lydia*, and *sp03m2Reggie* to the library.

**e.** Create a new page on the site titled **Adoptions**.

**f.** Type **Dogs Ready for Adoption** and apply the **Heading 1 Style** to the title. Add a **2×2 Table** to the page.

**g.** Click in the **first row, first column**, and add a **Text Filter Web Part**. In the second row, first column, add the **Available Dogs app part**. Edit the properties of the Available Dogs list to not show the toolbar. Edit the properties of the Text Filter following these specifications:

- Filter Name and Title: **Search by Breed**
- Connect the Search by Breed Text Filter Web Part to the Available Dogs list app, using the field **Breed**

**h.** Click in the **second column, second row**, and add a **Picture Library Slideshow Web Part** using the following specifications:

- Duration: **10**
- Picture Library: **../Cuddly_Cats**
- Display with No Title or Description
- Deselect the Show Toolbar option
- Title: **Cats Are Available for Adoption Too**
- Height: **300 Pixels**

**i.** Type the following list in the **first row, second column**, and apply **numbered formatting** to the last 5 items:

**How to Arrange an Adoption:**

**Call the Shelter Pets office at (328)555-3829**

**Arrange for a meeting with your potential pet**

**Meet the pet, fill out the paper work, pay the fee**

**Prepare your home for a new arrival**

**Pick up your new family member after the approval process is complete**

**j.** Click after the phone number in the list you typed above, and add your email address as a hyperlink in the format of: **or email** your name.

**k.** Click the **FORMAT TEXT tab** and click **Select** in the Markup group. Select **Table** from the menu. Click the **DESIGN tab**, and apply **Table Style 4 - Light Lines** to the table.

**l.** Save the page. Test the filter using the breed **Husky mix**. Take a screen shot of the page, naming it **sp03m2ShelterPage_LastFirst**.

**m.** Sign out of your Office 365 account. Based on your instructor's directions, submit sp03m2ShelterPage_LastFirst.

# Beyond the Classroom

## Communication Skills Class

### GENERAL CASE

You are taking a communication skills class and must develop an end-of-semester demonstration speech that will prove your strong communication and collaboration skills, and your potential to work confidently with others. A demonstration speech is one in which you teach or direct the class how to do something. Because SharePoint Online is a relatively new technology, you decide to demonstrate some of its features. You will use PowerPoint to develop your presentation. After completing the presentation, save it as **sp03b1Speech_LastFirst** and submit as directed by your instructor. Develop a presentation with directions about the following topics:

- Customizing a Webpage
- Enhancing a Webpage with Media Assets
- Working with Web Parts and App Parts

Based on your instructor's directions, submit sp03b1Speech_LastFirst.

## Artist Site

### DISASTER RECOVERY

Your friend, Jannie Belkman, is an artist who is trying to market her art by creating a website. She is having trouble and asked for your advice. She has sent you a file named *sp03b2ArtistSite* with screenshots of the home page of her site. Open the file with a picture viewing application and increase the size as needed so you can review the page. Based on what you have learned, prepare a well-worded memo that offers her suggestions for improvement of the home page. Keep in mind the things you learned in this chapter. After completing the memo, save the document as **sp03b2ArtistMemo_LastFirst**. Based on your instructor's directions, submit sp03b2ArtistMemo_LastFirst.

# Capstone Exercise

You have been working with the team developing the curriculum for Project Investor, offered to young people by Wellington Finances. You have been asked to add to the home page by presenting quotations about investing and money. You will also add more information about Project Investor to this page.

## Create a Subsite

You will create a new site and update the page with a logo and a theme change.

**a.** Sign in to your Office 365 site and SharePoint, and create a new subsite with the following specifications:
- Title: **Project Investor Page**
- Description: **Updated by**, your name, and today's date
- URL: **project_investor_page**
- Template: **Team Site**

**b.** Add the logo *sp03c1Logo* to the site, with the description of **Project Investor logo**.

**c.** Change the theme to **Green**. Change the colors to **This palette is primarily White with Gray-80% and Green**. Change the site layout to **Oslo**. Change the font to **Blueprint MT Pro** and **Corbel**.

## Prepare a Library and a List

A number of quotations about investing have been created as .png files. You will upload the images into a library for use later in the exercise. You will also import an Excel worksheet to create a custom list.

**a.** Add a Picture Library app to the site named **Quotations**.

**b.** Upload five images *sp03c1Quote1* through *sp03c1Quote5* to the library.

**c.** Use the Import Spreadsheet app to import the file *sp03c1Schools* into a custom list named **School Districts**, and a description of **Area school districts that support Project Investor**.

## Work with Webpage Content

You will add a table to the home page to better organize the information you are going to include on the page. You will add a list and a hyperlink.

**a.** Open the home page for editing. Remove the *Get started with your site* web part. Add a **2×4 Table** in the content box under Edit Item.

**b.** Split the first row, second column into two cells. Place the picture *sp03c1Investors* in the first row, first column. Change the Horizontal Size of the photograph to **300 px** (with the Lock Aspect Ratio checked). Change the width of the column to **20%**.

**c.** Type the text **Project Investor will help you meet your savings goals through education, collaboration, and experience** in the first row, second column, and apply the **Heading 1 style**. Remove any blank lines that appear above the table. Change the width of the second column to **50%**.

**d.** Add the title **Upcoming Classes** to the second row, first column. Format this title as **Heading 2**.

**e.** Create a nested **3×4 Table** in the second column, second row. Type the following information in the nested table:

| Class | Date | Time |
|---|---|---|
| Be a Savvy Consumer | October 14 | 4:30-6:00 PM |
| The Value of Saving | November 15 | 6:00-7:30 PM |
| Avoiding Credit Card Debt | December 10 | 2:30-4:00 PM |

**f.** Format the column heading row of the nested table as **Heading 2**. Format the remaining text in the nested table with font size **11 pt**, and **Dark Green** from the Standard Colors gallery. Change the table style of the nested table to **Table Style 3 - Medium Two Tones**.

**g.** Merge all the cells in the third row of the larger table. Open *sp03c1Policies* and copy and paste the text into the merged column. Format the title as **Heading 2**. Format the remaining list items as a **bulleted** list. Change the font size of the list to **11 pt**.

**h.** Click in the row below the policy list and type **For more information contact:** followed by your name as a hyperlink to your email address. Do not apply a bullet to this line of text.

**i.** Select the larger table, and apply the **Table Style 1 - Clear** to the table.

**j.** Check the spelling of the page, and proofread it carefully. Correct any errors that you find.

## Add and Customize a Web Part

A customized web part will display the quotations in the Picture Library as if they were slides. You will customize the web part after adding it to the page.

**a.** Add the **Picture Library Slideshow Web Part** to the first row, third column. Change the column width for the third column to **30%**.

**b.** Edit the properties of the web part to show the quotations images in the Quotations Picture Library for **10** seconds each, in sequential order. Do not display a toolbar or title of the picture. Change the title to **Famous Investor Quotations**.

## Add and Connect an App Part

A Text Filter Web Part will enable students to see if their school participates in any Project Investor programs. You will add the app part and custom list to the last row of the table.

a. Merge the columns on the fourth row. Add a **Text Filter Web Part** to the fourth row of large table. Below the web part, insert the **School Districts app part**. Modify the School Districts app part so that the toolbar does not display.

b. Modify the Text Filter Web Part Filter Name and Title to be **Search School Districts that Participate in Project Investor**. Set the Chrome Type to **None**.

c. Set up a connection between the filter and the School Districts list using **Column1** to configure the connection.

d. Save the page. Test the filter using a school district name **Marion**. Take a screen shot of the webpage, naming it **sp03c1Investor_LastFirst**.(Note: You may have to take more than one screen shot to show all your work.) Name the second screenshot **sp03c1Investor2_LastFirst**.

e. Sign out of Office 365. Based on your instructor's directions, submit

sp03c1Investor_LastFirst

sp03c1Investor2_LastFirst

# SharePoint and Office 2016 Documents

## CASE STUDY | Daniela's Table Documents

Your work as the media expert for Daniela's Table continues with more opportunities to improve a team site to make it more functional for the users. You have heard about the extensive functionalities available for displaying lists and libraries, and you want to experiment with the options.

The team is generating a lot of documents in their desktop applications of Word, PowerPoint, Excel, and Access as they complete their work for the website. You decide that you should review the ways of saving files and data to SharePoint Online so that you can advise them on how to correctly upload and manage the data. You will provide a default template for a library so that they can easily create worksheets for the episode schedule. You want to be able to edit data contained in SharePoint lists and libraries when appropriate, and also to make it available for viewing without desktop applications. You also want to create custom views to display the lists and libraries. An Access database contains information you would like to add to the site, so you will create an Access custom web app. You will link a SharePoint Online list to an Access database.

# Integrating Microsoft Office 2016 Documents with SharePoint Sites

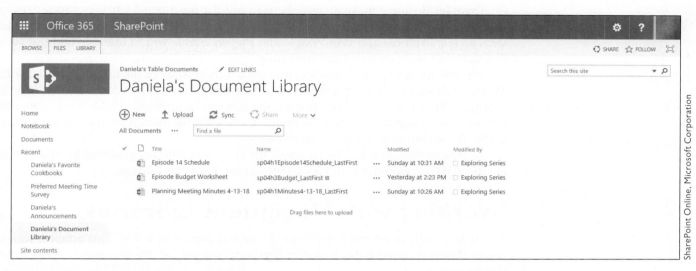

## CHAPTER 4

**FIGURE 4.1** Daniela's Table Documents

SharePoint Online, Microsoft Corporation

## CASE STUDY | Daniela's Table Documents

| Starting Files | Files to be Submitted |
|---|---|
| sp04h1EpisodeSchedule | sp04h1Episode14Schedule_LastFirst |
| sp04h1Minutes4-13-18 | sp04h1Minutes4-13-18_LastFirst |
| sp04h1UpcomingEpisodes | sp04h1DocumentLibrary_LastFirst |
| sp04h2Zucchini | sp04h1Filter_LastFirst |
| sp04h2Presentation | sp04h1Announcement_LastFirst |
| sp04h3Budget | sp04h1Survey_LastFirst |
| sp04h3Cookbooks | sp04h2WordRecipe_LastFirst |
| | sp04h2Blog_LastFirst |
| | sp04h2Link_LastFirst |
| | sp04h3Budget_LastFirst |
| | sp04h3Cookbooks_LastFirst |
| | sp04h3Episodes_LastFirst |
| | sp04h3UpcomingEpisodes_LastFirst |

# Work in SharePoint with Microsoft Office 2016 Documents

SharePoint 2016 tools enable you to effectively work with various Microsoft Office and Windows client applications. Office application files from Access, Excel, PowerPoint, Word, and OneNote can be loaded to SharePoint Online sites for access and collaboration. Files from other software applications, such as text files and PDFs, can be stored on SharePoint sites. Office 365 apps, such as Outlook, Calendar, People, and Newsfeed, enable you to stay in touch and work efficiently with people. Office Online apps and OneDrive for Business make it convenient to edit the documents whether you are using your desktop computer, laptop, tablet, or smartphone. The Windows client applications, such as File Explorer and Windows Media Player, enable you to manage and use your files as if they were on your local computer.

SharePoint document libraries can contain thousands of documents created with Microsoft Office or other applications. The documents can be uploaded individually or in groups. Within the SharePoint libraries, the files can be grouped in folders and they can be sorted and filtered as needed. Different views of the file listings enable you to customize the list to your organization's specifications.

In this section, you will learn about the tools and features provided by SharePoint Online 2016 for working with Word, PowerPoint, Excel, and Access.

## Working with Document Libraries

You will usually need more than one document library in a site. This enables you to assign different access rights to different groups of people at different stages in the life of the document.

A travel reimbursement document is an example of one where different people will need different access rights at different times. In most businesses, anyone can submit a travel reimbursement document, and when using SharePoint Online, it can be stored in the main shared document library. Once the travel reimbursement is signed by the department head, it should be moved to another document library so that only the department head and administrative assistant can edit the document. This protects the document from being modified later by the person who originally submitted it. Access rights to this document library might enable people to only view the document so they will know it is being processed. Once the travel reimbursement is completely processed, it should be moved to yet another document library and the access rights should change to read-only for all groups.

Using multiple document libraries also enables you to define different default document template types, as will be discussed in the next section. These content types can also be used to organize libraries, as discussed later in this chapter.

### Create a New Document Library

**STEP 1** ⟩⟩ When you create a collaboration team site, a default document library (Documents) is created. As you create additional document libraries, be sure to use descriptive names that enable you and others to understand the purpose of the library. This helps keep things organized.

> **TIP: USE THE CLASSIC VIEW**
> The new experience menu in SharePoint Online 2016 is still under development, with some commands and menus not available. The classic SharePoint view, available through a link at the bottom of the Site Contents Quick Launch, will enable you to create and edit pages with a full range of commands.

The Site contents page displays all of the document libraries and lists for a site. Click Site contents on the Quick Launch or click the Settings icon and select Site contents from the menu.

A name for the new library is requested in the Create document library dialog box. Also note that there is a setting for Advanced Options. These additional options enable you to further customize the library as you create it by providing a detailed description, selecting whether to use versioning, and selecting a default document template for all new files created in the document library. As shown in Figure 4.2, there are document templates for Microsoft Office applications (with the exception of Access), and different versions of these applications. You can also select a SharePoint Designer Web page, Basic page, or Web Part page as the default document template.

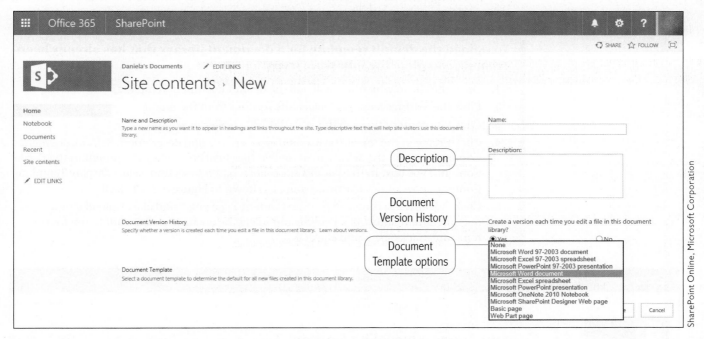

**FIGURE 4.2** Advanced Property Options for a New Document Library (Classic View)

The ***default template*** defines the default content type for the library. SharePoint creates this type of file when you click New Document while viewing the library's content listing. Only one default template can be selected per library. Keep in mind that even with the default template defined, you can still store other types of files within the document library.

> **TIP: DEFAULT DOCUMENT TEMPLATES**
> You might wonder why some Office applications are shown twice in the Document Template list. The various versions of Office use different file formats. For example, Word 2007–2016 uses the .docx format, whereas prior versions of Word use the .doc format.

The selected document template option opens a blank template or webpage when the user clicks New Document on the FILES tab in the library. You are not just locked into Office application templates for this option. The site administrator can add other document templates, such as the travel reimbursement form discussed earlier, which can be set to open as the default template.

Once you have selected the options for the library, click Create and the library will open automatically. Two tabs appear on the Ribbon in the classic SharePoint view:

- The FILES tab contains options for managing and editing your documents. You can upload documents from your local computer or network drive. New documents can be created using the default templates in the New group on the FILES tab.

- The LIBRARY tab enables you to manage the way the library appears on the screen. You can define different views, manage tags and notes, share and track the documents, connect and export the documents, customize the library, and work with the settings, including with whom the library is shared.

## Change the Default Template for a Document Library

As previously indicated, the default template can be changed to any type of document that a user's computer recognizes. For instance, the default template in a SharePoint library for the accounting department might be set to open an Excel document or other accounting software application document.

To change the default template to a document that you want to use, you must first upload the new document template.

**To upload the default template for a document library that has already been created, complete the following steps:**

1. Open the site to which you will add the default document template.
2. Click the Settings icon, and select Site settings from the menu.
3. Click Site content types in the Web Designer Galleries section.
4. Click Create at the top of the list, and type a name and description. Select Document Content Types in the *Select parent content type from* box. Select Document in the Parent Content Type box. In the *Put this site content type into* section, select Display Template Content Types under Existing group, as shown in Figure 4.3. Click OK.
5. Click Advanced settings on the Site Content Type page, and click Upload a new document template. Click Browse and select the document you want to use for the template. Click Open, and click OK.

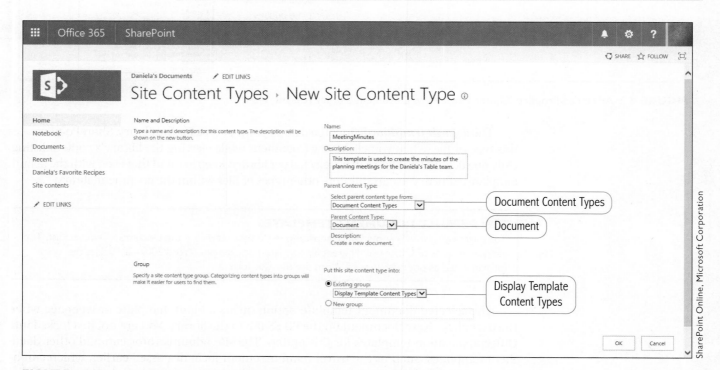

**FIGURE 4.3** Uploading a Document Template to a Document Library (Classic View)

After the new document template is uploaded, you change the settings so that it is assigned as the default template. This is accomplished on the Library Settings page.

> **To change the default template document, complete the following steps:**
>
> 1. Open the library where you want to change the default document template. Click the LIBRARY tab.
> 2. Select Library Settings in the Settings group.
> 3. Click Advanced settings in the General Settings section on the Settings page and click Yes under *Allow management of content types?* Click OK.
> 4. Scroll to the Content Types section on the Settings page and click *Add from existing site content types*.
> 5. Select Display Template Content Types in the *Select site content types from* box. Select the name of the document template you previously uploaded in the Available Site Content Types box, and click Add, as shown in Figure 4.4. Click OK.
> 6. Click *Change new button order and default content type* in the Content Types section on the Settings page. Change the Position from Top to 1 for the document template you previously uploaded. Click OK.

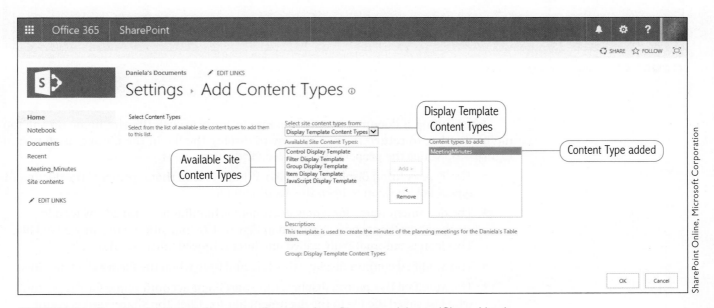

**FIGURE 4.4** Changing the Default Document Template for a Document Library (Classic View)

## Create a New Document in a Document Library

**STEP 2 ❯❯** Depending on whether the new document library was set up to appear on the Quick Launch, you may or may not be able to see it when working with the site. If the Recent category is on the Quick Launch, the document library will appear in that list. If it is visible on the Quick Launch, click the document library name to open it. If it is not visible, click Site contents, and click the document library link on the Site contents page to open the library. New document libraries do not contain any files until you create a new document or upload documents to the library.

To create a new document with the default document template, you use New on the library page to select the template to open on your computer and display the new blank document template in the Online version of the application. You complete your edits using the software application. Click the name of the file (next to the word Document) in the top navigation bar and type a meaningful file name, as shown in Figure 4.5. The word Saved will appear on the top navigation bar.

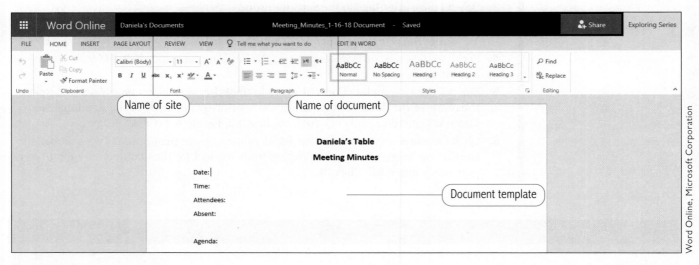

**FIGURE 4.5** Saving a New Document

After saving a document to the document library, click the site name on the top navigation bar to return to the site view to display the file in the library, as shown in Figure 4.6. Notice the properties displayed for the document:

- The Type column displays a familiar Windows icon that represents the document type. Click the icon to open the document file.
- The document name for a new document is highlighted with a New icon in classic SharePoint view, as shown in Figure 4.6, indicating a recently added file. This icon is automatically added and later removed (after two days).
- The Modified column displays the date and time when the file was last modified.
- The Modified By column displays the SharePoint account name for the person who last saved the file to the document library. Click the SharePoint account name for the person to view the profile information about the user.

**FIGURE 4.6** New Document Properties (Classic View)

## Add Columns to a View

Your users will very often need to see more properties of the documents than are displayed in the default document library list (refer to Figure 4.6). **Views** enable you to define which document property columns are displayed and whether the documents displayed are sorted or filtered. You can manage the views using the LIBRARY tab, Manage Views group. Select All Documents in the Manage Views group, and click Modify View to display the Edit View page, as shown in Figure 4.7. Check the columns you want to add to the view, or deselect the columns you do not want to include. Click the Position from Left arrow to change the arrangement of the columns on the page. This page can also be used to set up filters and sorting. You can change the name of the view as well.

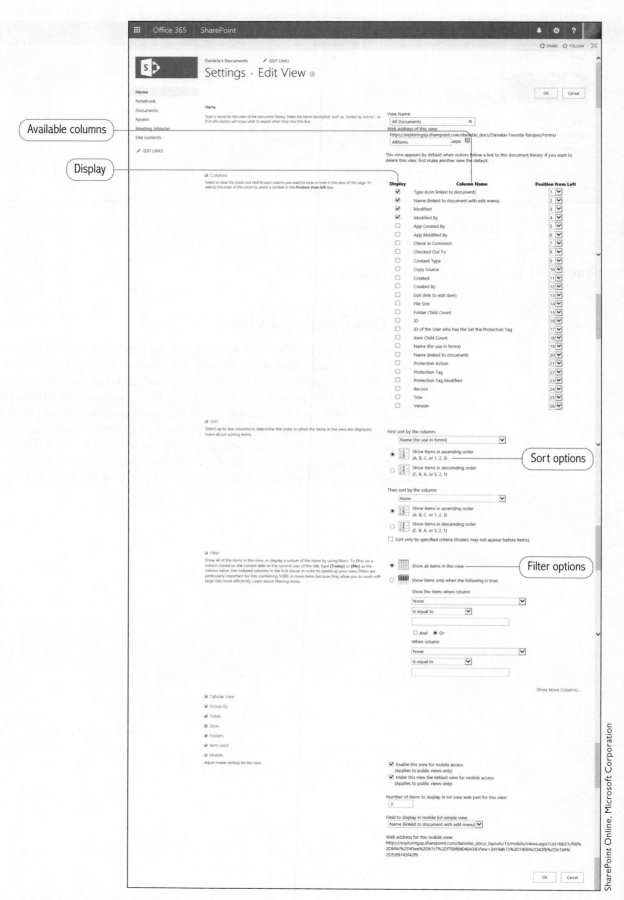

**FIGURE 4.7** Adding Columns to a View (Classic View)

As shown in Figure 4.8, the new column (Checked Out To, in this case) is displayed. Now it will be easy to figure out who has a document checked out, and you can contact them for additional information on the status of the document. If you have items checked out, you can check them in on the page where they are viewed. You can select individual items to check in by clicking the More Options icon next to the document name, clicking the More on the menu, and selecting Check In. If you want to check in multiple items in classic SharePoint view, click the check box next to each document, and click Check In on the FILES tab. Once you have checked in the documents, they will be available to other people who have access to the site.

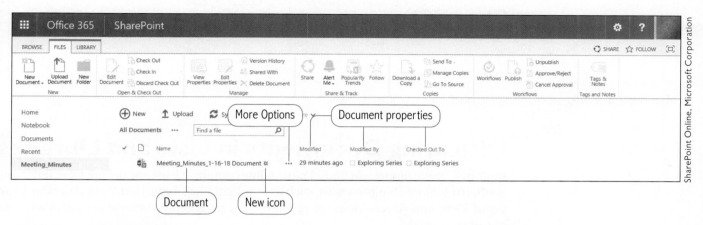

**FIGURE 4.8** Checked Out To Column Added (Classic View)

As you add more columns to the view, the width of the window expands, and you can scroll to see the additional column information.

## Sort and Filter the Documents in a Library

As discussed previously, SharePoint enables you to upload existing documents to document libraries. Whenever you want to change the sorting order of the documents in the document library listing, click the column header of the column you want to use as the sorting field (also known as the sort key) and select the method of sorting. The documents will appear in the specified order, based on the sort field column. Click the column header again to display the column in the opposite order. A small arrow to the right of the column name indicates the direction of the sort, as shown in Figure 4.9. If you prefer to use a menu, point to the column header and click the arrow that appears to the right. Select the sort direction from the menu, as shown in Figure 4.9.

You can also use the column header menu to filter the document list to show only the documents that meet a certain criterion. For instance, you can filter the document list to show only Excel files, or files that were modified on a certain date. When the column is currently filtered, a funnel appears to the right of the column name, as shown in Figure 4.9. Point to the column header, and select Clear Filters on the menu to remove the filter.

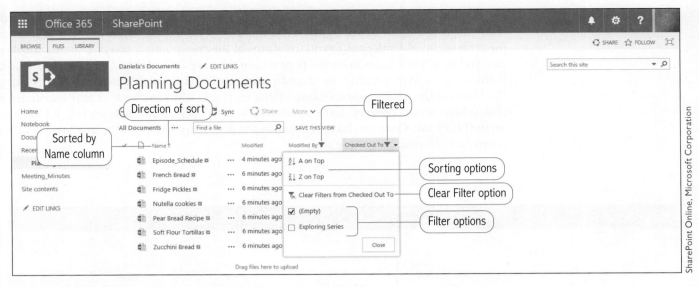

**FIGURE 4.9** Sorting and Filtering the Document List (Classic View)

# Displaying Documents in Lists and Libraries

Built-in lists and libraries in SharePoint Online contain at least one default view, but many contain additional built-in views, such as Standard View, Datasheet View, Calendar View, Gantt View, and Access View. Using SharePoint Designer, you can also customize views to suit your needs.

**To create a new view, complete the following steps:**

1. Open the site and library where you want to create the new view.
2. Click the LIBRARY tab, select Library Settings in the Settings group, and then click Create View in the Views section at the bottom of the window.
3. Select the view you want to apply to the document library from the list, as shown in Figure 4.10.
4. Name the view and make selections for the features of the view (refer to Figure 4.7). Each view type has different property options.

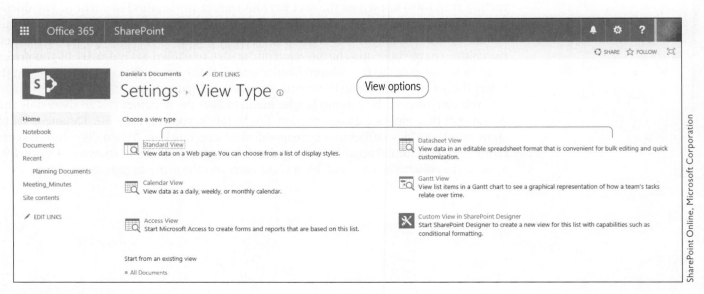

**FIGURE 4.10** View Options

After creating a view, it can be modified by clicking LIBRARY tab, selecting Library Settings in the Settings group, and then clicking the name of the view in the Views section at the bottom of the window. This opens the Edit View page, where you can change the properties of the view. Each view type will have somewhat different property options. The view can also be deleted from the site using the Edit View page.

## Working with Views

**STEP 3** ▶▶ ***Standard View*** displays the contents of lists and libraries as lists included in a webpage, as shown in Figure 4.11. The Standard View is the default view for the Team Site lists and libraries and is available for all SharePoint Online lists and libraries, except Survey and Discussions.

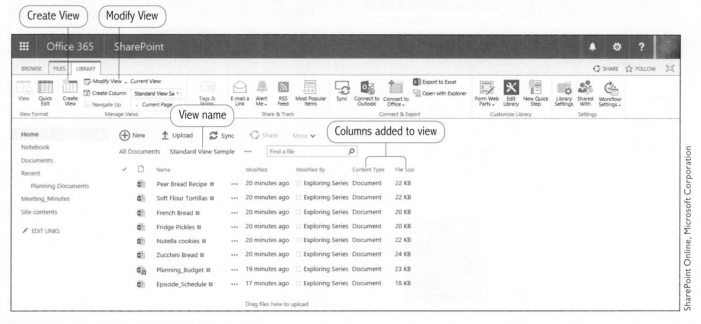

**FIGURE 4.11** New Standard View (Classic View)

***Datasheet View*** displays list or library items using a grid-like layout that enables you to easily edit the whole table, as shown in Figure 4.12. Datasheet View can be used with any list or library type other than the Picture Library, External List, and Survey view types.

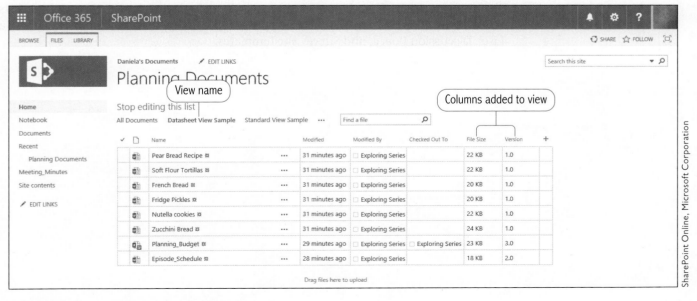

**FIGURE 4.12** New Datasheet View (Classic View)

***Calendar View*** can be used to display list data when at least one field is a date field, such as Modified or Created, with the files arranged on the calendar by the date they were last modified, as shown in Figure 4.13. The view is not available on the External List, Discussion Board, or Survey site templates. The Calendar View is the default view for the Calendar List. The options on the Create View and Edit View pages are somewhat different and require that you select the Calendar Columns for the Month View Title, Week View Title, Day View Title, and subheadings for the Week View and the Day View. You also select the Time Interval, specifying the columns used to place items in the calendar.

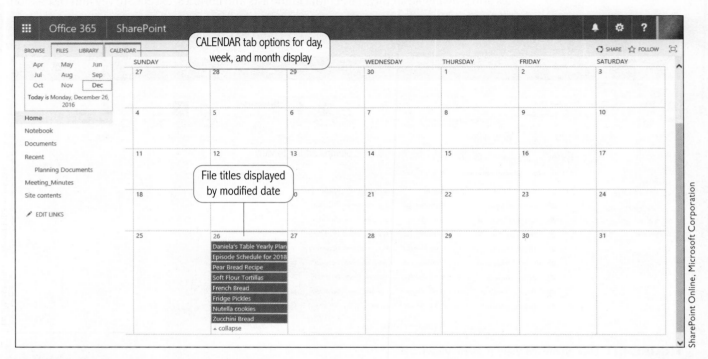

**FIGURE 4.13** New Calendar View (Classic View)

SharePoint Online, Microsoft Corporation

A ***Gantt View***, like a Gantt chart (www.ganttchart.com), is used to provide a graphical representation for a project timeline, as shown in Figure 4.14. You can build Gantt charts in Excel. The SharePoint Gantt View is the default view for the Project Tasks lists. It is available for all SharePoint list and library types except the Picture Library, External Lists, Discussion Board, and Survey site templates.

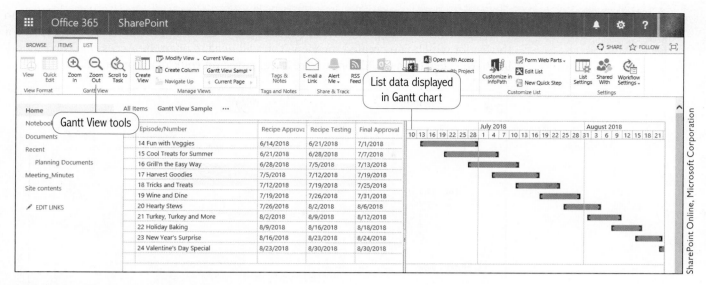

**FIGURE 4.14** New Gantt View (Classic View)

SharePoint Online enables you to create a list or library view using Access 2016. With *Access View*, you can use the Access advanced tools for generating reports and views. Data in the lists and libraries will be automatically updated when you edit content in Access View. You can use Access View for all SharePoint Online lists and libraries, except the External List and Survey. For instance, you can create an Access View to use on a Task List file. It is important to note that you will need the Access desktop application installed on your computer to use this view.

When you click Access View on the LIBRARY tab, the list opens in an Access application window, as shown in Figure 4.15, and you must provide a file name in a location on your local computer. The Create Access View dialog box opens to enable you to select the type of view you want. When you have selected the view you want to use to display

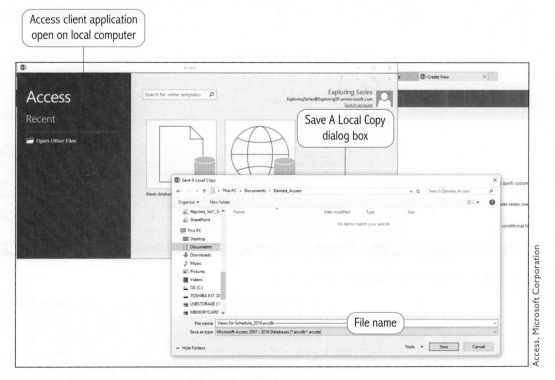

**FIGURE 4.15** Saving the Access View to Local Computer

the data, click OK, as shown in Figure 4.16. The data is displayed in Access View and can be edited, as shown in Figure 4.17. Access View does not appear in the existing views of the list for which you created the view. You will need to open the Access file corresponding to the view from the library where it was saved on your local computer.

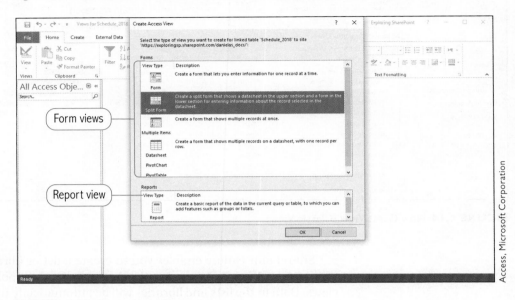

**FIGURE 4.16** Access View Types

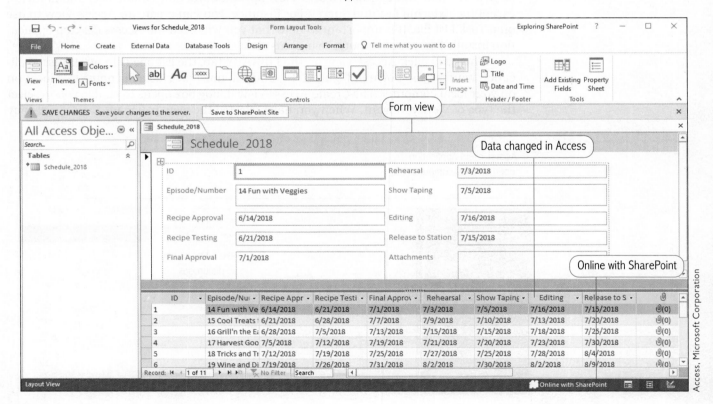

**FIGURE 4.17** List Data Displayed in Access View

The final option is to create a Custom View using SharePoint Designer. SharePoint Designer, as shown in Figure 4.18, is an application that can be downloaded for free from Microsoft and installed on your local computer. It has many of the same functions and features of SharePoint Online, but contains some unique capabilities for designing webpages. After you design the webpage with the Custom View, you can open the view from within SharePoint Online.

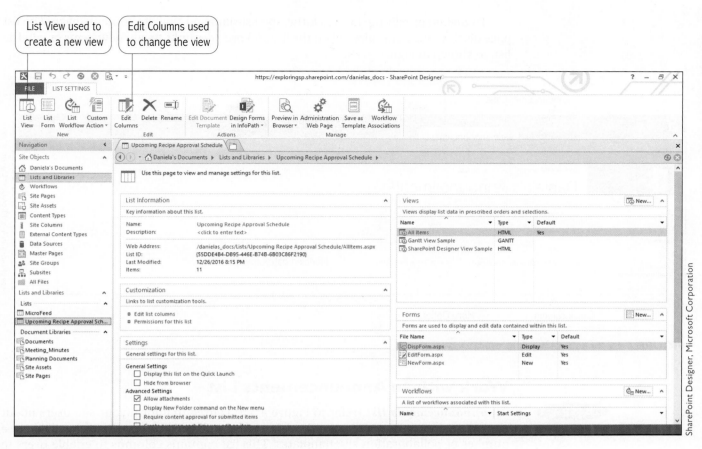

List View used to create a new view

Edit Columns used to change the view

**FIGURE 4.18** Work with a List in SharePoint Designer

# Working with SharePoint Built-in List Apps

Lists provide the easiest way to create and store information in SharePoint, using the familiar list paradigm such as important work tasks at the office, grocery items to buy on your way home, and home improvement projects for a weekend. SharePoint Online provides a variety of ways to keep this information electronically in predefined app lists.

Each SharePoint Online list app is arranged in columns. Some columns appear in almost every list, whereas other columns add unique capabilities to a list. Site templates have specialized libraries or list apps designed specifically for the type of site, but you can also create custom lists for the site. The only required column is the Title column, which you should use to give a descriptive name to the item. Additional columns can be added to meet the requirements of the users.

**To add a list app to a site, complete the following steps:**

1. Open the site, and click Site contents on the Quick Launch.
2. Click New under the banner (in the new experience view) and click App, or click *add an app* (in the classic SharePoint view).
3. Select the list tile that you want to install on the site.
4. Provide a name for the list and click Create.

The list app tile appears on the Site contents page in the site. You can add multiple list apps of the same type with different names. You can also add as many different list apps as needed to fulfill the needs of the users of the site.

To update or edit the list, click the app list name on the Site contents page. The list page displays the items already on the list and provides links to add new items or edit the list, as shown in Figure 4.19.

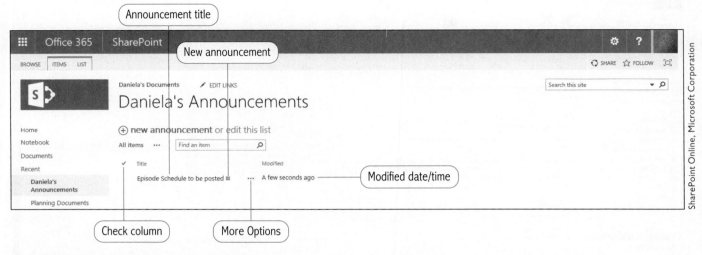

FIGURE 4.19 Announcements List (Classic View)

## Work with an Announcements List

**STEP 4** ⟩⟩ An **announcements list** (refer to Figure 4.19) is used to inform your site users about upcoming events, news, or activities. This is a popular type of list that is available in a number of collaboration site templates. This list contains columns to enable users to organize and view the posted announcements. An **announcement item** initially contains a title, body, and optional expiration date. Attachments can also be added to the item.

On the Announcements page, click new announcement to create an announcement item. Click the title link of an announcement item in the list to display the complete item, as shown in Figure 4.20. Click the More Options icon on the Announcements list to open a menu (refer to Figure 4.19), which enables you to view or edit the item, create an alert, follow the item, display who it is shared with, or delete the item. The check mark to the left of the title indicates that the item is selected. You can turn the check mark column off as you customize this list. The Modified column displays the date and time of the last modification to the item.

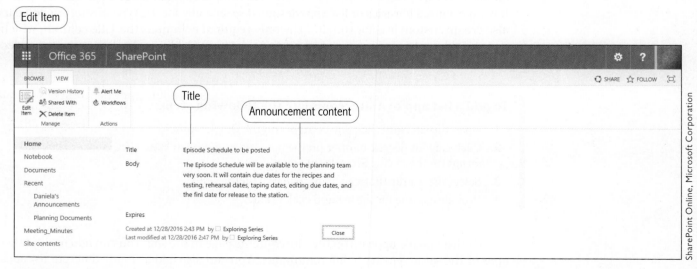

FIGURE 4.20 Announcement Displayed (Classic View)

You can edit an open announcement by clicking Edit Item in the Manage group (refer to Figure 4.20) on the VIEW tab. You can also review the version history, see who the item is shared with, and delete the item in the Manage group. The Actions group enables you to set up an alert on the item and add the item to a workflow.

As you edit an item, keep in mind that the title is required, but everything else is optional. The Body field provides space for text to describe the item in detail, as shown in Figure 4.21. For example, you might give the details for a meeting, seminar, or party in the body of the announcement item. Click within the body of the announcement, and you can format the text using familiar tools and insert tables, pictures, video and audio, links, files, and embed code. Using the Clipboard group tools, you can cut, copy, and paste text into the fields. The Expires field enables you to set a date for the announcement to be removed from the list, generally after the event takes place or after a certain period of time if the announcement is not related to an event. If you do not set an expiration date, SharePoint Online will not remove the item from the list. To add an attachment, such as a map or meeting agenda, click Attach File in the Actions group on the EDIT tab. The file is uploaded to SharePoint Online and will display in the appropriate Office Online app when clicked.

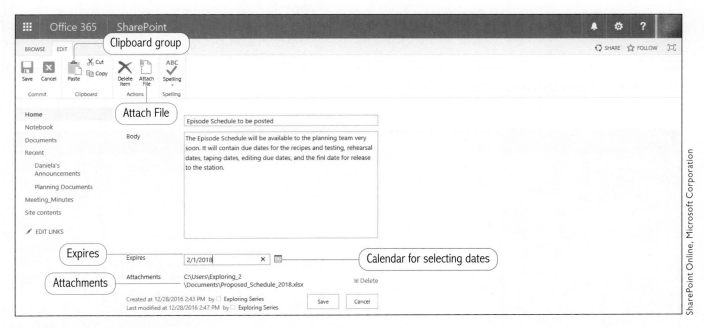

**FIGURE 4.21** Editing an Announcement (Classic View)

## Work with a Contacts List

The *contacts list*, created using the Contacts app, contains columns that enable you to manage contact information such as name, company, phone numbers, email addresses, and much more. You can add columns to the list by clicking *edit this list* on the contacts page and clicking Add Column (+) at the end of the columns list, as shown in Figure 4.22. Select the type of data, and when the field is created, type a descriptive name in the column heading. To see additional types of data, click More Column Types on the Add Column menu to quickly customize the view by creating your own column names, selecting the type of information, and providing a description, as shown in Figure 4.23. You can also require that the column contains information. Click OK to add the column to the list.

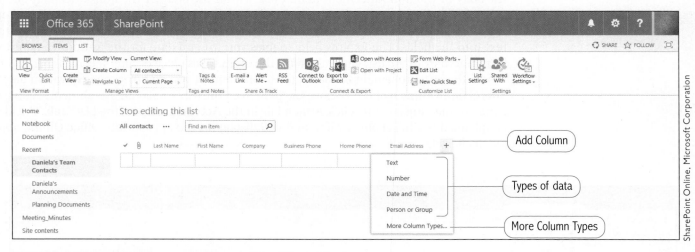

**FIGURE 4.22** Adding Columns to a Contacts List (Classic View)

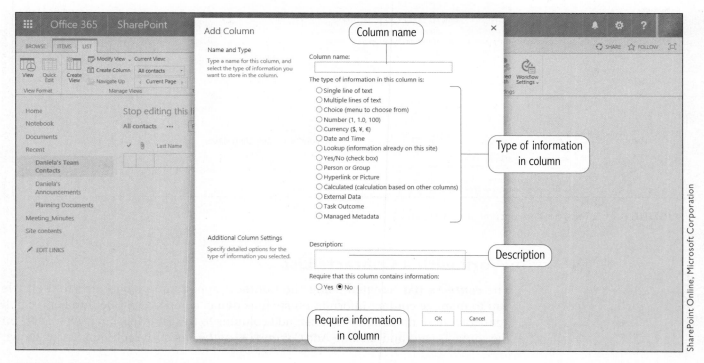

**FIGURE 4.23** Add Column Dialog Box

Some column choices open additional selections on the Add Column dialog box. The Choice option, selected in Figure 4.24, enables you to create a menu of options that a user can select from when using the list. The Lookup option enables the user to find information already on the site from the contacts list. The Calculated option enables you to create calculations based on other columns in the list.

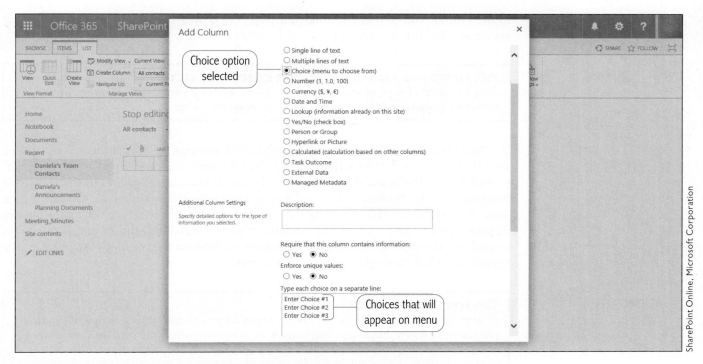

FIGURE 4.24 Choice Option in the Add Column Dialog Box

Click *Stop editing this list* to save the changes and return to the contacts list. As an alternative, you can click the More Options icon on the contacts page and click Modify this View. This opens the Edit View page that enables you to change the name of the view, select the columns you want to display in the view, change the sorting order or filtering of the contacts list, and more, as you have seen previously in this chapter. The Modify View option is also available on the LIST tab.

You may need to modify column headings. Click *edit this list* on the contacts page and click the arrow next to the column heading you want to modify. Select Rename Column and type the new column name. Click *Stop editing this list* after you have made the necessary adjustments. As an alternative, click the LIST tab and click Quick Edit in the View Format group to change the column names, as shown in Figure 4.25. Again, click *Stop editing this list* when you have completed your modifications.

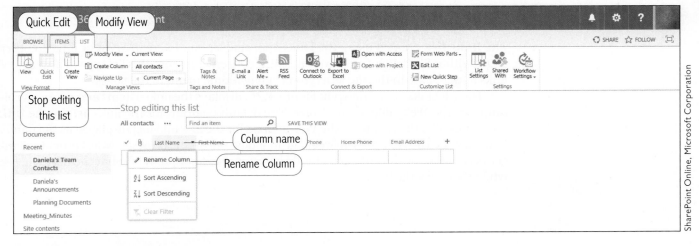

FIGURE 4.25 Quick Edit of View (Classic View)

At some point, you may not want to display a column. Click the LIST tab and click Modify View in the Manage Views group. Deselect the columns you do not want to display in the Columns section of the Edit View page. Click OK when you have completed your selections, and the contacts list page will display.

> **TIP: FILTERING AND SORTING THE CONTACTS LIST**
> Using the Edit View page, you can also sort or filter the view of the list. This becomes important as the contact list grows to enable your users to find the person they want.

To add a new contact to the contacts list, click *new item* on the contacts page, or click the ITEMS tab and click New Item. The Clipboard commands enable you to cut, copy, and paste data into the fields. You can attach a file, such as a resume or article, to the contact information. The Spelling command is also available on the Ribbon as you add a new item. You will notice that you may have more fields for different types of data than are displayed on the contacts list. Although this data is not viewable on the contacts list, it is available if the individual contact is opened by clicking on the contact's last name in the contact list. Click Save after completing the entries.

> **TIP: HYPERLINK FIELDS**
> As items are added to a list, SharePoint creates a hyperlink that enables the user to open the contact information to display the content. This happens for all list items, usually on the column named Title, or in the case of the contacts list, Last Name. You can change the title to make it more descriptive, so users can clearly understand the purpose of the link. Another link column that can be displayed in a list is an email address column. Hyperlinks have two parts: a descriptive name displayed to the user, and the actual email address that opens the default email client when a user clicks the link. Email links always begin with mailto:. Yet another type of hyperlink column links to Web addresses. These addresses can be SharePoint addresses or other URLs on the Internet. These hyperlinks begin with http:// or https://, depending on the security settings of the site.

## Import a Spreadsheet List

Excel worksheets can be used to populate data quickly into SharePoint, saving you the trouble of retyping the data. The Import Spreadsheet app enables you to import data into a custom list. You can decide if you want to import a range of cells, a named range, or an Excel table. Later in this chapter, an in-depth discussion of importing Excel data will show you how to import data into a list, how to export a list to an Excel spreadsheet, and how to synchronize data from a SharePoint list to Excel spreadsheets.

## Work with a Links List

The **links list**, created using the Links app, enables you to create a list of links to other pages within SharePoint or to websites. It is convenient to use this list type to display the links to webpages in the site as a type of navigational menu to the pages.

The All Links view, shown in Figure 4.26, displays the linked items and contains columns for the Web address and Notes. The default columns for the links list are the URL and Notes. The URL contains the Web address for the link and text displayed as the name. You click the URL to open the webpage in a new tab on the browser. Notes provide a longer description of the link, and should be a concise description of what the user will see when they click the link.

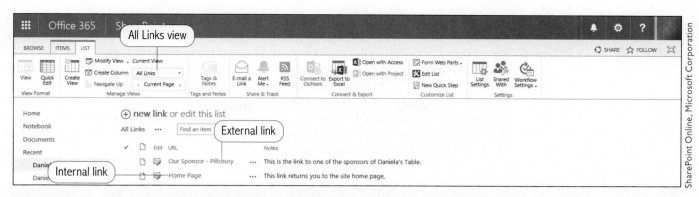

**FIGURE 4.26** Links List View (Classic View)

Links can be arranged in folders or displayed as a long list that can be sorted by the displayed URL. This can be cumbersome, so a better option is to create a custom column that provides views that filter the links.

A good implementation of a links list is including it on a Web Part page of the site, as shown on the home page in Figure 4.27. This way you can provide users with a list of the most relevant site-related links. Using the ITEMS tab on the links list view, you can change the order of the items, by clicking Change Item Order in the Actions group. This enables you to place more important links at the top of the list because people usually begin scanning at the top of a list. You can create multiple views of the list, with a different order of items on the list.

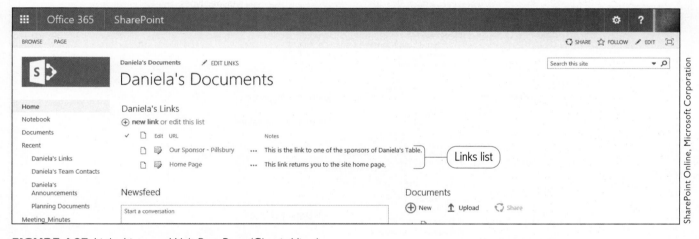

**FIGURE 4.27** Links List on a Web Part Page (Classic View)

> **TIP: MORE ABOUT LINKS LIST**
> A Wiki page template, used to build pages for collaboration, enables you to link to other page sites without using a links list. For external links to other websites, you should consider using a links list to make the links easy to find, use, and update.

## Work with a Survey List

The ***survey list*** displays columns as a questionnaire or poll rather than a list of columns and rows. After creating the survey list using the Survey app, click Settings, and click Add Questions. There are 13 built-in answer types, including text, rating scales such as the Likert scale, Yes/No, Number, Date and Time, Lookup, and External Data. The New Question page enables you to type the question text, select the type of answer the question will accept, require a response, determine how the choices will be displayed, and set up branching logic and column validation, as shown in Figure 4.28. Some questions, such as multiple choice and rating scales, require that you add the text of the answers. For example, a rating scale question would have text answers such as "Strongly Agree," "Neutral," and "Strongly Disagree." Minimum and maximum value limits can be added to numeric answers. The answer lists can be set to display as drop-down menus, radio buttons, or check boxes. Surveys in SharePoint enable branching based on the responses someone makes. As you add questions, you can determine branching triggers to customize the survey. Click Next Question to add an additional question to the survey list, or click Finish to make the survey available to the users.

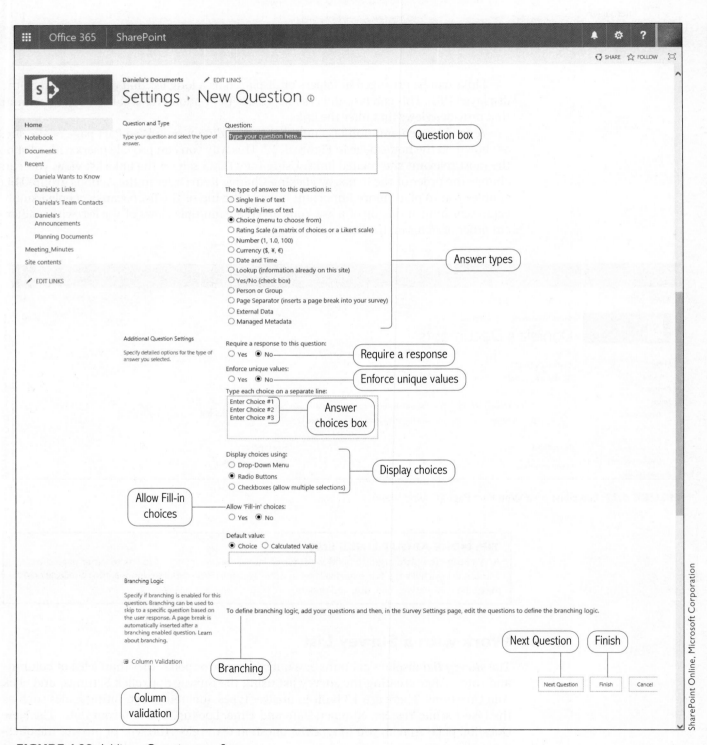

**FIGURE 4.28** Adding a Question to a Survey

When a user views the survey list, the name of the survey, a description, and the date it was created are displayed, as shown in Figure 4.29. If other people have answered the survey, a number indicates the number of responses to the survey. When a user clicks Respond to this Survey, SharePoint displays the questions on a new page. The user selects the appropriate answers and clicks Finish when they have completed the survey, or Cancel to discard any changes made to the survey.

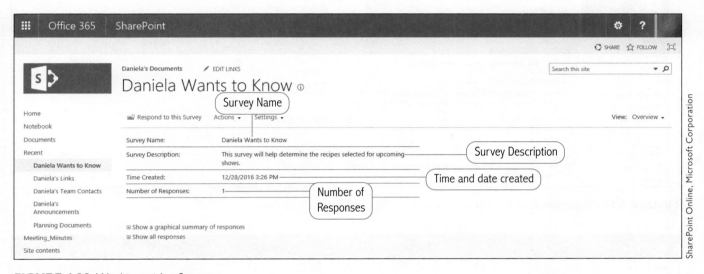

**FIGURE 4.29** Working with a Survey

Once people have completed the survey, the Actions menu enables you to review the results in one of three ways:

- Export to Spreadsheet: The export option moves the results of the survey to Excel so that you can complete analysis of the items.

- View RSS Feed: This option enables you to add an RSS feed to the survey so you can be notified when users complete the survey.

- Alert Me: This option sends you a notification when items change.

## Work with a Discussion Board List

The ***discussion board list*** supports message postings related to list topics. If you have used newsgroups, social media, or education learning management systems, you have probably participated in discussion boards. The discussion board list enables you to group messages and responses in the order in which they arrived, or by threads. The default discussion board list has columns for the subject, body, the name of the user who created the message, and the date the message was created. Additional columns can be added to the discussion board lists.

After installing the Discussion Board app, the discussion board list enables you to elicit feedback, questions, answers, and ideas from your users. Click new discussion to add a new posting. Figure 4.30 shows a discussion board with three added topics, in the default Subject view, with a response made to the first topics. The responses are viewed by clicking the subject title. A new page displays the messages related to the topic clicked, as shown in Figure 4.31. This page displays a flat view of the messages.

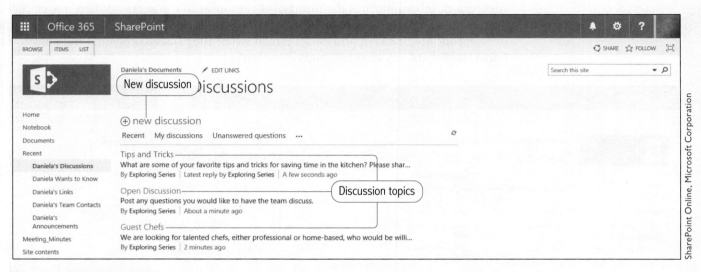

**FIGURE 4.30** Discussion Board List (Classic View)

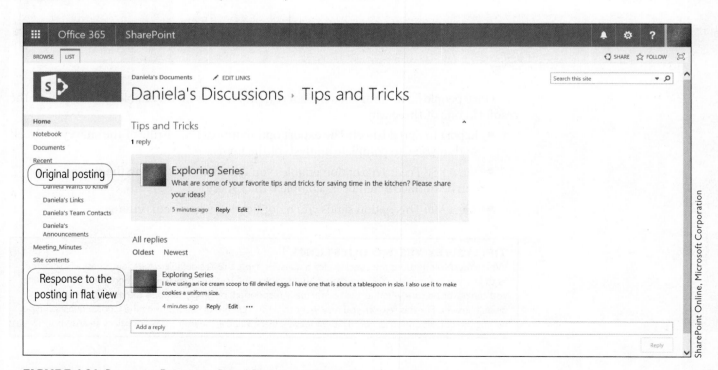

**FIGURE 4.31** Reviewing Discussion Board Responses (Classic View)

By default, the messages are displayed in a *flat view*, which displays the postings in sequence based on the date and time they were added to the discussion board list. This enables users to view the conversation as it occurred. Two additional public views of the discussion board are the Management view and the Featured Discussions view. Click the LIST tab, and click the Current View arrow to display the additional default views.

## Work with a Calendar List

The *calendar list* displays events and activities in day, week, or month layout. It is similar to an announcements list in that it displays a title, description, and time and date information when an event is displayed. Items are added to the calendar list using the EVENTS tab. Figure 4.32 shows the default calendar list view displaying the event title on the calendar date. Click the event link to display additional information such as description, location, start and end time, and category. Events can be set up as all-day events or as recurring events as the list item is added to the calendar.

**FIGURE 4.32** Calendar List in Calendar View (Classic View)

Two additional built-in views enable you to display All Events (past, present, and future) as shown in Figure 4.33, or Current Events (present and future), as shown in Figure 4.34.

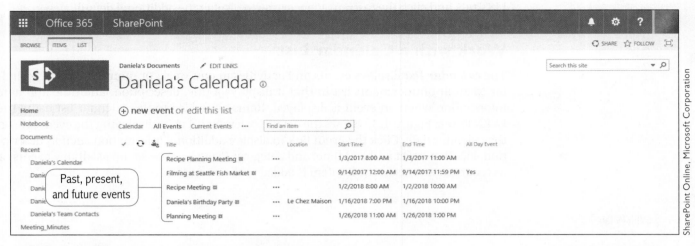

**FIGURE 4.33** Calendar List in All Events View (Classic View)

**FIGURE 4.34** Calendar List in Current Events View (Classic View)

**Quick Concept**

1. What are two advantages to setting up a default document template for a library? *p. 213*

2. What are three advantages of modifying or creating views in a document library? *p. 217*

3. What are the differences between a standard view and a datasheet view of a list? *p. 221*

# Hands-On Exercises

## 1 Work in SharePoint with Microsoft Office 2016 Documents

The planning team for Daniela's Table is growing, and more people are accessing SharePoint for information and collaboration. You will add a site devoted to working with documents, creating a document library, and providing a default document template that will be used by the team to plan upcoming episodes. You will also create a custom view for the document library. You will then create a survey to query the team about an upcoming activity.

---

**STEP 1 ›› ADD A NEW DOCUMENT LIBRARY**

You will create a new document library and change its default document template. Refer to Figure 4.35 as you complete Step 1.

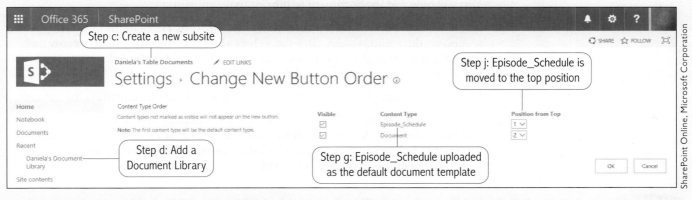

**FIGURE 4.35** Add a New Document Library (Classic View)

a. Open Internet Explorer, navigate to your Office 365 site, and then open SharePoint. Open the Team Site.

b. Click **Site Contents** on the Quick Launch. Click **Return to classic SharePoint** at the bottom of the Quick Launch.

c. Click **new subsite**. Type **Daniela's Table Documents** in the title box. Type **This site contains the documents used by the planning team** in the Description box. Type **danielas_documents** in the URL name box. Confirm that the Team Site template is selected. Accept the remaining default values. Click **Create**.

   You are creating a subsite so you can provide access to the site to all of the team members. The new site opens, and you will add a new document library to the site using the Document Library app.

d. Click **Site contents** on the Quick Launch. Click **add an app**, and click the **Document Library tile**. Type the name **Daniela's Document Library** and click **Create**.

   The newly created document library appears on the Site contents page. You will now change the site settings so that you can upload a new default document template.

e. Click the **Settings icon**, and select **Site settings** from the menu. Click **Site content types** in the Web Designer Galleries section of the Site Settings page.

**f.** Click **Create**. Type **Episode_Schedule** in the Name box. Type **This is the default template for Daniela's Document Library.** in the Description box. Click the **Select parent content type from arrow**, and select **Document Content Types**. Click the **Parent Content Type arrow**, and select **Document**. Click the **Existing group arrow** and select **Display Template Content Types**. Click **OK**.

**g.** Click **Advanced settings** on the Site Content Type page. Click **Upload a new document template**, and click **Browse**. Navigate to the student data files and select *sp04h1EpisodeSchedule*. Click **Open**, and click **OK**.

You have copied the template for the episode schedule to the library. You will now change the library settings to enable the document to be the default document that opens when you click New Document on the FILES tab.

**h.** Click **Daniela's Document Library** on the Quick Launch. Click the **LIBRARY tab**, and click **Library Settings** in the Settings group. Click **Advanced settings** in the General Settings column on the Settings page. Click **Yes** to select **Allow management of content types**, scroll to the bottom of the page, and then click **OK**.

> **TROUBLESHOOTING:** If you do not see Daniela's Document Library on the Quick Launch, click Site contents on the Quick Launch and click the Daniela's Document Library tile.

You will now add the document to the Content Types list.

**i.** Scroll down and click **Add from existing site content types** in the Content Types section on the Settings page. Click the **Select site content types from arrow** and select **Display Template Content Types**. Click **Episode_Schedule** in the Available Site Content Types box and click **Add**. Click **OK**.

The document template you created has now been fully implemented on the library.

**j.** Scroll down the Daniela's Document Library Settings page and click **Change new button order and default content type** in the Content Types section. Deselect the **Visible box** next to Document. Click the **Position from Top** arrow for Episode_Schedule and select **1**. Click **OK**.

**STEP 2** ▶▶ **ADD DOCUMENTS TO THE DOCUMENT LIBRARY**

You will create a new document based on the default template of the document library. You will upload another document to the document library. Refer to Figure 4.36 as you complete Step 2.

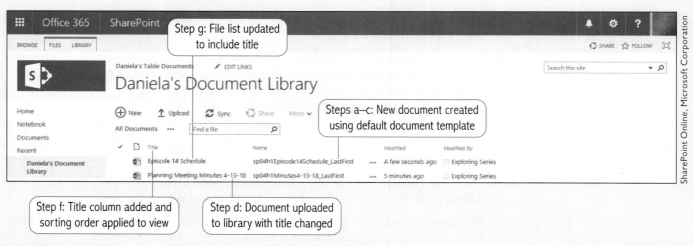

**FIGURE 4.36** Documents Added to the Document Library (Classic View)

**a.** Click **Daniela's Document Library** on the Quick Launch, and click the **FILES tab**. Click **New Document** in the New group.

The episode schedule document template opens for editing.

**b.** Click **cell B6** and type **Introduction of guest chef Charles Bonham**. Press **Ctrl+Enter** to enter the cell contents, but remain in the cell for further editing. Click the **Fill Color arrow** in the Font group and select **Blue, Lighter 80%**. Select the range **B7:B12**, and click the **Fill Color arrow**. Select **Blue, Darker 50%**.

You have updated the document. You will now save it to the library so that others can add to the file.

**c.** Click the word **Book** on the Excel Online top navigation bar. Type **sp04h1Episode14Schedule_LastFirst** for the file name, and click **cell A1**. Click **Daniela's Table Documents** on the Excel Online top navigation bar to return to the Daniela's Document Library page.

The file name appears in the document library. You will now upload another document to the library.

**d.** Click the **FILES tab** and click **Upload Document** in the New group. Browse to the location of the student data files and select *sp04h1Minutes4-13-18*. Click **Open**, and click **OK**. Add your last name and first name to the file name as **sp04h1Minutes4-13-18_LastFirst**. Type **Planning Meeting Minutes 4-13-18** in the Title box and click **Save**.

The file is displayed on the file list.

**e.** Click **sp04h1Minutes4-13-18_LastFirst** in the file list. Click **Edit Document**, and select **Edit in Browser**. Replace the words **Student Name** with your first name and last name in the Attendees list. Click **Daniela's Table Documents** on the top navigation bar.

You have edited the file to include your name. The file was saved automatically. You returned to the Document Library page. You will now add columns to the view to display the title.

**f.** Click the **More Options icon** next to All Documents on the Daniela's Document Library page, and select **Modify this View**. Click the check box next to **Title** in the Display column to select it, and click the **Position from Left arrow** for Title. Select **2** on the list of numbers. Click the **First sort by the column arrow**, and select **Title**. Click **OK**.

You modified the view of the file listing. You will now add a title to the file that is missing a title.

**g.** Click the **More Options icon** next to the file name sp04h1Episode14Schedule_LastFirst, and click the **More Options icon** on the dialog box that displays. Select **Properties** on the menu and type the title **Episode 14 Schedule** in the Title box. Click **Save**.

The two file names are displayed in the library in ascending sorted order by title.

**h.** Right-click the file name **sp04h1EpisodeSchedule_LastFirst**, and select **Download**. Click **Save As**, and navigate to the location where you store your files. Click **Save**. Repeat this step for the file **sp04h1Minutes4-13-18_LastFirst**. Take a screen shot of the Daniela's Document Library page, naming the file **sp04h1DocumentLibrary_LastFirst**. You will submit these files at the end of the last Hands-On Exercise.

You will upload a custom list and create a Datasheet View for the custom list. Refer to Figure 4.37 as you complete Step 3.

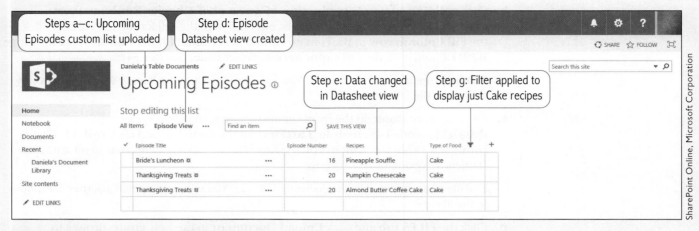

**FIGURE 4.37** Filtered Data Sheet (Classic View)

SharePoint Online, Microsoft Corporation

a. Click **Site contents** on the Quick Launch, and click **add an app**. Click the **Import Spreadsheet tile** (you may have to navigate to a second page of apps).

b. Type **Upcoming Episodes** in the Name box. Type **This is the planned listing of upcoming episodes for Daniela's Table.** Click **Browse** and navigate to the location of the student data files. Select *sp04h1UpcomingEpisodes*, click **Open**, and then click **Import**.

> **TROUBLESHOOTING:** If an error message displays, reset your Internet Explorer settings. Click Tools (the gear icon) on the browser window, select Internet Options, click the Advanced tab, and click Reset.

c. Click the **Select Range arrow**, and click **Sheet1!Table1**. Click **Import**.

   The custom upcoming episode list is displayed. You will now change the view to enable you to work with the list.

d. Click the **LIST tab** and click **Create View** in the Manage Views group. Click **Datasheet View**. Type **Episode View** in the View Name box. In the Columns section, click the **Position from Left arrow** next to Episode Title and select the number **1**. Click **OK**.

   In a few moments, the custom list is displayed in Datasheet View with the changes you made to the view. You will now update information on the list.

e. Click **Marshmallow Chocolate Roll** in the Bride's Luncheon row. Type **Pineapple Souffle**. Click **Stop editing this list**.

f. Click the **LIST tab**, click the **Current View arrow**, and then select **All Items** in the Current View menu. Review the changes to the custom list.

   The episode number appears at the far left in this view of the custom list. You cannot change any of the data in this view.

g. Click the **LIST tab** and select **Episode View** under Current View in the Manage Views group. Point to the column heading **Type of Food**, and click the arrow for the column. Select **Cake**. Click away from the menu. Take a screen shot of the filtered list, naming it **sp04h1Filter_LastFirst**.

   The custom list has been filtered to display just the episodes that have cake recipes. You will now clear the filter to display the entire list.

**h.** Point to the column heading **Type of Food**, and click the arrow for the column. Select **Clear Filter**.

The Datasheet View displays all of the episode information.

## STEP 4 》 WORK WITH SHAREPOINT BUILT-IN LIST APPS

You will modify the Announcements list view. You will create a new Survey list, customize it, and add a question to the list. Refer to Figures 4.38 and 4.39 as you complete Step 4.

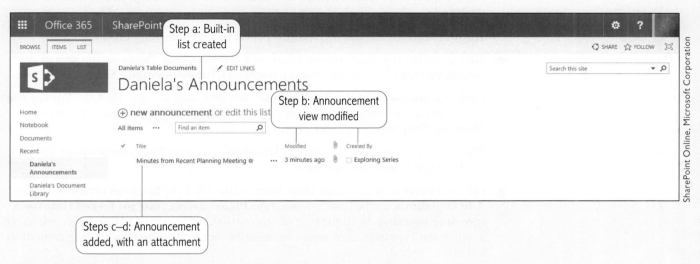

**FIGURE 4.38** Announcement Created with Custom View (Classic View)

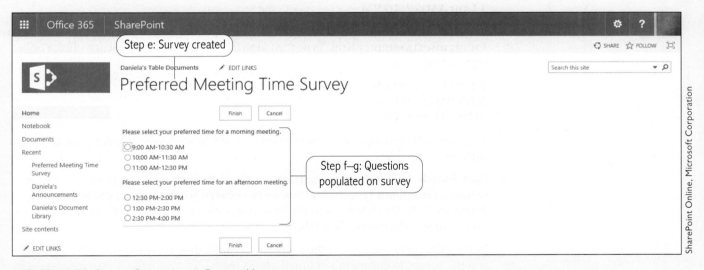

**FIGURE 4.39** Survey Created with Custom View

**a.** Click **Site contents** on the Quick Launch, and click **add an app**. Click the **Announcements tile**. Type **Daniela's Announcements** in the Name box, and click **Create**.

The app appears on the Site Contents page in an app tile.

**b.** Click the **Daniela's Announcements tile**. Click **edit this list** next to new announcement. Click the **More Options icon** and select **Modify this View** from the menu. Click the check box next to **Attachments** in the Columns list to select it, and click the check box next to **Created By**. Click **OK**.

**c.** Click **new announcement** and add the following information:

- Title: **Minutes from Recent Planning Meeting**
- Body: **Please review the minutes from the recent planning meeting we had with WKRE-TV. Contact Firstname Lastname** (replace with your name) **for more information or changes.**
- Expires: Click the **calendar icon**, and select a date using the selection calendar that is three weeks from today's date.

**d.** Click the **EDIT tab**. Click **Attach File** in the Actions group. Click **Browse**, and navigate to the student data files. Select *sp04h1Minutes4-13-18*, click **Open**, and then click **OK**. Click **Save**.

The announcement is displayed with a paperclip icon indicating the attachment.

**e.** Click the **Minutes from Recent Planning Meeting link**. Take a screen shot of the page displaying the message, naming it **sp04h1Announcement_LastFirst**.

**f.** Click **Site contents** on the Quick Launch, and click **add an app**. Click the **Survey tile** (you may have to navigate to a second page of apps), and type the name **Preferred Meeting Time Survey**. Click **Create**.

The Preferred Meeting Time Survey tile is displayed on the Site Contents page. You will now add questions to the survey.

**g.** Click the **Preferred Meeting Time Survey tile**. Click the **Settings arrow**, and select **Add Questions**. In the Question box, type **Please select your preferred time for a morning meeting.** With the type of answer to this question of **Choice** selected, scroll down to the Type each choice on a separate line box and replace the existing content as follows:

**9:00 AM-10:30 AM**
**10:00 AM-11:30 AM**
**11:00 AM-12:30 PM**

**h.** Click **Next Question**, and in the Question box type **Please select your preferred time for an afternoon meeting.** Type the following choices in the Type each choice on a separate line box:

**12:30 PM-2:00 PM**
**1:00 PM-2:30 PM**
**2:30 PM-4:00 PM**

You have added two questions to the survey, and you are ready to make some advanced settings.

**i.** Click **Finish**. Click **Advanced settings** on the Settings page in the General Settings column. Click **Read responses that were created by the user** in the Item-level Permissions section. Click **No** in the Search section for Allow items from the survey to appear in search results. Click **OK**.

You set the survey up so that the users can see only their replies to the survey. You will test the survey to ensure that it functions correctly.

**j.** Click **Site contents** on the Quick Launch. Click the **Preferred Meeting Time Survey tile**, and click **Respond to this Survey**. Select a response for each question, and click **Finish**.

**k.** Click **Show all responses** on the Preferred Meeting Time Survey page. Click **View Response #1** to review the response. Take a screen shot of the completed survey, naming the file **sp04h1Survey_LastFirst**. Click **Close**.

**l.** Click **SharePoint** on the top navigation bar to return to the top-level team site, if you plan to continue to the next Hands-On Exercise. If not, sign out of your Office 365 account and close the browser.

# Integration of Word and PowerPoint Files in SharePoint Sites

One of the biggest strengths of SharePoint Online is its integration with Microsoft Office applications, including Word, PowerPoint, Excel, and OneNote. Features in Office 2016 enhance document sharing with SharePoint 2016. When you store documents in a SharePoint document library, users can open the document and see who else is editing the document on the status bar. SharePoint Online enables you to take content offline so you can work on both documents and list items without an Internet connection. You can collaborate simultaneously, with other users, in editing Word or PowerPoint files in a process known as "coauthoring." PowerPoint presentations can also be streamed over the Web using SharePoint Online sites.

Word and PowerPoint support a large number of file formats that can be integrated into a SharePoint site. For example, the Portable Document Format (PDF) and XML Paper Specification (XPS) formats are supported by both Word and PowerPoint, and can be easily integrated into a SharePoint site.

***Portable Document Format (PDF)*** and ***XML Paper Specification (XPS)*** are both fixed-layout file formats that preserve document formatting and enable file sharing. The PDF and XPS formats ensure that whether the file is viewed online or printed, the format remains exactly as you created it. In addition, the data in the file cannot be easily changed. The PDF format is used when the document will be commercially printed.

---

**TIP: MORE ABOUT MICROSOFT OFFICE 2016, PDF AND XPS**
To read more about the Microsoft XPS format, see the Microsoft webpage "XML Paper Specification: Overview" https://msdn.microsoft.com/en-us/library/windows/hardware/dn641615(v=vs.85) .aspx. The add-in used to create the PDF and XPS file formats is a part of Office 2016, so no additional downloads or applications are needed to create documents in these formats.

---

In this section, you will learn how you can work with SharePoint Online, Word, and PowerPoint to integrate Word and PowerPoint documents into SharePoint sites.

## Integrating Word Files in SharePoint Sites

Microsoft Word enables users to create a regular Word document (.docx file format), a webpage (.htm or .html file format), or an XML file (.xml file format). It also offers three options for saving a Word document as a webpage: Single File Web Page; Web Page; and Web Page, Filtered. You can also save and export a Word document as a PDF (.pdf file format) or XPS Document (.xps file format). When you are creating a webpage in Word, work in the Web Layout view because it gives you a good idea of how the document will look when it is viewed in a browser.

The ***Single File Web Page option*** saves the entire document into a single .mht or .mhtml format file, which is supported only by Internet Explorer. The ***Web Page option*** saves the document as an .htm or .html file with a set of files (grouped in a folder having the same name as that of the .htm or .html file), which enables you to rebuild the original Word document (for example, but not limited to, all graphic files included in the original Word document, and .xml files defining the color scheme used by the original Word document). Word metadata includes information about the document, such as the full name, path, smart tags, hyperlinks, track changes, comments, hidden text, and the last 10 authors. The ***Web Page, Filtered option*** saves the document in an .htm or .html file format and saves an additional set of files grouped in a folder, but it filters and removes all the Word-specific metadata.

# Add Word Documents to a SharePoint Site

Microsoft Office 2016 and SharePoint are closely integrated and enable you to save, open, and share documents easily. You can open documents on portable devices, such as tablets and smartphones, and make modifications. A connection between a SharePoint Online library and Microsoft Office application enables you to open and save Office documents directly to the SharePoint library. This ensures that the most up-to-date version is stored in a central location for access by everyone. Through coauthoring, multiple authors can work on the same document at the same time, using either the desktop application or an Office web app.

---

**TIP: CONNECT OFFICE TO SHAREPOINT ONLINE**

By connecting a SharePoint Online library to Office, you can establish a connection that adds a short-cut to the Office desktop programs that enables you to open and save the Office documents directly to the SharePoint library. Navigate to the library you want to connect with in SharePoint Online. Click the LIBRARY tab and click the Connect to Office arrow in the Connect & Export group. Click Add to SharePoint Sites to add the shortcut to the library to the Office desktop applications. You can also use this command to remove shortcuts you have previously used to connect and to manage the list of shortcuts, as shown in Figure 4.40.

---

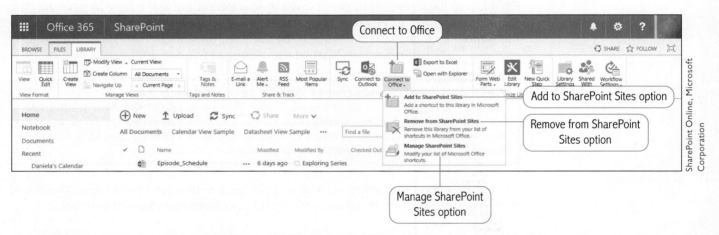

**FIGURE 4.40** Setting Up a Shortcut Connection between Office and SharePoint Online (Classic View)

As you create documents in the desktop application of Word, you can save the file directly to SharePoint.

---

**To save a Word document to SharePoint, complete the following steps:**

1. Open or create the document in Word.
2. Click the File tab, and click Save As, as shown in Figure 4.41.
3. Click the SharePoint site name in the left pane.
4. Click Browse or select a folder from the Recent Folders list.
5. Navigate to the location where you want to place the file.
6. Type a document name and select the appropriate Save as type if you are saving it as something other than a Word document.
7. Click Save. You may be prompted to select a Content Type, such as Document. Click OK after making a selection.

---

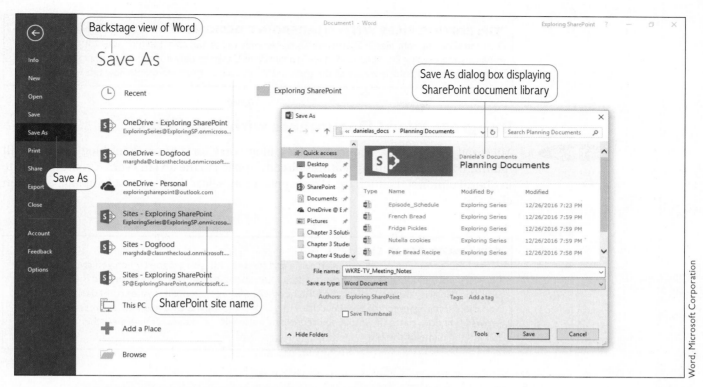

**FIGURE 4.41** Saving a Word Document to SharePoint Online Using Backstage View

> **TIP: WORKING WITH THE WORD WEB PAGE OR WEB PAGE, FILTERED FORMATS**
> When you are working with a document saved as a Web Page, or as a Web Page, Filtered format, the supporting files are not automatically uploaded or imported for you by SharePoint Online from the *filename_files* folder. Therefore, you must upload/import this folder as well.

SharePoint enables you to upload any Word file format to a document library. From a Web designer's point of view, the process of uploading a document saved as a PDF, XPS Document, and Single File Web Page is identical. The graphic files are embedded in these documents so there is no need to upload/import them separately.

When a Word document is opened in a SharePoint Online site, the document is opened, by default, in Word Online. You can then select whether you wish to edit the document using the Word Online app or using the Word desktop application. Click Edit Document when the document opens and select the option you want to use. There are some advantages of using each option. If you just have a few items that need to be updated, the Word Online app is a good option to select. The Ribbon in Word Online is not as full-featured but still very functional. As you work in Word Online, your work is automatically saved back to the file location in SharePoint Online. If you have a lot of editing to complete, use the option to edit in the Word application on your desktop computer. You will have a fully functioning Ribbon. You will have to save the document back to SharePoint using Backstage view when you have completed the editing process.

To open an uploaded .pdf or .xps file in SharePoint, click the file name in the document library. The .pdf file will display in a Reader window, and the .xps file will display in an XPS Viewer window. If you want to modify any document in Word's .pdf or .xps file format, edit the original .docx source file of the webpage in Word, save it again as a .pdf or .xps file, and then import the updated file into your website, replacing the existing file.

If you want to modify any uploaded document created in Word's .mht file format, edit the original .docx source file of the webpage in Word, save it again as an .mht file, and then import the updated file into the website, replacing the existing file.

## Integrate Word Documents with Blog Sites

**STEP 2** ≫ Microsoft Word enables you to create a blog entry for a SharePoint blog site that will maintain all the formatting features already applied to the text in Word. Create a blog site in SharePoint first. Launch the Word application, select the Blog post template, and then click Create.

**If this is the first time you have created a blog post, complete the following steps to register your blog account:**

1. Click Register Now on the Register a Blog Account dialog box, as shown in Figure 4.42.
2. Click SharePoint blog in the New Blog Account dialog box, and click Next.
3. Type or paste the URL of your SharePoint blog in the Blog URL box of the New SharePoint Blog Account dialog box, and click OK. A Microsoft confirmation box indicating that your account was successfully registered will display when the connection has been made to the SharePoint blog.

**FIGURE 4.42** Registering a SharePoint Blog Site

The Blog Post tab displays in the Word window, as shown in Figure 4.43. Type the title and text you want to post to the blog, and click Publish in the Blog group. A confirmation of your post appears at the top of the Word document.

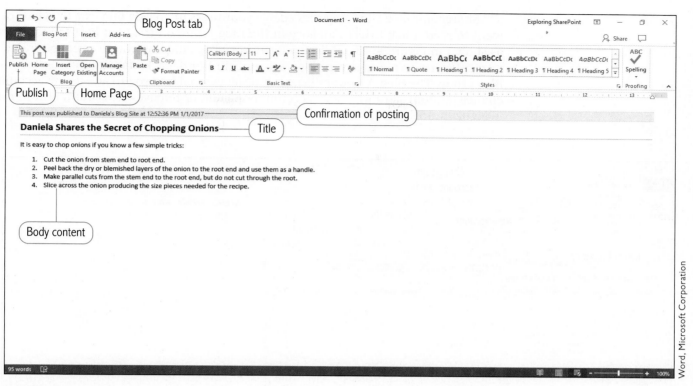

**FIGURE 4.43** Creating a Blog Post

Click Home Page in the Blog group (refer to Figure 4.43) to see your post on the Blog site, as shown in Figure 4.44.

**FIGURE 4.44** Reviewing a Blog Posting in SharePoint Online (Classic View)

---

**TIP: SHAREPOINT BLOG SITE RSS FEEDS**

By default, RSS feeds are enabled for SharePoint blog sites. When the RSS feed icon is orange (refer to Figure 4.44), users can subscribe to this RSS feed.

---

SharePoint Blog site categories enable your users to quickly find exactly what they want to read. Click Insert Category in the Blog group on the Blog Post tab in Word, as shown in Figure 4.45, to display a category list, enabling you to select or create a new category. To manage your blog accounts in Word, click Manage Accounts in the Blog group. The Blog Account dialog box displays, enabling you to add a new account, change account settings, set an account as default, or remove an account, also shown in Figure 4.45.

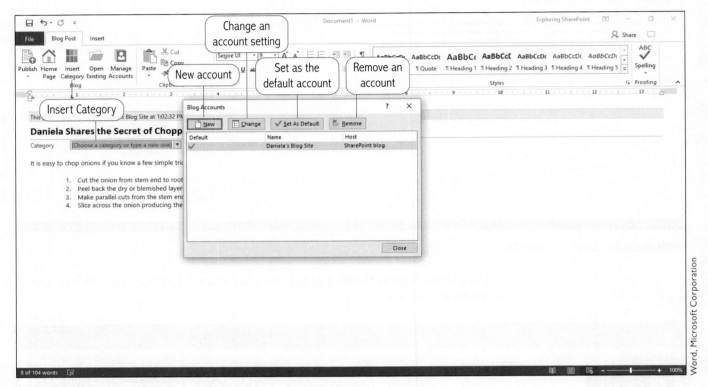

**FIGURE 4.45** Selecting a Category and Managing Blog Accounts

# Integrating PowerPoint Files in SharePoint Sites

**STEP 3** ➤➤ PowerPoint, a popular Office application, is so versatile that a nine-year-old child could use it to prepare a show-and-tell school presentation, a PhD candidate could use it to prepare his or her thesis dissertation, or a corporate communications team could use it to prepare a company's annual report to shareholders. PowerPoint enables you to save a presentation directly from PowerPoint to a SharePoint Online document library. You can also add a link to a PowerPoint presentation.

The PowerPoint Backstage view enables you to save a presentation to a SharePoint library, using Save As and browsing to the location where you want to save the presentation on the SharePoint site.

Depending on the size of the presentation, it can take a few moments to upload the presentation to SharePoint Online, as indicated on the status bar at the bottom of the PowerPoint window. The presentation file name is displayed in the document library list. Click the name of the presentation to open the file in PowerPoint Online. It can then be displayed as a slide show, edited using PowerPoint Online or the PowerPoint desktop application, or shared with others.

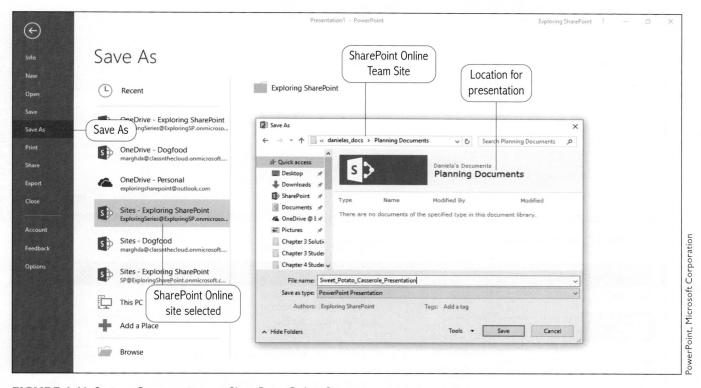

**FIGURE 4.46** Saving a Presentation to a SharePoint Online Site

You can add a link to a PowerPoint presentation saved in original PowerPoint format (.pptx) or PowerPoint Show format (.ppsx) on a SharePoint page. By doing this, you can provide access to a presentation on any page in your site.

**To add a link that points to a PowerPoint presentation, complete the following steps:**

1. Open the SharePoint page where you want the link to appear for editing. Place the insertion point in the location where you want the link to be displayed.
2. Click the INSERT tab, and click Link in the Links group.
3. Click From SharePoint and navigate to the location of the PowerPoint presentation using the Select an Asset dialog box, as shown in Figure 4.47.
4. Select the presentation and click Insert. The link appears on the page where you placed the insertion point. Save the page, and test the link. When you click a link to the presentation, the file opens in the desktop application of PowerPoint, as shown in Figure 4.48.

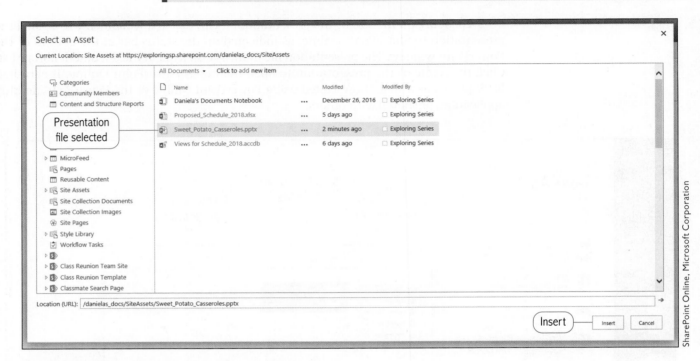

**FIGURE 4.47** Select an Asset Dialog Box (Classic View)

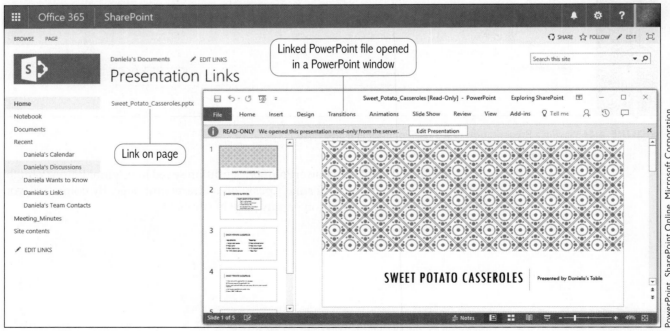

**FIGURE 4.48** Opening a Presentation from a Link

You can also save a PowerPoint presentation as a Windows Media Video (.wmv) file, retaining the animations, narrations, and other multimedia elements. You can then upload the file into a SharePoint library and add a link on a webpage. When you click the link, the Windows Media Player window displays, enabling the user to play the .wmv video file.

---

**TIP: SHARE A PRESENTATION**

PowerPoint presentations can be uploaded to a document library and shared with others for collaboration and display. Select the presentation in the document library and click Share, as shown in Figure 4.49. Type the addresses of the people you want to share the file with, select the editing rights, and click Share in the dialog box.

---

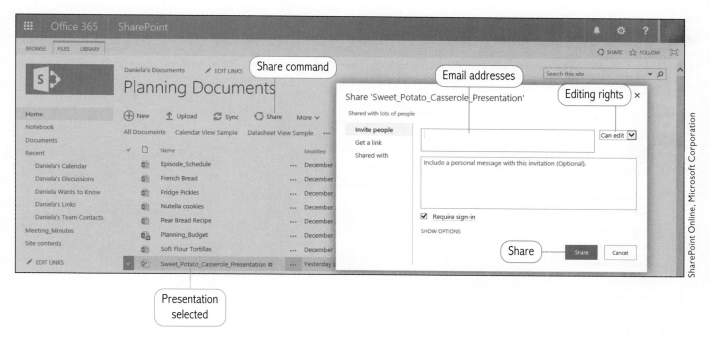

**FIGURE 4.49** Share a Presentation

*Quick Concept*

4. What are two fixed-layout file formats and why would you use each of them? *p. 243*

5. Why would you create a blog post in Word rather than in SharePoint? *p. 246*

6. What is the advantage of saving a PowerPoint presentation as a Windows Media Video file and uploading it to a SharePoint library? *p. 251*

# Hands-On Exercises

**Skills covered:** Add a
Word Document • Create a Blog
Subsite • Publish a Blog Post
• Save a Presentation to a Site

## 2 Integration of Word and PowerPoint Files in SharePoint Sites

Many documents are needed to support the Daniela's Table television broadcast. Viewers will want to see recipes, tips, and more. You will integrate Word and PowerPoint files into SharePoint to enable the viewers to find what they want. You will create a blog on the site and make a post to the blog from Word.

### STEP 1 ▶▶ ADD A WORD DOCUMENT TO A SHAREPOINT SITE

You will modify a Word document and save it directly to SharePoint Online as a Single File Web Page. Refer to Figure 4.50 as you complete Step 1.

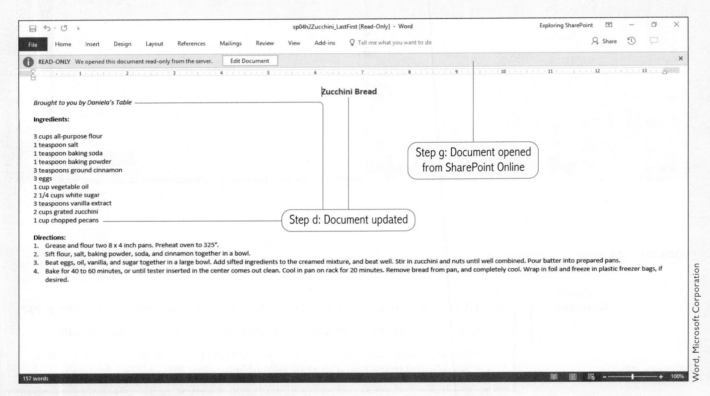

**FIGURE 4.50** Single File Web Page Word Document

a. Open a browser and navigate to your Office 365 site, if you exited after the previous Hands-On Exercise. Click the **Team Site tile**.

b. Click **Site Contents** on the Quick Launch, and ensure the classic SharePoint view is displayed. Scroll down, and click the subsite link to **Daniela's Table Documents**.

c. Open the Word desktop application and open the Word document *sp04h2Zucchini* from the student data files.

You will make some minor modifications to this Word file before saving it to the SharePoint site.

**d.** Select the title **Zucchini Bread** and change the font color to **Dark Blue, Text 2**. Insert a new paragraph after the title, and type **Brought to you by Daniela's Table**. Select the text you just typed and apply *italic* formatting to it. Select the word *walnuts* in the second column of the ingredients list, and type **pecans**.

**e.** Click the **File tab** to open Backstage view, and click **Save As**. Click **SharePoint** on the taskbar to display the Daniela's Table Document site. Right-click the **URL** in the address bar of the browser and select **Copy**. Minimize the browser window to return to the Word Backstage view. Click **Browse**. Right-click the **address bar** in the Save As dialog box, and click **Edit address**. Right-click the **address bar** again in the Save As dialog box and click **Paste**. Delete the address text to the right of the site name (*danielas_documents*) and click the **Go to arrow** on the right side of the address box. Double-click **Documents** under Document Libraries to select the folder.

**f.** Click the **Save as type arrow** and select **Single File Web Page**. Click **Open**. Add your last and first name to the file name in the format **sp04h2Zucchini_LastFirst**. Click **Save**.

The document format changes in the Word desktop application. You will now review the page in SharePoint Online.

**g.** Close Word. Click **Site contents** on the Quick Launch of the SharePoint Online window and click the **Documents tile**. Click **sp04h2Zucchini_LastFirst** in the file list. Review the document and take a screen shot displaying it, naming it **sp04h2WordRecipe_LastFirst**. Close Word.

---

**STEP 2 »  INTEGRATE A WORD DOCUMENT WITH A BLOG SITE**

You will add a subsite using the Blog template, and then add a document to the blog using the Word desktop application. Refer to Figure 4.51 as you complete Step 2.

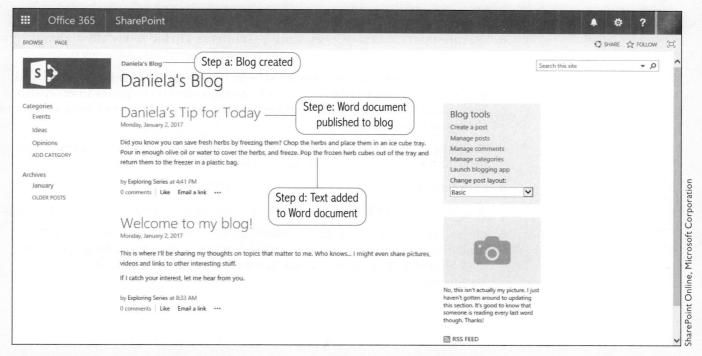

**FIGURE 4.51** Posting to a Blog Using Word

**a.** Click **Site contents** on the Quick Launch of the Daniela's Table Documents site. Click **new subsite** and create a site using the following specifications:

- Title: **Daniela's Blog**
- Description: **Daniela writes a weekly blog with tips and tricks.**
- URL name: **daniela_blog**
- Select a template: **Blog**
- Accept all other default values

**b.** Open the desktop application of Word. Click **Blog post** on the template list, and then click **Create**.

You will register your blog in Word so that the posting is placed on the site.

> **TROUBLESHOOTING:** If you do not see Blog post listed among the templates, type blog in the Search for online templates box and search for the template.

**c.** Click **Register Now** in the Register a Blog Account dialog box. Click the **Blog arrow** and then select **SharePoint blog**. Click **Next**. Open the SharePoint Online window that displays the blog site you just created and copy the URL from the address bar. Paste the URL in the Blog URL box in the New SharePoint Blog Account dialog box in Word and delete /default.aspx from the URL you just pasted. Click **OK**. Click **OK** after the account registration process is complete.

A message briefly displays indicating that the blog provider is being contacted. It can take a few moments for the registration process to finish.

> **TROUBLESHOOTING:** If you already have a blog account listed in Word, click Manage Accounts in the Blog group and click New to register a new account.

**d.** Click the title *Enter Post Title Here* and type **Daniela's Tip for Today**. Click below the line that separates the title from the body of the posting and type the following posting:

**Did you know you can save fresh herbs by freezing them? Chop the herbs and place them in an ice cube tray. Pour in enough olive oil or water to cover the herbs, and freeze. Pop the frozen herb cubes out of the tray and return them to the freezer in a plastic bag.**

Click **ABC** in the Proofing group and make any spelling corrections that are necessary. Read the document to ensure it is accurate before you post it to the blog.

**e.** Click **Publish** in the Blog group on the BLOG POST tab.

A notification that the blog has been posted is displayed at the top of the Word document.

**f.** Close Word without saving the document. Refresh the browser view and review the blog. Take a screen shot of the blog posting, naming the file **sp04h2Blog_LastFirst**. Click **SharePoint** on the top navigation bar and navigate back to the Daniela's Table Documents site.

You will open, modify, and save a PowerPoint presentation to the Daniela's Table Documents site. Refer to Figure 4.52 as you complete Step 3.

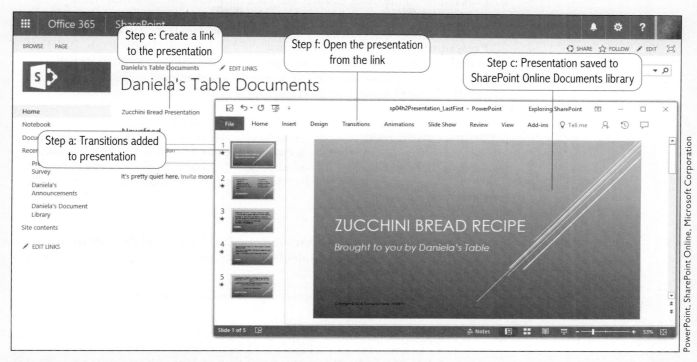

**FIGURE 4.52** PowerPoint Presentation Opened from SharePoint Online Link

a. Navigate to the PowerPoint presentation *sp04h2Presentation* in the student data files and double-click the file name to open it in the desktop application of PowerPoint. Click **Slide 1** in the left pane, hold Shift, and then click **Slide 5** in the left pane to select all of the slides in the presentation. Click the **Transitions tab**, and click **Split** in the Transition to This Slide group. Click **Slide 2**, and select the ingredient list on the left. Click the **Animations tab**, and click **Wipe** in the Animation group. Select the ingredient list on the right and apply the same animation to the list.

You have modified the presentation to make it a little more interesting.

b. Click the **File tab** to open Backstage view, and click **Save As**. Display the SharePoint window and copy the URL from the top of the browser window. Minimize the SharePoint window. Click **Browse** on the Save As page, right-click the **address bar** on the Save As dialog box, and then select **Paste**. Remove the text after the name of the site (danielas_ documents). Click the **Go to arrow** to the right of the address bar. Select **Documents** in the Documents Libraries list and click **Open**.

c. Add your last name and first name to the file name in the format **sp04h2Presentation_LastFirst**. Click the **Save As type arrow** and select **PowerPoint Show**. Click **Save**. Close the PowerPoint desktop application.

d. Display the SharePoint Online browser window and click **Documents** on the Quick Launch of the Daniela's Table Documents site. Click the **sp04h2Presentation_ LastFirst link** to open the presentation in PowerPoint Online. Click **Start Slide Show** and navigate through the slides to ensure that the transitions and animations work. Click **Daniela's Table Documents** on the top navigation bar to return to the SharePoint Online Documents library.

After successfully loading the presentation onto SharePoint, you decide to place a link to the presentation on the home page of the site.

> **TROUBLESHOOTING:** If a security warning displays at the bottom of the screen when you start the slide show, click Allow once.

**e.** Click **Home** on the Quick Launch, and click the **PAGE tab**. Click **Edit**. Click **REMOVE THIS** to remove the Get started with your site Web Part and click **OK**. Click in the content placeholder that you just cleared and type **Zucchini Bread Presentation**. Select the words you just typed and click the **INSERT tab**. Click **Link** in the Links group and select **From SharePoint**. In the left pane, navigate to the Daniela's Table Documents site and double-click **Documents** in the right pane. Click **sp04h2Presentation_LastFirst** and click **Insert**.

> **TROUBLESHOOTING:** If you do not see From SharePoint when you click Link, you will need to navigate to the Documents library, click More Options next to the file name sp04h2Presentation_LastFirst, and copy the URL in the link box (below *Shared with lots of people*). Open the Home page again for editing, click the INSERT tab, and then click Link in the Links group. Paste the URL into the Address box and click OK.

**f.** Click the **PAGE tab**, and click **Save**. Click the **Zucchini Bread Presentation** hyperlink on the Home page of Daniela's Table Documents, and click **Open** on the security bar at the bottom of the window.

The file is downloaded to your local computer and opened in the PowerPoint desktop application.

**g.** Resize the PowerPoint window so that you can see the presentation and the SharePoint page with the link, as shown in Figure 4.52. Take a screen shot of the window, naming the file **sp04h2Link_LastFirst**. You will submit all of the files created at the end of the last Hands-On Exercise.

**h.** Click **SharePoint** on the top navigation bar to return to the top-level team site if you plan to continue to the next Hands-On Exercise. If not, sign out of Office 365.

# Integration of Excel and Access Files in SharePoint Sites

Microsoft Excel 2016 and Access 2016 enable you to easily import data from and export data to SharePoint Online lists. Excel provides only one-way synchronization between SharePoint lists and Excel spreadsheets, whereas Access provides developers with two-way synchronization between SharePoint lists and Access databases. Access also enables developers to create SharePoint data-driven applications.

In this section, you will learn about the different approaches you can take to integrate Excel and Access with SharePoint Online sites, from copying and pasting content to a SharePoint page, to importing and exporting data from Excel and Access files into SharePoint lists.

## Integrating Excel Files in SharePoint Sites

Excel is one of the most in-demand Microsoft applications in the business world. Its versatility enables students from elementary school through college, home and business owners, or scientists to fulfill a wide variety of tasks. With its friendly user interface and comprehensive set of features, Excel can assist you in building a spreadsheet for tracking your household expenses or sophisticated business and scientific statistical studies and charts.

Excel enables integration with other applications. Its capability to create documents that can be cut and pasted onto a webpage, or even to create a document ready to be published on the Web, has consistently improved in each new version of Office. Excel 2016 enables you to export to and import data from a SharePoint list. You can also edit Excel file data offline and then synchronize it with a SharePoint list.

### Add Excel Content to a Webpage

You can take advantage of the Microsoft Excel and SharePoint Online content integration features and use content created in Excel in your webpages. The easiest way to add Excel content to a SharePoint Online page is by using traditional copy and paste commands. Launch Excel, open the workbook you want to use the data from, and copy the data onto the Clipboard. Launch SharePoint Online and create a new Wiki page or open an existing one. Paste the information into position in the content box on the page, as shown in Figure 4.53.

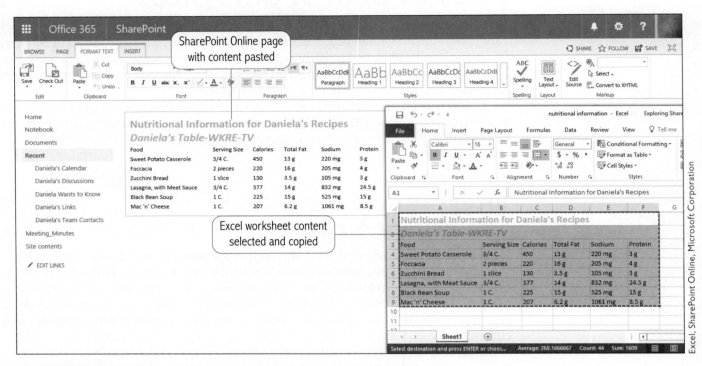

**FIGURE 4.53** Copy and Paste from Excel to SharePoint Online (Classic View)

As you paste information onto a SharePoint Online page, you have three paste options. You can paste the information, which reproduces the content much like it is shown on the worksheet (refer to Figure 4.53). If you select the Paste Clean option, the information appears in a grid format, as shown in Figure 4.54. The third option you have in SharePoint Online is Paste Plaintext, which removes all column formatting and places the text in rows, as shown in Figure 4.55.

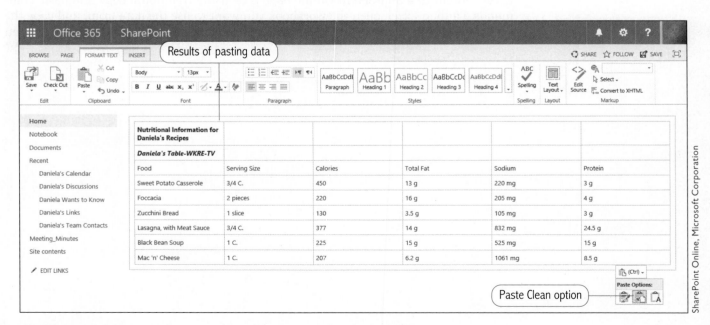

**FIGURE 4.54** Pasting Information Using the Paste Clean Option (Classic View)

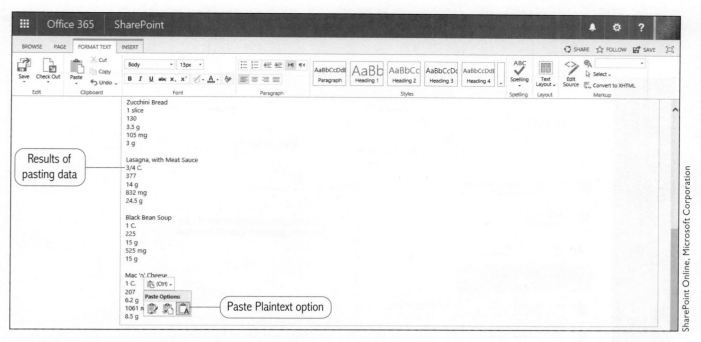

**FIGURE 4.55** Pasting Information Using the Paste Plaintext Option (Classic View)

## Upload Excel Files to a SharePoint Library

SharePoint Online enables you to upload any Excel file format into a library. Microsoft Excel 2016 enables users to create XML formats, such as an Excel Workbook (.xlsx). Many options are available for saving or exporting an Excel document as an Excel Binary Workbook (.xlsb) as XML Data, as a Web Page (.htm or .html) or Single File Web Page (.mht or .mhtml), or as a PDF (.pdf) or an XPS document (.xps).

If you use the Web Page option, the document is saved as an .htm or .html file with a set of files grouped in a *filename_files* folder that includes Excel metadata, which enables you to rebuild the original Excel document. Excel metadata includes information about the document, such as the full name, path, smart tags, hyperlinks, track changes, comments, hidden text, and the last 10 authors.

The Single File Web Page option saves the entire Excel document into a single .mht or .mhtml format file, which is supported only by Internet Explorer version 6.0 and higher. When you save an Excel document as a Single File Web Page or Web Page, you can choose to save the Entire Workbook, or as a Selection: Sheet (the active worksheet). When you click Publish, the Publish as Web Page dialog box opens, enabling you to select the AutoRepublish check box so the webpage is automatically republished every time the corresponding workbook is saved, as shown in Figure 4.56.

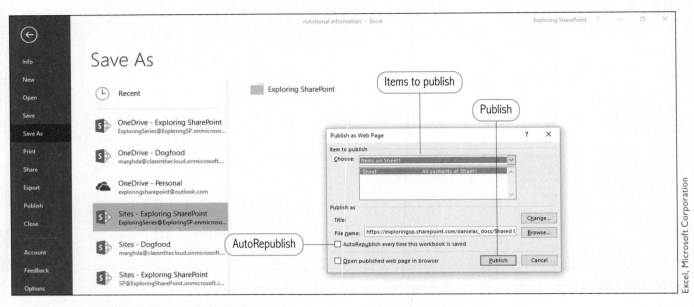

**FIGURE 4.56** Publishing a Single File Web Page

When you save an Excel document as a PDF or an XPS Document, click Options to open the Options dialog box, as shown in Figure 4.57. Within the sections of this dialog box, you can select the Page range, if you want to publish the Active sheet(s), the Entire workbook, or just a selection (range of cells) within a workbook. A **range** is a group of adjacent or contiguous cells. If a table is selected in a workbook, you can also publish the table. A **table** is a range that contains related data, structured to allow easy management and analysis.

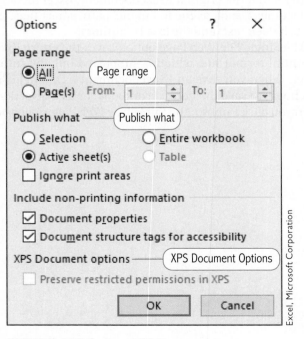

**FIGURE 4.57** Saving a XPS Document

To upload an Excel document to a SharePoint Online library, you apply the same procedure explained previously for Word document uploads. From a developer's point of view, the process of importing an Excel document saved as an XLSX, PDF, XPS Document; Single File Web Page; or Web Page format is identical. When you are working with a document saved as a Web Page format, the supporting files are not automatically imported for you from the *filename_files* folder. These files must be individually uploaded.

The Save As tab of Excel's Backstage view enables you to directly save the whole workbook, selected sheets, or named items in the workbook to a SharePoint document library, as shown in Figure 4.58.

**To save the document to SharePoint Online, complete the following steps:**

1. Click the File tab and click Save As.
2. Select the SharePoint server in the Save As list.
3. Click the folder in the right pane to open the Save As dialog box.
4. Scroll to select the site where you want to save the document and double-click the icon next to the site name.
5. Navigate to the document library where you want to save the document, and double-click the icon next to the folder name. Click Save.

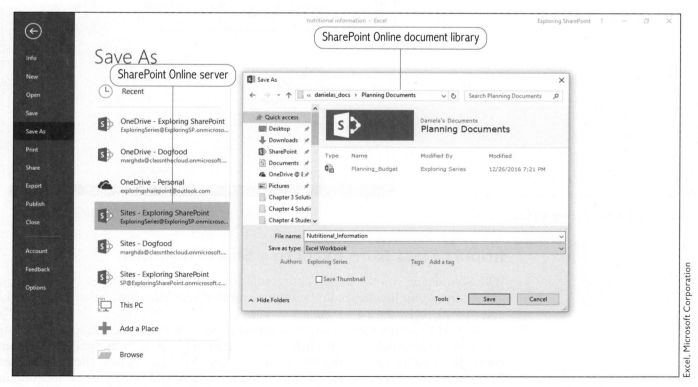

**FIGURE 4.58** Saving Directly to SharePoint Online

When you click the link to the uploaded Excel document in SharePoint Online, the file opens in Excel Online with options to edit the workbook in the browser or the Excel desktop application, as shown in Figure 4.59.

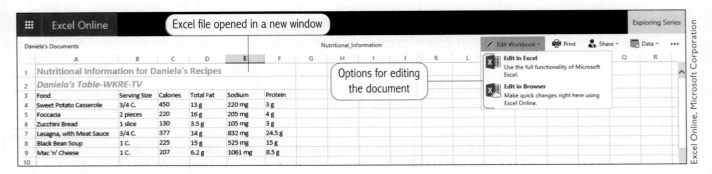

**FIGURE 4.59** Opening an Excel File

You can add a link to an Excel workbook (.xlsx) that you have previously uploaded to a SharePoint document library using the procedure introduced for PowerPoint files. When you click the link, the Excel file will open in a Excel desktop application window, as shown in Figure 4.60.

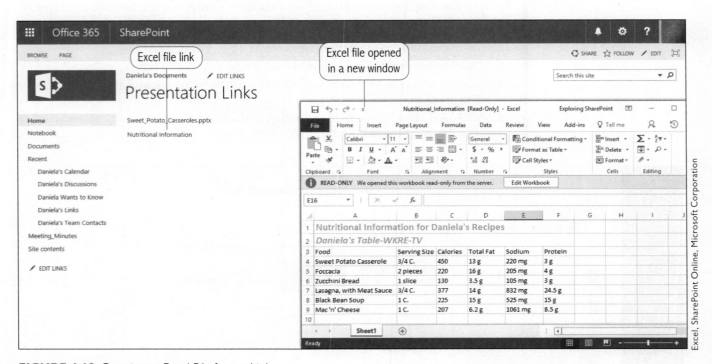

**FIGURE 4.60** Opening an Excel File from a Link

## Import Data from Excel to a SharePoint List

With SharePoint, you can import data contained in an Excel spreadsheet, range, or table into a SharePoint list. Depending on the permission level they hold, other users will be able to read, revise the list, or enter new data.

Open the site in which you wish to import Excel data in Internet Explorer, click Site contents on the Quick Launch, click New, and then select App, or in classic SharePoint view, click add an app on the Site contents page. Navigate to and click the Import Spreadsheet tile. Type a name for the list, a description, and browse to the location of the Excel file. Click Import. Select a Range Type in the Import to Windows SharePoint

Services list, and then select the range. Click Import, as shown in Figure 4.61. The list is displayed on the site, as shown in Figure 4.62, and available as a tile by clicking Site contents on the Quick Launch. You can manage the list by adding new items, editing existing items (use the More Options icon next to the item, or click *edit this list* to modify multiple items), or by modifying the view (click the More Options icon next to the search box).

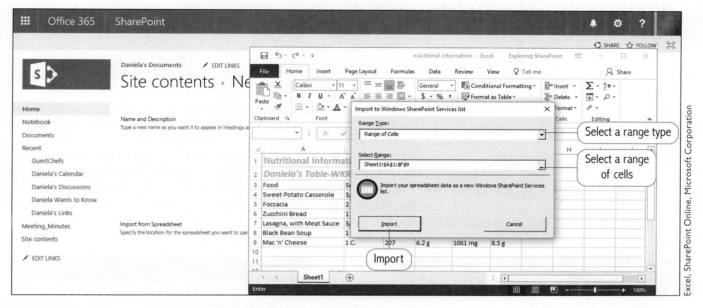

**FIGURE 4.61** Importing an Excel Spreadsheet into a List

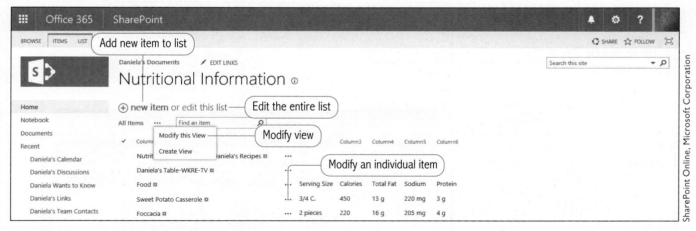

**FIGURE 4.62** Viewing the List (Classic View)

## Export Data from a SharePoint List to an Excel File

**STEP 2** ➤➤ Excel enables you to create a saved *Web query (.iqy)*, which extracts data from text or tables on a webpage and imports that data into Excel. With SharePoint Online, you can export the contents of SharePoint lists, document libraries, and survey results to an Excel worksheet as an Excel Web query that will automatically be updated anytime you make changes to the original list or library. This automatic update is realized by a connection maintained by Excel between the spreadsheet that becomes a linked object and the SharePoint list.

This export method applies only to the columns and rows included in the current view of the list. That means you will need to create a list view that includes all the columns and rows that you want to export, or export an existing view and then filter the data in Excel.

**To export data from a list, complete the following steps:**

1. Open the list in SharePoint Online in classic SharePoint view.
2. Click the LIST tab, and click Export to Excel in the Connect & Export group.
3. Click the Save arrow (at the bottom of the window) and select Save As.
4. Navigate to the location where you want to save the file and click Save.

The file downloads into Excel as an owssvr.iqy web query file and is ready to be saved to your local computer, as shown in Figure 4.63. The Design tab is active, and each column has an AutoFilter arrow in the header row, enabling you to further refine the display of the exported data. Any change you make to the Excel spreadsheet will not show in the source SharePoint list. However, any changes you make to the SharePoint list will automatically be made to the linked worksheet. After editing the SharePoint Online list, click Refresh in the External Table Data group on the Table Tools Design tab to view the updated information.

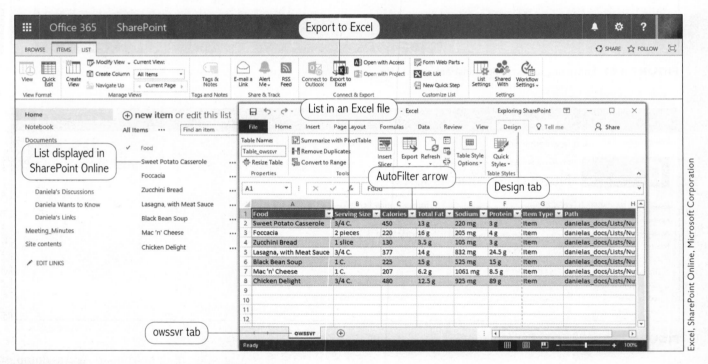

**FIGURE 4.63** Exporting a List to Excel (Classic View)

Excel enables you to modify the way data will be synchronized between the SharePoint list and the linked Excel spreadsheet. Click the Data tab in Excel and click Properties in the Connections group, as shown in Figure 4.64, to display and select the settings in the External Data Properties dialog box.

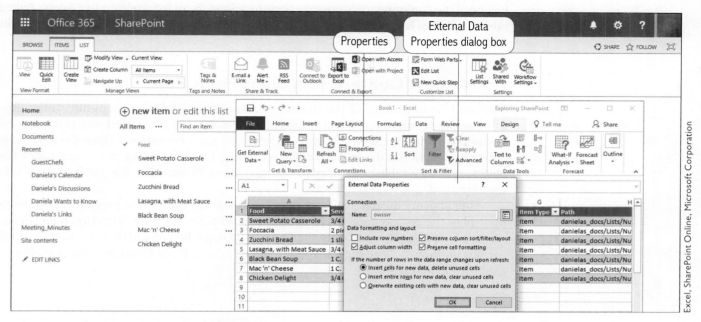

**FIGURE 4.64** External Data Properties Dialog Box

# Integrating Access Files in SharePoint Sites

In response to the boom of the Internet, with applications built on real-time access to databases for e-commerce and e-trading in recent years, the SharePoint database capabilities have been upgraded. Access is one of the most in-demand, powerful, yet easy-to-use relational databases. Profit and nonprofit organizations use databases to keep track of their employees, volunteers, events, sales, product inventories, and acquisitions. A **database** is a file of related data containing objects such as tables, queries, reports, and forms. All records in a database table consist of the same set of database fields. Usually databases display their records as rows within tables. A **database table** is a set of related data containing records arranged in rows and columns, which are fields.

Access requires a Windows environment to run. Access provides wizards that walk users through the setup of simple relational databases. Access is a product suitable for the development of small-scale databases that are used in office workgroups with relatively few numbers of users. However, because of its ease of use, Access is often used to develop prototypes of larger-scale databases. Migration of data from an Access database into another database (such as SQL Server or Oracle) can be accomplished relatively easily. Therefore, Access can be a good choice for small-scale databases that will eventually require a more robust environment.

Access 2016 provides you with considerable SharePoint connectivity enhancements and a wizard that enables you to fully take advantage of SharePoint Online list improvements. You can export a table, report, or a query object to a wide range of formats, such as an external file, an Excel workbook, a Rich Text Format (.rtf), a text file, a PDF, or XPS file. You can also export into formats for an email attachment, an Extensible Markup Language (XML) document, an Open Database Connectivity (ODBC) data source, or Hypertext Markup Language (.html). You can also export a table to a SharePoint Online site by creating a new list.

Access enables you to create a new table by importing data from an external source, such as an Excel workbook, an XML document, an ODBC data source, or a SharePoint site.

Access and SharePoint do not provide any data synchronization between their two data locations. If you do not need to keep copies of the data in both locations and you just need the content-synchronized access to a SharePoint list, you can use Access linked tables. A *linked table* provides only the connection to a SharePoint list and synchronizes data changes.

## Add Access Content to a SharePoint Page

You can take advantage of the Access and SharePoint Online content integration features and use content created in Access on your webpages. The easiest way to add Access content to a SharePoint page is by using copy and paste commands. Open the Access file database containing the content you want to use in a SharePoint site. Double-click the object, such as a table or a query in the Navigation Pane. Select the data and copy it to the Clipboard.

After copying the data, launch SharePoint and navigate to the page where you want to display the Access data or create a new Wiki page. With the insertion point in the content box, paste the data onto the SharePoint page. Just as with Excel, you have three options for how to paste the data onto the page: Paste, Paste Clean, and Paste Plaintext, as shown in Figure 4.65.

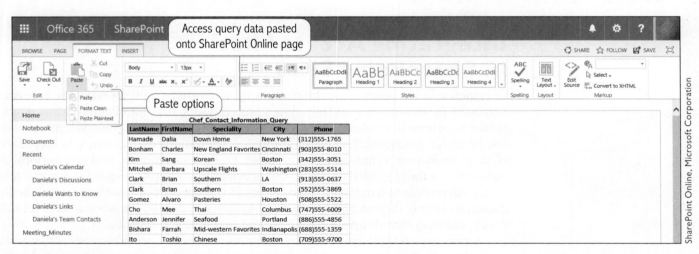

**FIGURE 4.65** Working with Access Content (Classic View)

## Upload Access Files to a SharePoint Library

You can create an HTML document in Access and export it to a SharePoint library. Click More in the Export group on the External Data tab. When you export an Access document as a HTML document, the Export - HTML Document dialog box enables you to specify export options, as shown in Figure 4.66. When you select an option,and click OK, the HTML Output Options dialog box opens, as shown in Figure 4.67, enabling you to select the HTML Template, as well as the encoding you wish to use for saving the file, making any further export from the document easier. You can then save the export steps if you know you will be exporting the file again. The Access HTML file is created on your local computer for transfer to SharePoint Online, as shown in Figure 4.68.

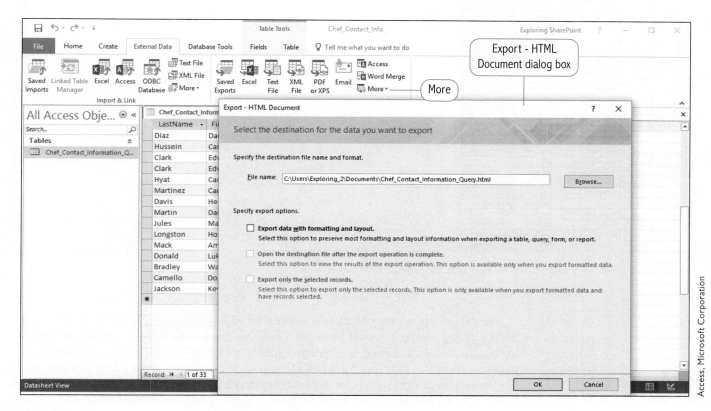

**FIGURE 4.66** Export HTML Document Options

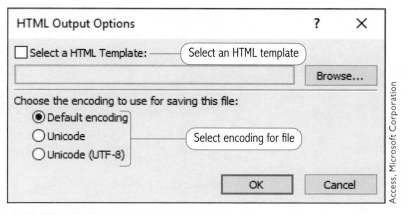

**FIGURE 4.67** HTML Output Options

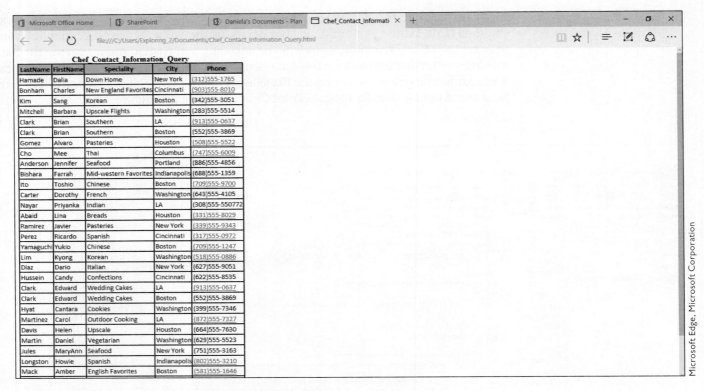

| LastName | FirstName | Speciality | City | Phone |
|---|---|---|---|---|
| Hamade | Dalia | Down Home | New York | (312)555-1765 |
| Bonham | Charles | New England Favorites | Cincinnati | (903)555-8010 |
| Kim | Sang | Korean | Boston | (342)555-3051 |
| Mitchell | Barbara | Upscale Flights | Washington | (283)555-5514 |
| Clark | Brian | Southern | LA | (913)555-0637 |
| Clark | Brian | Southern | Boston | (552)555-3869 |
| Gomez | Alvaro | Pasteries | Houston | (508)555-5522 |
| Cho | Mee | Thai | Columbus | (747)555-6009 |
| Anderson | Jennifer | Seafood | Portland | (886)555-4856 |
| Bishara | Farrah | Mid-western Favorites | Indianapolis | (688)555-1359 |
| Ito | Toshio | Chinese | Boston | (709)555-9700 |
| Carter | Dorothy | French | Washington | (643)555-4105 |
| Nayar | Priyanka | Indian | LA | (308)555-550772 |
| Abaid | Lina | Breads | Houston | (331)555-8029 |
| Ramirez | Javier | Pasteries | New York | (339)555-9343 |
| Perez | Ricardo | Spanish | Cincinnati | (317)555-0972 |
| Yamaguchi | Yukio | Chinese | Boston | (709)555-1247 |
| Lim | Kyong | Korean | Washington | (518)555-0886 |
| Diaz | Dario | Italian | New York | (627)555-9051 |
| Hussein | Candy | Confections | Cincinnati | (622)555-8535 |
| Clark | Edward | Wedding Cakes | LA | (913)555-0637 |
| Clark | Edward | Wedding Cakes | Boston | (552)555-3869 |
| Hyat | Cantara | Cookies | Washington | (399)555-7346 |
| Martinez | Carol | Outdoor Cooking | LA | (872)555-7327 |
| Davis | Helen | Upscale | Houston | (664)555-7630 |
| Martin | Daniel | Vegetarian | Washington | (629)555-5523 |
| Jules | MaryAnn | Seafood | New York | (751)555-3163 |
| Longston | Howie | Spanish | Indianapolis | (802)555-3210 |
| Mack | Amber | English Favorites | Boston | (581)555-1646 |

**FIGURE 4.68** Access Table Saved as an HTML Document

Microsoft Edge, Microsoft Corporation

To export an Access object as a PDF or an XPS Document, click PDF or XPS in the Export group on the External Data tab. Click Options on the Publish as PDF or XPS dialog box to select the range, which can include all records, selected records, or specific pages, as shown in Figure 4.69. Click Publish to create the document. You can also select the Document structure tags for accessibility check box. Access metadata includes information about the document such as the full name, path, smart tags, hyperlinks, track changes, comments, hidden text, and the last 10 authors.

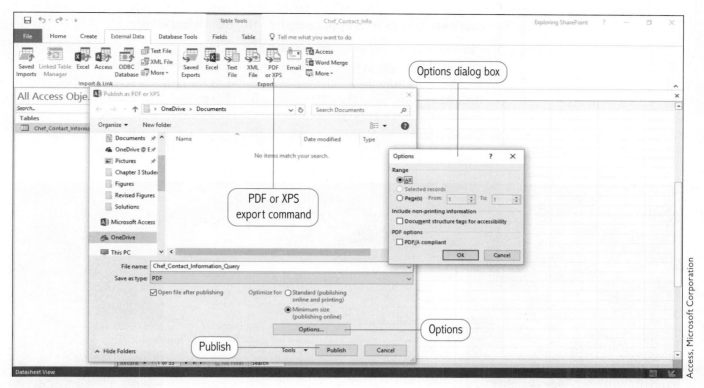

**FIGURE 4.69** Exporting an Access Object as a PDF Document

SharePoint Online enables you to upload any Access file format to a document library. To upload an Access document to a SharePoint library, you apply the same procedures explained previously for Word and Excel documents. From a developer's point of view, the process of uploading an Access document saved as a PDF, XPS Document, or HTML document is identical.

---

**TIP: GRAPHIC FILES AND IMPORTED ACCESS DOCUMENTS**
If you import a .html, .pdf, or .xps Access document, the graphic files are embedded in the document so there is no need to import them separately.

---

## Create an Access Web App

**STEP 3** ➤➤ When you need to add a functioning database to SharePoint Online, you create a web app in Access and place it on your site. The web app requires SharePoint Server 2016 or an Office 365 Business or Enterprise SharePoint site. The process for creating a web app database has two parts. First you create the app, and then you populate it with the tables of the database. Users can view or modify the data in the web app based on their permissions to the SharePoint site.

**To create an Access web app, complete the following steps:**

1. Open Access and click Custom web app in the templates pane.
2. Type an App Name in the Custom web app dialog box, as shown in Figure 4.70.
3. Select the site from the Available Locations box. If the right site is not available, type the URL to your site in the Web Location box or copy and paste it from the SharePoint Online site, deleting everything after the site name in the pasted address.
4. Click Create.

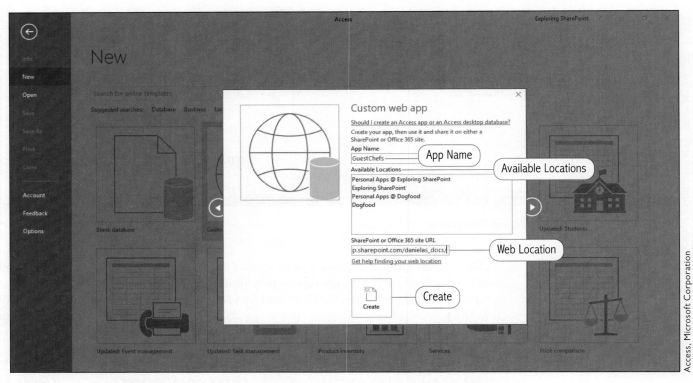

**FIGURE 4.70** Creating a Custom Web App

After creating the Access web app, you add tables to the app from Access. You can create a new table using templates or you can create a table using an existing source, as shown in Figure 4.71. Note that you can create a table from Access or from Excel, in addition to using an SQL Server/ODBC Data source, a text or CSV file, or a SharePoint list. The table can easily be created by using existing tables in an Access database. Click Access in the Add Tables pane to open the Get External Data - Access Database dialog box, which enables you to browse to the Access database on your local computer. The other selections will provide different dialog boxes that enable you to navigate to and select the data.

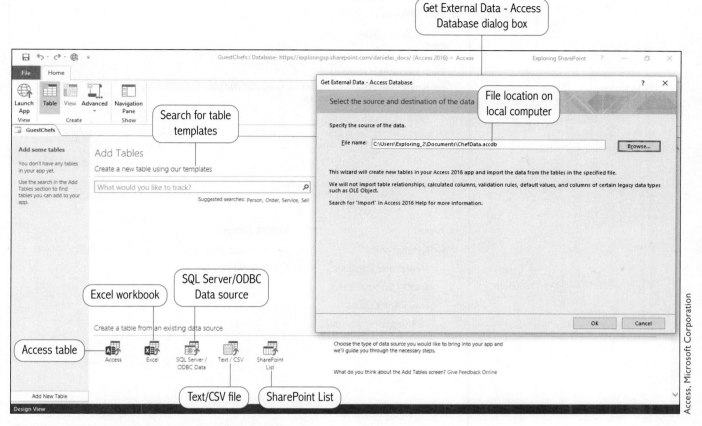

**FIGURE 4.71** Adding a Table to a Custom Web App

The Import Objects dialog box opens after you click OK in the External Data - Access Database dialog box, and enables you to select the tables you want to make available in the custom web app, as shown in Figure 4.72. You can select all of the tables by clicking Select All, or you can select one table by selecting it and clicking OK. Use Options to select the Import options, table definitions, and data. When the tables are uploaded, click Close on the Get External Data - Access Database dialog box.

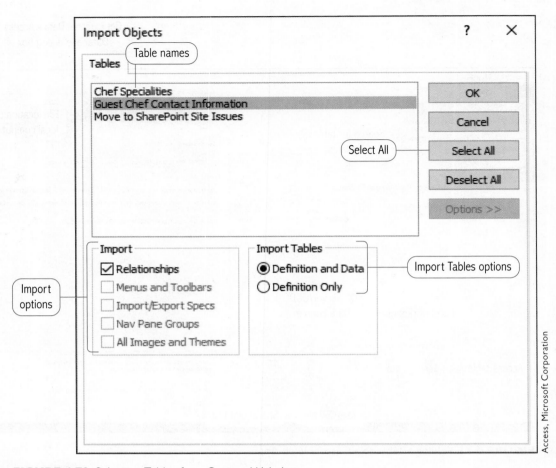

**FIGURE 4.72** Selecting Tables for a Custom Web App

After the tables are uploaded, you can edit the table list or datasheet view in Access, as shown in Figure 4.73. Select the table you want to edit in the left pane. Select the view you want to edit, and then click Edit. For instance, you can add a custom action, change the data source, format the ActionBar (by either hiding it or changing the caption) and create a new action. You can move the fields within the app and you can add or delete fields from the list. For example, in Figure 4.74, the Specialty field was added to the Chef Contact Information list. Click Save when you have completed your edits.

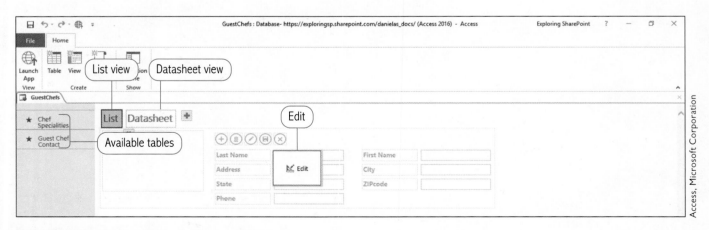

**FIGURE 4.73** Views of Tables in Custom Web App

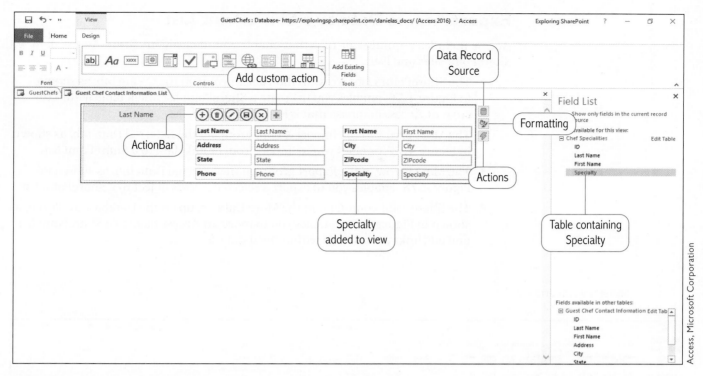

**FIGURE 4.74** Modifying a View

After your edits are finished, click the Home tab and click Launch App in the View group to open the database in SharePoint Online. You can also open the custom web app from your SharePoint Online Site contents page. With the site open in SharePoint, as shown in Figure 4.75, you can select between a list view and a datasheet view. The ActionBar at the top of the page enables you to add a new record, delete a record, edit an existing record, save, and cancel edits you may have made. The tables in the database are accessed by clicking the table name in the left pane. Click Back to Site on the top navigation bar to return to the SharePoint Online site where the database is located.

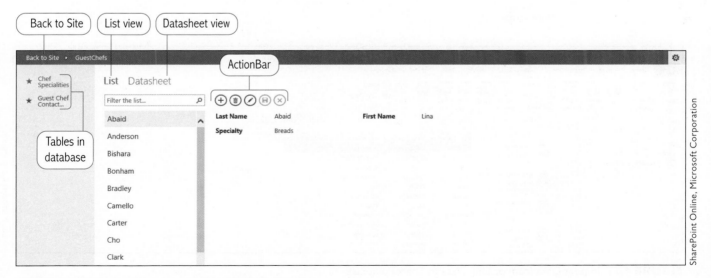

**FIGURE 4.75** Access Database in SharePoint Online Site

# Export Access Data to a SharePoint List

Access includes a number of tabs that enable you to easily integrate Access data with SharePoint sites and lists:

- The SharePoint Lists arrow in the Tables group on the Create tab, as shown in Figure 4.76, enables you to create a SharePoint list and a table within the current Access database that is linked to the new list.
- The More arrow in the Import & Link group on the External Data tab, as shown in Figure 4.77, enables you to import from or link data to a SharePoint list.
- The More arrow in the Export group on the External Data tab, as shown in Figure 4.78, enables you to export a selected Access object to a SharePoint list.
- The SharePoint command in the Move Data group on the Database Tools tab, as shown in Figure 4.79, enables you to move an Access table to a SharePoint list and add links to this table within the database.

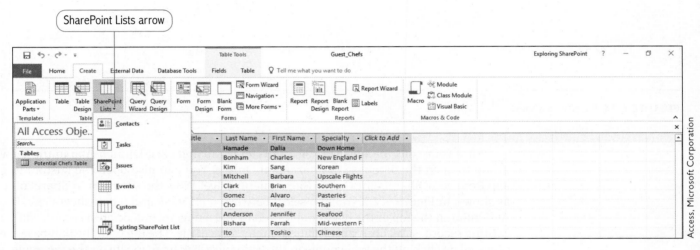

**FIGURE 4.76** Create a SharePoint List and Table Linked to a New List

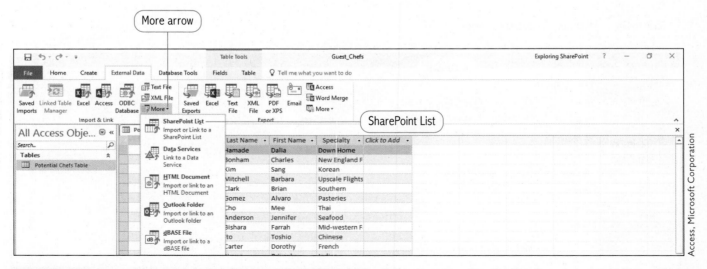

**FIGURE 4.77** Import Data from or Link Data to SharePoint List

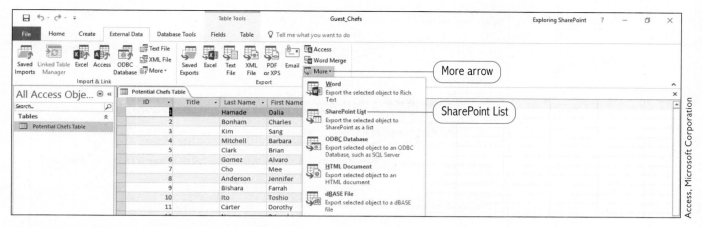

**FIGURE 4.78** Export Access Object to a SharePoint List

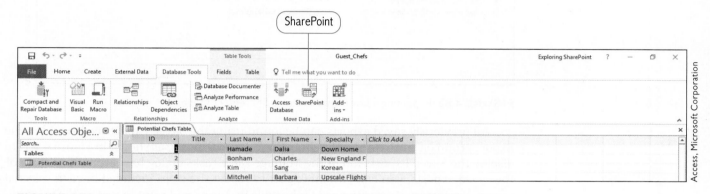

**FIGURE 4.79** Move an Access Table to a SharePoint List and Add Links to the Table

You can export an Access table to SharePoint Online. In Access, open the table you want to export to a SharePoint list, click the External Data tab, and click More in the Export group. Click SharePoint List. The Export - SharePoint Site dialog box is displayed, as shown in Figure 4.80. Select the site in the Specify a SharePoint site list box, or type (or copy and paste) the URL to the site in the box below the list box. Type a name for the list, leave the Open the list when finished check box checked, and then click OK. The page is displayed in a new browser window in editing mode. Click *Stop editing this list* to save the list to SharePoint Online. After completing the upload of the list, you can save the export steps using the Save Export Steps dialog box in Access. It is helpful to provide a description of the purpose of the export for future reference.

Access, Microsoft Corporation

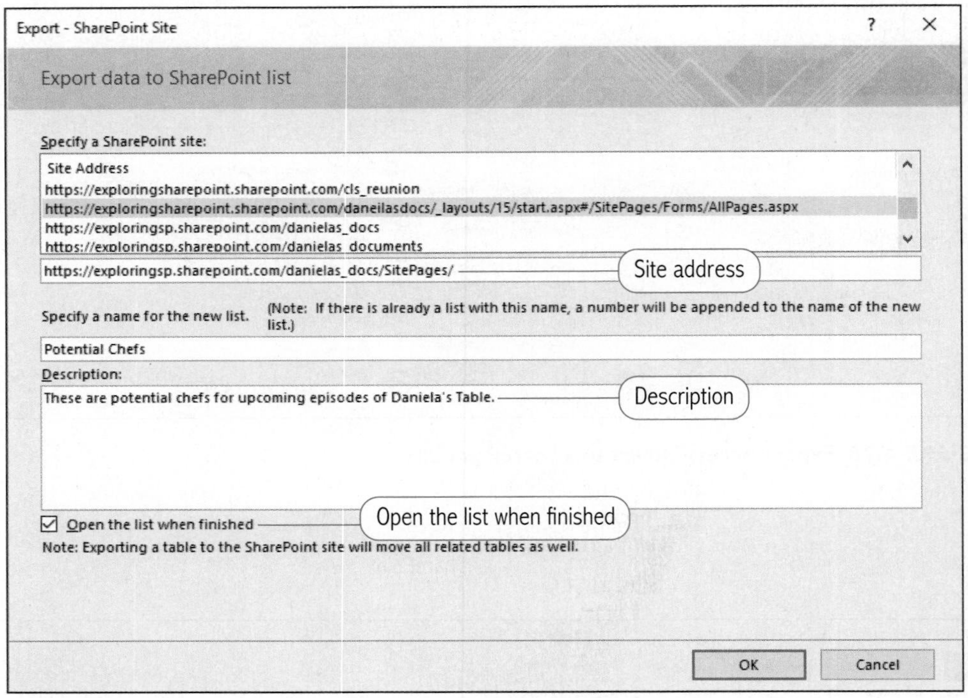

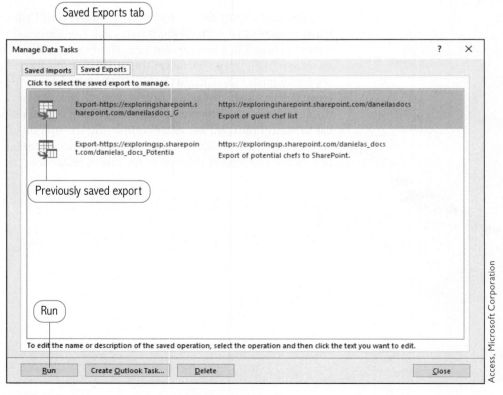

**FIGURE 4.80** Exporting a List from Access to SharePoint Online

All previously saved exports can be found using the Saved Exports command in the Export group on the External Data tab. Click Saved Exports, as shown in Figure 4.81, to display the Saved Exports tab in the Manage Data Tasks dialog box. From this listing of the saved exports, you can run an export to repeat the steps included in each selected export. For instance, you may add to the table in Access and want to update the information in SharePoint, making the saved export an efficient way to update the page.

Access, Microsoft Corporation

**FIGURE 4.81** Using Previously Saved Exports

## Import a SharePoint List to Access

When you create a new Access database table by importing data from a SharePoint list, that table automatically becomes a part of your database, but the data is not synchronized with the SharePoint list after it is imported.

**To create a new Access database table with data from SharePoint, complete the following steps:**

1. Click the External Data tab in Access, and click More in the Import & Link group. Click SharePoint List. The Get External Data - SharePoint Site dialog box is displayed.
2. Select the site address in the *Specify a SharePoint site* list box, or type (or copy and paste) the site URL into the box below.
3. Select the *Import the source data into a new table in the current database* option, as shown in Figure 4.82, and click Next.
4. Select the source list from SharePoint in the Import data from list page in the Get External Data - SharePoint Site dialog box, as shown in Figure 4.83, and click OK.

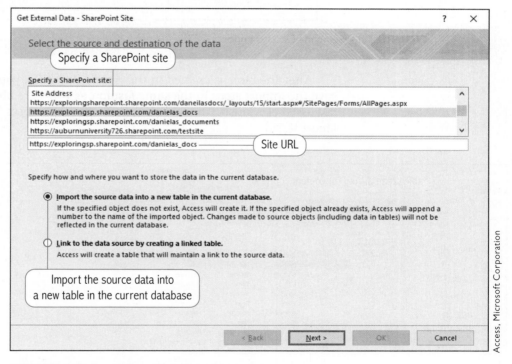

**FIGURE 4.82** Importing a SharePoint List into Access

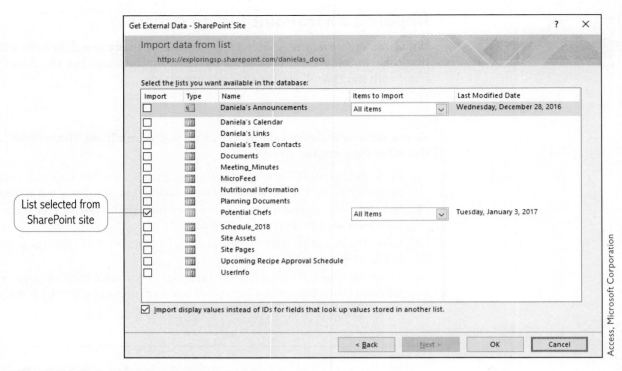

**FIGURE 4.83** Selecting Data to Import

After the table is created in the Access database, you will have the opportunity to save the import steps in the same fashion as you were able to save the export steps, as discussed previously. The table is displayed in the Access Navigation Pane, as shown in Figure 4.84.

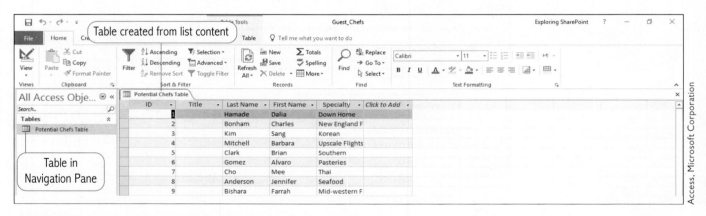

**FIGURE 4.84** Access Table with SharePoint Online List Content

## Link SharePoint Lists to Access

The previous two methods for importing/exporting data did not allow for any type of synchronization between the Access and SharePoint site data. Access provides you with enhanced features (by caching the linked table data) for using linked tables:

- When connectivity with the SharePoint server is activated, Access automatically synchronizes data changes.
- When connectivity with the SharePoint server is lost, the Access database automatically goes offline.

The linking process begins with closing all the Access objects in the Access database.

**To link a SharePoint list to Access, complete the following steps:**

1. Click the External Data tab, click More in the Import & Link group, and then click SharePoint List.
2. Select the SharePoint site or type (or copy and paste) the URL into the Specify a SharePoint site box.
3. Select *Link to the data source* to create a linked table and click Next.
4. Select the check box corresponding to the list you want to link, as shown in Figure 4.85, and then click OK.

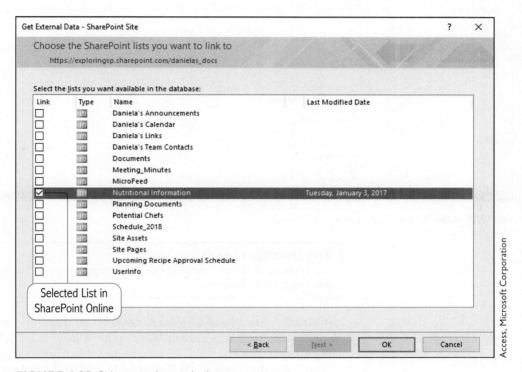

**FIGURE 4.85** Selecting a List to Link

The linked table is displayed in the Navigation Pane in Access, and the text Online with SharePoint is displayed on the right edge of the status bar, as shown in Figure 4.86.

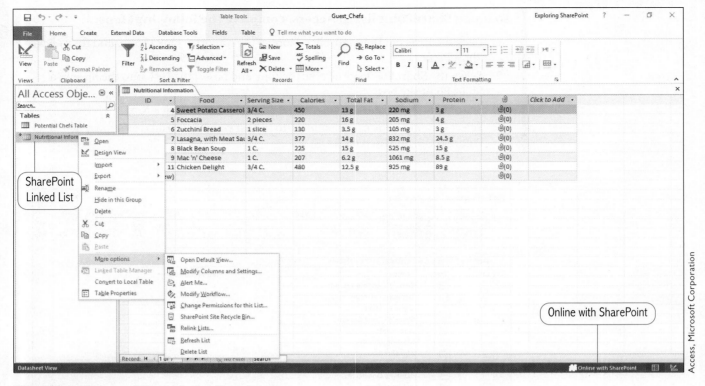

**FIGURE 4.86** Access Table Linked to SharePoint

---

> **TIP: LINKED TABLES**
> If the linked table uses information from other supporting tables, all those tables will show as linked in the Access Navigation Pane.

To see the results of a linked Access and SharePoint object, right-click the linked table in the Navigation Pane, select More options, and then click Open Default View (refer to Figure 4.86). The SharePoint list is displayed in a browser window. In the Access window, double-click the name of the linked table, and make a change to the table data by changing the value in a cell, deleting a row, or adding a new row. Save the table. Activate the browser window and click Refresh. The modifications will be updated in the SharePoint list, as shown in Figure 4.87.

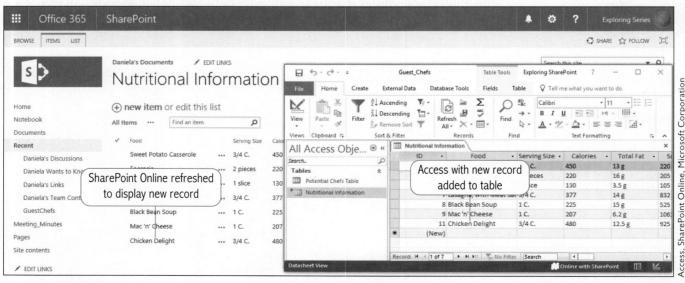

**FIGURE 4.87** Updating Access and SharePoint Online List Data (Classic View)

## Move an Access Database to SharePoint Online

Although Access is a powerful application for managing data, it was not designed to enable users to work concurrently on the same database. Moving Access databases to SharePoint sites enables you to take advantage of both Access and SharePoint tools for managing and sharing data.

In Access, click the Database Tools tab, and click SharePoint in the Move Data group. The Export Tables to SharePoint Wizard is launched and the *Where do you want to move your data* page is displayed. Select the target site in the *What SharePoint site do you want to use* box (or type, or copy and paste the URL of the site), as shown in Figure 4.88, and click Next. The Moving Data to SharePoint site dialog box displays the progress of this process in the following steps:

- A SharePoint list is created for each Access table.

- Data is moved from each Access table to its corresponding SharePoint list. Each row of an Access table is moved to an item in the corresponding list.

- The Access tables are replaced by linked tables that target their corresponding SharePoint lists, as shown in Figure 4.89.

- A backup copy of the database is created on your computer.

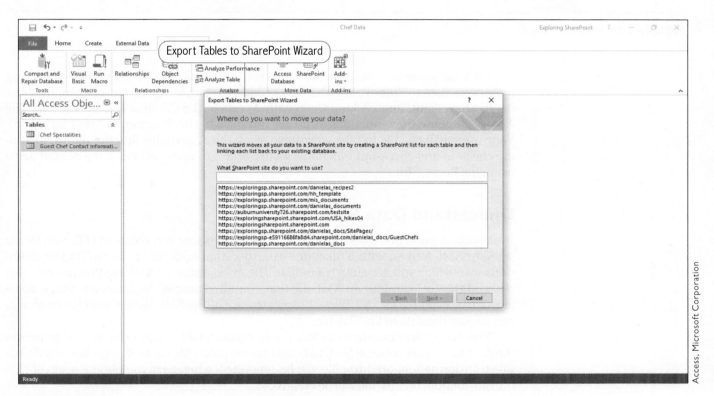

**FIGURE 4.88** Moving an Access Database to SharePoint Online

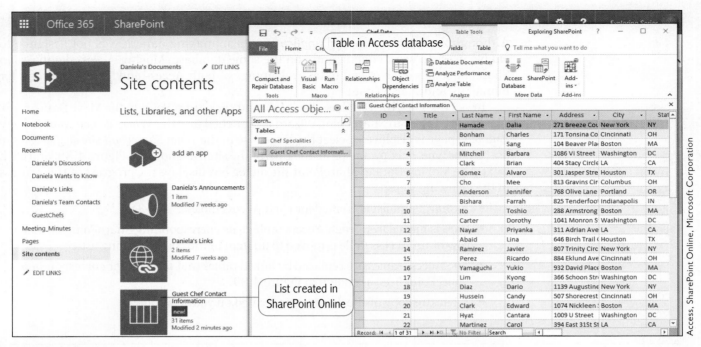

**FIGURE 4.89** Database Objects

Click the Show Details check box, and click Finish to complete the process of moving the Access data to SharePoint. The Access database can be opened by clicking the LIST tab in SharePoint, and clicking Open with Access in the Connect & Export group. The Access database now functions as a user interface to the data moved into SharePoint. Your users will be able to take advantage of all the SharePoint functionalities, including check-in and check-out functions, secure access to data, and restoring deleted items using the Recycle Bin.

## Understand Data Sources

By default, documents, workbooks, and presentations that you create in Office 2016 are saved in XML format, with a file name extension that adds an "x" or "m" to the extensions with which you are already familiar. The "x" signifies an XML file that has no macros, and the "m" signifies an XML file that contains macros. All Microsoft Office 2016 files can be exported as XML files. Through the use of the XML Viewer Web Part app, you can display the data in an XML file.

The Access user interface enables you to export a table as an XML file and generates the data file (.xml), schema file (.xsd), and presentation file (.xsl). If you choose a client-side transformation, an .html file will be generated, whereas if you choose a server-side transformation, an .asp file will be created.

To export an Access table to XML, open the table you want to export from Access in the Navigation Pane. Click the External Data tab and click XML File in the Export group. Click OK to continue; the Export XML dialog box appears, as shown in Figure 4.90. Select all three check boxes to generate all three types of files. Click More Options and click the Presentation tab on the Export XML dialog box. If you want to generate a client-side transformation, click the Client (HTML) option. If you want a server-side transformation, click Server (ASP), as shown in Figure 4.91. Click Browse and navigate to the location where the export will be stored, clicking OK to close the Browse dialog box when you are finished. Click OK to close the Export XML dialog box. So that you can reuse the export, click the Save export steps check box and then provide additional information, such as a description or an alternative file name. Click Save Export to complete this process. The transformation is complete, and the files are shown in the destination location. Preview the .xml file in a browser, as shown in Figure 4.92. The content of the .xml file is an accurate representation of the original Access data.

**FIGURE 4.90** Export XML Dialog Box

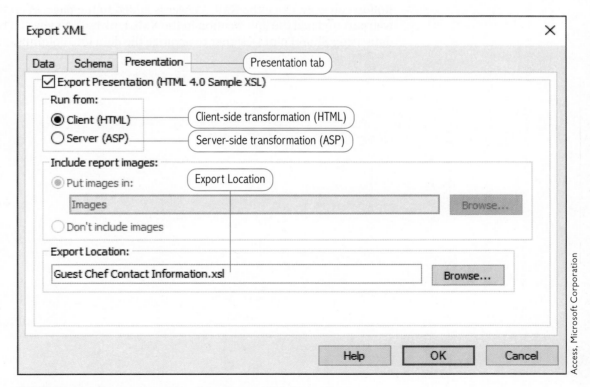

**FIGURE 4.91** Presentation Tab of the Export XML Dialog Box

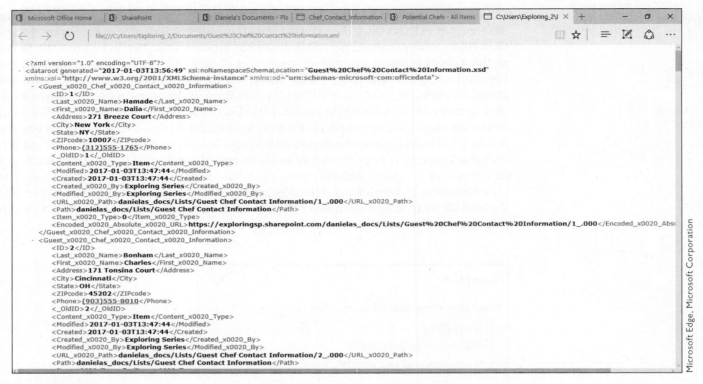

```
<?xml version="1.0" encoding="UTF-8"?>
- <dataroot generated="2017-01-03T13:56:49" xsi:noNamespaceSchemaLocation="Guest%20Chef%20Contact%20Information.xsd"
  xmlns:xsi="http://www.w3.org/2001/XMLSchema-instance" xmlns:od="urn:schemas-microsoft-com:officedata">
  - <Guest_x0020_Chef_x0020_Contact_x0020_Information>
        <ID>1</ID>
        <Last_x0020_Name>Hamade</Last_x0020_Name>
        <First_x0020_Name>Dalia</First_x0020_Name>
        <Address>271 Breeze Court</Address>
        <City>New York</City>
        <State>NY</State>
        <ZIPcode>10007</ZIPcode>
        <Phone>(312)555-1765</Phone>
        <_OldID>1</_OldID>
        <Content_x0020_Type>Item</Content_x0020_Type>
        <Modified>2017-01-03T13:47:44</Modified>
        <Created>2017-01-03T13:47:44</Created>
        <Created_x0020_By>Exploring Series</Created_x0020_By>
        <Modified_x0020_By>Exploring Series</Modified_x0020_By>
        <URL_x0020_Path>danielas_docs/Lists/Guest Chef Contact Information/1_.000</URL_x0020_Path>
        <Path>danielas_docs/Lists/Guest Chef Contact Information</Path>
        <Item_x0020_Type>0</Item_x0020_Type>
        <Encoded_x0020_Absolute_x0020_URL>https://exploringsp.sharepoint.com/danielas_docs/Lists/Guest%20Chef%20Contact%20Information/1_.000</Encoded_x0020_Abso
    </Guest_x0020_Chef_x0020_Contact_x0020_Information>
  - <Guest_x0020_Chef_x0020_Contact_x0020_Information>
        <ID>2</ID>
        <Last_x0020_Name>Bonham</Last_x0020_Name>
        <First_x0020_Name>Charles</First_x0020_Name>
        <Address>171 Tonsina Court</Address>
        <City>Cincinnati</City>
        <State>OH</State>
        <ZIPcode>45202</ZIPcode>
        <Phone>(903)555-8010</Phone>
        <_OldID>2</_OldID>
        <Content_x0020_Type>Item</Content_x0020_Type>
        <Modified>2017-01-03T13:47:44</Modified>
        <Created>2017-01-03T13:47:44</Created>
        <Created_x0020_By>Exploring Series</Created_x0020_By>
        <Modified_x0020_By>Exploring Series</Modified_x0020_By>
        <URL_x0020_Path>danielas_docs/Lists/Guest Chef Contact Information/2_.000</URL_x0020_Path>
        <Path>danielas_docs/Lists/Guest Chef Contact Information</Path>
```

**FIGURE 4.92** XML File

After you have created the XML file, you upload it to the Site Assets library or a document library. You can display the raw data in SharePoint Online by adding the XML Viewer to a Wiki page, as shown in Figure 4.93. The web part is inserted from the Content Rollup category. Once the XML Viewer is added to the page, open the properties for the web part and add the link location in the XML Link box. A view can be applied to the XML data using SharePoint Designer to arrange the data into columns.

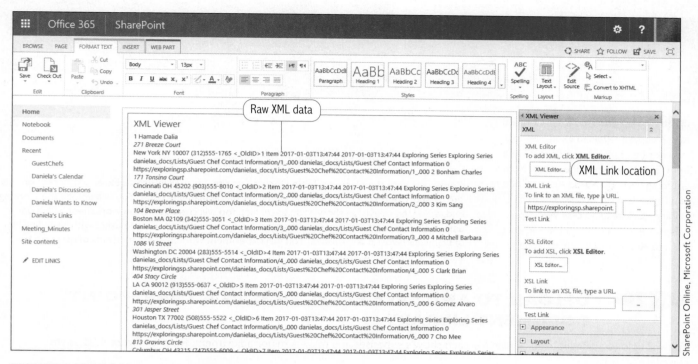

**FIGURE 4.93** XML Viewer Web Part (Classic View)

7. What are three ways you can use Excel data on a SharePoint Online site? *pp. 257–262*

8. What are the basic steps required to create an Access web app? *p. 270*

9. Why would you link a SharePoint list to Access? *p. 278*

# Hands-On Exercises

**Skills covered:** Add Excel Content to a Webpage • Upload Excel Files to a Library • Edit Excel Data • Import Data from Excel to a List • Export Data from a List to an Excel File • Add Access Content to a Page • Upload Access Files to a Library • Create an Access Web App • Export Access Data to a List • Import a List to Access • Link Lists to Access

## 3 Integration of Excel and Access Files in SharePoint Sites

Continuing with the Daniela's Table Documents site, you will integrate Excel and Access on the site to improve the functionality for members of the planning team. You will upload the working budget for the television show as an Excel file. You will create an Excel worksheet based on data in a SharePoint list. You will create an Access web app to provide users with a reading list of Daniela's favorite cookbooks. You will experiment with different methods of using Access data on a SharePoint site.

**STEP 1** ≫ **UPLOAD TO AND SAVE EXCEL FILES IN A SHAREPOINT DOCUMENT LIBRARY**

You will upload a budget used to plan for each show's expenses and make a minor adjustment. Refer to Figure 4.94 as you complete Step 1.

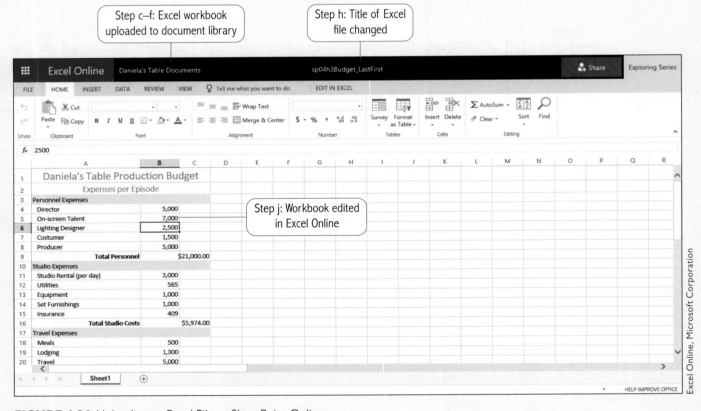

**FIGURE 4.94** Uploading an Excel File to SharePoint Online

a. Open Internet Explorer and navigate to your Office 365 site, if you exited after the previous Hands-On Exercise. Click the **Team Site tile**.

b. Click **Site Contents** on the Quick Launch, click **Return to classic SharePoint**, and then click the subsite link to **Daniela's Table Documents**.

You will upload an Excel budget document to the site.

c. Open the file *sp04h3Budget* from the student data files in the Excel desktop application. Click the **File tab** to open Backstage view, and click **Save As**.

d. Display the SharePoint browser window and copy the URL. Minimize the browser window and click **Browse** in the Excel Backstage view. Right-click the **address bar** and select **Edit Address**. Right-click the **address bar** again, select **Paste** to add the URL into the address bar of the Save As dialog box, delete everything after danielas_documents in the address, and then click the **Go to arrow**.

e. Click **Daniela's Document Library** in the Document Libraries list and click **Open**. Type your last name and first name after the file name in the format **sp04h3Budget_LastFirst** and click **Save**.

f. Click the **Content Type arrow** and select **Document**. Click **OK**. Close Excel.

The Excel file is now uploaded to SharePoint Online.

g. Display the SharePoint browser window, click **Site contents**, and then click the **Daniela's Document Library tile**.

The Budget document does not currently have a title. The Excel file displays in the list.

h. Click the **More Options icon** next to the sp04h3Budget_LastFirst file name and select the **More actions icon** on the menu. Select **Properties** and type the title **Episode Budget Worksheet**. Click **Save**.

i. Click the **sp04h3Budget_LastFirst link** to open the Excel file in Excel Online. Click the **Edit Workbook arrow** and select **Edit in Browser**.

j. Click **cell B5**, type **7000**, and press **Enter**. Click **Daniela's Table Documents** on the top navigation bar to return to the site.

The Excel workbook has been modified in SharePoint Online, and a new total for personnel expenses was calculated.

k. Right-click the **sp04h3Budget_LastFirst link** and select **Download**. Click the **Save arrow** (at the bottom of the window) and select **Save As**. Navigate to the location where you save your files and click **Save**. Close the notification at the bottom of the window.

You decide to export the Upcoming Episodes list to Excel so you can work on the data on your local computer. Refer to Figure 4.95 as you complete Step 2.

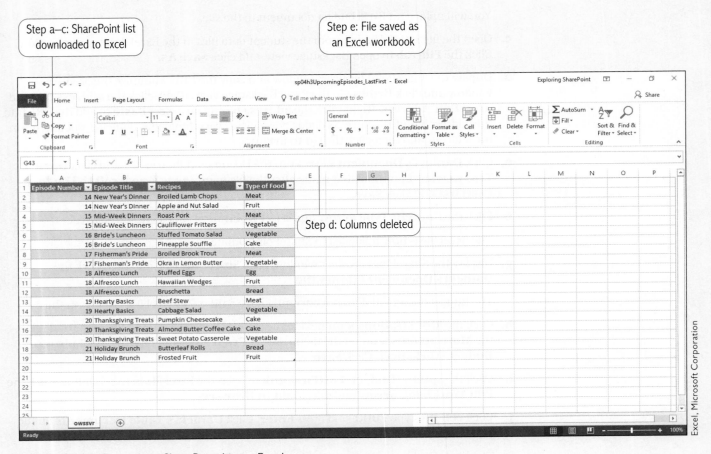

**FIGURE 4.95** Exporting a SharePoint List to Excel

a.  Click **Site contents** on the Quick Launch and click the **Upcoming Episodes tile**.

You will export the Upcoming Episodes list to Excel.

b.  Click the **LIST tab** and click **Export to Excel** in the Connect & Export group. Click the **Save arrow** (at the bottom of the window) and select **Save As**. Navigate to the location where you store your files. Click **Save**.

The message bar at the bottom of the window informs you that download is complete.

c.  Click **Open** (at the bottom of the window) and click **Enable**.

The workbook opens with *owssvr* as the tab name. You will modify the file to display only the information that you need before saving it.

d.  Right-click the column header for **column E** and select **Delete**. Repeat this process to remove the new **column E** (Path).

e.  Click the **File tab** to open Backstage view, click **Save As**, and then navigate to the location where you save your files. Type **sp04h3UpcomingEpisodes_LastFirst** for the file name and click **Save**.

f.  Close Excel.

You will create an Access web app and experiment with methods for using Access data in lists. You will create a linked list for easy updating from Access. Refer to Figures 4.96, 4.97, and 4.98 as you complete Step 3.

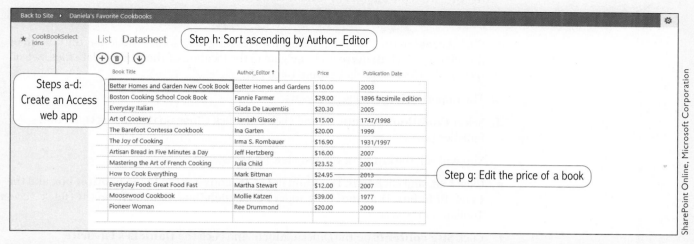

**FIGURE 4.96** Sorted Datasheet View

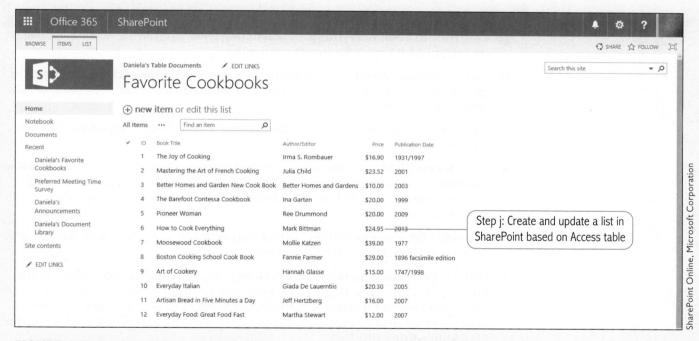

**FIGURE 4.97** List Created from an Access Table

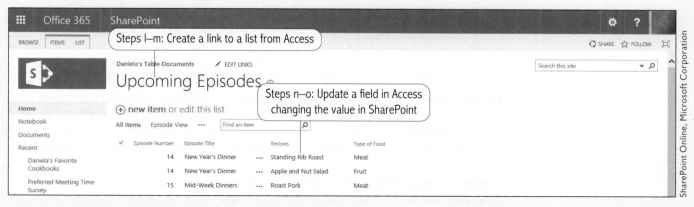

**FIGURE 4.98** List Updated in SharePoint Online by Access

**a.** Open **Access 2016** and click the **Custom web app template**.

**b.** Type the App Name **Daniela's Favorite Cookbooks**. Type the URL to the Daniela's Table Documents site in the Web Location box. As an alternative, you can copy and paste the URL from the SharePoint Online site, removing text after the site name. Click **Create**.

After a few moments, the Add Tables window opens in Access.

**c.** Click **Access** in the Create a table from an existing data source section at the bottom of the window. Click **Browse** and navigate to the location of the student data files. Select *sp04h3Cookbooks* and click **Open**. Click **OK**.

The Import Objects dialog box opens.

**d.** Select **CookBookSelections** and click **OK**. Click **Close** on the Import Operation Finished page.

You will edit the layout of the List view in Access.

**e.** Click **List**, and click **Edit**. Press and hold **Ctrl** and click the **Price caption box** and the **Price field box**. Drag the boxes under Publication Date. Click **Save** on the Quick Access Toolbar. Close Access.

**f.** Click **Site contents** on the Quick Launch, and click the **Daniela's Favorite Cookbooks tile** to open the web app.

The web app opens in List view. You will now edit an entry in the web app.

**g.** Click **How to Cook Everything**. Click **Edit** (the pencil icon) on the ActionBar. Change the price to **24.95**. Click **Save** on the ActionBar.

**h.** Click **Datasheet**. Point to the column heading **Author_Editor**, click the arrow next to the column heading, and then select **Sort Ascending** on the menu. Click **Back to Site** on the top navigation bar.

You decide to experiment more with the Access database. You will export the data to a SharePoint list.

**i.** Open **Access 2016** and open *sp04h3Cookbooks* from the student data files. Click **Enable Content**. Save the file as **sp04h3Cookbooks_LastFirst** in the location where you store your files. Double-click the **CookBookSelections table** in the Navigation Pane to open the table.

You notice the new price for the cookbook did not appear in the Access database because the list is not linked to the Access database.

**j.** Click the **External Data tab**, and click **More** in the Export group. Select **SharePoint List**. Type the URL to the Daniela's Table Documents site in the Specify a SharePoint site box. Type **Favorite Cookbooks** in the Specify a name for the new list box. Click **OK**. Click the **Price field** for the How to Cook Everything book, and type **24.95**. Press **Enter**. Click **Stop editing this list**.

> **TROUBLESHOOTING:** If you are asked to sign on to your SharePoint account, do so to display the Favorite Cookbooks page.

The data is shown as a SharePoint list and updated.

**k.** Click **Daniela's Favorite Cookbooks** on the Quick Launch and click **Datasheet**. Point to the space between the columns where the information is not completely visible and drag the size of the columns to display all text. Take a screen shot of the Daniela's Favorite Cookbooks page in Datasheet view, naming the file **sp04h3Cookbooks_LastFirst**.

> **TROUBLESHOOTING:** If you do not see Daniela's Favorite Cookbooks under Recent on the Quick Launch, click Site Contents and click the Daniela's Favorite Cookbooks Access app tile.

**l.** Open the Access 2016 window and click **Close** to close the Save Export Steps dialog box. Ensure the CookBookSelections table is displayed, and click **Refresh All** in the Records group on the Home Tab.

The price is not updated in the Access database. You will further your experiment by linking a SharePoint list to Access. This time you will import the Upcoming Episodes list into Access.

**m.** Close the **CookBookSelections** table. Click the **External Data tab** and click **More** in the Import & Link group. Select **SharePoint List** and ensure that the SharePoint site is for danielas_documents. Click **Next**.

**n.** Select the **Upcoming Episodes check box**, and click **OK**.

**o.** Double-click the **Upcoming Episodes table** in the Access Navigation Pane. Change the Recipes field for the first record to **Standing Rib Roast**. Click **Save**.

**p.** Open the SharePoint Online window, click **Back to Site** on the top navigation bar, click **Site contents** on the Quick Launch, and then click the **Upcoming Episodes tile**.

The first recipe for the New Year's Dinner has been modified to Standing Rib Roast.

**q.** Take a screen shot of the Upcoming Episodes page, naming the file **sp04h3Episodes_LastFirst**.

**r.** Sign out of your Office 365 account. Based on your instructor's directions, submit the following:

sp04h1Announcement_LastFirst

sp04h1Episode14Schedule_LastFirst

sp04h1Minutes4-13-18_LastFirst

sp04h1DocumentLibrary_LastFirst

sp04h1Filter_LastFirst

sp04h1Survey_LastFirst

sp04h2WordRecipe_LastFirst

sp04h2Blog_LastFirst

sp04h2Link_LastFirst

sp04h3Budget_LastFirst

sp04h3Cookbooks_LastFirst

sp04h3Episodes_LastFirst

sp04h3UpcomingEpisodes_LastFirst

# Chapter Objectives Review

After reading this chapter, you have accomplished the following objectives:

1. **Working with document libraries.**
   - Create a new document library: You can create multiple document libraries, providing a method of organization.
   - Change the default template for a document library: Each document library can have a different default document template type, enabling you to customize the library to the needs of the users.
   - Create a new document in a document library: New documents are created using the FILES tab on the library page. To create a new document using the default template type, click New Document. As you save the document, you can select to save it to the library, OneDrive for Business, or your local computer. You can also upload documents of any type to a document library regardless of the default template type.
   - Add columns to a view: Views enable you to define which document property columns are displayed. You can add or delete columns from a view.
   - Sort and filter the documents in a library: Using sorting and filtering, you can organize documents and find what you are looking for quickly.

2. **Display documents in lists and libraries.**
   - Built-in lists and libraries contain at least one default view that enables you to display the documents.
   - Working with views: Many lists and libraries contain additional built-in views, such as Standard View, Datasheet View, Calendar View, Gantt View, and Access View.

3. **Work with SharePoint built-in list apps.**
   - Lists are a familiar way to display many types of data, and SharePoint Online contains app lists that display data in columns. Some columns (such as Title) appear in almost every list, whereas others add unique capabilities to the list. List apps are added from the Site contents page, and include an announcements list, contacts list, links list, survey list, discussion board, and import spreadsheet list.
   - Work with an announcements list: An announcements list is used to inform site users about upcoming events, news, or activities.
   - Work with a contacts list: The Contacts app enables you to manage contact information. Additional columns can be added, or columns can be deleted to the list view to provide exactly the type of information you want to display.
   - Import a spreadsheet list: A quick way to populate data into a SharePoint list is to import an Excel worksheet.
   - Work with a links list: Using the Links app, you can create a specialized list of links to webpages within SharePoint or to other websites.

   - Work with a survey list: A survey list displays a questionnaire or poll with a wide variety of question types. The results of the survey can be exported to a spreadsheet, viewed as an RSS feed, or have an Alert Me notification that signals you when someone posts their responses.
   - Work with a discussion board list: A discussion board list enables you to group messages and responses from the site users. The discussions can be shown in flat view or conversation view.
   - Work with a calendar list: Using the Calendar app, you can develop a list of events and activities that are displayed in familiar calendar layouts.

4. **Integrate Word files in SharePoint sites.**
   - Word documents can be integrated with SharePoint Online sites in a variety of ways.
   - Add Word documents to a SharePoint site: Documents can be saved as .docx, .htm, .html, .xml, .mht, .mhtml, .pdf, or .xps and saved directly to the site.
   - Integrate Word documents with blog sites: Blog sites can also be integrated with Word, enabling you to retain the formatting applied to the Word document in the blog posting. Each blog account is registered in the desktop Word application prior to publishing the blog post.

5. **Integrate PowerPoint files in SharePoint sites.**
   - Similar to Word, PowerPoint files can be saved in a variety of formats and saved directly to the SharePoint site using the PowerPoint Backstage view. A presentation saved as a Windows Media Video (.wmv) retains the animations, narrations, and other multimedia elements and is played using the Windows Media Player.

6. **Integrate Excel files in SharePoint sites.**
   - Add Excel content to a webpage: Content created in Excel files can be copied and pasted onto SharePoint pages.
   - Upload Excel files to a SharePoint library: Excel files can be uploaded to a library as Excel files, Excel Binary Workbooks, XML Data, a Web Page, a Single File Web Page, a PDF file, or a XPS document.
   - Import data from Excel to a SharePoint list: Data from an Excel spreadsheet, range, or table can be imported into a SharePoint list, and enable users to read, revise, or enter new data into the list.
   - Export data from a SharePoint list to an Excel file: Content in a SharePoint list can also be exported to Excel, using a Web query. This method of integrating data enables a connection to be made between Excel and SharePoint that changes the data in the Excel file when changes are made to the list in SharePoint Online.

7. **Integrate Access files in SharePoint sites.**
   - Using Access 2016, you can export database content to a table, report, or a query object to a wide range of formats, such as an external file, an Excel workbook, a Rich Text Format (.rtf), a text file, a PDF, or an XPS file. You can also export into formats for an email attachment, an Extensible Markup Language (XML) document, an Open Database Connectivity (ODBC) data source, or Hypertext Markup Language (.html).
   - Add Access content to a SharePoint page: The easiest way to add Access content to a SharePoint page is to copy and paste the data from Access into a Wiki page content area.
   - Upload Access files to a SharePoint library: HTML documents created in Access can be exported to a SharePoint library using the Export commands on the External Data tab.
   - Create an Access web app: An Access web app adds the functionality of a database to SharePoint Online. Use the Custom web app template in Access to create a SharePoint app that contains tables from the database.
   - Export Access data to a SharePoint list: You can export a table to a SharePoint Online site by creating a new list.
   - Import a SharePoint list to Access: Data from a SharePoint list can be imported into Access, but the data is not synchronized after the import.
   - Link SharePoint lists to Access: To synchronize data between Access and SharePoint, link the SharePoint list to Access.
   - Move an Access database to SharePoint Online: Moving Access databases to SharePoint sites enables you to manage and share data by enabling users to work concurrently on the same database.
   - Understand data sources: Microsoft Office Access 2016 enables you to export a table as an XML file and generates data (.xml), schema (.xsd), and presentation (.xsl) files. If you specify a client-side transformation, an .htm file will be generated. The raw data can be displayed using the SharePoint Online XML Viewer Web Part.

# Key Terms Matching

Match the key terms with their definitions. Write the key term letter by the appropriate numbered definition.

a. Access View
b. Announcements list
c. Calendar list
d. Calendar View
e. Contacts list
f. Database
g. Database table
h. Datasheet View
i. Default template
j. Discussion board list

k. Gantt View
l. Links list
m. Portable Document Format (PDF)
n. Range
o. Single File Web Page option
p. Standard View
q. Survey list
r. Table
s. Webpage option
t. Web query

1. _____ A display of a list that provides a graphical representation for a project timeline. **p. 222**

2. _____ A display of list data where at least one field is a date field. **p. 222**

3. _____ A display of list or library items using a grid-like layout that enables you to edit the table. **p. 221**

4. _____ A file format option in which the document is saved as an .htm or .html file with a set of files grouped into a folder that enables you to rebuild the original document in a browser. **p. 243**

5. _____ A file format that saves the entire document into a single .mht or .mhtml file. **p. 243**

6. _____ A file of related data containing objects such as tables, queries, reports, and forms. **p. 265**

7. _____ A file of extracted data from text or tables on a webpage which is imported into Excel. **p. 263**

8. _____ A fixed-layout file format used when the document will be commercially printed. **p. 243**

9. _____ A group of adjacent or contiguous cells. **p. 260**

10. _____ A list that contains information such as name, company, phone numbers, email addresses, and more about people. **p. 227**

11. _____ A list that contains links to other pages within a SharePoint site or to websites. **p. 230**

12. _____ A list that displays columns as a questionnaire or poll. **p. 231**

13. _____ A list that displays events and activities in day, week, or month layout. **p. 235**

14. _____ A list that is used to inform your site users about upcoming events, news, or activities. **p. 226**

15. _____ A list that supports message postings related to list topics. **p. 233**

16. _____ A range in an Excel workbook that contains related data, structured to allow easy management and analysis. **p. 260**

17. _____ A set of related data containing records arranged in rows and in columns, which are fields. **p. 265**

18. _____ The display of the content of lists and libraries as lists included in a webpage. **p. 221**

19. _____ The type of file that defines the default content type for a document library. **p. 213**

20. _____ A view that enables you to use advanced tools for generating reports and views. **p. 223**

# Multiple Choice

**1.** What view of a list is displayed as a grid and enables users to easily update the properties?

(a) Access View

(b) Datasheet View

(c) Gantt View

(d) Standard View

**2.** What view enables you to use advanced tools for generating reports and views of data?

(a) Access View

(b) Datasheet View

(c) Gantt View

(d) Standard View

**3.** What list type enables you to relate news about upcoming events or activities?

(a) Announcements List

(b) Contacts List

(c) Links List

(d) Survey List

**4.** What view would you use to display a timeline related to project deadlines?

(a) Access View

(b) Calendar View

(c) Gantt View

(d) Standard View

**5.** What type of template defines the content type for a library?

(a) Access template

(b) Default document template

(c) Portable Document Format

(d) Single File Web Page

**6.** What is the icon that indicates a column in a view is filtered?

(a) An arrow pointing up

(b) An arrow pointing down

(c) A funnel

(d) A star

**7.** As you copy and paste cell data from Excel onto a SharePoint page, which option removes all formatting?

(a) Paste

(b) Paste Clean

(c) Paste Special

(d) Paste Plaintext

**8.** You can integrate a SharePoint blog with which of the following Microsoft Office desktop applications?

(a) Access

(b) Excel

(c) PowerPoint

(d) Word

**9.** How do you retain the transitions, animations, narrations, and other multimedia elements in a PowerPoint presentation you are posting on SharePoint Online?

(a) Publish the presentation to a media library.

(b) Save the presentation as a PowerPoint Show.

(c) Save the presentation as a Single File Web Page.

(d) Save the presentation as a Windows Media Video.

**10.** A Web query:

(a) Creates a webpage with search results.

(b) Extracts data from text or tables on a webpage.

(c) Imports Excel data into a SharePoint site.

(d) Opens Access and selects information you requested.

# Practice Exercises

## 1   Adding Microsoft Documents to a SharePoint Online Site for an Introduction to Management Information Systems Course

 **FROM SCRATCH**

As a graduate teaching assistant in the Introduction to Management Information Systems course, you have been working on the development of a SharePoint site for the course. Your faculty supervisor gave you different types of Microsoft Office files that will need to be uploaded to the site. Some of the files will be displayed on the site pages using different formats. You will also add a class survey. You will add a blog to the site and make a posting from Word. Refer to Figures 4.99, 4.100, and 4.101 as you complete this exercise.

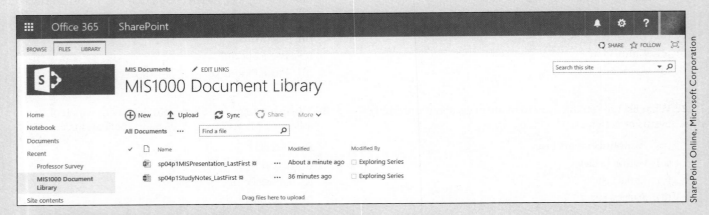

**FIGURE 4.99** Document Library (Classic View)

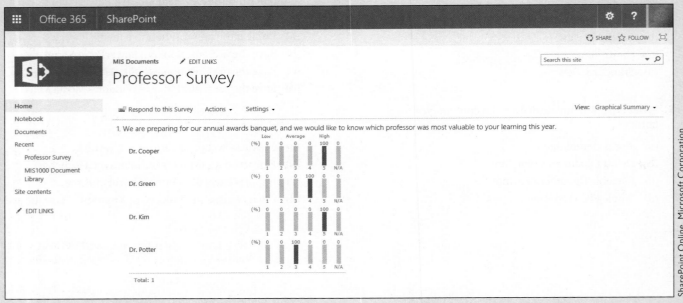

**FIGURE 4.100** Survey Results

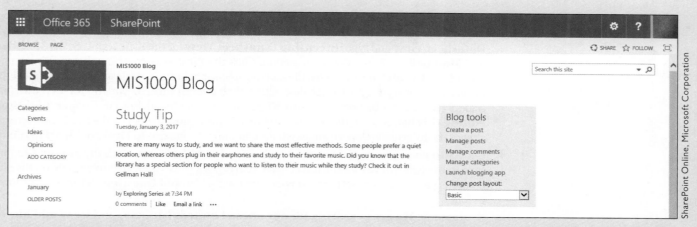

**FIGURE 4.101** Blog Post

a. Open **Internet Explorer**. Sign into your Office 365 account and open SharePoint.

b. Click the **Team Site tile**. Click **Site Contents** on the Quick Launch, ensure the classic view is displayed by clicking Return to classic SharePoint at the bottom of the Quick Launch, and then click **new subsite** to add a new subsite.

c. Type **MIS Documents** in the Title box. Type **This site manages the documents for the MIS1000 course** for the Description. Type **mis_documents** for the URL name. Accept all of the remaining default values and click **Create**.

d. Click **Site contents** on the Quick Launch and click **add an app**. Click the **Document Library tile** and type **MIS1000 Document Library** in the Name box. Click **Create**.

e. Click the **Settings icon** and select **Site settings** on the menu. Click **Site content types** in the Web Designer Galleries section of the Site Settings page. Click **Create**, and type **Study_Notes** in the Name box. Type the description **This template document helps you organize your notes.** Select **Document Content Types** for Select parent content type from. Select **Document** for the Parent Content Type. Select **Display Template Content Types** for Existing group, and click **OK**.

f. Click **Advanced settings** on the Site Content Type page, and click **Upload a new document template**. Click **Browse**, and navigate to *sp04p1StudyNotesTemplate*. Click **Open** and click **OK**.

g. Click **Site contents** and click the **MIS1000 Document Library tile**. Click the **LIBRARY tab** and click **Library Settings** in the Settings group. Click **Advanced settings** on the Settings page. Click **Yes** to answer the question Allow management of content types, and click **OK**.

h. Scroll down and click **Add from existing site content types** in the Content Types section on the Settings page. Click the **Select site content types from arrow** and select **Display Template Content Types**. Click **Study_Notes** in the Available Site Content Types list, click **Add**, and then click **OK**. Scroll down and click **Change new button order and default content type** in the Content Types section, click the **Visible check box** for Document to deselect it, and then click **OK**.

i. Click **Site contents** on the Quick Launch and click the **MIS1000 Document Library tile**. Click the **FILES tab** and click **New Document** in the New group. Type **MIS1000** after Course. Type **today's date** after Date. Select the word **Document** on the top navigation bar, and type **sp04p1StudyNotes_LastFirst** for the file name. Click within the document to save the file. Click the **MIS Documents link** on the top navigation bar to display the MIS1000 Document Library.

j. Click **Site contents** on the Quick Launch and click **add an app**. Click the **Import Spreadsheet app** and type **Internship Opportunities** for the name. Type **This list displays the current internship opportunities offered to our students.** for the description. Click **Browse**, navigate to and select *sp04p1Internships* in the student data files, and then click **Open**. Click **Import**.

**k.** Select **Table Range** in the Range Type box. Select **Sheet1!Table1** in the Select Range box. Click **Import**. Click the **LIST tab** and click **Create View** in the Manage Views group. Click **Datasheet View** and type **Internship Datasheet View** for the View Name. Select **Modified** and **Modified By** in the Columns section. Click the **First sort by the column arrow** and select **Faculty Advisor**. Click **OK**. Click in the Sponsor column in the last (blank) row, and type **Lewis Web Design**. Type the job description **Web design intern**, work hours **4 - 8 PM**, pay scale **$10-$12**, contact person **Nadir Klem**, and the faculty advisor **Dr. Cooper**. Click **Stop editing this list**. Refresh the browser and review the changed order of the list. Take a screenshot of the Internship Opportunities window, naming the file **sp04p1Internships_LastFirst**.

**l.** Click **Site contents** on the Quick Launch and click **add an app**. Click the **Survey tile** and type **Professor Survey** for the title. Click **Create**. Click the **Professor Survey tile** on the Site contents page, click the **Settings arrow**, and then select **Add Questions**. Complete the form as follows:

  - Question: **We are preparing for our annual awards banquet, and we would like to know which professor was most valuable to your learning this year.**
  - Type of answer to this question is: **Rating Scale (a matrix of choices or a Likert scale)**
  - Type each sub-question on a separate line:

    **Dr. Cooper**

    **Dr. Green**

    **Dr. Kim**

    **Dr. Potter**
  - Click **Finish**.

**m.** Click **Respond to this Survey**. Select a rating for each of the professors, and click **Finish**. Click **Show a graphical summary of responses** and review the ratings. Take a screen shot of the Professor Survey responses page, naming it **sp04p1Survey_LastFirst**.

**n.** Click **Site contents** on the Quick Launch, and click **new subsite**. Create a blog site based on the following specifications.

  - Title: **MIS1000 Blog**
  - Description: **This blog is used to share study information.**
  - URL name: **mis_blog**
  - Template: **Blog**
  - Click **Create**.

**o.** Open **Word 2016**, click the **Blog post template**, and then click **Create**. Type the Post Title **Study Tip**, and then type the content: **There are many ways to study, and we want to share the most effective methods. Some people prefer a quiet location, whereas others plug in their earphones and study to their favorite music. Did you know that the library has a special section for people who want to listen to their music while they study? Check it out in Gellman Hall!**

**p.** Click **Manage Accounts** in the Blog group on the BLOG POST tab. Click **New**. Click the **Choose your blog provider arrow**, select **SharePoint blog**, and then click **Next**. Type the **URL** to the blog or copy and paste it from the address box in the SharePoint window into the box, removing default.aspx. Click **OK**, and then click **OK** when you are notified the account registration was successful. With MIS1000 Blog selected, click **Set As Default**, and click **Close**. Click the **Account arrow** next to the currently listed default blog, and select **MIS1000 Blog**. Click **Publish** in the Blog group. Close Word without saving the document. Open the SharePoint Online window, and refresh the browser. Take a screen shot showing the Study Tip blog posting, naming the file **sp04p1Blog_LastFirst**. Click **SharePoint** on the top navigation bar and navigate to the MIS Documents site.

**q.** Open the PowerPoint presentation *sp04p1MISPresentation*. Click the **File tab**, and click **Save As**. Select your SharePoint site in the left pane, and click the folder in the right pane. Navigate to the MIS Documents site and double-click the icon for the site. Double-click the **MIS1000 Document Library**. Add **_LastFirst** to the file name and click **Save**. Click the **Content Type**

**arrow** and select **Document**. Click **OK**. Close PowerPoint after the uploading to SharePoint completes. Open the SharePoint Online window and click **MIS1000 Document Library** on the Quick Launch. Click the **sp04p1MISPresentation_LastFirst** link to the presentation, review the slides, and then click **MIS Documents** on the top navigation bar to return to the SharePoint site.

**r.** Take a screenshot of the MIS1000 Documents window, naming the file **sp04p1Documents_LastFirst**. Sign out of your Office 365 account. Based on your instructor's directions, submit the following:

sp04p1Blog_LastFirst

sp04p1Documents_LastFirst

sp04p1Internships_LastFirst

sp04p1Survey_LastFirst

As one of the members of the reunion planning team, you have been working on a SharePoint Online site that enables all of the team members to communicate and share documents. The date of the class reunion is quickly approaching. People have been paying for their reservations, and you will implement an Access database to enable the team to track the reservations. Using a PowerPoint presentation as a template in a document library, classmates will be able to create and save a slide to the site with their current information. You will also place the Excel worksheet budget on the site, so that any necessary changes can be viewed by all of the users. Refer to Figures 4.102, 4.103, and 4.104 as you complete this exercise.

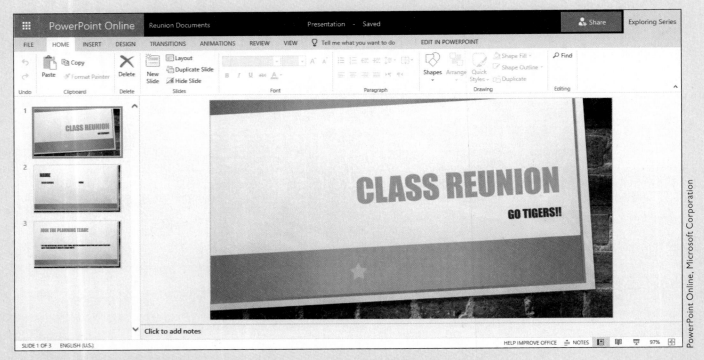

**FIGURE 4.102** PowerPoint Document Template

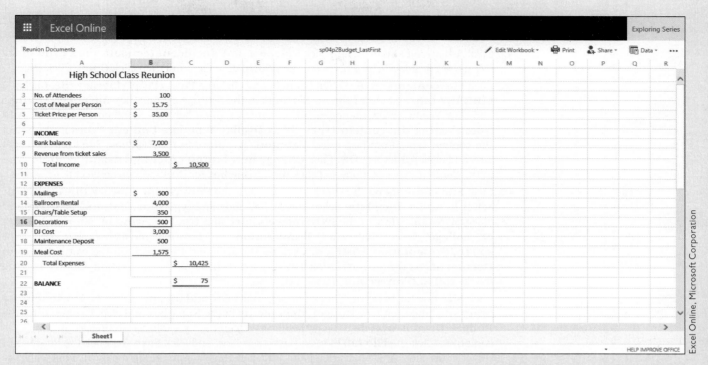

**FIGURE 4.103** Excel File Saved to the Budget_Documents Library

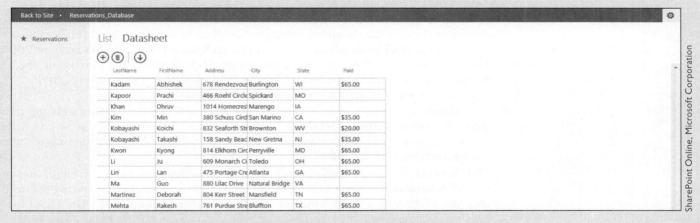

**FIGURE 4.104** Record Displayed in Access Web App

a. Navigate to and sign into your Office 365 account. Open SharePoint and click the **Team Site tile**.

b. Click **Site Contents** on the Quick Launch, ensure the classic SharePoint view is displayed, and then click **new subsite** to add a new subsite.

c. Type **Reunion Documents** in the Title box. Type **This site manages the documents for the class reunion.** for the Description. Type **reunion_documents** for the URL name. Accept all of the remaining default values and then click **Create**.

d. Click **Site contents**, and click **add an app**. Click the **Document Library app**, and type **PowerPoint_Library** for the name of the library. Click **Create**.

e. Click the **PowerPoint_Library tile**. Click the **Settings icon**, and select **Site settings**. Click **Site content types**, and click **Create**. Type **Reunion_Template** for the Name, **Use this template to create a personal slide.** for the Description. Select **Document Content Types** in the Select parent content type from box, select **Document** in the Parent Content Type box, and then select **Display Template Content Types** in the Existing group. Click **OK**.

f. Click **Advanced settings**, and click **Upload a new document template**. Click **Browse**, select *sp04p2ReunionPresentation* from the student data files, and then click **Open**. Click **OK**.

g. Click **Site contents** on the Quick Launch, and click the **PowerPoint_Library tile**. Click the **LIBRARY tab**, and click **Library Settings** in the Settings group. Click **Advanced settings** and click **Yes** for Allow management of content types. Click **OK**. Scroll down and click **Add from existing site content types**. Select **Display Template Content Types** in the Select site content types from box, select **Reunion_Template** in the Available Site Content Types box, and click **Add**. Click **OK**. Click **Change new button order and default content type** in the Content Types section, and click the **Visible box** for Document to deselect it. Click **OK**.

h. Click **Site contents** on the Quick Launch. Click the **PowerPoint_Library tile**. Click **New**. Select **Reunion Template**. Select the second slide and type **your first and last name** in place of NAME. Click in the **NOW placeholder** and type the **name of your university or college**. Select the word **Presentation** on the top navigation bar and type **sp04p2Presentation_LastFirst**. Click on the slide and then click on the words **Reunion Documents** on the top navigation bar. Take a screenshot of the PowerPoint_Library, naming the file **sp04p2PowerPoint_LastFirst**.

i. Click **Site contents** on the Quick Launch, and click **add an app**. Click the **Document Library tile**, and then type **Budget_Documents** in the Name box and click **Create**. Click the **Budget_Documents tile** to open the library. Open the Excel file *sp04p2Budget* on your local computer. Click the **File tab** to open Backstage view, and click **Save As**. Click the SharePoint server in the Save As list in the left pane, and click the folder in the right pane. Double-click the Reunion Documents site in the Save As dialog box. Double-click **Budget_Documents** in the library listing and add your last and first name in the format _LastFirst to the file name. Click **Save**. Close Excel after the upload completes.

j. Open the SharePoint Online window, and refresh the browser to see the Excel document in the document library. Click the **sp04p2Budget_LastFirst link** to open the file in Excel Online. Click the **Edit Workbook arrow** and select **Edit in Browser**. Click **cell B8** and type **7000**. Click **cell B16**, type **500**, and then press **Enter**. Click **Reunion Documents** on the top navigation bar to return to the SharePoint Online window. Take a screen shot of the Budget_Documents window, naming it **sp04p2BudgetDocs_LastFirst**.

k. Click **Home** on the Quick Launch. Open **Access 2016** and click the **Custom web app template**. Type **Reservations_Database** for the App Name. Type the Web location URL to the reunion_documents site, or copy and paste it from the SharePoint URL, removing any text after *reunion_documents*. Click **Create**.

l. Click **Access** in the Create a table from an existing data source section at the bottom of the window. Click **Browse** and navigate to and select the Access file *sp04p2Reservations* in the student data files. Click **Open** and click **OK**. Select the **Reservations table** and click **OK**. Click **Close**.

m. Click **List** and click **Edit**. Rearrange the field captions and fields into the following order:

| | |
|---|---|
| **LastName** | **FirstName** |
| **Address** | |
| **City** | **State** |
| **Paid** | |

**n.** Click **Save**. Open the SharePoint window, click **Site contents** on the Quick Launch, and click the **Reservations_Database tile**. Type **Martinez** in the Filter the list box and press **Enter**. Click the **Edit icon** on the ActionBar, and then type **$65.00** in the Paid field. Click the **Save icon** on the ActionBar. Click **Datasheet**, and then locate the record for **Lan Lin**. Click the **Paid field**, type **$65.00**, and press **Enter**. Take a screen shot showing both edited records, naming the file **sp04p2Data_LastFirst**. Click **Back to Site** on the top navigation bar.

**o.** Sign out of your Office 365 account. Close Access. Based on your instructor's directions, submit the following:

sp04p2PowerPoint_LastFirst

sp04p2BudgetDocs_LastFirst

sp04p2Data_LastFirst

# Mid-Level Exercises

## 1 Hope Hospital Documents, Blog Site, and Discussion Board

FROM SCRATCH As a Web designer for Hope Hospital, you are asked to create a SharePoint document library with a Word document template that nurses can use to keep track of patient blood pressure. You will create a Healthy Living blog for the Hope Hospital patients. You have also been asked to create a Discussion Board list where patients can share thoughts about healthy living. You will create an archive of the business office Excel documents related to the hospital expansion project, which are to be shared with all office employees. You will create a list from spreadsheet data and create a custom view. You have a very busy day ahead of you!

**a.** Log on to your Office 365 account using Internet Explorer, and create a new subsite under the team site, following these specifications:
   - Title: **Hope Hospital Documents**
   - Description: **This site provides access to Hope Hospital documents.**
   - URL: **hope_docs**
   - Template: **Team Site**

**b.** Create a blog subsite to the site you just created following these specifications:
   - Title: **Healthy Living Blog**
   - Description: **This is the blog site for Hope Hospital.**
   - URL: **hope_blog**
   - Template: **Blog**

**c.** Return to the Hope Hospital Documents site. Create a document library named **Hope Hospital Document Library** using the Site contents page. Create a new site content type following these specifications:
   - Name: **BloodPressureTracker**
   - Description: **This form helps track patient blood pressure levels.**
   - Select parent content type from: **Document Content Types**
   - Parent Content Type: **Document**
   - Put this site content type into: Existing group: **Display Template Content Types**

   After the site content type is created, use the Advanced settings to upload *sp04m1BloodPressureTracker* from the student data files. Use the LIBRARY tab to change the settings to allow management of content types, and then add the BloodPressureTracker as the default document template. Change the button order and default content type to specify the BloodPressureTracker as the only visible default document type.

**d.** Open the Hope Hospital Document Library, and create a new document using the BloodPressureTracker default document following these specifications:
   - Name: Replace Patient Name with your first and last name
   - Target Blood Pressure: Systolic **130** Diastolic **68**

   Save the document as **sp04m1BloodPressureTracker_LastFirst**.

**e.** Open Word 2016. Use the Blog post template to create a post to the hope_blog site you created in step b using the following specifications:
   - Title: **Tips for Healthy Living**
   - Content: **These tips, prepared by the Hope Hospital staff, will help you stay healthy. Always consult your doctor if you want additional information.**

   Manage the blog account, adding the URL to the blog you created for this exercise. Select the Healthy Living Blog below the title of the post and then publish the post to the blog site. Refresh the browser to review the post on the blog site. Make a screen shot of the blog posting, naming the file **sp04m1TipsBlog_LastFirst**.

**f.** Navigate to the Site contents page of the Hope Hospital team site, and add a Discussion Board app named **Healthy Living Discussions** to the site. Add a new item using the following specifications:

- Subject: **Tips for Healthy Living**
- Body: **Please share your favorite tips for staying healthy! What do you do for exercise? What foods do you regularly eat to improve your health? How do you reduce stress?**
- Question: Select the check box
- Add the following reply to the discussion board posting: **I keep a count of my calories throughout the day and eat a lot of vegetables.**

Return to the Healthy Living Discussions main Discussion Board page and add another discussion with the following specifications:

- Subject: **HIPAA Privacy Rule**
- Body: **The HIPAA Privacy Rule protects the information collected about you and your health. What thoughts do you have about the rule?**
- Question: Select the check box

Take a screen shot of the Healthy Living Discussions page, naming it **sp04m1Discussion_LastFirst**. Open the Tips for Healthy Living Discussion and take a screen shot of the page, naming it **sp04m1Tips_LastFirst**.

**g.** Open the Word document *sp04m1HealthyLiving* from the student data files. Select the title and subtitle, change the font to **Calibri**, and apply the **Orange, Accent 6** color to the text. Type your first and last name below Prepared by Hope Hospital Staff. Save the file to the Hope Hospital Document Library with the file name **sp04m1HealthyLiving_LastFirst** and the content type **Document**. Close Word. Navigate to the Hope Hospital Document Library and open the document in Word Online for editing. Below your first and last name, type **today's date**. Return to the Hope Hospital Document Library. Make a screen shot of the Hope Hospital Document Library page, naming the file **sp04m1DocLibrary_LastFirst**.

**h.** Use the Site contents page to add an app to upload a spreadsheet to the site as a list, using the following specifications:

- Name: **Hope Hospital Expansion**
- Description: **This list provides information about the expansion products that will be purchased.**
- File location: *sp04m1HopeHospitalExpansion*
- Range Type: **Table Range**
- Select Range: **Hope Hospital Expansion!Table1**

**i.** Create a Datasheet view of the Hope Hospital Expansion list using the following specifications:

- View Name: **Expansion Products View**
- Columns: **Product Category**, **Price per Item**, **Units to Order**, **Total**, **Created**, **Created By**, **Modified**, **Modified By**
- Sort: **Product Category**

Take a screen shot of the Hope Hospital Expansion page, naming the file **sp04m1Expansion_LastFirst**.

**j.** Sign out of your Office 365 account. Close any open desktop applications. Based on your instructor's directions, submit the following:

sp04m1TipsBlog_LastFirst

sp04m1Discussion_LastFirst

sp04m1Tips_LastFirst

sp04m1DocLibrary_LastFirst

sp04m1Expansion_LastFirst

## 2 Shelter Pets Online

FROM SCRATCH

As the volunteer Web designer for Shelter Pets Online, you have been developing a site to focus on animal adoption and how to incorporate a pet into the household. You will now work with a document library to upload and store documents, creating a default template document used for the intake of new animals to the shelter. You will create a view for the document library. You will add an Access custom web app to the site containing information about recent adoptions. You will alter the list view of the Access custom web app. You will also add a Calendar list to the site advertising opportunities to get involved with the organization. You will add a Contact list to the site. Finally, you will add a training PowerPoint presentation to the site in Windows Media Video (.wmv) format.

**a.** Log on to your Office 365 account, and create a new subsite under the team site following these specifications:
- Title: **Shelter Pets Documents**
- Description: **This site provides access to the Shelter Pets Online documents.**
- URL: **shelter_docs**
- Template: **Team Site**

**b.** Create a document library named **Shelter Pets Intake Documents**. Create a new site content type following these specifications:
- Name: **Intake_Form**
- Description: **This form is used as each new animal is surrendered to the shelter.**
- Select parent content type from: **Document Content Types**
- Parent Content Type: **Document**
- Put this site content type into: Existing group: **Display Template Content Types**

After the site content type is created, use the Advanced settings to upload *sp04m2IntakeForm* from the student data files. Use the LIBRARY tab to change the settings to allow management of content types, and then add the **Intake_Form** as the default document template. Change the button order and default content type to specify the **Intake_Form** as the only visible default document type.

**c.** Open the Shelter Pets Intake Documents library, and create a new document using the **Intake_Form** default document, following these specifications:
- Date: Today's date
- Name: **Lucy**
- Breed: **Collie**
- Age: **3**
- Sex: **Female**
- Color: **Brindle**
- Hair Type: **Long**
- House Trained: **Yes**
- Good with children: **Yes**
- Previous owner: Your name
- Details: **Owner is moving to an apartment that will not allow animals.**

Save the document as **sp04m2Intake_LastFirst**. Return to Shelter Pets Intake Documents.

**d.** Create a view for the Shelter Pets Intake Documents library using the following specifications:
- View: **Standard View**
- View Name: **Intake View**
- Columns: **Type**, **Name**, **Created**, **Created By**

Take a screen shot of the Shelter Pets Intake Documents page, naming the file **sp04m2IntakeDocs_LastFirst**.

e. Use Access 2016 to create an Access Custom web app using the following specifications:
- App Name: **Dog_Adoptions**
- Web Location: **URL to Shelter Pets Documents**
- Access table data source: *sp04m2AnimalAdoptions*
- Table: **DogAdoptions**

Edit the List view to resemble the following:

| **Name** | **Previous Owner** |
|---|---|
| **Breed** | |
| **Gender** | **New Owner** |
| **Approximate Age** | |

f. Use the List view to find the entry for **Bear** and add the new owner name **John Clark**. Display the DogAdoptions data as a Datasheet, and take a screen shot of the page, naming it **sp04m2Adoptions_LastFirst**.

g. Add a Calendar list app to the site, using the name **Shelter Pets Online Calendar**. Add the following events for next week:

| |
|---|
| Next Saturday |
|        Title: Adoption Event |
|        Location: Pets, Inc. |
|        Start Time: 10 AM |
|        End Time: 1 PM |
|        Description: Puppies and kittens available |
|        Category: Get-together |
| Next Wednesday |
|        Title: Volunteer Appreciation Dinner |
|        Location: Country Cooking Catering |
|        Start Time: 6 PM |
|        End Time: 10 PM |
|        Description: Dinner, awards, and entertainment. RSVP to Sally Millard |
|        Category: Get-together |
| Next Thursday |
|        Title: Board Meeting |
|        Location: Shelter Pets Conference Room |
|        Start Time: 2 PM |
|        End Time: 4 PM |
|        Description: Agenda distributed at meeting |
|        Category: Business |

Display the calendar in **All Events** view. Create a new view, based on the All Events view, named **Calendar Event View** with the following columns: **Title**, **Location**, **Start Time**, **End Time**, **Category**. Take a screen shot of the Calendar Event View page, naming the file **sp04m2Calendar_LastFirst**.

**DISCOVER**

**h.** Add the Contacts list app to the site with the name **Shelter Pets Online Contacts**. Create a Standard view named **Shelter Contact View** with the following columns in the order shown: **First Name**, **Last Name**, **Business Phone**, **Email Address**, and **Job Title**. Sort by **Last Name**. Add the following contact information:

- Last Name: Your last name
- First Name: Your first name
- Email Address: Your email address
- Job Title: **Volunteer Web designer**
- Business Phone: **(384)555-1465**

Take a screen shot of the Shelter Pets Online Contacts page, naming the file **sp04m2Contacts_LastFirst**.

**i.** Create a document library named **PowerPoint_Library**. Open the PowerPoint presentation *sp04m2Presentation*. Save the file to the library as a **PowerPoint Show** file named **sp04m2Presentation_LastFirst**. After the presentation uploads (watch the PowerPoint status bar for the progress), close PowerPoint, refresh the browser window, and open the presentation to review it. Return to the PowerPoint_Library page and take a screen shot of the page, naming the file **sp04m2Presentation_LastFirst**.

**j.** Sign out of your Office 365 account. Close any open desktop applications. Based on your instructor's directions, submit the following:

sp04m2IntakeDocs_LastFirst

sp04m2Adoptions_LastFirst

sp04m2Calendar_LastFirst

sp04m2Contacts_LastFirst

sp04m2Presentation_LastFirst

# Beyond the Classroom

## Integrating OneDrive for Business, Outlook, and SharePoint Online

**GENERAL CASE**

In this chapter, you have integrated the major Microsoft Office applications and SharePoint. OneDrive for Business and Outlook can also be integrated with SharePoint Online libraries, lists, and calendars. After completing research using the Internet and help files on SharePoint Online, write the steps of the process for syncing OneDrive for Business with a SharePoint library. Write a second procedure for connecting SharePoint Online libraries and lists such as a calendar list, with Outlook 2016. Save your file with the file name **sp04b1Research_LastFirst**. Based on your instructor's directions, submit sp04b1Research_LastFirst.

## SharePoint File Mayhem

**DISASTER RECOVERY**

Your supervisor called you in to discuss the lack of organization of the Documents library on the SharePoint Online site. She is dismayed that it is difficult to find documents and that everyone is using different forms to complete their work. Budgets are grouped with letters to customers and pictures used in advertising. People are using at least six different travel reimbursement forms, with none of them collecting all of the information. Prepare a memo (addressed to your instructor) that describes solutions to the problems in SharePoint Online. Use the subject line **sp04b2Recommendations_LastFirst** for the memo. Based on your instructor's directions, submit sp04b2Recommendations_LastFirst.

# Capstone Exercise

You have been working with the team developing the curriculum for Project Investor, an after-school class offered by Wellington Finances. You will add organization to a site and integrate Microsoft Office applications with the site.

## Create a Subsite with a Document Library and Default Document Template

You will create a site that you will share with your teammates. The site will contain a document library and you will set up a default document template to enable team members to track their volunteer hours on the project.

a. Sign on to your Office 365 site, and create a new subsite to the team site with the following specifications:
   - Title: **Project Investor Documents**
   - Description: **Updated by**, your name, and today's date
   - URL: **project_investor_docs**
   - Template: **Team Site**

b. Create a document library named **Volunteer_Documents**.

c. Upload and make the Excel worksheet *sp04c1Volunteer* the default document template for the document library. Name the template **Volunteer_Hours** and type the description **This form is for recording your volunteer hours for Project Investor.** Change the Volunteer_Hours document to be the only visible document on the New Document command.

d. Create a new document using the default document template by typing your name on the form, and typing the following volunteer information:
   - Project: **Curriculum**
   - Date: Today's date
   - Time In: **3:00 PM**
   - Time Out: **5:00 PM**

   Save the file as **sp04c1Volunteer_LastFirst**. Open the file in SharePoint Online, and add the following comment: **Completed Section 4**. Right-click the file link on the Volunteer_Documents page and download the file to your computer.

## Create a Links List

To help people find resources on investing, you will create a Links list and populate it with hyperlinks.

a. Create a links list named **Investing Resources**.

b. Add the following resource links to the links list:
   - URL: **http://www.usa.gov/Citizen/Topics/Money/Investing.shtml**

   - Description: **USA government investing information**

c. Create a Datasheet view named **Investing_Links**, with the following columns in the order listed:

   **Type, Edit, URL (URL with edit menu), Notes, Created, Created By**

d. Click the Edit icon on the blank row of the datasheet, and add the following link:
   - Address: **http://www.stockinvestment123.com**
   - Display text: **Stock Investment for Beginners**

   Take a screen shot of the Investing Resources page, naming the file **sp04c1Resources_LastFirst**.

## Import a Spreadsheet List and Create a Custom View

The team wants to review the participation of the schools in the area. You have a spreadsheet with the data, so you will import it as a spreadsheet list and then customize the view. You will update information on the list.

a. Import the spreadsheet *sp04c1Schools* using the following specifications:
   - Name: **Participating_Students**
   - Description: **The schools and participating student numbers are listed.**
   - Range Type: **Table Range**
   - Select Range: **Sheet1!Table1**

b. Create a view based on the Standard view, using the following specifications:
   - View Name: **Schools View**
   - Display columns in this order: **School (linked to item with edit menu), Student Population, Students Participating, Modified**
   - Sort by the **Students Participating** column in **descending order**, and then by **School** in **ascending order**.

c. Update the entry for the Marion School District, so the Student Population is **520**, and the Students Participating is **467**. Stop editing the list, and take a screen shot of the Participating_Students page, naming the file **sp04c1Students_LastFirst**.

## Create an Access Custom Web App and Link a SharePoint List to Access

An Access database contains information about student registrations for the upcoming session of Project Investor. You will add this data to the SharePoint site using an Access custom web app. You will then link a SharePoint list to Access to enable users to edit the Participating Students list in Access.

a. Create an Access custom web app, using the following specifications:
   - App Name: **Student_Registrations**
   - Web Location: **Project Investor Documents** SharePoint Online Site
   - Access Table data source: *sp04c1Registrations*, **RegisteredStudents table**
   - Edit the List view to display the **City**, **State**, **and ZIPcode** on the same line. Move the School caption and field next to the FirstName field.

   Display the record for Medina Hayek, and take a screen shot of the list view, naming the file **sp04c1Registrations_LastFirst**.

b. Create a blank Access database named **sp04c1StudentParticipants_LastFirst**. Import the SharePoint List **Participating_Students** as a linked table.

c. Locate the row for **Central Columbia School District**, and change the Students Participating field value to **45**. Save the database. Open the SharePoint Online window, refresh the browser, and review the update. Take a screen shot of the Participating_Students page showing the update has been made, naming the file **sp04c1Update_LastFirst**.

d. Sign out of Office 365. Close all open applications. Based on your instructor's directions, submit the following:

   sp04c1Volunteer_LastFirst
   sp04c1Resources_LastFirst
   sp04c1Students_LastFirst
   sp04c1Registrations_LastFirst
   sp04c1Update_LastFirst
   sp04c1StudentParticipants_LastFirst

# HTML, XHTML, XML, and CSS

## HTML and XHTML

In 1991, CERN released the first text-oriented browser. However, the explosive growth of the revolutionary hypertext approach started in 1992, when the first graphically oriented browser, Mosaic, was developed at the National Center for Supercomputing Applications at the University of Illinois at Urbana–Champaign. This approach later evolved into the fundamental method of sharing and retrieving information on the Internet.

This text introduces you to SharePoint tools that empower Web developers to create, edit, format, and optimize HTML/XHTML code without any actual HTML/XHTML knowledge. However, a minimum level of HTML knowledge is a good addition to any Web designer's portfolio. This appendix uses SharePoint Designer to explain the concepts of HTML, XHTML, and XML. SharePoint Designer provides a robust set of tools for working with webpages. It can be downloaded for free from microsoft.com. You can use it to design and edit your SharePoint Online pages at the code level. Additional materials available with this text describe how to use SharePoint Designer.

> **TIP: SHAREPOINT ONLINE DESIGN MANAGER**
> SharePoint Online includes Design Manager, which is available only on certain types of sites, such as publishing sites. Your administrator must give you access to the SharePoint Server Publishing Infrastructure for you to use this feature. Design Manager enables you to upload design files, edit master pages and display templates, and edit page layouts. Snippets, available in Design Manager, enable you to add code to pages to customize them.

The relationships among HTML, XHTML, and XML, as today's core markup languages, are still an area of considerable confusion, especially for beginners in Web development and design; thus, this section aims to clarify this confusion.

In this section, you will learn about the HTML and XHTML markup languages.

## Getting Started with HTML

A **markup language** describes the layout of webpage content using tags. **Tags** are specific codes that indicate how the text should be displayed when the document is opened in a Web browser. Browsers interpret the tags and display the content (including text, graphic elements, colors, and fonts) formatted on the webpage according to the tags. **Hypertext Markup Language (HTML)** is known as the "language of the Web" because it defines the page layout and graphic elements of the page and provides links to other documents on the Web.

HTML is the most common markup language. Because HTML documents are created using unformatted text, you can create them in a simple text program (such as Windows Notepad), in a word-processing program (such as Microsoft Word), or in a Web-design program (such as SharePoint Online 2016 or SharePoint Designer 2013). HTML documents normally have the file extension .htm or .html.

HTML was created to simplify the Standard Generalized Markup Language (SGML) so that anyone could learn to use it. HTML documents contain a combination of American Standard Code for Information Interchange (ASCII) text and tags. Computers

## SharePoint Tools for Working with HTML, XHTML, XML, and CSS

Burlingham/Fotolia

can understand only numbers. **ASCII**, which was created by the American National Standards Institute (http://www.ansi.org), is the common numeric code used by computers to represent characters. The standard ASCII character set consists of 128 decimal numbers ranging from 0 through 127 assigned to letters, numbers, punctuation marks, and the most common special characters. For instance, the lowercase letter "a" is &#97 in the ASCII character set, whereas the uppercase "A" is &#65. The extended ASCII character set also consists of 128 decimal numbers and ranges from 128 through 255, representing additional special, mathematical, graphic, and foreign characters.

> **TIP: PHYSICAL AND LOGICAL TAGS**
> Physical tags indicate the way information should be displayed and provide no indication about the type of information. HTML tags are physical tags that format specific character selections. These tags, such as <b> and <i>, are used for formatting. Although less common than physical tags, you can also use logical tags to format text in an HTML document. Logical tags, such as <strong> and <em>, concentrate on the type of information being displayed rather than how the information should be displayed. You are encouraged to use logical tags because the browser can then pick the best way to display the text on the screen. Logical tags are supported by HTML 4.01 and HTML5 and by all core browsers (see also http://www.w3schools.com/html/default.asp).

> **TIP: WHAT IS SHTML?**
> You may see webpages with the suffix of ".shtml." This webpage includes dynamic content, typically a "last modified date," added by the server before the webpage is sent to your browser.

HTML documents follow a specific syntax, which is a set of standards or rules developed by the **World Wide Web Consortium (W3C),** an organization that provides leadership through an open forum of groups with a vested interest in the Internet, with the mission of leading the Web to its full potential. Many HTML tags are used in pairs, and the basic syntax of these pairs is <tag>*text*</tag>. HTML tags are not case sensitive, so they can be written in uppercase, lowercase, or mixed case. Some HTML tags are not used in pairs, such as the <br> tag, which forces a break in the current line of text. These tags are referred to as *empty element tags.* The W3C has created a set of standards indicating the correct format that should be applied to standard tags.

### To review W3C standards, complete the following steps:

1. Open a browser window and type www.w3.org/standards/webdesign.
2. Click HTML & CSS.
3. Click HTML in the right-side pane.

> **TIP: W3C HTML STANDARDS**
> If you want to read more about the W3C HTML standards and specifications, you can check them out at the W3C website (http://www.w3.org). SharePoint Designer assists you in developing webpages in line with W3C standards and specifications.

In addition to the tags that define webpage elements, HTML enables you to use attributes that further define the way elements are displayed in Web browsers. The *attributes* are placed within the start tag in an HTML tag pair: <tag attributes>*text*</tag>. You can use these attributes to define the style, color, size, width, height, and source of the elements on your webpage. Specific values are assigned to each attribute. For instance, you can specify the height of a graphic in pixels, or a table width as a percentage. You can also specify the style characteristics of the elements on your webpage using a Cascading Style Sheet (CSS). W3C guidelines and standards clearly indicate that CSS styles are preferred over setting the attributes within the HTML code.

Over the years, millions of webpages have been, and continue to be, created with HTML, which remains the most popular markup language. However, despite its popularity, HTML has some drawbacks. All Web developers should be aware of the following limitations and flaws when using HTML:

- HTML does not enable users to structure, define, and process data. For example, you can use HTML to build forms, but you cannot fully validate, send, and retrieve the form's information to and from a database. To accomplish these types of tasks, a Web developer must use code written in a scripting language, such as JavaScript, Microsoft Active Server Pages (ASP), or Sun Java Server Pages (JSP).

- HTML is not extensible. In other words, it includes a finite set of tags and does not enable users to create new custom tags; thus, it cannot be changed to meet specific developers' needs for describing data content. The extensibility issue is discussed in greater detail later in this appendix.

- Although HTML includes a wide range of syntax rules, it does not enforce these rules. If you forget an HTML rule, you can use the W3C Validation Service (http://validator.w3.org), or manually validate the way the HTML code is displayed in one or more browsers.

- HTML features are still not consistently supported by all browsers; thus, an HTML document might be displayed differently in one browser than in another. For example, some browsers require the </p> end tag and some do not. Also, some of the HTML5 new features are not supported by all browsers.

---

**TIP: WHAT IS A SCRIPTING LANGUAGE?**

A *scripting language* is less powerful than traditional programming languages, such as Java and C++. Traditional programming languages are sets of commands compiled and then executed one by one. Each scripting language employs a scripting engine and does not require compilation as does a traditional programming language. Depending on where a script code is interpreted (which means also where the scripting engine is located), scripting languages are divided into two main categories: client-side and server-side. A script code written in a server-side scripting language is interpreted on the Web server before the requested webpage is sent back to the client. When an HTML document containing code written in a client-side scripting language is loaded in a browser, a scripting engine built in the browser interprets the code. A *scripting engine* (or *interpreter*) is a program that translates code one line at a time into an executable format each time the program runs. Consequently, scripting languages commonly run more slowly than traditional programming languages do.

---

*Microsoft Active Server Pages (ASPX)* and *Java Server Pages (JSP)* are two of the most popular server-side scripting languages used to develop interactive websites that interface with databases or other data sources (such as an XML document). JavaScript is one of the most popular client-side scripting languages, and its scripting engine is supported by all major browsers, such as Microsoft Edge, Internet Explorer, Chrome, and Firefox. Developers from Netscape and Sun Microsystems created JavaScript as a Java subset that is simpler to use than the Java programming language. It is able to meet the needs of most Web developers who want to create dynamic webpages. JavaScript is used by Web developers for such things as automatically changing a formatted date on a webpage, causing a linked page to appear in a pop-up window, causing text or a graphic image to change during a mouse rollover, obtaining information about the current Web browser, navigating to webpages that have been opened during a Web browser session, or validating data submitted via an HTML form.

# Getting Started with XHTML

***Extensible Hypertext Markup Language (XHTML)*** is a newer markup language that overcomes some of the problems generated by HTML. XHTML is a transitional language between HTML and XML. Thus, until all browsers are upgraded to fully support XML, XHTML will continue to be a worthy solution.

Although there are many similarities between HTML and XHTML, there are also some important differences (see Figure A.1), such as

- Well-formed and valid XHTML can be read by all XML-enabled applications.
- XHTML code has to be well-formed and valid to avoid generating errors.
- XHTML tags and attribute names must be lowercase.
- XHTML tags are case sensitive.
- In XHTML, the empty element tags that were inherited from HTML, such as <img>, <br>, and <hr>, have the following syntax: <img/>, <br/>, and <hr/>.

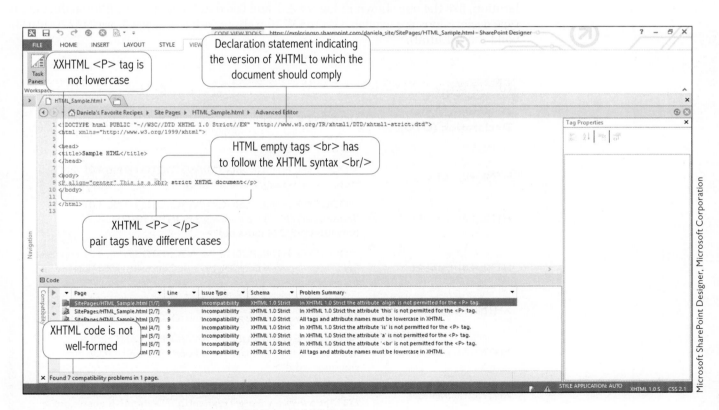

**FIGURE A.1** Main Differences between HTML and XHTML Documents

---

**TIP: CREATING AN XHTML DOCUMENT**
XHTML documents are also XML documents. The first line of XHTML coding includes a declaration statement indicating that the document complies with XML syntax rules (as shown in Figure A.1).

---

# Developing Standard HTML/XHTML Documents

The way a webpage is displayed by different browsers and on different platforms can vary. Fonts, colors, tables, and hyperlinks are only a few of the many webpage elements that can appear differently between browsers—for instance, between Firefox and Microsoft Edge. The same webpage might also be displayed differently on computers using different operating systems. Fonts and colors are some of the webpage elements that might look different on an Apple computer or a Sun workstation than they do on a computer that uses Windows. Although organizations and corporations around the world are working on ways to eliminate cross-browser and cross-platform issues, they still pose a problem for Web developers.

To overcome the cross-browser and cross-platform issues, W3C declared many older HTML tags and tag attributes as deprecated, meaning that they might not be supported by all browsers. To learn more about the HTML elements and their status, visit the W3C Index of Elements website (http://www.w3.org/TR/REC-html40/index/elements.html). To learn more about HTML attributes and their status, visit the W3C Index of Attributes website (http://www.w3.org/TR/REC-html40/index/attributes.html).

W3C has defined three variations of HTML 4.01 (http://www.w3.org/TR/REC-html40) and XHTML 1.0 (http://www.w3.org/TR/xhtml1): strict, transitional, and frameset. In the strict version, deprecated tags are not allowed. If you specify transitional or frameset declarations, deprecated tags can be used. The only difference between transitional and frameset is the latter allows frames. When developing an XHTML or HMTL webpage, you indicate which version and variation you are using with a DOCTYPE declaration, like the one shown in Figure A.1 and listed in Table A.1. Additional document type declarations are available on the W3C website (http://www.w3.org/QA/2002/04/valid-dtd-list.html).

| TABLE A.I  DOCTYPE Declarations for HTML and XHTML | |
|---|---|
| **Document Type Declaration (DTD)** | **DOCTYPE Statement** |
| HTML 5.0 | <!DOCTYPE html> |
| HTML 4.01 strict | <!DOCTYPE HTML PUBLIC "-//W3C//DTD HTML 4.01//EN" "http://www.w3.org/TR/html4/strict.dtd"> |
| HTML 4.01 transitional | <!DOCTYPE HTML PUBLIC "-//W3C//DTD HTML 4.01 Transitional//EN" "http://www.w3.org/TR/1999/REC-html401-19991224/loose.dtd"> |
| HTML 4.01 frameset | <!DOCTYPE HTML PUBLIC "-//W3C//DTD HTML 4.01 Frameset//EN" "http://www.w3.org/TR/1999/REC-html401-19991224/frameset.dtd"> |
| XHTML 1.0 strict | <!DOCTYPE HTML PUBLIC "-//W3C//DTD XHTML 1.0 Strict//EN" "http://www.w3.org/TR/xhtml1/DTD/xhtml1-strict.dtd"> |
| XHTML 1.0 transitional | <!DOCTYPE HTML PUBLIC "-//W3C//DTD XHTML 1.0 Transitional//EN" "http://www.w3.org/TR/xhtml1/DTD/xhtml1-transitional.dtd"> |
| XHTML 1.0 frameset | <!DOCTYPE HTML PUBLIC "-//W3C//DTD XHTML 1.0 Frameset//EN" "http://www.w3.org/TR/xhtml1/DTD/xhtml1-frameset.dtd"> |

Pearson Education, Inc.

The latest version of HTML released by the W3C is HTML5 (http://www.w3schools.com/html/html5_intro.asp). In HTML5, there is only one DOCTYPE: <!DOCTYPE html>. HTML5 replaces HTML 4.01 and XHTML. SharePoint 2016 supports HTML5 as defined by the W3C. The focus of HTML5 is on coding for all types of devices, from desktop computers to mobile devices, such as tablets and smartphones. HTML5 is supported by browsers from Microsoft, Apple, Mozilla, Google, and others. HTML5 uses the same syntax as previous versions, but adds new elements that replace the use of browser plug-ins, with both HTML5 video and Silverlight players supported.

Once you finish a draft of your webpage, you can use a validator application to evaluate the page and see if it complies with the version and variation you used. W3C offers a freeware Markup Validation Service (http://validator.w3.org) that can be used to check HTML, XHTML, and more. The webpage can be validated by supplying URI (Uniform Resource Identifier) or Web address, uploading the page, or typing HTML code into the validator application.

To help eliminate cross-browser and cross-platform issues, all browser manufacturers should comply with the W3C standards. Unfortunately, this is not always the case; thus, Web developers need to continue their efforts to develop standard websites that overcome cross-browser and cross-platform challenges.

# Getting Started with Common HTML and XHTML Elements and Attributes

The W3C provides an updated list of the common HTML and XHTML elements and attributes for the current version of HTML. Search the W3C site using the key words *index of elements* and select the most recent HTML version from the results. Shown in Figure A.2 is a portion of the element list for HTML5. Click the element link for more information about each element. The description column gives you an idea of how the element is used, whereas the Attributes column describes the possible settings for the element.

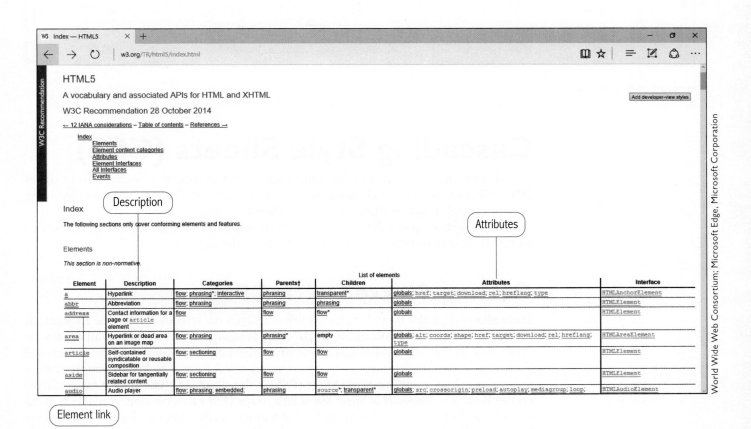

**FIGURE A.2** W3C HTML5 Elements List

Special characters, such as language accent marks, fractions, or copyright symbols, have unique coding that begins with an ampersand (&). These entity codes can be used to place special characters within the webpage. A comprehensive and updated list of all special characters, used in HTML can be found at the W3C website by searching HTML5 entities and selecting the W3C Character Entity Reference Chart link (see Figure A.3).

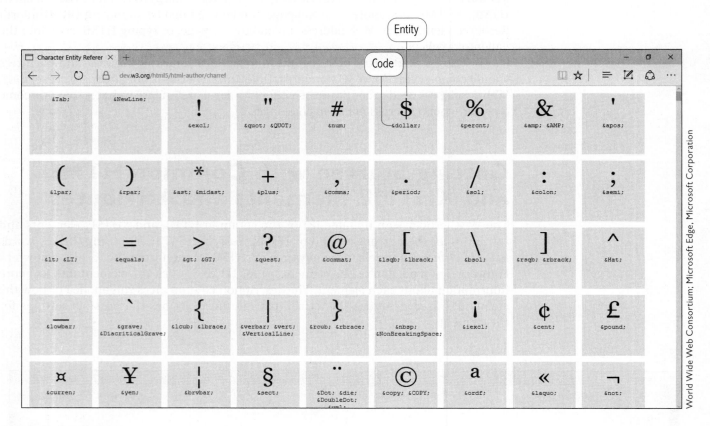

**FIGURE A.3** W3C Special Character Entities

# Cascading Style Sheets (CSS)

This chapter introduces you to the comprehensive set of tools that SharePoint Designer 2013 offers to empower Web developers to create, edit, modify, and optimize Cascading Style Sheet (CSS) styles without any actual CSS knowledge.

In this section, you will learn about this style sheet language and how it is linked to an HTML page to provide styles to the elements on the page.

## Getting Started with CSS

*Style sheets* describe how documents are displayed on screens, presented in print, or even how words are pronounced. *Style sheet languages* are computer languages for expressing style sheets. Although several style sheet languages have been developed, CSS is a robust formatting language that successfully separates a webpage's content from its appearance. *Cascading Style Sheet (CSS)* is the standard style sheet language used on the Web. The *Extensible Style Sheet Language (XSL)* was developed by the W3C as an improved method for formatting XML documents, allowing developers to transform XML data files into a wide variety of popular file formats, such as HTML and Portable Document Format (PDF). XSL is still supported by fewer browsers than CSS.

Although CSS was initially developed for HTML, it is currently used in HTML, XML, and XHTML. CSS2, the newest release from the W3C, is supported in SharePoint 2016. CSS2 offers features that enable screens to render pages accurately, regardless of the size of the screen. These features are important to display pages on devices such as TVs, desktop computer monitors, tablets, and smartphones. W3C is offering CSS Validation Service (https://jigsaw.w3.org/css-validator).

You can use four different types of CSS style codes to format the HTML/XHTML code of your webpages: inline styles, embedded styles, external styles, and imported styles.

*Inline style* codes are included in the start tag by using the tag's style attributes. Inline style codes override the styles defined in internal and external styles. **Embedded styles** are usually included in the <head> section of an HTML document and have the following syntax: <style>*style declarations*</style>. Embedded style codes override the format defined in a linked external style sheet. **External styles** are included in separate files used to specify the formatting of any HTML document to which they are linked. These style codes are kept in a document with a .css file extension and are linked to the HTML document using the <link> HTML tag. If you have two styles with the same weight in a document—for instance, two declared inline styles—the style declared last has precedence. **Imported styles** are similar to external styles with the styles being imported from a separate file at the time the webpage is downloaded. This text focuses on the first three styles because external styles and imported styles are so similar.

---

**TIP: USING METATAGS**

Metatags represent one of the tools that you can use to ensure that the content of your website has the proper topic identification and ranking by search engines, such as Google, Bing or Yahoo. SharePoint pages automatically include default metatags that indicate the language used and how the webpage should be displayed. A Web designer can add user-defined metatags to a webpage. These tags identify the kinds of topics included in the pages of the webpage.

---

A single style defines the look of one webpage element by simply telling a browser how to format that content on a webpage, from displaying a headline in blue to bordering a table with orange. A style consists of two elements:

- The webpage element that will be formatted by the browser, named the selector.
- The formatting instructions, named the declaration block.

However, even a simple style, like the one illustrated in Figure A.4, contains several elements:

- The **selector** indicates to a Web browser which element(s) within a webpage to style. In Figure A.4, the selector *a* refers to the tag <a>; therefore, the Web browser will format all <a> tags using the formatting directions included in this style.

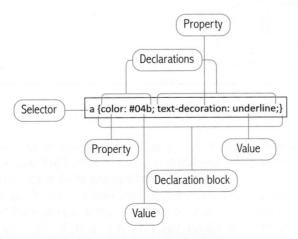

**FIGURE A.4** The Anatomy of a CSS Style

- The ***declaration block*** begins and ends with braces {}. It includes all the formatting options you want applied to the selector.
- A ***declaration*** is composed of one or more formatting instructions also known as declarations. Each declaration includes a property and a value.
- A ***property*** is a word or a group of hyphenated words indicating a style effect. In Figure A.4, color and text-decoration are properties of the <a> tag.
- A ***value*** is required to be assigned to any property. In Figure A.4, #04b is the value of the color property and underline is the value of the text-decoration property of the <a> tag.

The CSS style selectors allow you to single out one specific webpage element or a collection of similar webpage elements:

- ***Tag selectors*** apply to all occurrences of the HTML tag they specify, and they are easy to distinguish in a document because they have the same name as the HTML tag they style. For example, in the webpage shown in Figure A.5, a style was created for the <p> tag selector. Therefore, all the <p> tag occurrences implement this style.

> **TIP: TAG SELECTORS**
> Make sure you do not add the less than < and greater than > symbols to tag selectors.

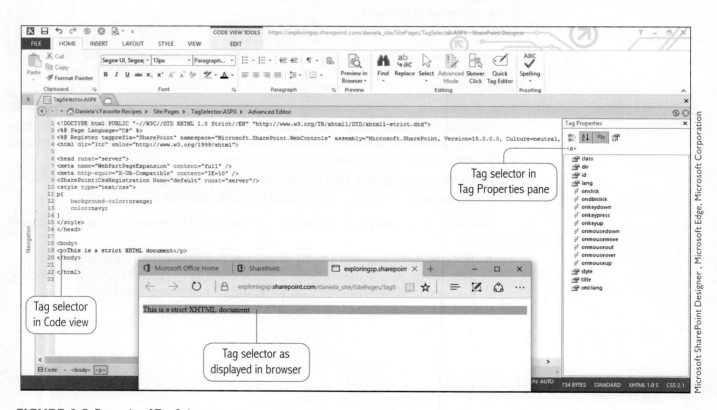

**FIGURE A.5** Example of Tag Selector

- ***Class selectors*** usually apply to HTML sections of your webpage that can be identified by the <div> or <span> tags. They start with a period, and they are case sensitive. After the period, the name must start with a letter and can include only letters, numbers, hyphens, and underscores. Class selectors are usually defined in the head section of a webpage or in an external style sheet. For example, in the webpage shown in Figure A.6, a .style_italic class selector was created in the webpage's attached external style sheet and applied using the <p> and </p> tags.

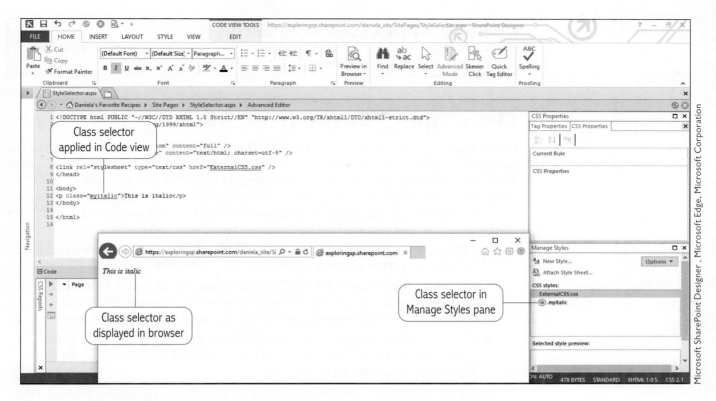

**FIGURE A.6** Example of Class

- **ID selectors** are used to identify unique parts of your webpage such as banners, navigation bars, or main content area. An element is connected to a unique ID. For example, in the webpage shown in Figure A.7, a #navigation ID selector style was created in the webpage's attached external style sheet and applied to the section <div id = "navigation">.

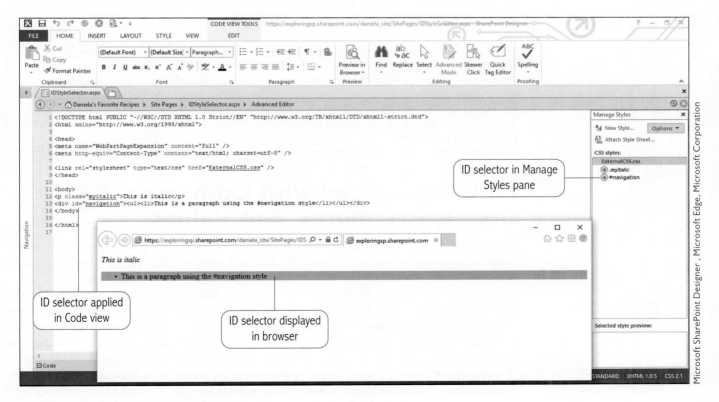

**FIGURE A.7** Example of ID Selector

> **TIP: SHOULD I USE A CLASS OR AN ID?**
> When you want to use a style several times in a page or site you must use a class. When a browser encounters a class and an ID for the same tag, it gives priority to the ID.

# Developing Standard CSS

One of the biggest advantages to using CSS is that when the style sheet is changed, all the webpages created with that style sheet are automatically updated. To learn more about W3C CSS standards and which browsers support CSS, visit this webpage of the W3C (http://www.w3.org/Style/CSS) and search with the key term *browsers*.

The specifications for CSS are maintained by the W3C and are made up of various levels or versions and profiles. Desktop browsers implement CSS level 1, 2, or 3:

- CSS level 1 (http://www.w3.org/TR/CSS1) was the earliest level developed, and includes properties for fonts, margins, colors, and more.
- CSS level 2 (http://www.w3.org/TR/CSS21) was introduced in 1998, and includes all of CSS level 1, as well as new styles for absolutely positioned elements, automatic numbering, page breaks, right to left text, and more.
- CSS level 3 (http://www.w3.org/Style/CSS/current-work), currently under development, encompasses all of CSS level 2, and provides new styles for user interaction, accessibility, and speech.

Three CSS profiles have been developed for alternative platforms, such as PDAs, cellphones, televisions, printers, and speech synthesizers. They include:

- CSS Mobile Profile 2.0 (http://www.w3.org/TR/css-mobile), which enables display on mobile devices, such as cell phones and PDAs.
- CSS TV Profile 1.0 (http://www.w3.org/TR/css-tv), which is for browsers that run on television displays.
- CSS Print Profile (http://www.w3.org/TR/css-print), which is in the draft stage and will provide styles to low-cost printers.

> **TIP: ALWAYS THINK ABOUT THE USERS' NEEDS**
> You should be aware that a visitor can override any style applied to your webpages. People with disabilities often use the Internet Explorer Accessibility dialog box to apply their own style sheet to the webpage display. The visitor's style sheets take precedence over your style sheet and their browser's default styles. Thus, as discussed in Appendix B, your webpages should be able to display properly with or without a style sheet.

# Getting Started with Common CSS Styles, Attributes, and Values

If you do not specify a style for an element on your webpage, the element inherits the style of its parent element. For example, all the styles specified for the <body> element will apply to any included <p> element that does not have a specified style.

Common CSS styles, their common attributes, and standard values are found on the W3C website. Some attributes use CSS units of measure to indicate properties, such as color, length, and spacing. To learn about the CSS units of measure, visit the Wired CSS Units of Measure website (https://www.wired.com/2010/02/css-units-of-measure).The W3C working group is a dynamic one, frequently generating new styles and standards. To keep up with the CSS most recent developments, visit the W3C Cascading Style Sheets website (http://www.w3.org/Style/CSS), or search for CSS 2.2 and select the CSS level you want to learn about in the search results.

# SharePoint Designer Tools for Working with HTML, XHTML, and CSS

One of the greatest strengths of SharePoint Designer is that Web developers can use the graphical user interface to create a wide variety of webpages and websites without extensive knowledge of HTML and XHTML. The SharePoint Designer 2013 tools enable you to create, edit, format, and optimize HTML and XHTML code. SharePoint Designer also offers new and enhanced tools for creating and managing CSS styles to further refine your webpages.

In this section, you will review and learn more about SharePoint Designer tools for working with HTML, XHTML, and CSS.

## Working in SharePoint Designer with HTML and XHTML

SharePoint Designer 2013 excels in offering tools that enable all categories of Web developers, from beginners to professionals, to create, edit, format, and optimize the HTML/XHTML code of your webpages. Some of the most relevant tools are described here:

- **Code view** Code view is helpful for editing and formatting HTML/XHTML. Code view shows the HTML/XHTML code of the webpage and enables you to edit the code.

- **IntelliSense tool** The IntelliSense tool is a great built-in tutor for developers. It provides a content-specific list of HTML/XHTML code entries to select. If you type the opening tag < while editing, SharePoint Designer displays a list of appropriate HTML/XHTML tags for that specific HTML/XHTML section of the webpage. It provides the same type of assistance when typing attributes for HTML/XHTML tags.

- **Apply XML formatting rules** The Apply XML Formatting Rules tool is available in Code view(right-click the body of the webpage and then click Apply XML Formatting Rules) and applies XML formatting rules to the HTML/XHTML code, such as end tags.

- **Accessibility and Compatibility tools** The Accessibility Checker and Compatibility Checker are extremely powerful in assisting Web developers when creating accessible and usable websites.

- **Find and Replace HTML tags** The Find and Replace HTML tags tool assists Web developers in performing more sophisticated searches using the HTML rules feature. It enables you to create detailed search rules. With these detailed rules, you can refine the search to include HTML/XHTML tags, as well as their attributes and attribute values.

- **Reformat HTML** The Reformat HTML tool is available in Code view (right-click the body of the webpage and then click Reformat HTML). This command reformats the HTML code to follow predefined code formatting options as selected in the Code Formatting tab of the Page Editor Options dialog box, available by clicking Options on Backstage view. To comply with the W3C requirements for standardization, the tag names are lowercase and attribute names are lowercase. Click the appropriate checkboxes on the Code Formatting tab of the Page Editor Options dialog box.

## Working in SharePoint Designer with CSS

SharePoint Designer 2013 provides tools for working with CSS that you can use to further refine your webpage layouts and formatting. CSS tools, such as task panes, assist you in managing, applying, and editing CSS rules and style sheets to design the look of your page.

## Understand How SharePoint Designer Works with CSS

SharePoint Designer provides a CSS Style Application toolbar, CSS layout tools, and Microsoft IntelliSense for CSS. Some of the most relevant tools are described here:

- **Tag and CSS Properties tools** The Tag Properties and CSS Properties task panes enable you to apply HTML properties (attributes) and CSS properties (styles) to HTML tags.

- **Applying and managing style sheets tools** The Apply Styles and Manage Styles task panes enables you to easily create, apply, and manage CSS styles.

- **CSS Reports** The CSS Reports tool helps eliminate errors by providing a list of all unused styles, undefined classes, or mismatched cases (see Figure A.8 for an example). It also provides a comprehensive list of the CSS class, ID, and element selectors, as shown in Figure A.9.

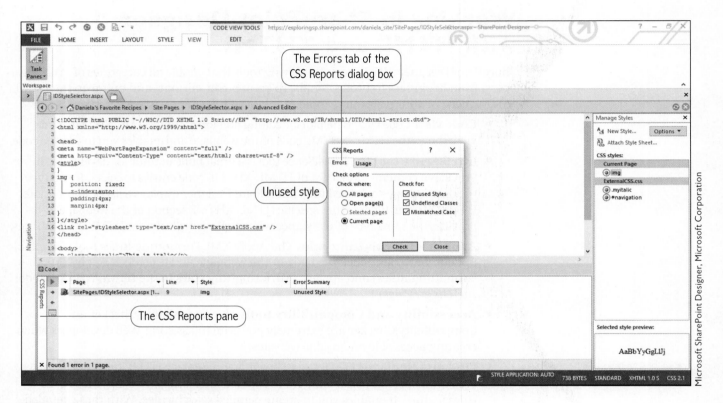

**FIGURE A.8** Using the CSS Reports to Eliminate Errors or Omissions

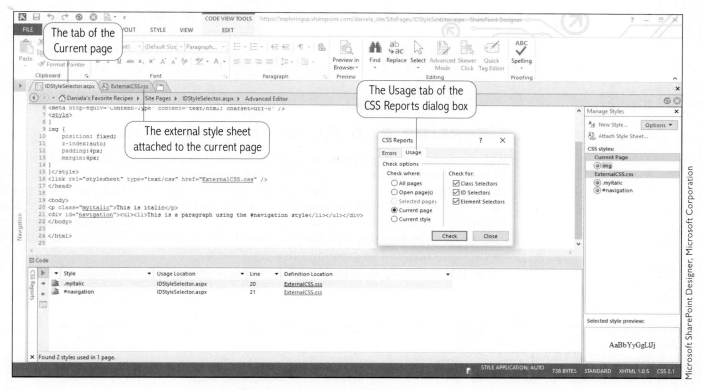

**FIGURE A.9** Using the CSS Reports to Generate a Comprehensive List of the CSS Class, ID, and Element Selectors

- **IntelliSense tool** The IntelliSense tool for CSS acts as a built-in tutor for developers. It provides a content-specific list of CSS code entries from which you can select as you complete the HTML/XHTML code (see Figure A.10).

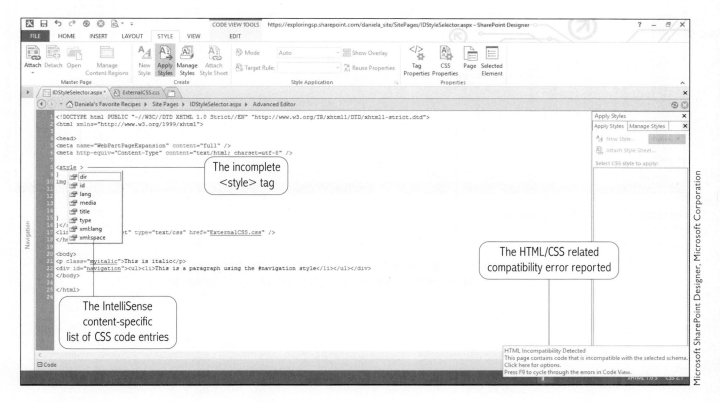

**FIGURE A.10** Using the IntelliSense Tool for CSS

- **Compatibility Checker** The Compatibility Checker enables you to detect areas of your site that do not comply with the Web standards you are targeting. For example, you can check to see that your pages are compatible with XHTML 1.0 Strict and CSS 2.1(or other combinations of CSS and HTML standards).

# Creating and Attaching CSS Files

Web developers place styles in an external file so they can have a centralized location for managing the styles and applying the styles as needed to any number of pages. After creating the CSS file, the developer attaches it to every page on which they want to use the styles. Once the CSS file is attached, the styles appear in the Manage Styles task pane so that they can be applied to areas on the webpage. SharePoint Online built-in templates mainly use styles that reside in external files. SharePoint Designer provides you with two user-friendly methods for creating a new style sheet:

- Using the New Style command on the Style tab, as shown in Figure A.11.

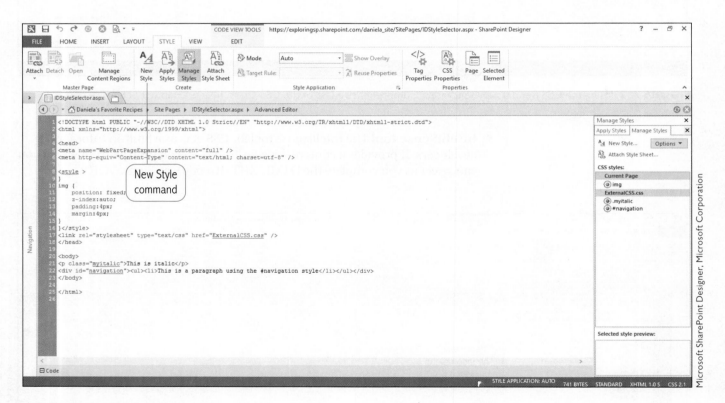

**FIGURE A.11** New Style Command

- Using the New Style dialog box that you open by clicking New Style on the Manage Styles or Apply Styles task pane, as shown in Figure A.12.

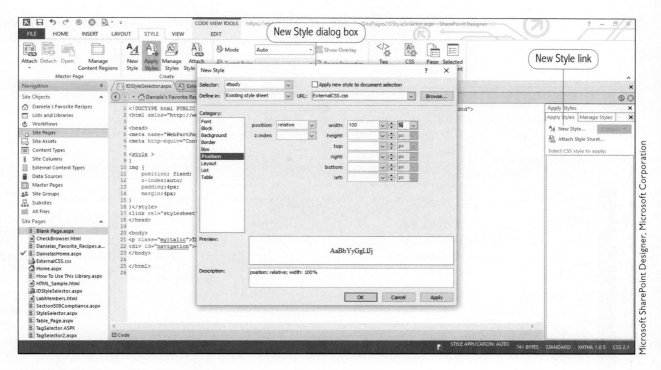

**FIGURE A.12** New Style Link and Dialog Box

Once you have created the styles in a CSS file, you attach the style sheet file to the webpages to apply the newly created styles, as shown in Figure A.13:

- Using the Attach Style Sheet command in the Create group on the Style tab.
- Using the Attach Style Sheet link in the Apply Styles or Manage Styles task pane.

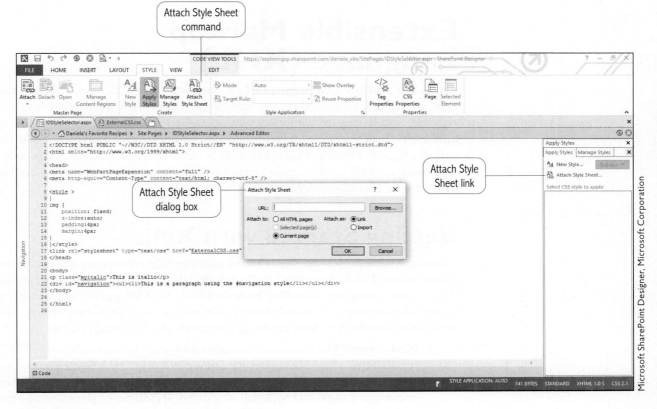

**FIGURE A.13** Attaching an External Style Sheet

After you attach the CSS file, the <link> tag shows in the Code view window and the new CSS file is listed in the Apply Styles task pane, as shown in Figure A.14.

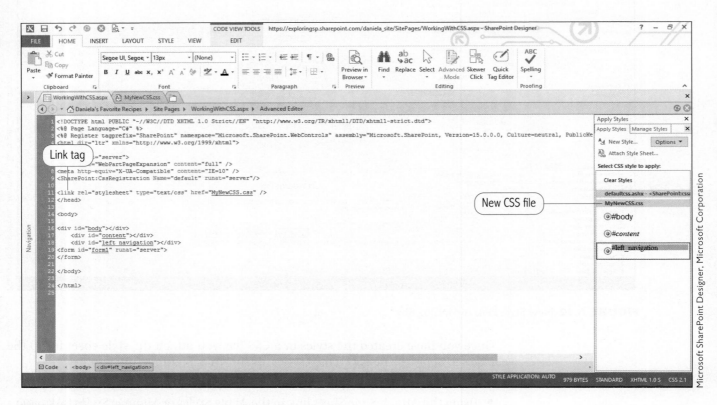

**FIGURE A.14** ASPX Page with an External Style Sheet Attached

# Extensible Markup Language (XML)

***Extensible Markup Language (XML)*** is based on the SGML standard and enables data to be shared and processed via the Internet and across software applications, operating systems, and hardware computer platforms. Because XML is an extensible language, unlike HTML, developers can create specific custom tags, describing the data content for each document. Developers also like XML because they can prevent many code errors by employing an XML parser, and because XML has the ability to define data content. In this section, you will explore XML.

## Getting Started with XML

As an extensible language, XML enables developers to create custom tags, describing the data contained in each document. By defining data content, developers can manipulate the contents using tags that they have specified. An ***XML parser*** is used after the document code is written, to identify any syntax errors. An XML parser interprets the document code to make sure that the document meets the following criteria:

- ***Well-formed*** The document contains no syntax errors and obeys all W3C specifications for XML code (http://www.w3.org/XML). Some common syntax errors can be caused by ignoring the case sensitivity of XML tags or by omitting one or more tags. As previously discussed, HTML never gives you any type of feedback regarding syntax errors.

- **Valid** The document is well formed and satisfies the rules included in the attached document type definition or schema.

XML supports an optional document type definition and XML schema. These documents define all the components that an XML document is allowed to contain, as well as the structural relationship between the components. A ***document type definition (DTD)*** specifies what tags and attributes are used to describe content in an XML document, where each tag is allowed, and which tags can appear within other tags, thus eliminating many code errors that occur. The DTD can be internal, included in the XML document itself; external, stored in an external .dtd file; or a combination of internal and external components. The power of a DTD is increased when using external components because the same external DTD can be applied to more than one XML file. A ***schema*** is an XML document that includes the definition of one or more XML document's content and structure. Two of the most popular schemas are the XML schema (http://www.w3.org/XML/Schema.html), developed by W3C in 2001, and the Microsoft schema, XDR.

---

### TIP: XML PARSERS

The Microsoft XML parser is called MSXML and is built into Internet Explorer versions 5.0 and above. However, it must be downloaded and installed separately. The Mozilla Firefox XML parser is called Expat. Although these are the most popular, many other XML editors and parsers are available, such as Altova® XMLSpy® (http://www.altova.com/products/xmlspy/xml_editor.html), an award-winning XML editor for modeling, editing, transforming, and debugging XML technologies.

---

HTML only defines the way webpage content is formatted and displayed on a page. In contrast, XML code describes the type of information contained in the document. The XML code does not indicate how data is to be formatted or displayed, as shown in Figure A.15. Consequently, CSS or Extensible Style Sheet (XSL) languages are used to build style sheets

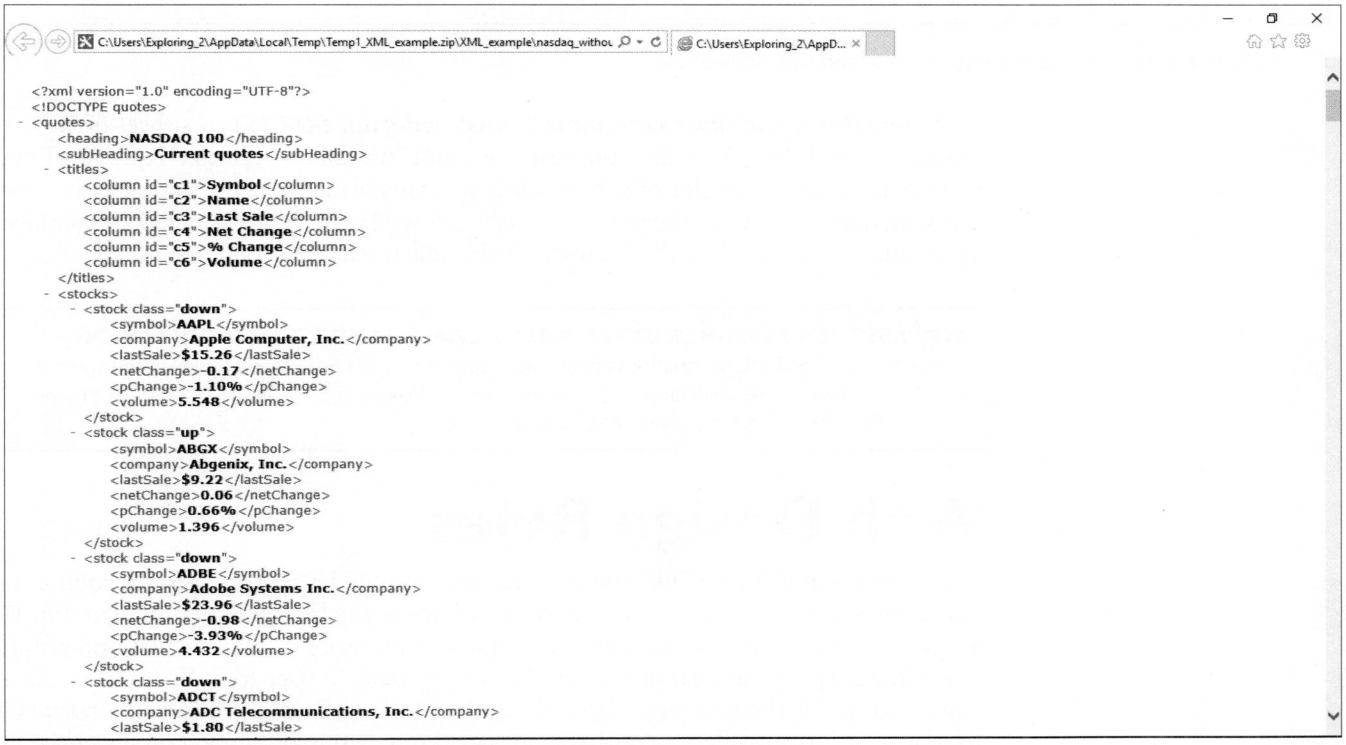

```
C:\Users\Exploring_2\AppData\Local\Temp\Temp1_XML_example.zip\XML_example\nasdaq_withou

<?xml version="1.0" encoding="UTF-8"?>
<!DOCTYPE quotes>
<quotes>
    <heading>NASDAQ 100</heading>
    <subHeading>Current quotes</subHeading>
    <titles>
        <column id="c1">Symbol</column>
        <column id="c2">Name</column>
        <column id="c3">Last Sale</column>
        <column id="c4">Net Change</column>
        <column id="c5">% Change</column>
        <column id="c6">Volume</column>
    </titles>
    <stocks>
        <stock class="down">
            <symbol>AAPL</symbol>
            <company>Apple Computer, Inc.</company>
            <lastSale>$15.26</lastSale>
            <netChange>-0.17</netChange>
            <pChange>-1.10%</pChange>
            <volume>5.548</volume>
        </stock>
        <stock class="up">
            <symbol>ABGX</symbol>
            <company>Abgenix, Inc.</company>
            <lastSale>$9.22</lastSale>
            <netChange>0.06</netChange>
            <pChange>0.66%</pChange>
            <volume>1.396</volume>
        </stock>
        <stock class="down">
            <symbol>ADBE</symbol>
            <company>Adobe Systems Inc.</company>
            <lastSale>$23.96</lastSale>
            <netChange>-0.98</netChange>
            <pChange>-3.93%</pChange>
            <volume>4.432</volume>
        </stock>
        <stock class="down">
            <symbol>ADCT</symbol>
            <company>ADC Telecommunications, Inc.</company>
            <lastSale>$1.80</lastSale>
```

**FIGURE A.15** XML Rendered without an Attached CSS Style Sheet

that can be embedded into the XML document or linked to it, as shown in Figure A.16. The style sheets contain formatting instructions for each element described in the XML document. Using a style sheet to format XML documents provides the same formatting features found in HTML, and provides greater flexibility:

- By attaching different style sheets to an XML document, you can change the way the XML document appears in a browser.
- By changing a style sheet attached to multiple XML documents, you can change the way all these XML documents are displayed in a browser.

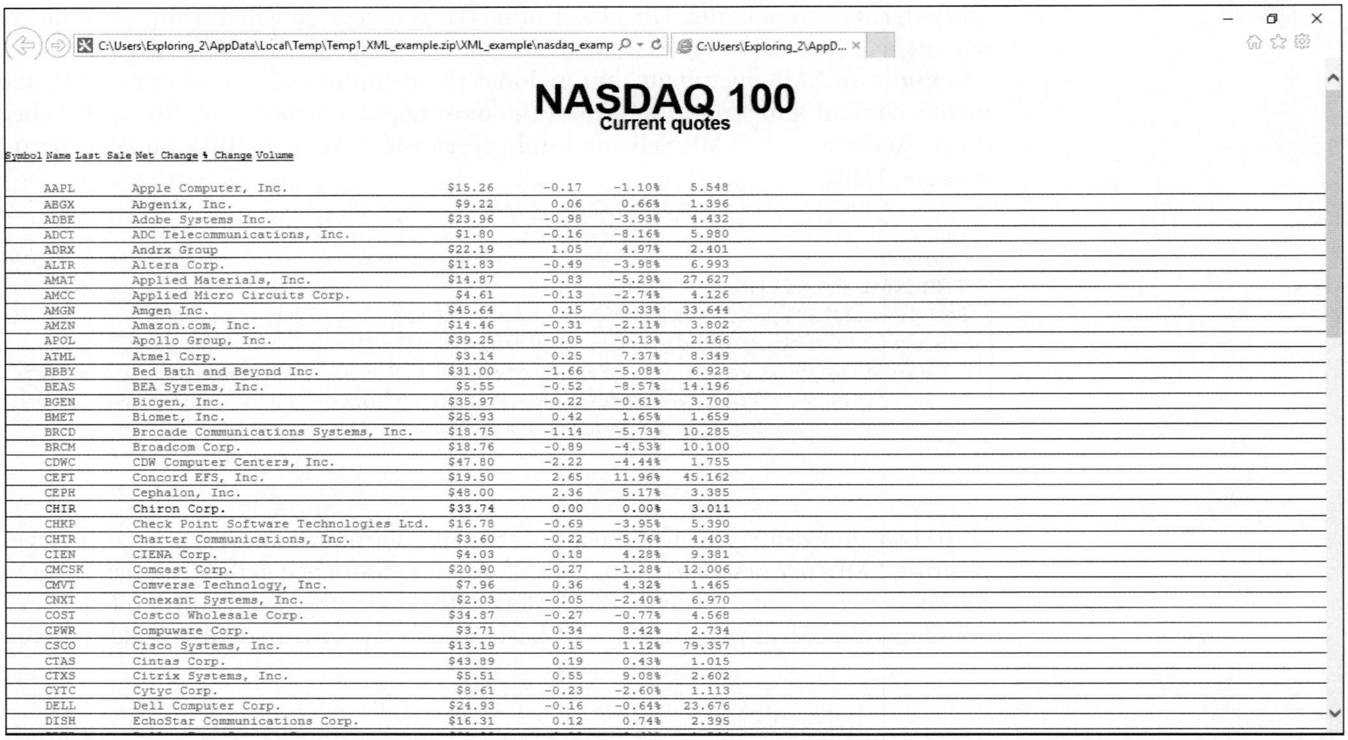

C:\Users\Exploring_2\AppData\Local\Temp\Temp1_XML_example.zip\XML_example\nasdaq_examp

**NASDAQ 100**

**Current quotes**

| Symbol | Name | Last Sale | Net Change | % Change | Volume |
|---|---|---|---|---|---|
| AAPL | Apple Computer, Inc. | $15.26 | -0.17 | -1.10% | 5.548 |
| ABGX | Abgenix, Inc. | $9.22 | 0.06 | 0.66% | 1.396 |
| ADBE | Adobe Systems Inc. | $23.96 | -0.98 | -3.93% | 4.432 |
| ADCT | ADC Telecommunications, Inc. | $1.80 | -0.16 | -8.16% | 5.980 |
| ADRX | Andrx Group | $22.19 | 1.05 | 4.97% | 2.401 |
| ALTR | Altera Corp. | $11.83 | -0.49 | -3.98% | 6.993 |
| AMAT | Applied Materials, Inc. | $14.87 | -0.83 | -5.29% | 27.627 |
| AMCC | Applied Micro Circuits Corp. | $4.61 | -0.13 | -2.74% | 4.126 |
| AMGN | Amgen Inc. | $45.64 | 0.15 | 0.33% | 33.644 |
| AMZN | Amazon.com, Inc. | $14.46 | -0.31 | -2.11% | 3.802 |
| APOL | Apollo Group, Inc. | $39.25 | -0.05 | -0.13% | 2.166 |
| ATML | Atmel Corp. | $3.14 | 0.25 | 7.37% | 8.349 |
| BBBY | Bed Bath and Beyond Inc. | $31.00 | -1.66 | -5.08% | 6.928 |
| BEAS | BEA Systems, Inc. | $5.55 | -0.52 | -8.57% | 14.196 |
| BGEN | Biogen, Inc. | $35.97 | -0.22 | -0.61% | 3.700 |
| BMET | Biomet, Inc. | $25.93 | 0.42 | 1.65% | 1.659 |
| BRCD | Brocade Communications Systems, Inc. | $18.75 | -1.14 | -5.73% | 10.285 |
| BRCM | Broadcom Corp. | $18.76 | -0.89 | -4.53% | 10.100 |
| CDWC | CDW Computer Centers, Inc. | $47.80 | -2.22 | -4.44% | 1.755 |
| CEFT | Concord EFS, Inc. | $19.50 | 2.65 | 11.96% | 45.162 |
| CEPH | Cephalon, Inc. | $48.00 | 2.36 | 5.17% | 3.385 |
| CHIR | Chiron Corp. | $33.74 | 0.00 | 0.00% | 3.011 |
| CHKP | Check Point Software Technologies Ltd. | $16.78 | -0.69 | -3.95% | 5.390 |
| CHTR | Charter Communications, Inc. | $3.60 | -0.22 | -5.76% | 4.403 |
| CIEN | CIENA Corp. | $4.03 | 0.18 | 4.28% | 9.381 |
| CMCSK | Comcast Corp. | $20.90 | -0.27 | -1.28% | 12.006 |
| CMVT | Comverse Technology, Inc. | $7.96 | 0.36 | 4.32% | 1.465 |
| CNXT | Conexant Systems, Inc. | $2.03 | -0.05 | -2.40% | 6.970 |
| COST | Costco Wholesale Corp. | $34.87 | -0.27 | -0.77% | 4.568 |
| CPWR | Compuware Corp. | $3.71 | 0.34 | 8.42% | 2.734 |
| CSCO | Cisco Systems, Inc. | $13.19 | 0.15 | 1.12% | 79.357 |
| CTAS | Cintas Corp. | $43.89 | 0.19 | 0.43% | 1.015 |
| CTXS | Citrix Systems, Inc. | $5.51 | 0.55 | 9.08% | 2.602 |
| CYTC | Cytyc Corp. | $8.61 | -0.23 | -2.60% | 1.113 |
| DELL | Dell Computer Corp. | $24.93 | -0.16 | -0.64% | 23.676 |
| DISH | EchoStar Communications Corp. | $16.31 | 0.12 | 0.74% | 2.395 |



**FIGURE A.16** XML Rendered with an Attached CSS Style Sheet

***Extensible Style sheet Language Transformation (XSLT)*** is a subset of XSL that enables you to display XML data on a webpage and "transform" it into HTML. XSLT pages are used to create client-side or server-side XML transformations. If you perform a server-side XML transformation, the server converts it into HTML; whereas when you perform a client-side transformation, the browser will handle the transformation.

> **TIP: XSLT (EXTENSIBLE STYLE SHEET LANGUAGE TRANSFORMATION)**
> The client-side XSLT transformations are still not supported by all browsers. However, the current versions of some of the most popular browsers (such as Microsoft Edge, Internet Explorer 11, and FireFox 50.0) do support client-side XSLT transformations.

# Web Design Rules

Web design principles include many of the same principles as print design, such as providing easy-to-read fonts and good contrast between the background and text, but Web design principles go further to address unique situations for displaying text and graphics on a screen. The main goal of Web design is to provide a user-friendly interface for the viewers to enable them to move throughout the site and access the information that they need or want. Intuitively, you probably already know what looks good on a website, and you probably avoid sites that appear cluttered or disorganized.

There are some excellent websites that synthesize best practices when it comes to Web design. Some of the best are Stefan Mischook's "The Dos and Don'ts of Web Site Design" (http://www.killersites.com/articles/articles_dosAndDontsWebDesign.htm) and "What & Why of Usability Guidelines" (http://guidelines.usability.gov). You can also learn a lot about Web design by thoughtfully observing sites that you visit. Find a site that you like and evaluate the colors, fonts, layout, and navigation as inspiration for creating your own site.

Although entire books have been written about Web design, as a new Web designer, you can focus on some of the main principles to guide you in your development of websites. In this section, you will review some Web design rules and principles.

# Designing Good Webpages

The principles of good Web design enable you to create sites that are useful and interesting to your audience. There are many considerations you make as you put together text, graphics, navigation, and layouts. A webpage is a representation of the designer's professional and personal background, expertise in solving technical design and development issues, and finally, personal creativity and artistic skills. However, there are certain key factors that all professional designers and Web developers consider essential to good webpage design, as described in Table A.2.

| TABLE A.2 | Key Design Factors for Developing Good Webpages |
|---|---|
| **Design Factor** | **Description** |
| Usability | A usable website is accessible and easy to navigate. You should always keep in mind that you design your webpages for the people who will be visiting them. The quality of your design will be measured by audience satisfaction and response. |
| Navigation | Webpages must be easy to navigate. Always consider using webpage templates, link bars, hyperlinks, and bookmarks to create a clear and robust navigational structure for your webpages. |
| Compatibility | Webpages should appear the same (or as close as possible) in all browsers, in all versions of the same browser, and on all computer platforms. |
| Accessibility | Webpages need to be accessible to all people, including those with different types of total and partial disabilities. You should consult the World Wide Web consortium's (W3C) website frequently to stay on top of the latest standards and requirements. |
| Consistency | Web users do not like surprises. They expect the information on a webpage to be laid out as it was on previous pages of the same website. To ensure the consistency of your webpages from the early stages of development, you should always sketch a draft of your webpages before starting the actual construction, and use webpage templates. |
| Validity | The validity of a webpage must be tested thoroughly before it is published. If a website does not display and function properly, it can cause more pain than gain for your audience, and they will leave your site to find another one. |
| Attractiveness | A webpage will be attractive only if it's designed as precisely as a NASA space shuttle and as beautifully as Leonardo da Vinci's *Mona Lisa*. Think like an engineer and an artist when you design a webpage; that's an important part of the key to success. |

Pearson Education, Inc.

Although it is often said that rules are made to be broken, there are guidelines that you should follow unless you have a good reason not to follow them. The following rules provide guidance in producing webpages that are well designed.

**The Do's**

- **Do** use color wisely. Colors should be used primarily for emphasizing text titles, sections, and keywords. Remember that people who are colorblind might not be able to see all colors. Use color as background for your webpages, but ensure that it does not diminish the readability of your webpage content.

- **Do** keep a balance between the need to use graphic, audio, and video files to enrich the content, the need to maintain the "look" of your webpage, and the need to keep the size and amount of time required to display your webpages at a reasonable level.
- **Do** use images as backgrounds for your webpages so long as they do not diminish the readability of your webpage content.
- **Do** add meaningful alternative text and caption text to all graphic, audio, and video files used in your webpages so visitors who are visually or hearing impaired can fully understand what is represented.
- **Do** regularly update the content of your webpages and remove any outdated or no longer relevant content.
- **Do** implement a consistent style for all the webpages included in a website by using webpage and website templates and CSS external style sheets.
- **Do** build easy-to-navigate webpages and websites.

### The Don'ts

The following guidelines enable you to produce webpages that enhance the user's experience as they visit your site:

- **Don't** allow broken links and, whenever possible, do not publish webpages still under development.
- **Don't** use the underline style for text on your webpages, because it might lead your users to believe that the underlined text is a hyperlink.
- **Don't** use sound as a background on your webpages if you do not want to annoy your visitors.
- **Don't** use unethical wording, and try to avoid using professional or "street" jargon.
- **Don't** use any kind of copyrighted material unless you have official permission to do so.

After designing and development are complete on your pages, it is important to seek feedback and to test the site thoroughly. Feedback can come from coworkers, supervisors, focus groups, or other people. It is especially helpful to observe a user of your site as he or she navigates through it to understand any difficulties they may encounter. You also should personally check every link on every page, including those in the navigation scheme, to ensure that they function as you expect.

Designing websites is a cycle that includes planning, development, implementation, testing, deployment, and maintenance. Once your site is published on the Web, revisit it often to determine if it is time to add new content, update links, or implement other elements.

# Key Terms Matching

Match the key terms with their definitions. Write the key term letter by the appropriate numbered definition.

**a.** Attribute

**b.** Cascading Style Sheet (CSS)

**c.** Class selector

**d.** Declaration block

**e.** Document Type Definition (DTD)

**f.** Embedded style

**g.** Extensible Hypertext Markup Language (XHTML)

**h.** Extensible Markup Language (XML)

**i.** External style

**j.** Hypertext Markup Language (HTML)

**k.** ID selector

**l.** Inline style

**m.** Markup language

**n.** Selector

**o.** Tag selector

**p.** Tag

**q.** World Wide Web Consortium (W3C)

**r.** XML parser

**1.** _____ A code placed within tags to define the style, color, size, width, height, or source of elements. *p. 314*

**2.** _____ A CSS style selector often used to signify sections of a webpage to be identified by <div> or <span> tags. *p. 320*

**3.** _____ A group of formatting instructions that begins and ends with braces {}, and contains all the formatting options you want applied to the selector. *p. 320*

**4.** _____ A language based on the SGML standard that enables data to be shared and processed via the Internet and across software applications, operating systems, and hardware computer platforms. *p. 328*

**5.** _____ Any language that describes the layout of webpage content using tags. *p. 312*

**6.** _____ A newer markup language that was designed to overcome some of the problems with HTML. *p. 315*

**7.** _____ A selector that is applied to all occurrences of the HTML tag it styles; easy to distinguish in a document because it has the same name as the HTML tag it styles. *p. 320*

**8.** _____ A selector used for identifying unique parts of your webpage such as banners, navigation bars, or main content area because they are connected to the id attribute of a webpage element and the id must be unique. *p. 321*

**9.** _____ A specific code that indicates how the text should be displayed when the document is opened in a Web browser. *p. 312*

**10.** _____ A statement that specifies what tags and attributes are used to describe content in an XML document, where each tag is allowed, and which tags can appear within other tags, thus eliminating many code errors that occur. *p. 329*

**11.** _____ A style code that is included in the start tag by using the tag's style attributes. *p. 319*

**12.** _____ A style code usually included in the <head> section of an HTML document and has the following syntax: <style>*style declarations*</style>. *p. 319*

**13.** _____ A style included in a separate file used to specify the formatting of any HTML document to which the external style sheet is linked. *p. 319*

**14.** _____ An indication to a Web browser which element(s) within a webpage to style. *p. 319*

**15.** _____ An application that evaluates XML documents. ***p. 328***

**16.** _____ An organization that provides leadership through an open forum of groups with a vested interest in the Internet, with the mission of leading the Web to its full potential. ***p. 313***

**17.** _____ The most common markup language used to create webpages, by defining the page layout and graphic elements of the page and providing links to other documents on the Web. ***p. 312***

**18.** _____ The standard style sheet language used on the Web. ***p. 318***

# Accessibility and Compatibility

The World Wide Web Consortium (W3C) has a mission of leading the Web to its full potential, and this includes accessibility by all people, regardless of disabilities that they may have. The W3C produced guidelines to assist Web developers in designing sites to be accessible. The United States government also wants to guarantee accessibility and passed a law to implement **Section 508** of the Rehabilitation Act of 1973, describing Web-based intranet and Internet information accessibility standards required from organizations that do business with the federal government. By understanding and following the guidelines and standards, you can create user-friendly, accessible, and compatible webpages and sites.

In this appendix, you learn about the Web design guidelines that are included in the W3C's **Web Accessibility Initiative (WAI)**, and subsection 1194.22 of Section 508 Standards and Telecommunications Act concerning Web-based intranet and Internet information and applications. This appendix explains what it means to design for accessibility and compatibility, while discussing the SharePoint Designer 2013 Accessibility Reports tool and Compatibility Reports tool to maximize the accessibility and compatibility of your webpages. You are also introduced to some of the most popular assistive and adaptive technologies. At the time this manuscript was finalized, the United States Access Board was working on updating electronic and information technology guidelines (https://www.access-board.gov/guidelines-and-standards/communications-and-it/about-the-section-508-standards). Upon the official publishing of the revised Section 508, this appendix and any related information published in this textbook will be updated as soon as possible.

# Web Accessibility Guidelines

According to the 2016 United States Census estimates, approximately 19 percent of non-institutionalized people have a disability. To learn more about the Census and people who have disabilities, go to http://factfinder2.census.gov, and perform a search using the Guided Search or Advanced Search tools. As Article 27.1 of the Universal Declaration of Human Rights (http://www.un.org/en/universal-declaration-human-rights/index.html) states, "Everyone has the right freely to participate in the cultural life of the community, to enjoy the arts and to share in scientific advancement and its benefits." Today, the Internet is an important component of our professional and personal lives, so it is "essential that the Web be accessible to provide equal access and equal opportunity to people with diverse abilities" according to the W3C (http://www.w3.org/standards/webdesign/accessibility). Accessibility is so important that the United Nations Convention on the Rights of Persons with Disabilities (https://www.un.org/development/desa/disabilities/convention-on-the-rights-of-persons-with-disabilities.html) recognized Web accessibility as a basic human right. To learn more about the social, technical, financial, legal, and policy factors of Web accessibility, review "Developing a Web Accessibility Business Case for Your Organization: Overview" on the W3C website (http://www.w3.org/WAI/bcase).

In this section, you are introduced to the W3C Web Accessibility Initiative guidelines and Section 508 law. The More Information section of this appendix provides you with a resource list of related websites.

> **TIP: INTERNATIONAL ACCESSIBILITY AND DISABILITY INITIATIVES**
> Efforts around the world focus on raising awareness of accessibility and disability and maximizing World Wide Web (WWW) accessibility. The W3C WAI strives to maximize the accessibility of the WWW in five primary areas: technology, guidelines, education, outreach, and research and development. The W3C Web Content Accessibility Guidelines 2.0 are being adopted by many governments around the world, including the United Kingdom, Japan, Canada, and Australia.

# Understanding the W3C Web Accessibility Initiative (WAI)

In 1997, the W3C launched the Web Accessibility Initiative to improve Web functionality for people with disabilities (http://www.w3.org/WAI) by producing the **Web Content Accessibility Guidelines 1.0 (WCAG 1.0)**. These guidelines have since been updated to WCAG 2.0 (http://www.w3.org/TR/WCAG20).

The original WCAG 1.0 defined three priorities, which are listed in Table B.1. Checkpoints were defined, and each was assigned a priority level by the Web Content Accessibility Guidelines Working Group (WCAG WG) based on its impact on the webpage's accessibility.

| TABLE B.1 | WCAG 1.0 Priority Levels |
|---|---|
| **Priority Level** | **Description** |
| I | Checkpoint must be satisfied. It is a basic requirement to enable some groups to access Web documents. |
| II | Checkpoint should be satisfied, removing significant barriers to accessing Web documents. |
| III | Checkpoint might be addressed, improving access to Web documents. |

Pearson Education, Inc.

When organizations revisit or create Web accessibility policies, the W3C recommends using WCAG 2.0. Rather than focus on checkpoints, the WCAG 2.0 is based on the four layers of principles, guidelines, success criteria, and sufficient and advisory techniques.

- Four principles provide the foundation for Web accessibility: perceivable, operable, understandable, and robust. These principles are detailed at http://www.w3.org/TR/UNDERSTANDING-WCAG20/intro.html#introduction-fourprincs-head
- Twelve guidelines are listed under the principles and provide basic goals for making content more accessible to users with different disabilities. These goals provide a framework and overall objectives to guide Web developers. The guidelines are explained at http://www.w3.org/TR/WCAG20.
- Each guideline is supplemented with testable success criteria, which can be used where requirements and conformance testing are necessary. There are

three levels of conformance: A (lowest), AA, and AAA (highest). Additional information is available at http://www.w3.org/TR/UNDERSTANDING-WCAG20/conformance.html#uc-levels-head

- Techniques are provided by WCAG 2.0 for meeting the success criteria and the guidelines. The techniques are identified as sufficient for complying with the success criteria or as advisory. Refer to http://www.w3.org/TR/UNDERSTANDING-WCAG20/intro.html#introduction-layers-techs-head for additional information.

Web content developers can elect to comply with WCAG 1.0, WCAG 2.0, or both. The W3C currently recommends the use of WCAG 2.0 standards, especially as new content is developed or as content is updated. This means that in some cases the legacy content may comply with WCAG 1.0, whereas the newest information on the website complies with WCAG 2.0.

## Reviewing Section 508 Law

In 1998, the Section 508 law (https://www.section508.gov) was enacted by Congress as an amendment to the Rehabilitation Act of 1973, "to require Federal agencies to make their electronic and information technology accessible to people with disabilities." This amendment ensures that all Americans have access to information, particularly from Federal agencies and organizations that do business with the Federal government. Under Section 508 (29 U.S.C. 794d), agencies must give people with disabilities access to information that is comparable to the access available to others. Subsection 1194.22 of the Section 508 Guidelines discusses maximizing the accessibility of websites.

The United States Access Board (https://www.access-board.gov) is a federal agency that develops and maintains design requirements and access standards for a variety of environments, including electronic and information technology. It also provides technical assistance and training, as well as enforces accessibility standards for federally funded facilities. These standards, covered by Section 508 of the Rehabilitation Act (https://www.access-board.gov/guidelines-and-standards/communications-and-it/about-the-section-508-standards), initially published in 2000, cover products and technologies procured by the Federal government, including computer hardware and software, websites, phone systems, fax machines, and copiers. The U.S. Access Board guidelines also affect telecommunications products and equipment covered by Section 255 of the Telecommunications Act (https://www.access-board.gov/guidelines-and-standards/communications-and-it). An advisory committee of the U.S. Access Board, the Telecommunications and Electronic and Information Technology Advisory Committee, or TEITAC, reviews telecommunications standards and guidelines, and recommends changes. The committee's membership included representatives from industry, disability groups, standard-setting bodies in the United States and abroad, and government agencies, among others.

## Designing for Compatibility

A computer platform is defined by the type of hardware and operating system in use on a given computer. Why do webpages look different when viewed on the same computer platform and when using different Internet browsers, or even different versions of the same browsers? What causes these problems, and is there a way you can correct them? These questions continue to challenge Web designers and developers.

The ***cross-platform incompatibility*** issue is the result of the way different browsers or browser versions display webpages on different computer platforms. The ***cross-browser incompatibility*** issue is the result of the way different browsers display the same webpages on the same computer platform. Because you cannot predict the computer platform and browser your users will be using when they view your website, it is your responsibility, as the designer, to address potential cross-platform and cross-browser compatibility issues in your design.

The W3C develops specifications, guidelines, software, and tools with a goal of eliminating the cross-browser and cross-platform incompatibility issues. The W3C joined with companies, such as Microsoft, IBM, and Oracle, and governmental organizations, such as the U.S. Department of Health & Human Services (https://www.hhs.gov/Accessibility.html), to develop a universal standard for Web design and compatibility. Despite these efforts, Web designers often need to develop different versions of the same webpage to make sure their page has the same appearance and functionality in all browsers and on all platforms.

SharePoint Designer has tools that help Web designers avoid some of the cross-platform and cross-browser incompatibility issues. The Compatibility Reports tool enables you to verify that the webpages in your site are in compliance with the W3C Web standards. In SharePoint Designer, click the View tab, click Task Panes, and then select Compatibility from the menu. The Run Compatibility Checker command, as shown in Figure B.1, on the Compatibility task pane, displays the Compatibility Checker dialog box in which you can identify any areas of your website that you want to check. The Compatibility Report displayed in the task pane gives details on the parts of the website that do not behave as anticipated so you can address these issues.

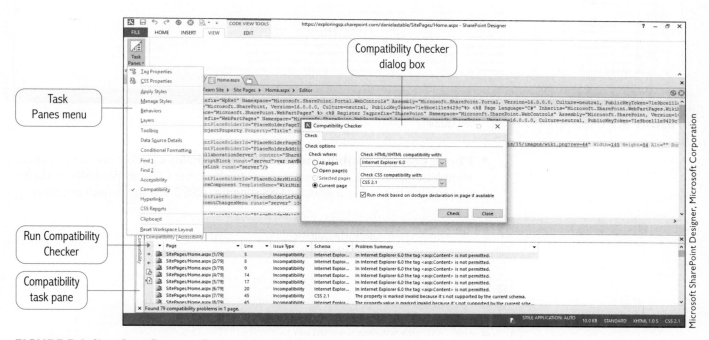

**FIGURE B.1** SharePoint Designer Compatibility Task Pane

Using the Compatibility Checker dialog box, you first select the page(s) that will be checked for compatibility under Check where. You then select the appropriate criteria for compatibility checking:

- **Check HTML/XHTML compatibility with:** This Compatibility Checker dialog box option, shown in Figure B.2, enables designers to improve the HTML/XHTML compatibility of their webpages with the browsers and the W3C HTML/XHTML standards.

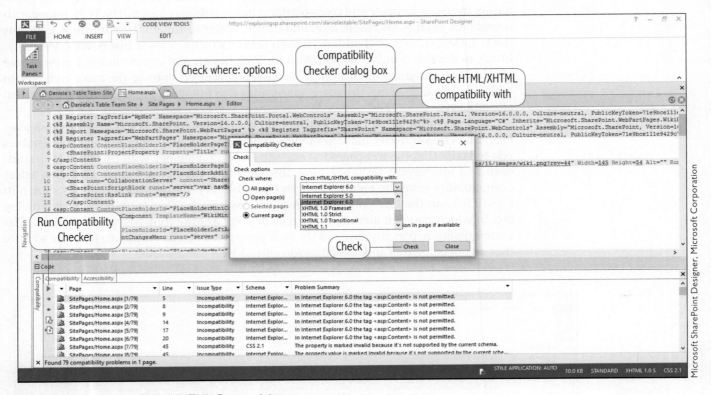

**FIGURE B.2** Check HTML/XHTML Compatibility

- **Check CSS compatibility with:** This Compatibility Checker dialog box option, shown in Figure B.3, enables designers to check the CSS compatibility of their webpages when using a selected CSS schema (CSS 2.1 is the default schema).

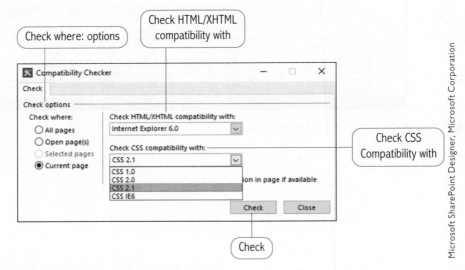

**FIGURE B.3** Check CSS Compatibility

When you run the Compatibility Checker, your pages are searched for errors and reported in the Compatibility task pane. If you see an error listed in the Compatibility task pane, click the Generate HTML Report button. SharePoint Designer generates an HTML Compatibility report in HTML code, which you can open in a browser window, as shown in Figure B.4. To fix a compatibility error, double-click the listed error in the Compatibility task pane. SharePoint Designer opens the document (if it is not already open) and selects the code section where the incompatibility is located. You can also right-click an error in the Compatibility task pane and choose Go to page or you can manually switch to Code view and scroll to the indicated line number.

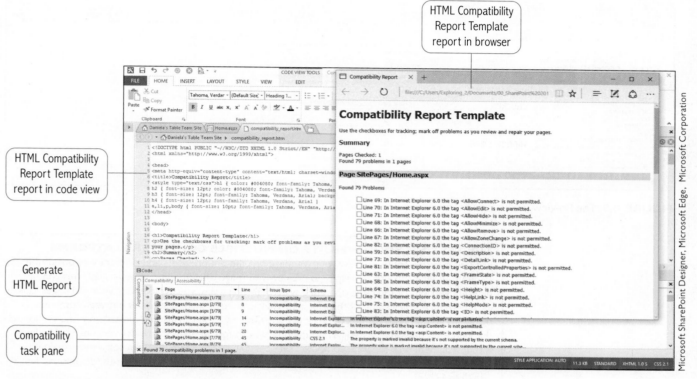

**FIGURE B.4** Working with the Compatibility Report

Preview in Browser is also a useful compatibility feature, included in the Preview group on the Home tab, that enables you to select the browser, the browser version, and screen resolution you want to use to preview your webpage. You can also preview a webpage in multiple browsers at the same time, as shown in Figure B.5. The browsers you want to test need to be installed on your computer to use the Preview in Browser feature. Browsers installed on your computer are added to the SharePoint Designer browser list using Add (see Figure B.5). Click the Preview in Browser arrow, select the browser, browser version, and screen resolution to preview a webpage.

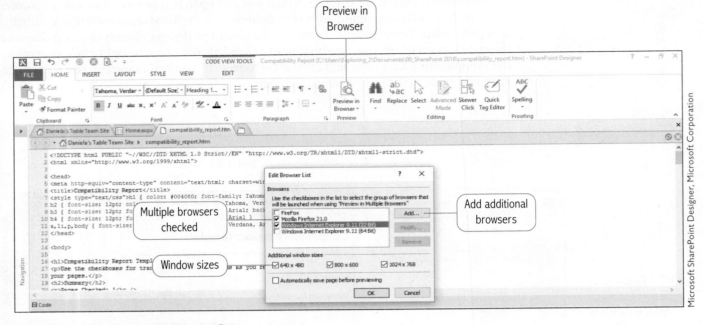

**FIGURE B.5** The Preview in Browser Feature

---

**TIP: TESTING YOUR WEBSITE ON MULTIPLE COMPUTER PLATFORMS**

Just as it is important to preview your webpage on different browsers and different versions of the same browser, it can also be helpful to preview your page on different computer platforms and on different versions of the same operating system. By doing this, you avoid having your webpages looking different or losing some of their functionalities caused by incompatibilities between computer platforms and versions of the operating system. On a PC, you can normally install only one version of the Windows operating system. Thus, the only way to test webpages on older versions of Windows is to install them on a separate computer, set up a dual-boot system, or run a software virtualization solution such as Windows 10 Client Hyper-V (https://www.microsoft.com/en-us/download/details .aspx?id=48128).

Client Hyper-V is the virtualization technology built into Windows 10 and Windows 8.x. It is the same virtualization technology previously available only in Windows Server. Client Hyper-V enables you to run more than one 32-bit or 64-bit x86 operating system at the same time on the same host computer. The Mac computers support Windows operating systems. To read more about how Microsoft products are supported by Mac computers, see the Apple Boot Camp Support (http://www.apple.com/support/bootcamp).

---

# Designing for Accessibility

The Disability Statistics Center projects that there are 6.8 million Americans with visual impairments, 10.8 million with hearing impairments, and 20.6 million with impairments affecting the mobility of shoulders and upper extremities. These kinds of impairments are likely to affect the ability of people to browse the Internet and access your website. If your website does not comply with the accessibility guidelines, these people might not be able to access your webpages.

---

**TIP: DIFFERENCES BETWEEN ACCESSIBILITY AND USABILITY**

Although accessibility and usability have many related requirements and goals, they are not identical. Usability issues, such as navigation, affect all Web users equally. Accessibility applies only to people with disabilities.

---

What does accessibility have to do with webpages? **Accessibility** means that a page can be accessed—read and used—by any person regardless of special needs or disabilities. An accessible webpage has to be compatible with screen reading and screen magnification software—applications that help people with visual challenges—and with natural language speech applications that people with poor arm or finger motion use. It also must offer text equivalents for multimedia content for people with hearing impairments.

---

**TIP: MICROSOFT'S OFFICIAL RESPONSE TO SECTION 508 REGULATIONS**

Microsoft has a strong commitment to accessibility. To read more about the history of Microsoft's dedication to accessibility, visit Microsoft's Section 508 of the Rehabilitation Act webpage (https://enterprise.microsoft.com/en-us/industries/government/section-508-vpats-for-microsoft-products). Scroll down to see the list of every Microsoft product that supports accessibility. Click the Microsoft SharePoint 2013 VPAT link to download and read the Section 508 SharePoint 2013 Voluntary Product Accessibility Template (VPAT). The VPAT is an informational document developed by a group of companies and government agencies to support the responsibilities of Federal employees and private organizations as they comply with Section 508.

---

SharePoint Designer 2013 contains an Accessibility Report feature. This tool can tell you how well your design complies with the existing W3C and government standards. In SharePoint Designer, click the View tab, click Task Panes, and then select Accessibility from the menu. Click Run Accessibility Checker, on the Accessibility task pane, to display the Accessibility Checker dialog box shown in Figure B.6. To use the Accessibility Checker, you select which pages you want the Accessibility Checker to validate. The Accessibility Checker can check specific pages or the whole site. Select the accessibility guidelines you want to check against: High Priority, Medium Priority, or Failure to meet minimal level. Indicate if you wish to view errors, warnings, or a manual checklist.

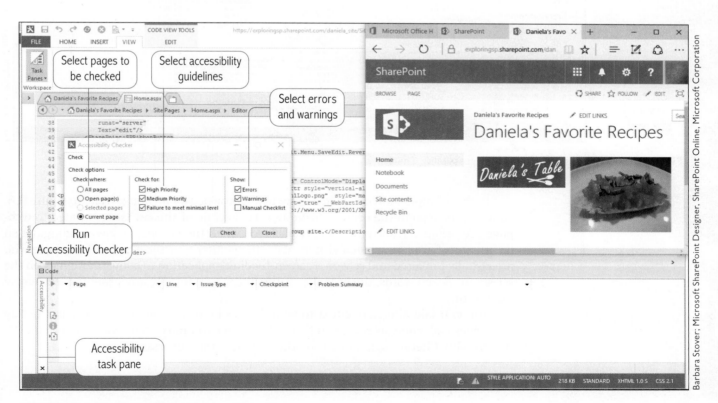

**FIGURE B.6** The Accessibility Checker Dialog Box

When you click Check on the Accessibility Checker dialog box, the checker searches your page(s) for errors and, if you have any errors, they appear in the Accessibility task pane. If you see an error list in the Accessibility task pane, click the Generate HTML Report button, shown in Figure B.7. SharePoint Designer generates an Accessibility Report. The report can then be opened in a browser window, just as the Compatibility Report was opened.

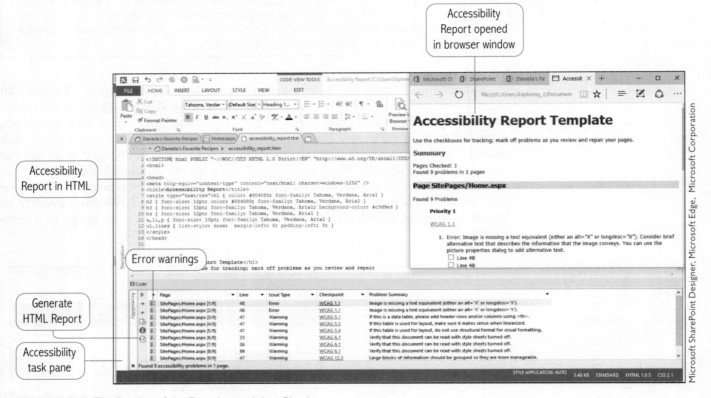

**FIGURE B.7** The Results of the First Accessibility Check

In the example shown, no alternative text is provided for an image (refer to Figure B.6, showing the logo in the browser window). This is one of the key issues related to webpage accessibility. Alternative text is displayed when the graphic is downloading, when it cannot be found, or when a visitor moves the pointer over the graphic. For people who are visually impaired and rely on a screen-reading application to convert graphics on the screen to spoken words, the presence of the alternative text for any graphic is extremely important.

You can add alternative text to your figures by using the alt attribute in the Tag Properties task pane, as shown in Figure B.8. After you make your corrections, run the Accessibility Checker again to ensure there are no other errors.

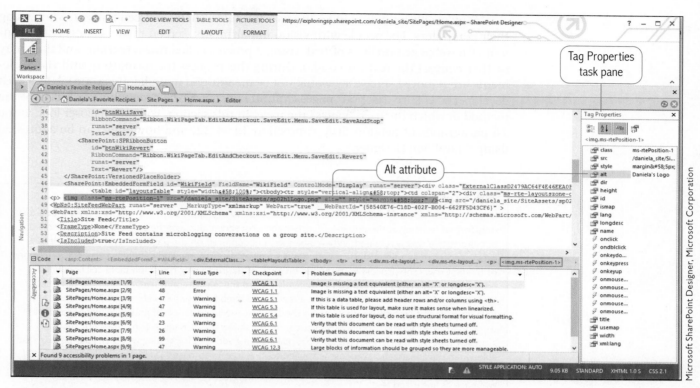

**FIGURE B.8** Correcting Accessibility Errors

# SharePoint Tools for Developing Webpages in Compliance with Section 508

Microsoft has a strong commitment "to enable people and businesses throughout the world to realize their full potential." This commitment particularly applies to people who have disabilities. In 2003, Microsoft commissioned a study to better understand and address the computing-related needs of people with disabilities (https://www.microsoft.com/enable/research/phase2.aspx). The study revealed that among the adult computer users in the United States, one in four has a vision impairment, one in five has a hearing impairment, and one in four has dexterity difficulty (with pain or complete loss of feeling in their fingers, hands, wrists, or arms).

---

**TIP: MICROSOFT'S "USING ACCESSIBLE TECHNOLOGY: GUIDES FOR EDUCATORS"**

Microsoft's "Using Accessible Technology: Guides for Educators" download (https://www.microsoft.com/download/en/details.aspx?id=1447) is an excellent source of information for accessibility features and assistive technology products that help individuals with specific disabilities.

---

The Microsoft and Section 508 website provides in-depth documentation about the way each Microsoft application's design, including SharePoint Designer 2013 (there is no SharePoint Designer 2016), complies with the Section 508 law (https://www.microsoft.com/enable/microsoft/section508.aspx). The SharePoint Designer 2013 Accessibility Reports tool enables you to maximize the accessibility of your webpages by identifying the design elements that do not comply with WCAG 1.0 Priority 1, WCAG 1.0 Priority 2, and Section 508. The Compatibility Reports tool checks for cross-platform and cross-browser usability.

Many people with disabilities use assistive tools, such as screen readers, when using their computers. For people with vision impairments, screen readers convert the content of a webpage into lines of text, using a process called *linearization*, and then may further convert the text into audio. During this process the formatting and visual elements are removed since they would not be meaningful in audio. It is your job as a Web developer to ensure that your pages continue to convey their meaning regardless of the method in which the user "views" the page. In this section, you take a closer look at the 16 paragraphs of Section 508, subsection 1194.22, and how they can be addressed using SharePoint Designer.

---

**TIP: THE WEBPAGE LINEARIZATION PROCESS**

In the webpage linearization process, an assistive technology application converts the page into a text-only format, starting at the upper-left corner and proceeding through the page. Images are ignored, but alternative text is retained. When tables are encountered on the page, the text in the table is processed a line at a time, starting with the first cell of the first row and continuing across the columns of the first row. The process is continued on each of the remaining rows. If a table cell contains a nested table, this table is linearized completely before the application moves to the next table cell. Lynx (http://www.lynxbrowser.com) is a text-based Web browser, available for UNIX, DOS, and Windows operating systems, that can be used to test the linearization of an entire webpage. It was developed by Academic Computing Services at the University of Kansas. Lynx does not support graphics, plug-ins, JavaScript, Java, or CSS, making it a good tool for testing whether your page is readable when the linearization process is applied to it. A free Web-based Lynx viewer, developed by DJ Delorie (http://www.delorie.com/web/lynxview.html) enables you to submit a URL and view the webpage as linearized text.

---

# Working with Graphics and Images

**1194.22 (a) A text equivalent for every non-text element shall be provided (e.g., via "alt," "longdesc," or in element content).**

The first paragraph of subsection 1194.22 requires that all graphic images have alternative text attached. If no alternative text is present, the screen reader applications attempt to read the graphic image file, which will not help a visually impaired user. You can use the alt attribute for short descriptions, or the longdesc attribute if a longer description is required. A long description is a URL that points the viewer to another webpage where more detail about the graphic is available. Keep in mind that not all browsers support the long description attribute, so you should always include an alternative attribute as well. Some decorative graphic elements that you use repeatedly, such as graphic bullets, do not require alternative attributes. You can simply add the alternative attribute and assign it an empty text string (alt=" ").

SharePoint Designer automatically opens the Accessibility Properties dialog box when you insert a picture on a webpage, enabling you to add the alt or longdesc attribute, as shown in Figure B.9.

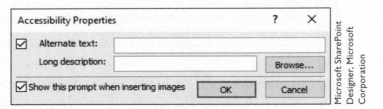

**FIGURE B.9** SharePoint Designer Accessibility Properties Dialog Box

In SharePoint Designer, you can also add or edit the alt or longdesc attribute for an inline image after the image has been placed on the page.

**To add or edit the alt or long description, complete the following steps:**

1. Select the img code <img> on the Quick Tag Selector bar.

2. Click the Picture Tools Format tab.

3. Click Properties in the Picture group.

4. Click the General tab in the Picture Properties dialog box, as shown in Figure B.10. In browsers that support the longdesc attribute, the value assigned to the attribute is displayed as a link.

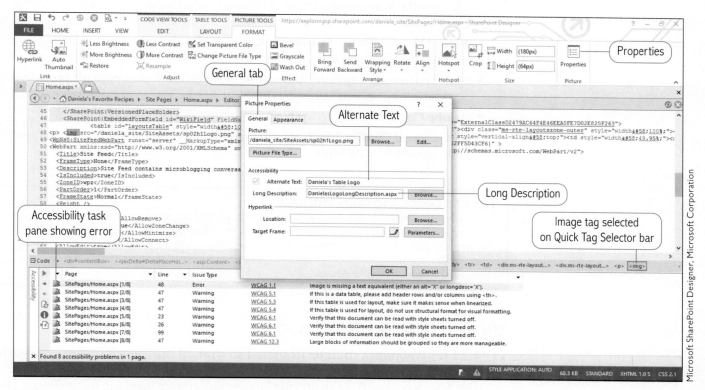

**FIGURE B.10** SharePoint Designer Accessibility Checker and Inline Images

---

**TIP: ANIMATED IMAGES AND THUMBNAILS**

Avoid using animations, which can cause problems for some users who have disabilities. You should provide access to large images via thumbnails or text links (keep in mind that large images still take a long time to download). In SharePoint Designer, you can easily generate a thumbnail image by clicking the original image code, and clicking Auto Thumbnail in the Link group on the Picture Tools Format tab of the Ribbon.

---

# Working with Multimedia

**1194.22 (b) Equivalent alternatives for any multimedia presentation shall be synchronized with the presentation.**

If your webpage features audio, consider the users who have hearing impairments by supplying a text transcript for the audio content. If video is a part of your webpage, you should provide captions for this group of users. For users with visual impairments, include synchronized descriptions of the action on the video as separate text descriptions as well as an audio transcript. The Caption It Yourself™ website (https://www.dcmp.org/ciy) provides you with tips for captioning your videos, the benefits of captioning, as well as directs you to software application options for the task. To learn more about audio content transcripts and captions for video content, check out the following websites:

- **Captions and Audio Descriptions for PC Multimedia** (https://msdn .microsoft.com/en-us/library/ms971317.aspx)
- **The National Captioning Institute** (http://www.ncicap.org)
- **Relay Conference Captioning** (http://www.fedrcc.us/FedRcc)
- **WGBH's Media Access Group** (http://access.wgbh.org)
- **Microsoft SAMI 1.0** (https://msdn.microsoft.com/en-us/library/ms971327 .aspx)
- **The Media Access Generator (MAGpie)** (http://ncam.wgbh.org and search for MAGpie)
- **WebAIM—Captions, Transcripts, and Audio Descriptions** (http://webaim .org/techniques/captions)
- **How to turn on captions and audio description in a media player** (https:// www.washington.edu/accessit/print.html?ID=1251)
- **Adobe Captivate** (http://www.adobe.com/products/captivate)
- **CPC Closed Captioning & Subtitling Software** (http://www.telestream.net/ captioning/overview.htm)

---

**TIP: CSS LEVEL 3 SPEECH MODULE**

The CSS level 3 Speech Module (https://www.w3.org/TR/css3-speech) enables you to specify to screen readers how content should be presented in audio to the user. Although CSS level 3 modules are currently under development (https://www.w3.org/TR/css-2015), it includes all of CSS level 2, and provides many new formatting features, including CSS properties for speech formatting such as voice types, volume, pauses, and rests.

---

# Working with Color

**1194.22 (c) Webpages shall be designed so that all information conveyed with color is also available without color, for example from context or markup.**

Web developers use color to provide interest and convey meaning on webpages, but for people who are blind or who have vision impairments, such as color blindness, the use of color may only hinder their understanding of the content. For instance, a chart that contains various colors can prove difficult for someone who cannot see the difference between the colors. By using color thoughtfully, you make your pages more user-friendly to all of the viewers of your website. For example, by selecting colors for text and backgrounds that provide contrast, you make it easier to read for people who have visual impairments, while also making the pages quicker to read for people who do not have impairments. You should always consider the following options as you use color on your webpages:

- Set colors of your webpages in style sheets. With SharePoint, you can create a CSS file and attach it to the webpages throughout the site. This enables the viewer to override the color choices so that colors they are capable of seeing better can be used. When colors are defined in HTML, your users cannot override color settings.
- Provide a black and white or grayscale alternative version of your webpage for users who are color blind. You can create a webpage template using black and white or grayscale colors and images using an image editing program. You can find out more about using image editing programs at the Web Developers Notes website (http://www.webdevelopersnotes.com) and search the website for image editing programs.

- Use brighter colors when possible, because they are easier for users who are color blind to differentiate.

- Make sure you offer text equivalent clues if you use important color clues in your webpage. For example, if you use a statement such as "Click the red button to log out" in your webpage, the red button must be identified with a text label that makes it recognizable to people who are color blind.

- Provide sufficient contrast between text colors and backgrounds.

- Avoid using red and green, which are challenging for the majority of color blind people. For instance, when filling out a form, fields that are not validated will often appear with red text, indicating that the user should provide the correct information. If the user cannot see the color red, they will not be able to find their mistakes and complete the form successfully. As a designer, you can improve the webpage by showing these visual messages in bold as well as red, making them more user-friendly for all viewers.

Two simple methods can help you verify that your webpage is in compliance with guideline (c). Because the content is the most important part of your webpage message, even more important than the design, you should convert your webpage into a black and white or grayscale version and review it to see that all content continues to make sense in this format. This is especially important if charts convey information, or if tables are color-coded. Try viewing the webpage on a black and white monitor, or printing the webpage on a black and white printer. If the usability of the webpage is not affected by the removal of color, your webpage should be easy to use by people who are color blind. If meaning is lost in the black and white or grayscale format, consider creating a separate webpage in black and white, using graphic elements in place of colors, for users who are color blind.

Several websites enable you to test the accessibility of your website for color blind users. aDesigner (http://www.eclipse.org/actf/downloads/index.php) is one of the best disability simulators to use for testing webpages for accessibility and usability problems related to visual and color deficiencies. There are two modes available in aDesigner:

- **Blind** The blind mode runs three types of tests on webpages: blind usability visualization, accessibility and usability checking, and compliance checking. This setting helps you understand how blind users who depend on voice browsers and screen readers experience their webpages. By using this setting, you can correct the most crucial factor in improving usability for the blind—navigability.

- **Low Vision** The low vision mode simulates how users with weak eyesight, color vision deficiencies, cataracts, and combinations of impairments perceive webpages. This mode enables you to detect accessibility problems from simulated webpages or images.

The Vischeck (http://www.vischeck.com/downloads) website provides you with free downloadable software tools that enable you to see how your webpages appear to people with different types of color blindness.

# Working with Style Sheets

**1194.22 (d) Documents shall be organized so they are readable without requiring an associated style sheet.**

By using style sheets to separate content from presentation, webpages load faster and are more usable and accessible in most browsers. However, you must ensure that pages display properly even if your visitor is using a browser that does not support style sheets, has style-sheet support turned off, or has to use another custom style sheet. When using cascading style sheets in developing your webpages, you should always consider the following recommendations:

- Do not rely on specific fonts or colors to convey relevant information, because the specified fonts and colors might not exist on all computers. If they do not exist, the browser uses its default colors and fonts. For instance, the decorative font *Gigi* will be substituted with the default font on computers that do not have *Gigi* as an installed font. If the use of a special font is critical to the design of your webpage, create the stylized text in a graphics program, and insert it as a graphic onto your webpage. Be sure to use alternative tags to describe the graphic so screen readers can process it. This process is often used for headings, organization names, and other text that is emphasized.

- Do not fix the size of your text in points or pixels. In some cases, people with low vision rely on changing the font size on their browsers to enable them to see the text more clearly. You can see what this is like by clicking View on the Menu bar while viewing a website in Internet Explorer, clicking Text Size, clicking a size option on the menu, and then reloading the page. Webpages that are set up with fixed text sizes in points or pixels cannot be altered by this simple method. As you design pages, use the em unit to set font sizes as required by CSS Techniques for Web Content Accessibility Guidelines 2.0 (https://www.w3.org and search for CSS Techniques for WCAG 2.0).

- The heading tags (<h1>–<h6>) should be used to emphasize the organization of your webpage, not to modify the text font size.

- Use an adjustable layout (relative length units and percentages of the browser window size) that shrinks or expands as necessary so that visitors with different browser window sizes and screen resolutions can properly see your webpages. To test this with your webpages, click Restore Down on the browser window (next to the Close button) to view the page in a smaller window. See the Units of Measure section of the CSS Techniques for Web Content Accessibility Guidelines 2.0 for more information.

- Use linked style sheets rather than imported style sheets or embedded styles on each webpage.

Linked style sheets offer the best solutions for maximizing the universal usability of your webpages. Reasons for choosing linked style sheets over embedded styles or imported style sheets include the following:

- Linked style sheets enable alternative views for different types of devices (such as printers and mobile devices), different options for viewing your webpages (such as larger size fonts or higher color contrast), or different browsers.

- Linked style sheets are supported by all CSS-capable browsers in contrast with the style sheets imported (using the @import method) that works only in Microsoft Edge, Internet Explorer 5.0 or later browsers, Firefox, Opera, and Safari.

- Linked style sheets minimize the time needed to download your webpages because they are downloaded only one time and applied to each linked webpage of your website as it is accessed.

- Linked style sheets help maximize the consistency of your website. Your users will need to get acquainted with only one design.

However, even when using CSS linked style sheets you might have to deal with browser incompatibilities that will force you to create alternate versions of your webpage for different browsers. SharePoint Designer can help you identify these incompatibilities and create alternate versions of your webpages with the Preview in Multiple Browsers command. Click the Preview in Browser arrow on the Home tab, and select Edit Browser List. Select the browsers you want to use to preview the webpages from the installed browsers list, as shown in Figure B.5. Click OK, click the Preview in Browser arrow again, and then click a size under Preview in Multiple Browsers. The page will open in the browsers. If there is obviously a problem with the way a page is displayed—for example, between Internet Explorer, Microsoft Edge, and Mozilla Firefox—you can address the problem by creating an alternate webpage by modifying the external style sheet.

For example, to ensure that your webpage will display correctly in Mozilla Firefox, you can use the SharePoint Designer Check Browser behavior to automatically determine the browser when the webpage is accessed and open the appropriate webpage for the viewer's browser.

> **To add the Check Browser behavior to an HTML webpage, complete the following steps:**
>
> 1. Create the alternate version of the webpage and click Task Panes on the View tab.
> 2. Click Behaviors.
> 3. Select the <body> tag on the Quick Tag Selector bar.
> 4. Click Insert on the Behaviors task pane to open the Check Browser dialog box.
> 5. Select the browser for which the webpage does not display correctly in the *If the current browser type is* box. From the Version list, check a specific version, if required. Click the first Go to URL check box, click Browse to navigate to the location of the alternate page, as shown in Figure B.11, and click OK to apply the behavior.

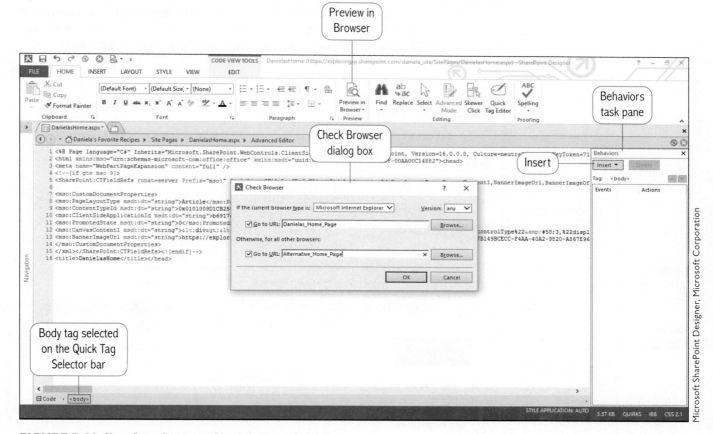

**FIGURE B.11** SharePoint Designer Check Browser Behavior

# Working with Image Maps

**1194.22 (e) Redundant text links shall be provided for each active region of a server-side image map.**
**1194.22 (f) Client-side image maps shall be provided instead of server-side image maps except where the regions cannot be defined with an available geometric shape.**

*Image maps* enable the viewers to click a region of a graphic to navigate to a different location. Client-side image maps are starting to replace server-side image maps, especially because client-side image maps enable polygon hotspots and therefore all shapes can be defined on a client-side map. Image maps provide a challenge for people with disabilities, especially if screen readers are used to access websites. To make a webpage containing a client-side image map accessible, you must add alternative text to the original map image and each hotspot within the map.

# Working with Tables

**1194.22 (g) Row and column headers shall be identified for data tables.**

Chapter 3 covers using tables to organize data, as well as using tables that include one or more levels of nested tables. To comply with guideline (g), when using data tables, use the <th> tag for any cell that contains a row or column header, even if the cell occurs in a nested table.

By default, SharePoint Designer uses the <td> tag as rows and columns are created. You can modify the HTML code by selecting the cell and clicking Header Cell in the Cell Layout group of the Table Tools Layout tab, as shown in Figure B.12. Adding a table caption can also help visually impaired users by providing them with more information about the table's content, as shown in Figure B.12. Click Insert Caption in the Rows & Columns group on the Table Tools Layout tab to add a caption. Providing a table summary using the summary attribute, in the Tag Properties pane, is useful for non-visual browser applications (the summary is not displayed and it is used only by screen reader users).

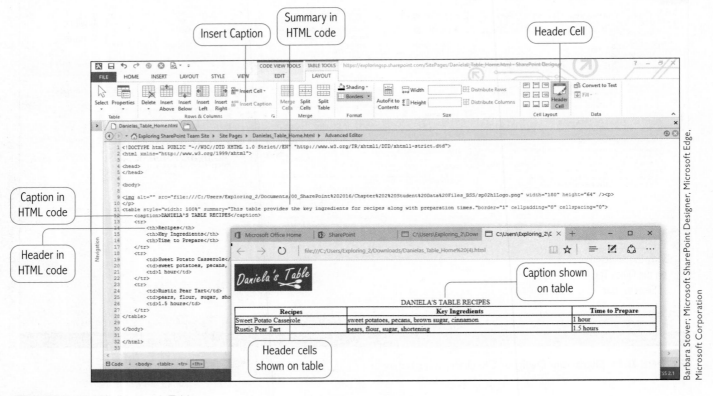

**FIGURE B.12** Working with Tables

---

**TIP: FLEXIBLE VIEWING CONDITIONS**

You should use flexible measurements for tables so your webpages can easily adapt to your users' screen resolution and size. The Layout section of the Insert Table and Table Properties dialog box enables you to specify the width and height of tables in percentages of the document window.

---

**1194.22 (h) Markup shall be used to associate data cells and header cells for data tables that have two or more logical levels of row or column headers.**

To comply with guideline (h), use the <th> tag for any cell that contains a row or a column header in any nested table. This can be tedious and might convince you that nested tables should be used only when absolutely necessary. As previously discussed, an excellent way to test that your webpage is accessible is by viewing it in the Lynx browser.

If a table is used as a layout tool, do not use any structural HTML tags (for example, the <th> tag that displays its content visually as centered and bold) for the purpose of visual formatting, as this can be confusing to someone using a screen reader. For a browser to render a table's side-by-side text correctly, you will need to linearize the table. To learn more about how to linearize a table, see the Creating Accessible Tables section of the WebAIM website (http://www.webaim.org and search for Creating Accessible Tables). One of the best tools for creating accessible tables is the WebAIM free online WAVE Accessibility Tool (http://www.webaim.org and search for WAVE Web Accessibility Evaluation Tool).

# Working with Frames

**1194.22 (i) Frames shall be titled with text that facilitates frame identification and navigation.**

Frames are a layout tool for creating webpages based on the structure of a frameset. A *frameset* is the actual layout that lets the browser know how to display the framed pages. Sometimes Web designers want to include the contents of one webpage in another webpage (using all the display features of a frame) without having to build a frameset layout. The inline frame, also known as a *floating frame*, is basically a frame that does not need to be framed in a frameset and embeds a document or another webpage into an HTML document so that embedded data is displayed inside a subwindow of the browser's window. The two documents are absolutely independent, and both are treated as complete documents.

When opening a frames page, assistive technologies applications for people who are visually impaired enable users to open only one frame at a time. Thus, it is important to provide information about the contents of each frame and inline frame included in your webpage. You can do this by adding the title or name attribute to each frame using the Tag Properties pane in SharePoint Designer. Because some browsers and assistive technology applications support the title attribute and others support the name attribute, it is wise to add both. Users without access to frames should still have access to the webpage content if appropriate navigation links are provided in the <noframes> tag.

The W3C added the <frames> tag to the list of deprecated tags; therefore, even though the accessibility issues related to frames can be addressed, it is highly recommended not to use frames if you wish to build standard and accessible webpages.

---

**TIP: FRAMES OR NO FRAMES**
It is not uncommon for users to not use frames or to use browsers that do not support frames. Therefore, you should always provide access to an alternate webpage using the <noframes> tag.

---

# Working with Animation and Scrolling Text

**1194.22 (j) Pages shall be designed to avoid causing the screen to flicker with a frequency greater than 2 Hz and lower than 55 Hz.**

Using flashing or flickering elements, such as animated GIF images, blinking text, and scrolling text, can affect the accessibility of your webpages. People with photosensitive epilepsy can have seizures caused by elements that flicker, flash, or blink with an intensity and frequency outside the range indicated by guideline (j). The majority of screen reader applications cannot read moving text. People with cognitive disabilities might also find it challenging to read moving text.

## Working with Text-Only Versions

**1194.22 (k) A text-only page, with equivalent information or functionality, shall be provided to make a website comply with the provisions of this part, when compliance cannot be accomplished in any other way. The content of the text-only page shall be updated whenever the primary page changes.**

A text-only webpage must contain all the information included in the original page and must have the same functionality the original page has. Anytime you update a webpage, you must also update its text-only version. A link to the text-only version must be included in the original webpage. The BeTobaccoFree.gov site converts all infographics on the site to text-only versions so that the information is available regardless of how you access the site, as shown in Figure B.13.

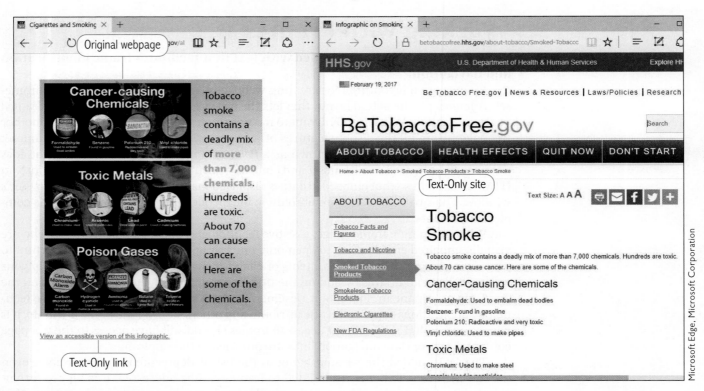

**FIGURE B.13** Working with Text-Only Webpages

## Working with Scripts, Applets, and Plug-ins

**1194.22 (l) When pages utilize scripting languages to display content, or to create interface elements, the information provided by the script shall be identified with functional text that can be read by assistive technology.**

**1194.22 (m) When a webpage requires that an applet, plug-in, or other application be present on the client system to interpret page content, the page must provide a link to a plug-in or applet that complies with §1194.21(a) through (l).**

A *scripting language* is less powerful than traditional programming languages, such as Java and C++. Traditional programming languages are sets of commands that are compiled and then executed one by one. Each scripting language employs a scripting engine and does not require compilation, as does a traditional programming language.

Microsoft Active Server Pages (ASPX) and Sun Java Server Pages (JSP) are two of the most popular server-side scripting languages used to develop interactive websites that interface with databases or other data sources (such as an XML document). ***JavaScript*** is one of the most popular client-side scripting languages, and its scripting engine is supported by all major browsers such as Chrome, Microsoft Edge, Internet Explorer, and Firefox. It is able to meet the needs of most Web developers who want to create dynamic webpages.

Scripting languages are used to develop webpages in the following ways:

- They automatically change a formatted date on a webpage.
- They cause a linked-to page to appear in a pop-up window.
- They cause text or a graphic image to change during a mouse rollover.
- They obtain information about the current Web browser.
- They enable navigating to webpages that have been opened during a Web browser session.
- They process data submitted via an HTML form.
- They retrieve data from a database via an HTML form.

Many of these scripting language applications require the use of the mouse. Some people with motor disabilities might not be able to use a mouse. Furthermore, some assistive technology applications have browsers with scripting turned off; thus, you should provide alternative methods for users with disabilities. Your webpages should include access keys (keyboard shortcuts) that enable users to achieve the same functionality.

The SharePoint Designer IntelliSense tool enables you to assign keyboard shortcuts (accesskey attributes) to the links and form fields on each webpage, so keyboard users can navigate the page by using a combination of the Alt key + a letter key. For consistency and usability, use the same access keys for the same links on all webpages included in a website. You can add an access key attribute to a hyperlink, as shown in Figure B.14, by clicking at the end of the hyperlink (before the </a> tag) in the code, selecting accesskey from the IntelliSense tool, and typing the letter used as the shortcut key. This produces a hyperlink tag that contains the accesskey=" " attribute with the letter between the quotation marks, as shown in Figure B.15. You can also type accesskey=" " (with a letter to indicate the keyboard shortcut between the quotation marks) directly into the hyperlink tag in the Code view. To add an access key attribute to a form field, add the accesskey to the form field tag, as shown in Figure B.16, using the method you prefer.

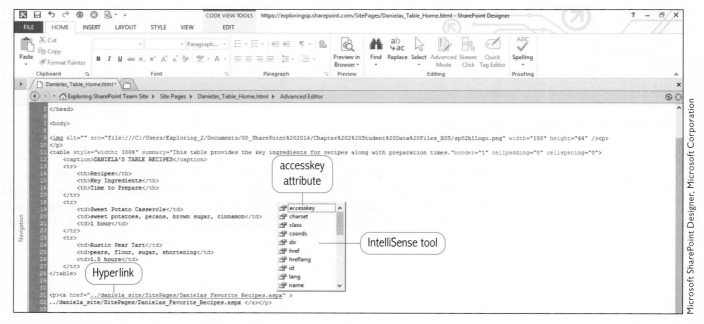

**FIGURE B.14** Assigning an accesskey to a Hyperlink

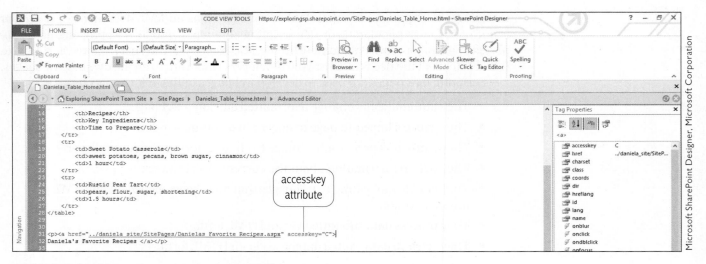

**FIGURE B.15** Assigning an accesskey Using Tag Properties

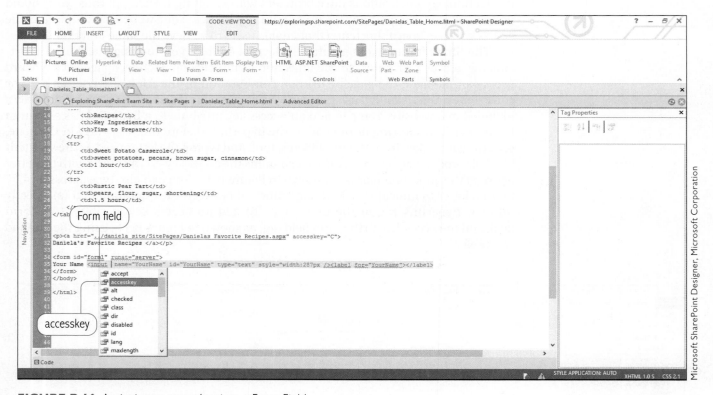

**FIGURE B.16** Assigning an accesskey into a Form Field

Chapter 3 covers the SharePoint Designer tools that enable you to add multimedia elements to webpages that might require a plug-in or another application to be displayed properly in a browser and empower the user with the decision when to access media. (http://www.access-board.gov/508.htm, click on Guide to the Section 508 Standards, and then click Web-based Intranet and Internet Information and Applications (1194.22).) When using any of these elements in a webpage, a link to the source of a required plug-in or application, such as Flash, Java, or Shockwave, should be added to the webpage. Plug-ins can be detected in the HTML code of a webpage by searching for the <object> tag, <embed> tag, or <iframe> tag.

---

**TIP: EMBED VIDEO IN SHAREPOINT ONLINE**

In SharePoint, you should use the HTML <iframe> tag to embed multimedia in your pages, as shown in Figure B.17. There are a number of ways you can do that. The easiest and most reliable way, recommended by Microsoft as well, is to insert the embed code using SharePoint Online, as discussed in Chapter 3. See also this very useful tutorial on Add video or audio to a page (https://office .microsoft.com/en-us/office365-sharepoint-online-enterprise-help/add-video-or-audio-to-a-page-HA102785752.aspx).

---

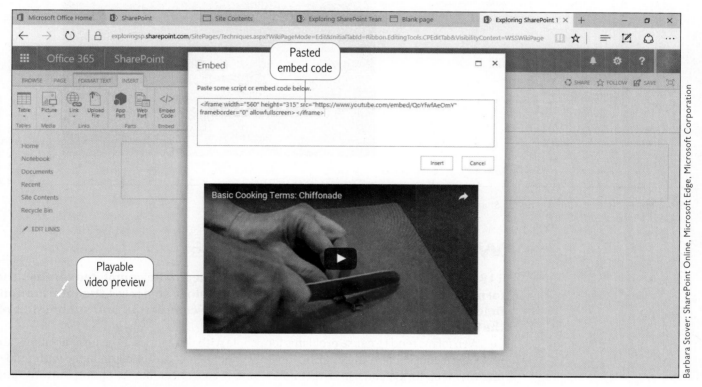

**FIGURE B.17** Embedding Video Code in SharePoint Online

You also have the option to add the embed code directly to the HTML coding in SharePoint Designer. Videos from YouTube provide the <iframe> embed code. Display the video, right-click and select Copy embed code. Open the SharePoint Designer page, and select the location where you want the video player to display. Right-click and paste the code. The <iframe> code embeds the player, as shown in Figure B.18, ensuring that it will play correctly.

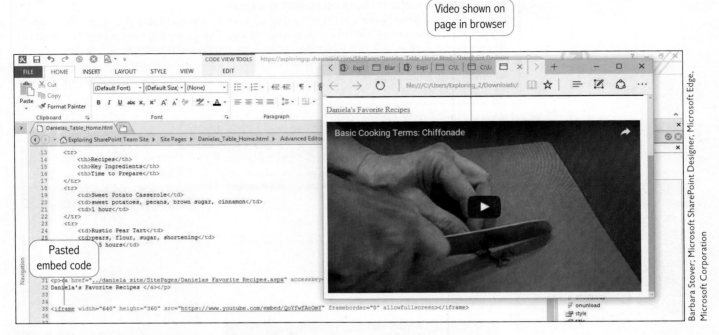

**FIGURE B.18** Embedded Video in SharePoint Designer

# Working with Web Forms

**1194.22 (n) When electronic forms are designed to be completed on-line, the form shall allow people using assistive technology to access the information, field elements, and functionality required for completion and submission of the form, including all directions and cues.**

Web forms tend to cause problems for people with disabilities if the form elements are improperly labeled and titled, or if they have not been coded in compliance with guideline (n). Web forms consist of text boxes, text areas, check boxes, option buttons, and drop-down menus. When form layouts are structured using a table, you must be careful to make sure the table is linearized. To improve a screen reader's ability to process an HTML form, each form element should have an initial default value to give the user guidance in completing the form.

All form elements must have adjacent labels (placed in the same table cell). The W3C HTML specifications (https://www.w3.org/wiki/HTML/Elements/label) require you to include a <label> tag associated with a form element. You can use the <label> tag in two distinctive ways:

- **Explicit labels** These labels can be implemented using the <label> tag with the *for* attribute. The id attribute of the form element is assigned as the value of the *for* attribute. The majority of assistive technology applications work extremely well with explicit labels.

- **Implicit labels** These labels can be implemented by including the form element and its associated label within the <label> tag. The majority of assistive technology applications, especially screen readers, do not support implicit labels properly.

SharePoint Designer cannot create explicit labels and does not add the id attribute to *form elements. You add explicit labels and the id attribute to the associated form elements manually in the code, as shown in Figure B.19.*

---

**TIP: ALTERNATIVE CONTACT METHODS**

It is not easy to design and develop accessible forms for users with different types of special needs. That is why you should always include an alternative contact method, such as a telephone number or email address, on your webpages with the forms.

---

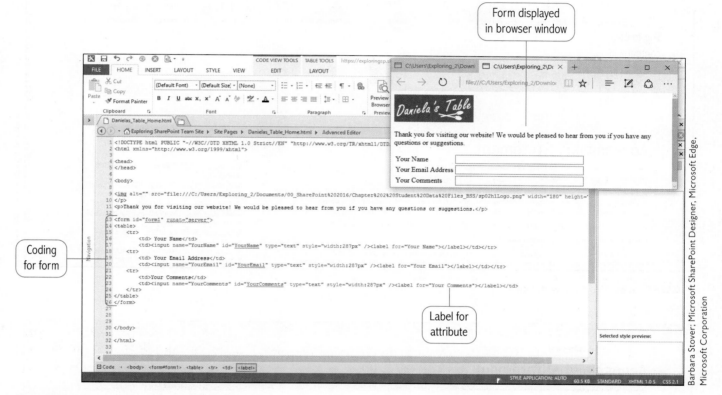

**FIGURE B.19** Working with Forms in SharePoint Designer

# Working with Links

**1194.22 (o) A method shall be provided that permits users to skip repetitive navigation links.**

Chapter 3 introduced bookmarks as hyperlinks that link to a specific location within a webpage. The most commonly used bookmark for accessibility is Skip Navigation Links. A Skip Navigation Links link enables a user to skip the webpage title and navigation links by directing the focus to the main contents of the webpage being viewed. This link is especially important for people who are visually impaired and use a screen reader application. In the example shown in Figure B.20, the Skip to Page Content link enables visually impaired users to skip directly to the main content of a webpage so that they are not forced to listen to the webpage title and navigation links each time they access the webpage. The resulting page is shown in Figure B.21.

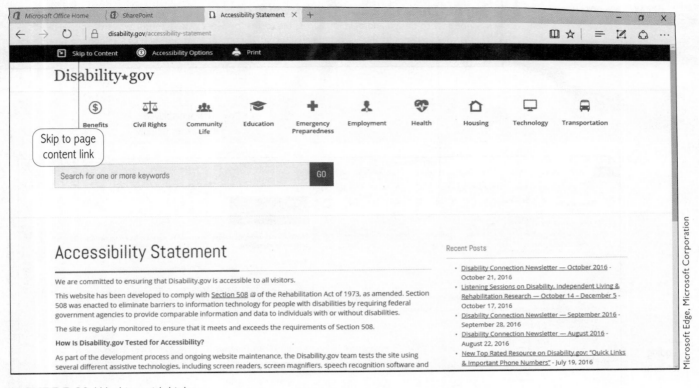

**FIGURE B.20** Working with Links

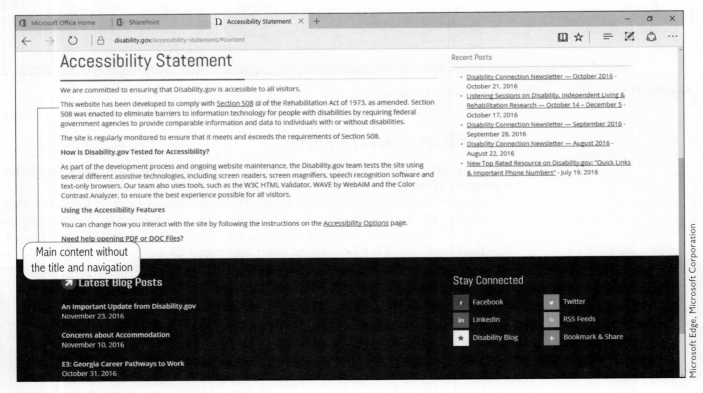

**FIGURE B.21** Skip to Page Content Results

# Working with Timed Response

**1194.22 (p) When a timed response is required, the user shall be alerted and given sufficient time to indicate more time is required.**

For security reasons and to accommodate visitor traffic on busy servers, Web developers use scripts that disable the functionality of webpages when a response is not received within a certain time limit. People with cognitive disabilities or different levels of visual impairment might need more time to provide a response. Consequently, you should always alert users if there is a time limit for providing a response. You should also consider establishing a response time that accommodates all users or enables them to change the time. For an excellent resource on this topic, go to the W3C "How People with Disabilities Use the Web" webpage (https://www.w3.org) and search for How People with Disabilities Use the Web.

# Assistive Technology and Accessibility Evaluation Tools

Webpages designed in compliance with Section 508 and the WCAG guidelines can be made accessible to the majority of people with disabilities using software applications and devices that are grouped under the umbrella of assistive technologies:

- Screen readers use text-to-speech (TTS) technology to verbalize screen text and textual representations of graphical elements if available.
- Speech-to-text converters automatically transform dialogue into text.

Browser extensions and other plug-in evaluation tools, such as the Web Accessibility Toolbar for IE - 2012 (http://www.visionaustralia.org, search for Web accessibility using the site search form, and then click Web Accessibility Toolbar for IE), WAVE Extension for Chrome (http://wave.webaim.org/extension), or Web Developer Extension for Chrome, Firefox, and Opera (http://chrispederick.com/work/webdeveloper) provide functionality to help perform many manual accessibility checks.

> **TIP: 25 WAYS TO MAKE YOUR WEBSITE ACCESSIBLE**
> Dennis E. Lembree, an accomplished Web developer and accessibility expert, published a down-to-earth article on "25 Ways to Make Your Website Accessible" (http://www.webhostingsearch.com/articles/25-ways-to-make-your-site-more-accessible.php).

Accessibility and Evaluation Tools refer to the tools used to make the Web accessible to people with a variety of disabilities, with some examples listed in Table B.2. W3C provides two free online validation services: The Markup Validation Service (http://validator.w3.org) and Cascading Style Sheet (CSS) Validation Service (https://jigsaw.w3.org/css-validator). The Markup Validation Service checks documents like HTML and XHTML for conformance to W3C recommendations and other standards. The CSS Validation Service checks CSS in HTML and XHTML documents or standalone CSS documents for conformance to W3C recommendations.

| TABLE B.2 | Examples of Assistive Technologies & Accessibility and Evaluation Tools | |
|---|---|---|
| **Category** | **Application** | **URL** |
| **Accessibility and evaluation tools** | aDesigner designed by IBM | http://www.ibm.com/us/en and search aDesigner |
| **Screen readers** | JAWS for Windows developed by Freedom Scientific | http://www.freedomscientific.com |
| | Dolphin Pen by Dolphin Computer Access | https://yourdolphin.com and search Dolphin Pen |
| | Window-Eyes developed by GW Micro | http://www.gwmicro.com |
| **Speech-to-text converters** | Dragon Naturally Speaking developed by Advanced Speech | http://www.nuance.com/index.htm |
| | Dragon for Mac by Nuance Communications | http://www.nuance.com/index.htm |

Pearson Education, Inc.

# More Information

The task of building accessible webpages is not an easy one. Web developers are required to accumulate a lot of knowledge to accomplish this task successfully. The good news is that increasingly more companies and organizations are developing competitive assistive and accessibility technology applications that can help you to assist people with disabilities and special needs.

W3C provides an "Evaluating Websites for Accessibility: Overview" collection of pages that includes general procedures and tips for evaluating the accessibility of your sites (https://www.w3.org/WAI/eval/Overview.html). This site also includes a "Complete List of Web Accessibility Evaluation Tools" (https://www.w3.org/WAI/ER/tools).

The following list presents some of the most resourceful websites that Web developers use to develop accessible websites, and includes the websites of software companies that are providing successful assistive and accessibility technologies, of organizations and institutions developing accessibility guidelines and laws, up-to-date articles, and Web accessibility online forums.

- **Microsoft Accessibility** https://www.microsoft.com/enable and click on Mission & Strategy in the Accessibility at Microsoft section
- **IBM Human Ability and Accessibility Center** http://www-03.ibm.com/able/access_ibm/disability.html
- **W3C Web Accessibility Initiative (WAI) Guidelines and Techniques** https://www.w3.org/WAI and click on Guidelines & Techniques in the vertical navigation bar
- **Web Accessibility in Mind (WebAIM)** http://www.webaim.org

- **Web Content Accessibility Guidelines** https://www.w3.org/WAI, click on Guidelines & Techniques in the vertical navigation bar, then click on Web Content (WCAG) in the vertical navigation bar
- **Freedom Scientific: JAWS for Windows** http://www.freedomscientific.com
- **IBM Alpha Works: aDesigner** http://www.ibm.com/us/en and search aDesigner
- **HiSoftwareCynthiaSays portal** http://www.cynthiasays.com
- **LIFT: Accessibility Evaluation Tool** http://usablenet.com
- **Window-Eyes** http://www.gwmicro.com
- **Lynx—Internet Software Consortium** http://lynx.invisible-island.net
- **Lynx Viewer** http://www.delorie.com/web/lynxview.html
- **Dragon: Dragon Naturally Speaking** http://www.nuance.com/dragon/index.htm
- **Section 508** https://www.section508.gov
- **WAVE: Web Accessibility Evaluation Tool** http://wave.webaim.org/help
- **Vischeck** http://www.vischeck.com/vischeck
- **ACM Special Interest Group on Computer-Human Interaction (SIGCHI)** http://www.sigchi.org
- **ACM Special Interest Group on Accessible Computing, SIGACCESS** http://www.sigaccess.org

# Key Terms Matching

Match the key terms with their definitions. Write the key term letter by the appropriate numbered definition.

**a.** Accessibility

**b.** Cross-browser incompatibility

**c.** Cross-platform incompatibility

**d.** Image map

**e.** JavaScript

**f.** Linearization

**g.** Scripting language

**h.** Section 508

**i.** Web Accessibility Initiative (WAI)

**j.** Web Content Accessibility Guidelines (WCAG)

**1.** _____ A computer language that does not require compilation as does a traditional programming language. *p. 354*

**2.** _____ A federal law (enacted by Congress as an amendment to the Rehabilitation Act of 1973) "to require Federal agencies to make their electronic and information technology accessible to people with disabilities." *p. 336*

**3.** _____ A graphic that enables the viewers to click a region of the graphic to navigate to a different location. *p. 352*

**4.** _____ The ability of a webpage to be accessed, read, and used by any person regardless of special needs or disabilities. *p. 343*

**5.** _____ A lack of consistency resulting in different browsers displaying webpages differently on the same computer platform. *p. 339*

**6.** _____ A lack of consistency resulting in different browsers or browser versions displaying webpages differently on different computer platforms. *p. 339*

**7.** _____ A process in which screen readers convert the content of a webpage into lines of text for people with vision impairment. *p. 346*

**8.** _____ Guidelines that describe priority levels and four layers of principles, guidelines, success criteria, and sufficient and advisory techniques to enable Web designers to create accessible webpages. *p. 337*

**9.** _____ Web design guidelines issued by the World Wide Web Consortium that help designers create accessible webpages. *p. 336*

**10.** _____ A client-side scripting language used by popular browsers. *p. 355*

# Glossary

**Absolute URL**  A URL that provides a full path to a webpage or file.

**Access View**  A view that enables you to use advanced tools for generating reports and views.

**Accessibility**  The capability of a webpage to be accessed, read, and used by any person, regardless of special needs or disabilities.

**Adobe Flash**  A popular application used for displaying multimedia content, usually for animated graphics.

**Announcement item**  Information on a list that contains a title, body, and optional expiration date.

**Announcements list**  A list that is used to inform your site users about upcoming events, news, or activities.

**App**  A small, easy to use Web application with a specific purpose.

**App part**  A web part used to display the contents of a list or library on a webpage.

**ASCII**  A common numeric code used by computers to represent characters.

**Attribute**  A code placed within tags to define the style, color, size, width, height, and source of elements.

**Basic Search Center template**  A site template that provides general search capabilities.

**Blog**  A website or webpage used to post information for comment and discussion.

**Blog template**  A site template that enables you to post information for comment and discussion.

**Breadcrumb navigation**  A navigation trail that enables you to see the path leading to the current page and to keep track of the current page location easily within the site.

**Calendar list**  A list that displays events and activities in day, week, or month layout.

**Calendar View**  A display of list data where at least one field is a date field, arranged on a calendar.

**Cascading Style Sheet (CSS)**  The standard style sheet language used on the Web.

**Cell**  The intersection of a column and a row in a table.

**Class selector**  A CSS style selector used to signify sections of a webpage to be identified by <div> or <span> tags.

**Cloud computing**  A network of remote servers that provide software applications through a Web browser and file storage on servers you connect to through the Internet.

**Color theme**  The color selections that affect page elements such as backgrounds, text, hyperlinks, and some graphic elements such as bullets and horizontal rules (or lines).

**Community Site template**  A site template that enables community members to congregate and discuss common interests.

**Contacts list**  A list created using the Contacts app that contains information such as name, company, phone numbers, email addresses, and more about people.

**Content section**  The main body of the site page that includes all of the elements you want to make available through the site.

**Contextual command**  A command that changes based on the page you are viewing.

**Conversation view**  The Outlook view that enables you to see your responses as a partial message.

**Cross-browser incompatibility**  A lack of consistency resulting in different browsers displaying webpages differently on the same computer platform.

**Cross-platform incompatibility**  A lack of consistency resulting in different browsers or browser versions displaying webpages differently on different computer platforms.

**Database**  A file of related data containing objects such as tables, queries, reports, and forms.

**Database table**  A set of related data containing records arranged in rows and columns, which are fields.

**Datasheet View**  A display of list or library items using a grid-like layout that enables you to edit the table.

**Declaration**  Formatting instructions that include a property and a value.

**Declaration block**  A group of formatting instructions that begins and ends with braces {}, and contains all of the formatting options you want applied to the selector.

**Default template**  The type of file that defines the default content type for the library.

**Discussion board list**  A list that supports message postings related to list topics.

**Document Center template**  A site template used to manage documents in a central location.

**Document type definition (DTD)**  A statement that specifies what tags and attributes are used to describe content in an XML document, where each tag is allowed, and which tags can appear within other tags, thus eliminating many code errors that occur.

**Dynamic Web Parts**  Web parts that can be placed on a Wiki page in a Web Part zone and are saved separately from the page in the SQL Server content database. This type of web part contains user-editable properties.

**Embedded style**  A style code usually included in the <head> section of an HTML document with the following syntax: <style>style declarations</style>.

**Enterprise Search Center template**  A site template that enables an enterprise-wide search experience through general, people, conversation, and video searches.

**Excel Online** An online application that enables you to develop spreadsheets that include text, values, formulas, functions, tables, charts, and surveys.

**Extensible Hypertext Markup Language (XHTML)** A newer markup language that overcomes some of the problems with HTML.

**Extensible Markup Language (XML)** A language based on the SGML standard that enables data to be shared and processed via the Internet and across software applications, operating systems, and hardware computer platforms.

**Extensible Style Sheet Language (XSL)** A language developed by the W3C as an improved method for formatting XML documents, allowing developers to transform XML data files into a wide variety of popular file formats, such as HTML and Portable Document Format (PDF).

**Extensible Stylesheet Language Transformation** A language that is a subset of XSL that enables you to display XML data on a webpage and "transform" it into HTML.

**External style** A style included in a separate file used to specify the formatting of any HTML document to which the external style sheet is linked.

**Flat view** A list of postings arranged in a sequence based on the date and time they were posted.

**Font theme** A theme that dictates the fonts used for heading and body text.

**Gantt View** A display of a list that provides a graphical representation for a project timeline.

**GIF (Graphics Interchange Format)** Format most often used for drawn graphics and animated images.

**Group** A collection of commands on the Ribbon related to a specific task.

**Hashtags** A common social networking tool that provides searchable categories of topics and help to organize posts.

**Home page** The first page displayed as user enters a site; it provides the navigational structure for the site.

**Hyperlink target** A file or page that opens when a hyperlink is clicked.

**Hypertext Markup Language (HTML)** The most common markup language used to create webpages, by defining the page layout and graphic elements of the page and providing links to other documents on the Web.

**ID selector** A selector used for identifying unique parts of your webpage, such as banners, navigation bars, or main content area, because they are connected to the ID attribute of a webpage element and the ID must be unique.

**Image map** A graphic that enables the viewers to click a region of a graphic to navigate to a different location.

**Imported style** A style that is obtained from a separate file that is downloaded at the time the webpage loads.

**Inline style** A style code that is included in the start tag by using the tag's style attributes.

**Insert Table grid** A graphical table that enables you to select the number of rows and columns for your table.

**Interlacing** A technology used for displaying images in stages.

**Interpreter** A program that translates code one line at a time into an executable format each time the program runs.

**Java Server Pages (JSP)** A popular server-side scripting language used to develop interactive websites.

**JavaScript** One of the most popular client-side scripting languages; its scripting engine is supported by all major browsers, such as Chrome, Microsoft Edge, Internet Explorer, and Firefox.

**JPEG (Joint Photographic Experts Group)** The file format can display all 16.7 million colors that are available, and it is the format most often used for photographs.

**Library** A collection of documents, pictures, or forms that can be shared with others.

**Linearization** A process in which screen readers convert the content of a webpage into lines of text for people with vision impairment.

**Linked table** An object that provides only the connection to a SharePoint list and synchronizes data changes.

**Links list** A list, created using the Links app, that contains links to other pages within a SharePoint site or to websites.

**List** A collection of announcements, links, survey questions, groups of discussions, or tasks that contains information arranged as records.

**List format** A common format seen on almost any webpage, usually as a numbered or bulleted list.

**Mailto link** A common type of hyperlink that opens the user's default email application.

**Markup language** A language that describes the layout of webpage content using tags.

**Menu** A group of hierarchical, customizable, drop down, or fly-out commands related to a specific task that is selected.

**Metadata** Information about the file, such as who created it and when.

**Microblog post** A short text message that you type to inform others of your activities, opinions, or ideas.

**Microsoft Active Server Pages (ASPX)** A Microsoft server-side scripting language used to develop interactive websites that interface with databases or other data sources.

**Microsoft Office** A collection of server platforms, desktop applications, and online services that all work together to improve productivity, make information sharing more effective, and facilitate the business decision-making process.

**Microsoft Office 365** A suite of apps that enable you to create documents and collaborate by sharing the documents with others.

**Multilingual User Interface (MUI)** The interface that enables you to specify support for various languages in the sites that you create and enables people to access the site interface in the language they select.

**Nested table** A table inserted in a cell of another table.

**Newsfeed stream** A display of updated information about people or documents you are following.

**Notification area** A display of messages that communicate the progress of the operation for a few seconds.

**Office Online** A suite of Web-based versions of Microsoft Word 2016, Excel 2016, PowerPoint 2016, and OneNote 2016 that enables you to edit and view documents.

**OneDrive for Business** An online application that enables you to create, sync, store, and share up to 1 TB of data in the cloud.

**OneNote Online** An online application that enables you to save notes in the form of text, pictures, and links in notebooks.

**Permission level** The rights within a site that can be assigned to individual users or groups.

**Plug-in** A software application that can be an integral part of a browser or can provide additional multimedia capabilities.

**PNG (Portable Network Graphics)** A newer file format that supports transparent colors, can display all 16.7 million colors available, and can contain animated images.

**Portable Document Format (PDF)** A fixed-layout file format that preserves document formatting and enables file sharing, used when the document will be commercially printed.

**PowerPoint Online** An online application that enables you to design a presentation with text, illustrations, images, SmartArt, transitions, and animations.

**Project Site template** A site template that focuses team collaboration on a specific project.

**Promoted link** A tile that enables users to enter sites or add tools to a site.

**Property** A word or a group of hyphenated words indicating a style effect.

**Quick Launch** A common pane throughout all sites in SharePoint that provides easy access to elements within the site.

**Range** A group of adjacent or contiguous cells.

**Records Center template** A site template that facilitates records management.

**Recycle Bin** A storage location that holds and enables you to restore deleted elements for a SharePoint site, such as files, lists, and libraries.

**Reghost** The action of resetting the pages to the original site definition, removing all customization, and reverting the page back to the configuration and layout of the template.

**Relative URL** A URL that provides the path to a webpage or a file in relation to another file.

**Ribbon** A display of contextual tabs available for the page you are viewing that enables you to select commands.

**SAP Workflow Site template** A site template that enables management of financial, asset, and cost accounting; production operations and materials; personnel; plants; and archived documents.

**Schema** An XML document that includes the definition of one or more XML document's content and structure.

**ScreenTip** A small box displaying descriptive and helpful text that appears when you point to a command, control, or hyperlink.

**Scripting engine** A program that translates code one line at a time into an executable format each time the program runs.

**Scripting language** A computer language that employs a scripting engine and does not require compilation as does a traditional programming language.

**Search field** A search tool that enables you to search the SharePoint sites you have permission to access.

**Section 508** A federal law (enacted by Congress as an amendment to the Rehabilitation Act of 1973) "to require Federal agencies to make their electronic and information technology accessible to people with disabilities."

**Selector** A tag that indicates to a Web browser which element(s) within a webpage to style.

**Send To** The command used to distribute documents to other libraries, making them available for other teams or in a centralized location.

**SharePoint** The Microsoft central information sharing and business collaboration platform for organizations.

**SharePoint collection** A mandatory top-level site and one or more optional subsites used by an organization to inform and foster collaboration.

**SharePoint Online** A component of Office 365 that provides you with the commonly used features of SharePoint while relieving you of the burden of installing the software and maintaining servers.

**SharePoint Online Ribbon** A fixed-position toolbar that appears across the top of each page in classic view and displays many of the most commonly used tools, controls, and commands.

**SharePoint site** A collection of related webpages, apps, and other components that enables you to organize and manage documents and information, and to create workflows for the organization.

**Single File Web Page option** A file format that saves the entire document into a single .mht or .mhtml format file, which is supported by Internet Explorer.

**Site hierarchy** A complete hierarchical infrastructure, including subsites, that shows the relationship between parent and child sites.

**Site theme** The theme that defines the layout, font, and color schemes for a site.

**Solution** A site template that can be distributed to others or archived on your local computer.

**Solution file** A template file for a site that has a .wsp (Web Solution Packet) extension.

**Standard View** The display of the content of lists and libraries as lists included in a webpage.

**Static Web Parts** Web parts that are placed directly on the webpage and saved as a part of the page. These web parts cannot be edited by the user, but rather the properties are fixed by the page designer.

**Status bar** A bar that provides the user with instant information in context, such as whether the page is checked out.

**Style sheet**  A collection of coding that describes how documents are displayed on screens, presented in print, or even how they are pronounced.

**Style sheet language**  A computer language used for expressing style sheets.

**Subsite**  A child site created within a top-level site.

**Survey list**  A list that displays columns as a questionnaire or poll.

**Tab**  A group of similar commands that can be performed on any page.

**Table**  A collection of rows having one or more columns that contains related data, structured to allow easy management and analysis.

**Tag**  A specific code that indicates how the text should be displayed when the document is opened in a Web browser.

**Tag selector**  A selector that is applied to all occurrences of the HTML tag it styles, and is easy to distinguish in a document because it has the same name as the HTML tag it styles.

**Team site**  A site that facilitates collaboration among people in an organization by providing tools for information sharing and management.

**Team site template**  A template that provides tools for information sharing and management, as well as other team collaboration activities.

**Template**  A beginning set of tools and a layout for a site or workspace.

**Top link bar**  A navigational bar that displays tab links to other sites and a Home button to enable you to return to the main page of the root site.

**Top-level site**  A site that is the top-most site (or parent site) in a site collection.

**Tree view**  A view that adds additional user-friendliness to your site by providing hierarchical navigation similar to a Folders list in File Explorer.

**Unghosted**  Pages that are customized pages and do not contain the characteristics of the standard configuration and layout of the site definition.

**Valid**  A document that is well-formed and satisfies the rules included in the attached document type definition or schema.

**Value**  A required element assigned to any property.

**Views**  The command that controls the display of document property columns and whether the documents displayed are sorted or filtered.

**Web Accessibility Initiative (WAI)**  Web design guidelines issued by the World Wide Web Consortium that help designers create accessible webpages.

**Web Content Accessibility Guidelines 1.0 (WCAG 1.0)**  Guidelines that describe priority levels and four layers of principles, guidelines, success criteria, and sufficient and advisory techniques to enable Web designers to create accessible webpages.

**Web Page option**  A file format option in which the document is saved as an .htm or .html file with a set of files grouped into a folder that enables you to rebuild the original document in a browser.

**Web Page, Filtered option**  A file format that saves the document as an .htm file and saves an additional set of files grouped in a folder, but filters and removes all the Word-specific metadata.

**Web Part Gallery**  A gallery that contains all the web parts available to the top-level site and its subsites.

**Web part page**  A page that contains Web Part zones that are containers for web parts and app parts.

**Web Part zone**  A container used to hold web parts.

**Web query (.iqy)**  A file of extracted data from text or tables on a webpage which is imported into Excel.

**Well-formed**  A document that contains no syntax errors and obeys all W3C specifications for XML code

**Wiki page**  A page that contains only a page content control into which you can insert text, media assets, web parts, and app parts.

**Word Online**  An online application used to create formatted documents, including text, pictures, tables, and links.

**Workflow**  A process that enables you to manage business processes and the associated content.

**World Wide Web Consortium (W3C)**  An organization that provides leadership through an open forum of groups with a vested interest in the Internet, with the mission of leading the Web to its full potential.

**XML Paper Specification (XPS)**  A fixed-layout file format that preserves document formatting and enables file sharing.

**XML parser**  An application that evaluates XML documents and identifies syntax errors.

# Index